GUY DEBORD AND THE SITUATIONIST INTERNATIONAL

OCTOBER BOOKS

Guy Debord and the Situationist International

Texts and Documents

edited by Tom McDonough

An OCTOBER Book

The MIT Press
Cambridge, Massachusetts
London, England

This book was set in Bembo by Graphic Composition, Inc., Athens, Georgia, and was printed and bound in the United States of America.

Library of Congress Cataloging-in-Publication Data
Guy Debord and the situationist international : texts and documents / edited by Tom McDonough.
    p. cm.
    "An October book."
    Includes bibliographical references.
    ISBN 0-262-13404-7 (alk. paper)
    1. Debord, Guy, 1931– 2. Internationale situationniste. 3. Radicalism. 4. Art, Modern—20th century. I. McDonough, Tom.
HN49.R33 G89 2001
303.48'4—dc21
                                                                          2001054649

Contents

Contents

Contents

Introduction: Ideology and the Situationist Utopia

Tom McDonough

"Dadaism," wrote Guy Debord in his foundational 1957 "Report on the Construction of Situations," "wished to be the refusal of all the values of bourgeois society, whose bankruptcy had just become so glaringly evident" on the battlefields of the First World War. From New York and Zurich to Paris and Berlin, that disgust with common values aimed at "the destruction of art and writing," at what in Benjaminian terms we might call the desacralization of culture. "Its historical role," Debord judged, "was to have dealt a mortal blow to the traditional conception of culture."[1] This "wholly negative definition" of its task was simultaneously dadaism's greatest success and most devastating error, in Debord's eyes, for while, on the one hand, it definitively confirmed the intellectual nullity of bourgeois cultural superstructures (doomed thereafter, in an anticipation of Peter Bürger's thesis, to "mere repetition"), on the other hand this negation came precisely too soon, positing the destruction of art before its most utopian promises had been fulfilled. This mutual destruction and fulfillment of art was a task that would fall to the avant-garde being constituted by Debord at that very moment.[2]

Yet despite this careful historical analysis, dadaism's negativity would always hold a powerful attraction for the founder of the Situationist International. In the late 1970s, amidst the ebbing of the revolutionary tide which crested around May

'68, Debord looked back with nostalgia to his own youth at the margins of a bohemian Paris of the 1950s, and saw there a kind of repetition of dadaism's moral revolt, of its refusal of bourgeois values. As he remembered it in 1978, "there was at that time, on the left bank of the river . . . , a neighborhood where the negative kept court." This court was founded on the determined refusal of society's "universally accepted assertions," and instead embraced as its sole principle of action the carefully guarded secret of the Old Man of the Mountain: "Nothing is true, everything is permitted." It could hardly be surprising that Debord's great model lay in Arthur Cravan, "deserter of seventeen nations," adventurer, boxer, and dadaist.[3]

It would seem, then, that fundamental to Debord's larger conception of society were the following linked dichotomies: bourgeoisie/revolutionary avant-garde, affirmation/negation. Each term faced the other across an unbridgeable divide, and over that chasm each was engaged in a mortal battle with its opposite. How devastating, then, to read the conclusions reached by historian Manfredo Tafuri regarding dadaism's destruction of the cultural heritage of bourgeois society; for in his view, this negation of the traditional conception of culture was not an element in that society's overthrow, but rather in its strengthening. As Tafuri argued, dadaist negativity comprised the "conditions for the *liberation* of the potential, but inhibited, energies" of the bourgeoisie—or rather, he wrote, "of a renewed bourgeoisie, capable of accepting doubt as the premise for the full acceptance of existence as a whole, as explosive, revolutionary vitality, prepared for permanent change and the unpredictable."[4]

The destruction of bourgeois values, undertaken as the highest aim of the avant-garde in culture, could function precisely as the prerequisite to a more effective operation within "that field of indeterminant, fluid, and ambiguous forces" that Tafuri described as capitalism itself. Not negation posed against affirmation, as Debord saw it, but negation as inherent in the system; not dadaist irrationality against bourgeois rationality, but "a wholly new type of rationality, which was capable of coming face to face with the negative, in order to make the negative itself the release valve of an unlimited potential for development."[5] It was Marx himself who, at the very commencement of modern industrial society, described how "the bourgeoisie cannot exist without constantly revolutionizing the instruments of production, and thereby the relations of production, and with them the whole relations of society. . . . Constant revolutionizing of production, uninterrupted disturbance of all social conditions, everlasting uncertainty and agitation distinguish the bourgeois epoch from all earlier ones."[6] Yet the salient characteristic of bourgeois society for Debord was predominantly not this sweeping away of "all fixed, fast-frozen relations," but the very opposite—what he called in a telling phrase "a freezing of life."[7] What is at issue here is the potential misrecognition on the part of the Situationist International of the role of the avant-garde in advanced capitalist society; rather than being the latter's absolute contestation, Tafuri raised the disturbing possibility that it was this society's necessary adjunct.[8]

The situationists themselves were forced by circumstances to face this very possibility throughout their history; even they could not remain blind to the continuing revolutionary character of bourgeois society. This placed the SI in an awkward position, in which their negativity appeared as simply the distorted reflection of capitalism's own inherent negativity. (The issue for both the SI and the bourgeoisie, then, was the technical problem of how to make this negativity work.)[9] Here are the editors of the first number of the *Internationale situationniste,* writing in 1958 of the capitalist avant-garde, of those scientists pioneering "new techniques of conditioning" the masses, from subliminal advertising to brainwashing: "It is the entire humanist, artistic, and juridical conception of the inviolable, unvarying personality that is being condemned. We will shed no tears over its passing. However, it must be understood that we will be present at, and take part in, a *sprint between independent artists and the police to test and develop the use of new techniques of conditioning.*"[10] What was here proposed in common by the situationists and "the police" was nothing less than complete integration of the subject with the mechanisms of socioeconomic rationalization, with what the SI called, in proper Marxist phraseology, "the domination of nature." Tafuri understood that integration as a project shared by the entirety of the historical avant-garde, from futurism to constructivism; to the extent that the SI was their heir, it, too, saw its task as planning "*the disappearance of the subject,*" that is, canceling "the anguish caused by the pathetic (or ridiculous) resistance of the individual to the structures of domination that close in upon him" through indicating "the voluntary and docile submission to those structures of domination as the promised land of universal planning," as the proletariat's domination of nature.[11] The subject must cease to be an obstacle in the rational functioning of the machine, must become completely moldable by the new science of the construction of situations. "The situationists," concluded the 1958 article, "will place themselves in the service of the necessity of *oblivion*."[12] Personality, memory, tragedy stood in the way of the utopias planned both by the police and by the SI.

There was, in fact, a curious strain of situationist thought, little remarked today, that was precisely concerned with the destruction of the subject, with the vision of a new, malleable humanity. This vision was particularly apparent in early discussions of the construction of situations and the linked problem of unitary urbanism, both of which were conceived as means of inciting new behaviors, and as such would have access to all the methods offered by modern technology and psychology. That peculiar neologism, "psychogeography," conveyed exactly this desire for rational control over ever greater domains of life; as the "study of the exact laws and precise effects of the geographical environment . . . acting directly on the affective deportment of individuals,"[13] it was a way of systematizing, of consciously organizing, what the surrealists had still experienced as random, as the marvelous. No less than a moralizing functionalist architecture, so despised by the situationists, their urban ideologies were devoted to reshaping the subject, to, in fact, envisioning an empty subject modeled by the influence of the surroundings.

Years later the group was still confronting this dilemma, and in 1964 returned to the ambivalent metaphor of the race to explain the difficulty of "differentiating ourselves clearly enough from *modern* tendencies of explanations and proposals regarding the new society to which capitalism has led us." In the collectively composed "Now, the SI," that murky differentiation was described as follows: "The path of complete police control over all human activities and the path of infinite free creation of all human activities is one: it is the same path of modern discoveries." The confusion that this might engender was little dispelled by adding that "we are inevitably on the same path as our enemies—most often preceding them—but we must be there, without any confusion, *as enemies.*"[14] The same path, a shared race, a mutual goal: how could one not be confused? When in the same article those modernist explanations and proposals were described as all, behind their varying masks, leading to more efficient integration into capitalist society, how could one not suspect with Tafuri that this was no less true of the revolutionary avant-garde? Four years earlier, in the spring of 1960, Dutch member Constant had been pressured into resigning from the SI over precisely this issue: his visionary urban designs (Tafuri would have called them "*partial utopias* of the plan"), central in the early history of the group, came to be criticized as "public relations for the integration of the masses into capitalist technological civilization."[15] Was this a mere "deviationist seed," as the SI wished to see it, or an indication of the fundamentally unified project of that civilization and its "negationist" avant-garde?

The situationist response to this question was, of course, resounding denial, and recourse to the concept of "recuperation," the idea that avant-garde innovations might be recovered for use by the reigning social order, that revolutionary negativity might be recouped to strengthen bourgeois affirmation. So we find the situationists conceding in "Now, the SI," that "it is quite natural that our enemies manage to partially use us . . . just like the proletariat, we cannot claim to be unexploitable within the given circumstances."[16] If they made the gesture of a refusal of ideological purity, by asserting that they would not "leave the current field of culture," they simultaneously emptied that gesture of meaning by the qualification that neither would they mix with their enemies. Only the tortured and self-justifying logic of recuperation could make sense of these competing claims, could, that is, reconcile the idea of being "on the same path as our enemies" with the insistence on an absolute distance from them. There is an irony in the use of the idea of recuperation to bolster the alleged purity of the situationist avant-garde, for what is recuperation other than a strategy of mixing, of blending—the heavy artillery with which bourgeois society batters down all Chinese walls of avant-gardist isolation? And, to take the argument a step further, could we not posit *détournement,* the situationist strategy of diverting elements of affirmative bourgeois culture to revolutionary ends, of distorting received meanings, as the exact corollary of recuperation? If power "creates nothing, it recuperates,"[17] then for the avant-garde "the impossibility of ex nihilo creation"[18] presented a precise symmetry. We can only conclude that the bourgeoisie was as adept at *détournement* as the situationists themselves, that, in fact, recuperation and *détournement* were one and the same, a shared cultural strategy. Against this blurring of boundaries, the SI's claims to a position of absolute contestation begin to falter.

The situationists' logic of recuperation rested on their belief in capitalism's fundamentally static, affirmative quality. It was a strategy of fragmentation, of *partial* use, whereby the dominant culture strove, as Debord wrote in 1957, "to divert [*détourner*] the taste for the new, which has in our era become a threat to it, into certain debased forms of novelty, which are entirely harmless and muddled."[19] The authentically new (as compared to mere "novelty") was understood as a threat to social order because each innovation only exacerbated that order's central contradiction between the immensity of productive forces and the stifling conditions of production, between the technological means unleashed by the bourgeoisie and its need as a class to preserve inequality. For the SI the twentieth century's avant-gardes, in both politics and culture, constituted a single, sustained attempt to overcome this contradiction, to construct what Debord called "a superior organization of the world," which would be in conjunction with "the development of the modern potentialities of production."[20] He expressed this viewpoint at length in the opening paragraphs of his "Report on the Construction of Situations": "We are living through a fundamental historical crisis, in which the problem of the rational domination of new productive forces, and of the formation of a civilization on the global scale, is each year formulated more clearly. . . . The new desires being defined are placed in an awkward position: the era's resources permit their realization, but the obsolete economic structure is incapable of exploiting them."[21] To the bourgeoisie's irrational refusal to extend the domination of new productive forces, the SI—like the historical avant-garde before it—rationally sought their full exploitation, and herein lay the perceived threat at the root of the dynamics of recuperation.

We have tended to see the Situationist International as a post-surrealist movement, as a group that inherited and pushed further a Bretonian program of chance, irrationality, and revolutionary experiment—a self-described "movement more liberating than the surrealism *of* **1924.**"[22] This perspective is not necessarily incorrect, but it has often kept us from perceiving the larger, rational utopia of a planned future which subtended the talk of free creativity, liberating play, and so forth. From the first issue of the *Internationale situationniste* in 1958, this call for the planification of the future could clearly be heard. "Ordinary life, conditioned until now by the problem of subsistence, can be rationally controlled (this possibility is at the heart of all the conflicts of our time)," one collectively written article reads;[23] or, further on in that same number: "The true fulfillment of the individual . . . depends upon the collective mastery of the world—before this, there are not yet individuals, only phantoms haunting things that have anarchically been given them by others."[24] (A statement in evident contrast to the formulation proposed elsewhere in the journal's pages, in which the humanist, rounded bourgeois subject was consigned to oblivion, replaced by the empty subject of the construction of situations.) The problem of subsistence, what we might call "natural" alienation, had been definitively resolved in the modern era and the struggle for survival against a hostile environment won; the possibility of a new formulation of ordinary life was appearing, only to be kept in check by the absence of a collectively organized control of resources. So the situationists came to see the contradiction between the forces and the relations of production as pronouncing "a sentence (whose carrying out remains to be attempted with the necessary weapons) on the parsimonious as well as dangerous development organized by the self-regulation of this production," a sentence whose verdict was determined by "the grandiose *potential development* that could rely upon the present economic infrastructure."[25]

"Ordinary life" (*la vie courante*) or, adopting the terminology of Henri Lefebvre (whose sociology seminar at Nanterre Debord audited in 1957–1958), "everyday life" (*la vie quotidienne*) was the stake of this potential development, its sphere of action. The SI saw everyday life as characterized by its indigence and underdevelopment; as Debord described it in his 1961 lecture (delivered via tape recorder) on the "Prospects for Conscious Modifications in Everyday Life," everyday life was "organized within the limits of a scandalous poverty," a poverty defined by the "scarcity of free time and scarcity of possible uses of this free time." And this condition was by no means accidental, but the necessary product of modern capitalist accumulation and industrialization. Such poverty, in Debord's words, "is the expression of the fundamental need for the lack of consciousness and for mystification in an exploitative society, in a society of alienation." If Lefebvre had first suggested that everyday life could be understood as the product of uneven development within capitalist society, Debord would extend this idea by further describing ordinary existence as "a colonized sector," as "a kind of reservation for the good savages who (without realizing it) make modern society, with the rapid increase in its technological powers and the forced expansion of its market, work."[26] Everyday life, then, marked a border, the "frontier of the controlled and the uncontrolled sectors of life"—between, that is, the planned sector of production and the as yet unplanned sector of lived experience, consumption, leisure. The situationist goal was "to substitute an always moving frontier for the present ghetto, to work continuously for the organization of new opportunities"[27]—in other words, to put uncertainty to work through the rational control of productive forces, to institute a regime devoted to eliminating the irrational, mythical holdovers still present in everyday life. No longer a colony, this sphere was to be fully integrated into the logical functioning of society, a complete planification of the future.

This "Tafurian" critique of situationist positions is not intended as a blanket dismissal, needless to say. The ground they shared with capitalism's rationalist utopias only indicates the extent of their inheritance from earlier twentieth-century avant-gardes, only indicates what they still shared with dadaism or constructivism. But there are other aspects, of course, to the situationist project, ones that mitigate against such an ideology of the plan. We will need to examine more closely, for example, the situationist interest in the concept of the baroque[28] or, particularly in Debord's writings, the sense of the irreversible passage of time. This introduction is meant polemically, as an initial foray into new interpretive territory, as a suggestion for moving beyond the stale categories into which we have compartmentalized our thought on the Situationist International.

Those categories—of avant-gardist purity, or of chronological and ideological division ("artistic" versus "political" phases or wings)—now simply hinder any understanding of this group; it is time to move beyond them.

When this anthology first appeared, in a shorter format some four years ago, as a special issue of the journal *October*, I opened my introductory text with a plea for the "careful analysis of the Situationist legacy, a project of archival retrieval, reconstruction, and historicization."[29] Written not long after Guy Debord's suicide at the end of November 1994, this plea was a direct response to the alternating disdain (Debord as the solitary paranoiac, guilty of "seeing spies everywhere")[30] and hagiographic adulation (Debord as the solitary dissident, the brilliant "stylist of pessimism")[31] that Debord and the situationists more generally seemed to inspire in equal proportions. It struck me then and it continues to now that such responses are simply two sides of the same coin—a fact only highlighted when the two opposite reactions can be manifested almost simultaneously by the same commentator, as Roger Pol-Droit did in *Le Monde*—that both sympathetic and hostile commentators have largely engaged in a mythologizing of this politico-aesthetic avant-garde (for lack of a better term), and that the most pressing task facing historians is to see the SI not as some theoretical absolute divorced from its own record, but rather—as I then wrote—as "engaged in a struggle over the possible meanings of culture, as over the legacy of the historical avant-garde, with a broad spectrum of postwar cultural producers. The situationists participated in this struggle . . . on a field *coextensive* with figures ranging from the *nouveaux romanciers* to the *noveaux réalistes*, 'behind enemy lines,' so to speak."[32] I can then only concur with the conclusion drawn by Jean-Marie Apostolidès, who at the end of a recent, provocative essay on Debord demanded that the latter "take his place among the other writers of his generation," that he "cease to be an absolute value, and enter into the world of relative values and intellectual exchange," that, finally, as scholars it is our responsibility "to pass from the phase of spectacular (i.e., laudatory or deprecatory) reception of his works, to another, the phase of *interpretation*."[33] A modest proposal, no doubt, but such a critical perspective has only recently begun (with a few notable exceptions) to mark a turn from the long-standing "spectacular" reception of the SI.

The situationists themselves, we should note, were as little interested in hagiography as in dismissal, and from 1971 onward—that is, from the moment of their autodissolution—they emphasized the importance of a critical historicization of their project. In the jointly composed "Theses on the Situationist International and Its Times" (1971), Debord and Gianfranco Sanguinetti wrote that "the SI has never presented itself as a model of revolutionary organization, but as a specific organization that applied itself in a definite era to definite tasks . . ."[34]—a judgment echoed and deepened seven years later in the script to Debord's film *In girum imus nocte et consumimur igni* (1978), in which he remarked that "avant-gardes will not endure, and the most fortunate thing that might happen to them is, in the full sense of the term, that they should have *served their times*. . . . An historical project certainly cannot claim to preserve an eternal youth shielded from blows."[35]

My thanks must go first and foremost to the contributors to this volume, who have each embarked on that historical project of interpretation, and to the translators who have made so much material newly available to us. The editorial board of *October,* in particular Benjamin H. D. Buchloh and Hal Foster, have provided continuing support and guidance in transforming an issue of their journal into this collection, as has Catherine de Zegher, executive editor of October Books, without whose aid this anthology would not have appeared. Finally, I must thank my partner, Aruna D'Souza, for both her critical acumen and her warm affection.

Notes

1. Guy Debord, "Report on the Construction of Situations and the Terms of Organization and Action of the International Situationist Tendency," trans. Tom McDonough, in this volume, 32.
2. Or, as Debord would write in the middle years of the 1960s, "the critical position since worked out by the situationists demonstrates that the abolition and the realization of art are inseparable aspects of a single transcendence of art." See Guy Debord, *The Society of the Spectacle,* trans. Donald Nicholson-Smith (New York: Zone Books, 1994), 136.
3. See Guy Debord, *In girum imus nocte et consumimur igni,* trans. Lucy Forsyth (London: Pelagian Press, 1991), 32–33 (translation modified).

4. Manfredo Tafuri, *Architecture and Utopia,* trans. Barbara Luigia LaPenta (Cambridge: MIT Press, 1976), 55–56.

5. Ibid., 56.

6. *Manifesto of the Communist Party,* in *The Marx-Engels Reader,* 2d ed., ed. Robert C. Tucker (New York: W. W. Norton, 1978), 476.

7. Debord, *The Society of the Spectacle,* 121.

8. The historical and philosophical causes of this misrecognition can only be suggested here. Mark Shipway, for one, is certainly correct when he asserts that "many of the situationists' theoretical preoccupations . . . can be understood by reference to social trends in postwar France, a society undergoing rapid 'modernization,'" that is, that this misrecognition consisted of the projection of historically particular social conditions onto bourgeois society as a whole. See Mark Shipway, "Situationism," in Maximilien Rubel and John Crump, eds., *Non-Market Socialism in the Nineteenth and Twentieth Centuries* (Houndmills, England: Macmillan, 1987), esp. 166–168.

9. See Tafuri, *Architecture and Utopia,* 61.

10. "Notes éditoriales: La lutte pour le contrôle des nouvelles techniques de conditionnement," *Internationale situationniste* 1 (June 1958), 8.

11. Tafuri, *Architecture and Utopia,* 73.

12. "Notes éditoriales: La lutte pour le contrôle . . . ," 8.

13. Debord, "Report on the Construction of Situations," 45.

14. "Now, the SI," in Ken Knabb, ed. and trans., *Situationist International Anthology* (Berkeley: Bureau of Public Secrets, 1981), 136 (translation modified).

15. "Editorial Notes: Critique of Urbanism," trans. John Shepley, in this volume, 104.

16. "Now, the SI," 136 (translation modified).

17. "Editorial Notes: All the King's Men," trans. Tom McDonough, in this volume, 154.

18. Raoul Vaneigem, quoted in "La cinquième conférence de l'I.S. à Göteborg," *Internationale situationniste* 7 (April 1962), 27.

19. Debord, "Report on the Construction of Situations," 31.

20. Ibid., 29.

21. Ibid., 29–30.

22. "The Sound and the Fury," in Knabb, ed., *Situationist International Anthology,* 42.

23. "Notes éditoriales: Contribution à une définition situationniste du jeu," *Internationale situationniste* 1 (June 1958), 8.

24. "Preliminary Problems in Constructing a Situation," in *Situationist International Anthology,* 44 (translation modified).

25. "Ideologies, Classes and the Domination of Nature," in ibid., 104 (translation modified). For a gloss on these points, see Shipway, "Situationism," 156–157.

26. Guy Debord, "Perspectives de modifications conscientes dans la vie quotidienne," *Internationale situationniste* 6 (August 1961), 22.

27. Ibid., 24.

28. A few scholars have already begun such investigations. See Anselm Jappe, *Guy Debord,* trans. Donald Nicholson-Smith (Berkeley: University of California Press, 1999), 114–115; and Gianfranco Marelli, *La dernière internationale,* trans. David Bosc (Arles: Éditions Sulliver, 2000), 56–58.

29. Tom McDonough, "Rereading Debord, Rereading the Situationists," *October* 79 ("Guy Debord and the Internationale situationniste: A Special Issue") (Winter 1997), 5.

30. As in Roger Pol-Droit, "Guy Debord: Le dernier des Mohicans," *Le Monde,* July 22, 1988, 11.

31. As in, again, Roger Pol-Droit, "Guy Debord ou le sens de la révolte," *Le Monde,* December 3, 1994, 17.

32. McDonough, "Rereading Debord," 13.

33. Jean-Marie Apostolidès, *Les tombeaux de Guy Debord* (Paris: Exiles Éditeur, 1999), 160–161.

34. Guy Debord and Gianfranco Sanguinetti, "Thèses sur l'Internationale situationniste et son temps" (1971), in *La véritable scission dans l'Internationale,* rev. ed. (Paris: Librairie Arthème Fayard, 1998), 74.

35. Debord, *In girum imus nocte et consumimur igni,* 63–64.

Guy Debord and the
Situationist International

The Long Walk of the Situationist International

GREIL MARCUS

In the USA the Situationist International is mostly known, if it is known at all, as a small group of dadaist provocateurs that had something to do with the May 1968 uprising in France. The name has been batted around in reference to punk, because Sex Pistol Svengali Malcolm McLaren was supposedly connected with the situationists—or was it that, like a lot of 1960s UK art students, he favored the situationist rhetoric about revolution arising out of the boredom of everyday life? The situationists were, ah, sort of like the Yippies, one hears. Or New York's Motherfuckers, who once tore into Berkeley, firebombed a cop, and left a black bystander holding the bag. Or the Frankfurt School—not known for its fire-bombings, but the ideas were similar, right?

1

I first became intrigued with the Situationist International in 1979, when I struggled through "Le bruit et la fureur," one of the anonymous lead articles in the first issue of the journal *Internationale situationniste.* The writer reviewed the exploits of artistic rebels in the postwar West as if such matters had real political consequences, and then said this:

The rotten egg smell exuded by the idea of God envelops the mystical cretins of the American "Beat Generation," and is not even entirely absent from the declarations of the Angry Young Men. . . . They have simply come to change their opinions about a few social conventions without even noticing the whole *change of terrain* of all cultural activity so evident in every avant-garde tendency of this century. The Angry Young Men are in fact particularly reactionary in their attribution of a privileged, redemptive value to the practice of literature: they are defending a mystification that was denounced in Europe around 1920 and whose survival today is of greater counter-revolutionary significance than that of the British Crown.

Mystical cretins . . . finally, I thought (forgetting the date of the publication before me), someone has cut through the suburban cul-de-sac that passed for cultural rebellion in the 1950s. But this wasn't "finally"—it was 1958, in a sober, carefully printed magazine (oddly illustrated with captionless photos of women in bathing suits), in an article that concluded: "If we are not surrealists it is *because we don't want to be bored.* . . . Decrepit surrealism, raging and ill-informed youth, well-off adolescent rebels lacking perspective but far from lacking a cause—boredom is what they all have in common. The situationists will execute the judgment contemporary leisure is pronouncing against itself."[1]

Strange stuff—almost mystifying for an American—but there was a power in the prose that was even more seductive than the hard-nosed dismissal of the Beat Generation. This was the situationist style—what one commentator called "a rather irritating form of hermetic terrorism," a judgment situationist Raoul Vaneigem would quote with approval. Over the next decade it never really changed, but only became more seductive and more hard-nosed, because it discovered more seductive and hard-nosed opponents. Beginning with the notion that modern life was boring and therefore *wrong,* the situationists sought out every manifestation of alienation and domination and every manifestation of the opposition produced by alienation and domination. They turned out original analyses of the former (whether it was the Kennedy-era fallout shelter program in "The Geopolitics of Hibernation"—what a title!—or the Chinese cultural revolution in "The Explosion Point of Ideology in China") and mercilessly criticized the timidity and limits of the latter. In every case they tried to link specifics to a totality—why was the world struggling to turn itself inside out, and how could it be made to succeed? What were the real sources of revolution in postwar society, and how were they different from any that had come before?

2

The attack on the Beat Generation and the Angry Young Men—in 1958, it is worth remembering, considered in the English-speaking world the very summa of "anti-Establishment" negation—was an opening round in a struggle the situationists thought was already going on, and a move toward a situation they meant to construct. "Our ideas are in everyone's mind," they would say more than once over the next ten years. They meant that their ideas for a different world were in everyone's mind as desires, but not yet as ideas. Their project was to expose the emptiness of everyday life in the modern world and to make the link between desire and idea real. They meant to make that link so real it would be acted upon by almost everyone, since in the modern world, in the affluent capitalist West and the bureaucratic state-capitalist East, the split between desire and idea was part of almost everyone's life.

Throughout the next decade, the situationists argued that the alienation which in the nineteenth century was rooted in production had, in the twentieth century, become rooted in consumption. Consumption had come to define happiness and to suppress all other possibilities of freedom and selfhood. Lenin had written that under communism everyone would become an employee of the state; that was no less capitalism than the Western version, in which everyone was first and foremost a member of an economy based in commodities. The cutting edge of the present-day contradiction—that place where the way of life almost everyone took for granted grated most harshly against what life promised and what it delivered—was as much leisure as work. This meant the concepts behind "culture" were as much at stake as the ideas behind industry.

3

Culture, the situationists thought, was "the Northwest Passage" to a superseding of the dominant society. This was where they started; this was the significance of their attack on the Beat Generation. It was a means to a far more
powerful attack on the nature of modern society itself: on the division of labor,
the fragmentation of work and thought, the manner in which the material success of modern life had leaped over all questions of the quality of life, in which
"the struggle against poverty . . . [had] overshot its ultimate goal, the liberation
of man from material cares," and produced a world in which, "faced with the alternative of love or a garbage disposal unit, young people of all countries have
chosen the garbage disposal unit."[2]

Unlike many with whom they shared certain notions—Norman Mailer,
the Marxist sociologist Henri Lefebvre, the *gauchiste* review *Socialisme ou Barbarie*—the situationists were bent on discovering the absolute ability to criticize
anyone, anywhere—without restraint, without the pull of alliances, and without
self-satisfaction. And they were bent on turning that criticism into events.

3

The situationists thought of themselves as avant-garde revolutionaries, linked as
clearly to dada as to Marx. One could trace them back to Saint-Just—the twenty-
two-year-old who arrived in Paris in 1789 with a blasphemous epic poem, *Organt*
(an account of the raping of nuns and of endless sexual adventures), and became
the coldest, most romantic, most brilliant, most tragic administrator of the Terror.
Prosecutor of Louis XVI, he gave his head to the same guillotine a year later.

More directly, situationist thinking began in Paris in the early 1950s, when
Guy Debord and a few other members of the Lettrist International—a group,
known mostly to itself, which had split off from the lettrists, a tiny, postwar neo-
dada movement of anti-art intellectuals and students—devoted themselves to
dérives: to drifting through the city for days, weeks, even months at a time, looking for what they called the city's psychogeography. They meant to find signs of
what lettrist Ivan Chtcheglov called "forgotten desires"—images of play, eccen-
tricity, secret rebellion, creativity, and negation. That led them into the Paris cat-

acombs, where they sometimes spent the night. They looked for images of refusal, or for images society had itself refused, hidden, suppressed, or "recuperated"—images of refusal, nihilism, or freedom that society had taken back into itself, coopted or rehabilitated, isolated or discredited. Rooted in similar but intellectually (and physically) far more limited surrealist expeditions of the 1920s, the *dérives* were a search, Guy Debord would write many years later, for the "supersession of art." They were an attempt to fashion a new version of daily life—a new version of how people organized their wishes, pains, fears, hopes, ambitions, limits, social relationships, and identities, a process that ordinarily took place without consciousness.

The few members of the grandiosely named Lettrist International wanted to reshape daily life according to the desires discovered and affirmed by modern art. Dada, at the Cabaret Voltaire, "a laboratory for the rehabilitation of everyday life" in which art as art was denounced and scattered, "wanted to suppress art without realizing it," Debord wrote in 1967, in his book *The Society of the Spectacle*. "Surrealism wanted to realize art without suppressing it."[3] In other words, dada wanted to kill off the claim that art was superior to life and leave art for dead. Surrealism wanted to turn the impulses that led one to create art into a recreation of life, but it also wanted to maintain the production of art works. Thus surrealism ended up as just another debilitated, gallery-bound art movement, a fate dada avoided at the price of being almost completely ignored. The Lettrist International thought art had to be both suppressed as separate, special activity, and turned into life. That was the meaning of supersession, and that was the meaning of a group giving itself up to the pull of the city. It was also the meaning of the LI's attack on art as art. Debord produced a film without images; with the Danish painter Asger Jorn, he created a book "'composed entirely of prefabricated elements,' in which the writing on each page runs in all directions and the reciprocal relations of the phrases are invariably uncompleted." Not only was the book supposedly impossible to "read," it featured a sandpaper jacket, so that when placed in a bookshelf it would eat other books.

In 1952, at the Ritz, the LI broke up a Charlie Chaplin press conference, part of the huge publicity campaign for *Limelight*. "We believe that the most urgent expression of freedom is the destruction of idols, especially when they present themselves in the name of freedom," they explained. "The provocative tone of our leaflet was an attack against a unanimous, servile enthusiasm." (Provocative was perhaps not the word. "No More Flat Feet," the leaflet Debord and others scattered in the Ritz, read: "Because you [Chaplin] identified yourself with the weak and the oppressed, to attack you was to strike the weak and oppressed, but in the shadow of your rattan cane some could already discern the nightstick of the cop.") The lettrist radicals practiced graffiti on the walls of Paris (one of their favorite mottoes, "Never work!," would show up fifteen years later during May 1968, and thirteen years after that in Bow Wow Wow's "W.O.R.K.," written by Malcolm McLaren). They painted slogans on their ties, shoes, and pants, hoping to walk the streets as living examples of *détournement*—the diversion of an element of culture or everyday life (in this case, simply clothes) to a new and displacing purpose. The band "lived on the margins of the economy. It tended toward a role of pure consumption"—not of commodities, but "of time."[4]

From *On the Passage of a Few People through a Rather Brief Period of Time,* Debord's 1959 film on the group:

> Voice 1: That which was directly lived reappears frozen in the distance, fit into the tastes and illusions of an era carried away with it.
> Voice 2: The appearance of events we have not made, that others have made against us, obliges us from now on to be aware of the passage of time, its results, the transformation of our own desires into events. What differentiates the past from the present is precisely its out-of-reach objectivity; there is no more should-be; being is so consumed that it has ceased to exist. The details are already lost in the dust of time. Who was afraid of life, afraid of the night, afraid of being taken, afraid of being kept?
> Voice 3: That which should be abolished continues, and we continue to wear away with it. Once again the fatigue of so many nights passed in the same way. It is a walk that has lasted a long time.
> Voice 1: Really hard to drink more.[5]

This was the search for that Northwest Passage, that unmarked alleyway from the world as it appeared to the world as it had never been, but which the art of the twentieth century had promised it could be: a promise shaped in countless images of freedom to experiment with life and of freedom from the banality and tyranny of bourgeois order and bureaucratic rule. Debord and the others tried to practice, he said, "a systematic questioning of all the diversions and works of a society, a total critique of its idea of happiness."[6] "Our movement was not a literary school, a revitalization of expression, a modernism," a Lettrist International publication stated in 1955, after some years of the pure consumption of time, various manifestos, numerous jail sentences for drug possession and drunk driving, suicide attempts, and all-night arguments. "We have the advantage of no longer expecting anything from known activities, known individuals, and known institutions."[7]

They tried to practice a radical deconditioning: to demystify their environment and the expectations they had brought to it, to escape the possibility that they would themselves recuperate their own gestures of refusal. The formation of the Situationist International—at first, in 1957, including fifteen or twenty painters, writers, and architects from England, France, Algeria, Denmark, Holland, Italy, and Germany—was based on the recognition that such a project, no matter how poorly defined or mysterious, was either a revolutionary project or it was nothing. It was a recognition that the experiments of the *dérive,* the attempts to discover lost intimations of real life behind the perfectly composed face of modern society, had to be transformed into a general contestation of that society, or else dissolve in bohemian solipsism.

4

Born in Paris in 1931, Guy Debord was from beginning to end at the center of the Situationist International, and the editor of its journal. *The Society of the Spectacle,* the concise and remarkably cant-free (or cant-destroying, for that seems to be its effect) book of theory he published after ten years of situationist activity, begins with these lines: "In societies where modern conditions of production prevail, all of life presents itself as an immense accumulation of spectacles.

Everything that was lived has moved away into a representation."[8] Determined to destroy the claims of twentieth-century social organization, Debord was echoing the first sentence of *Capital:* "The wealth of societies in which the capitalist mode of production prevails appears as an 'immense collection of commodities.'" To complain, as French Marxist critics did, that Debord misses Marx's qualification, "appears as," is to miss Debord's own apparent qualification, "presents itself as"—and to miss the point of situationist writing altogether. Debord's qualification turned out not to be a qualification at all, but rather the basis of a theory in which a society organized as appearance can be disrupted on the field of appearance.

Debord argued that the commodity—now transmuted into "spectacle," or seemingly natural, autonomous images communicated as the facts of life—had taken over the social function once fulfilled by religion and myth, and that appearances were now inseparable from the essential processes of alienation and domination in modern society. In 1651, the cover of Thomas Hobbes's *Leviathan* presented the manifestation of a nascent bourgeois domination: a picture of a gigantic sovereign being, whose body—the body politic—was made up of countless faceless citizens. This was presented as an entirely positive image, as a utopia. In 1967, *Internationale situationniste* no. 11 printed an almost identical image, "Portrait of Alienation": in a huge stadium, countless Chinese performing a card trick that produced the gigantic face of Mao Zedong.[9]

If society is organized around consumption, one participates in social life as a consumer; the spectacle produces spectators, and thus protects itself from questioning. It induces passivity rather than action, contemplation rather than thinking, and a degradation of life into materialism. It is no matter that in advanced societies, material survival is not at issue (except for those who are kept poor in order to represent poverty and reassure the rest of the population that they should be satisfied). The "standard of survival," like its twin, the "standard of boredom," is raised but the nature of the standard does not change. Desires are degraded or displaced into needs and maintained as needs. A project precisely the opposite of that of modern art, from Lautréamont and Rimbaud to dada and surrealism, is fulfilled.

The spectacle is not merely advertising, or propaganda, or television. It is a world. The spectacle as we experience it, but fail to perceive it, "is not a collection of images, but a social relationship between people, mediated by images."[10] In 1928 in *One-Way Street,* writing about German inflation, Walter Benjamin anticipated the argument:

> The freedom of conversation is being lost. If earlier it was a matter of course to take interest in one's partner, this is now replaced by inquiry into the price of his shoes or his umbrella. Irresistibly intruding upon any convivial exchange is the theme of the conditions of life, of money. What this theme involves is not so much the concerns and sorrows of individuals, in which they might be able to help one another, as the overall picture. It is as if one were trapped in a theater and had to follow the events on the stage whether one wanted to or not, had to make them again and again, willingly or unwillingly, the subject of one's thought and speech.[11]

Raoul Vaneigem defined the terrain of values such a situation produced: "Rozanov's definition of nihilism is the best: 'The show is over. The audience get up to leave their seats. Time to collect their coats and go home. They turn around. . . . No more coats and no more home.'"[12] "The spectator feels at home nowhere," Debord wrote, "because the spectacle is everywhere."[13]

The spectacle is "the diplomatic representation of hierarchic society to itself, where all other expression is banned"[14]—which is to say where all other expression makes no sense, appears as babble (this may be the ironic, protesting meaning of dada phonetic poems, in which words were reduced to sounds, and of lettrist poetry, in which sounds were reduced to letters). The spectacle says "nothing more than 'that which appears is good, that which is good appears.'"[15] (In a crisis, or when the "standard of survival" falls, as in our own day, hierarchic society retreats, but maintains its hegemony, the closing of questions. The spectacle "no longer promises anything," Debord wrote in 1979, in a new preface to the fourth Italian edition of his book. "It simply says, 'It is so.'") The spectacle organizes ordinary life (consider the following in terms of making love): "The alienation of the spectator to the profit of the contemplated object is expressed in the following way: the more he contemplates the less he lives; the more he accepts recognizing himself in the dominant images of need, the less he understands his own existence and his own desires. The externality of the spectacle in relation to the active man appears in the fact that his own gestures are no longer his but those of another who represents them to him."[16]

Debord summed it up this way: "The first phase of the domination of the economy over social life brought into the definition of all human realization the obvious degradation of *being* into *having*. The present phase of total occupation of social life by the accumulated results of the economy"—by spectacle—"leads to a generalized sliding of *having* into *appearing*."[17] We are twice removed from where we want to be, the situationists argued—yet each day still seems like a natural fact.

5

This was the situationists' account of what they, and everyone else, were up against. It was an argument from Marx's 1844 *Economic and Philosophical Manuscripts,* an argument that the "spectacle-commodity society," within which one could make only meaningless choices and against which one could seemingly not intervene, had succeeded in producing fundamental contradictions between what people accepted and what, in ways they could not understand, they wanted.

This was the precise opposite of social science, developed at precisely the time when the ideology of the end of ideology was conquering the universities of the West. It was an argument about consciousness and false consciousness, not as the primary cause of domination but as its primary battleground.

If capitalism had shifted the terms of its organization from production to consumption, and its means of control from economic misery to false consciousness, then the task of would-be revolutionaries was to bring about a recognition of the life already lived by almost everyone. Foreclosing the construction of one's own life, advanced capitalism had made almost everyone a member of a new proletariat, and thus a potential revolutionary. Here again, the discovery of the source of revolution in what "modern art has sought and promised" served as the axis of the argument. Modern art, one could read in *Internationale situationniste* no. 8, in January of 1963, had "made a clean sweep of all the values and rules of everyday behavior," of unquestioned order and the "unanimous, servile enthusiasm" Debord and his friends had thrown up at Chaplin; but that clean sweep had been isolated in museums. Modern revolutionary impulses had been separated from the world, but "just as in the nineteenth century revolutionary theory arose out of philosophy"—out of Marx's dictum that philosophy, having interpreted the world, must set about changing it—now one had to look to the demands of art.[18]

At the time of the Paris Commune in 1871, workers discussed matters that had previously been the exclusive province of philosophers—suggesting the possibility that philosophy could be realized in daily life. In the twentieth century, with "survival" conquered as fact but maintained as ideology, the same logic meant that just as artists constructed a version of life in words, paint, or stone, men and women could themselves begin to construct their own lives out of desire. In scattered and barely noticed ways, the desire to construct one's own life was shaping the twentieth century, or the superseding of it ("Ours is the best effort so far toward getting *out* of the twentieth century," an anonymous situationist wrote in 1964, in one of the most striking lines in the twelve issues of *Internationale situationniste*).[19] It was the desire more hidden, more overwhelmed and confused by spectacle, than any other. It had shaped the lettrist adventures. It was the Northwest Passage. If the spectacle was "both the result and the project of the existing mode of production,"[20] then the construction of life as artists constructed art—in terms of what one made of friendship, love, sex, work, play, and suffering—was understood by the situationists as both the result and the project of revolution.

6

To pursue this revolution, it was necessary to take all the partial and isolated incidents of resistance and refusal of things as they were, and then link them. It was necessary to discover and speak the language of these incidents, to do for signs of life what the Lettrist International had tried to do for the city's signs of "forgotten desires." This demanded a theory of exemplary acts. Society was organized as appearance, and could be contested on the field of appearance; what mattered was the puncturing of appearance—speech and action against the spectacle that was, suddenly, not babble, but understood. The situationist project, in this sense, was a quest for a new language of action. That quest resulted in the urgent, daring tone of even the lengthiest, most solemn essays in *Internationale situationniste*—the sense of minds engaged, quickened beyond rhetoric, by emerging social contradictions—and it resulted in such outrages as a six-word analysis of a leading French sociologist. ("M. GEORGES LAPASSADE," announced almost a full page of *IS* no. 9, "EST UN CON.")[21] It led as well to a style of absurdity and play, and to an affirmation that contestation was fun: a good way to live. The situationists delighted in the discovery that dialectics caused society to produce not just contradictions but also endless self-parodies. Their journal was filled with them—my favorite is a reproduction of an ad for the Peace o' Mind Fallout Shelter Company. And the comics that illustrated *IS* led to *détournement* of the putative heroes of everyday life. Characters out of *Steve Canyon* and *True Romance* were given new balloons, and made to speak passionately of revolution, alienation, and the lie of culture—as if even the most unlikely people actually cared about such things. In the pages of *IS,* a kiss suggested not marriage but fantasies of liberation: a sigh for the Paris Commune.

The theory of exemplary acts and the quest for a new language of action also brought the situationists' pursuit of extremism into play. *IS* no. 10, March 1966, on the Watts riots: "All those who went so far as to recognize the 'apparent justifications' of the rage of the Los Angeles blacks . . . all those 'theorists' and 'spokesmen' of international Left, or rather of its nothingness, deplored the irresponsibility, the disorder, the looting (especially the fact that arms and alcohol were the first targets for plunder). . . . But who has defended the rioters of Los Angeles in the terms they deserve? We will."[22] The article continued: "The looting of the Watts district was the most direct realization of the distorted principle, 'To each according to his false needs' . . . [but] real desires begin to be expressed in festival, in the potlatch of destruction. . . . For the first time it is not poverty but material abundance which must be dominated [and of course it was the relative affluence of the Watts rioters, at least as compared to black Americans in Harlem, that so mystified the observers of this first outbreak of violent black rage]. . . . Comfort will never be comfortable enough for those who seek what is not on the market."[23]

"The task of being more extremist than the SI falls to the SI itself," the situationists said;[24] that was the basis of the group's continuation. The situationists looked for exemplary acts which might reveal to spectators that that was all they were. They cited, celebrated, and analyzed incidents which dramatized what they saw as the contradictions of modern society, and which contained suggestions of what forms a real contestation of that society might take. Such acts included the Watts riots; the resistance of students and workers to the Chinese cultural revolution (a struggle, the situationists wrote, of "the *official owners of the ideology* against the majority of the *owners of the apparatus* of the economy and the state");[25] the burning of the Koran in the streets of Baghdad in 1959; the exposure of a site meant to house part of the British government in the event of nuclear war; the "kidnapping" of art works by Caracas students, who used them to demand the release of political prisoners; the Free Speech Movement in Berkeley in 1964; the situationist-inspired disruption of classes taught by French cyberneticians in 1966 at Strasbourg, and by sociologists at Nanterre in 1967 and 1968; and the quiet revolt of Berlin actor Wolfgang Neuss, who in 1963 "perpetrated a most suggestive act of sabotage . . . by placing a notice in the paper *Der Abend* giving away the identity of the killer in a television serial that had been keeping the masses in suspense for weeks."

Some of these actions led nowhere; some, like the assaults on the cyberneticians and sociologists, led to May 1968, when the idea of general contestation on the plane of appearances was realized.

The situationist idea was to prevent the recuperation of such incidents by making theory out of them. Once the speech of the spectacle no longer held a monopoly, it would be heard as babble—as mystification exposed. Those who took part in wildcat strikes or practiced cultural sabotage, the situationists argued, acted out of boredom, rage, disgust—out of an inchoate but inescapable perception that they were not free and, worse, could not form a real image of freedom. Yet there were tentative images of freedom being shaped which, if made into theory, could allow people to understand and maintain their own actions. Out of this, a real image of freedom would appear, and it would dominate: the state and society would begin to dissolve. Resistance to that dissolution would be stillborn, because workers, soldiers, and bureaucrats would act on new possibilities of freedom no less than anyone else—they would join in a general wildcat strike that would end only when society was reconstructed on new terms. When the theory matched the pieces of practice from which the theory was derived, the world would change.

7

The situationist program—as opposed to the situationist project, the situationist practice—came down to Lautréamont and workers' councils. On one side, the avant-garde saint of negation, who had insisted that poetry "must be made by all"; on the other, the self-starting, self-managing organs of direct democracy that had appeared in almost every revolutionary moment of the twentieth century, bypassing the state and allowing for complete participation (the Russian soviets of 1905 and 1917, the German *Räte* of 1919, the anarchist collectives of Barcelona in 1936, the Hungarian councils of 1956). Between those poles, the situationists thought, one would find the liberation of everyday life, the part of experience that was omitted from the history books.

These were the situationist touchstones—and, oddly, they were left unexamined. The situationists' use of workers' councils reminds me of those moments in D. W. Griffith's *Abraham Lincoln* when, stumped by how to get out of a scene, he simply had Walter Huston gaze heavenward and utter the magic words, "The Union!" It is true that the direct democracy of workers' councils—where anyone was allowed to speak, where representation was kept to a minimum and delegates were recallable at any moment—was anathema to Bolsheviks and fascists both, not to mention the managers of representative democracies. It may also have been only the crisis of a revolutionary situation that produced the energy necessary to sustain council politics. The situationists wrote that no one had tried to find out how people had actually lived during those brief moments when revolutionary contestation had found its form—a form that would shape the new society—but they did not try either. They spoke endlessly about "everyday life," but ignored work that examined it both politically and in its smallest details (James Agee's *Let Us Now Praise Famous Men,* Foucault's *Madness and Civilization,* the books of the *Annales* school, Walter Benjamin's *One-Way Street* and *A Berlin Chronicle*), and produced nothing to match it.

But if Lautréamont, workers' councils, and everyday life were more signposts than true elements of a theory, they worked as signposts. The very distance of such images from the world as it was conventionally understood helped expose what that world concealed. What appeared between the signposts of Lautréamont and workers' councils was the possibility of critique.

Pursued without compromise or self-censorship, that critique liberated the situationists from the reassurances of ideology as surely as the experiments of the Lettrist International had liberated its members from the seductions of the bourgeois art world. It opened up a space of freedom and was a necessary preface to the new language of action the situationists were after. A single example will do: the situationist analysis of Vietnam, published in *IS* no. 11, in March 1967—almost frightening in its prescience, and perhaps even more frightening in its clarity.

"It is obviously impossible to seek, at the moment, a *revolutionary* solution to the Vietnam war," said the anonymous writer:

> It is first of all necessary to put an end to the American aggression in order to allow the real social struggle in Vietnam to develop in a natural way; that is to say, to allow the Vietnamese workers and peasants to rediscover their enemies at home; the bureaucracy of the North and all the propertied and ruling strata of the South. The withdrawal of the Americans will mean that the Stalinist bureaucracy will immediately seize control of the whole country: this is the unavoidable

conclusion. Because the invaders cannot indefinitely sustain their aggression; ever since Talleyrand, it has been a commonplace that one can do anything with a bayonet except sit on it. The point, therefore, is not to give unconditional (or even conditional) support to the Vietcong, but to struggle consistently and without any concessions against American imperialism. . . . The Vietnam war is rooted in America and it is from there that it must be rooted out.[26]

This was a long way from the situationists' rejection of the Beat Generation, but the road had been a straight one.

If the situationists were fooled, it was only by themselves; they were not fooled by the world. They understood, as no one else of their time did, why major events—May 1968, the Free Speech Movement, or, for that matter, Malcolm McLaren's experiment with what Simon Frith has called the politicization of consumption—arise out of what are, seemingly, the most trivial provocations and the most banal repressions. They understood why the smallest incidents can lead, with astonishing speed, to a reopening of all questions. Specific, localized explanations tied to economic crises and political contexts never work, because the reason such events developed as they did was what the situationists said it was: people were bored, they were not free, they did not know how to say so. Given the chance, they would say so. People could not form a real image of freedom, and they would seize any opportunity that made the construction of such an image possible.

8

The role of the Situationist International, its members wrote, was not to act as any sort of vanguard party. ("The task of any avant-garde," they wrote, "is to keep abreast of reality.") The situationists "had to know how to wait," and to be ready to disappear in a common festival of revolt. Their job was not to "build" the SI, as the job of a Trotskyist or Bolshevik militant is to build his or her organization, trimming all thoughts and all pronouncements to that goal, careful not to offend anyone who might be seduced or recruited. Their job was to think and speak as clearly as possible—not to get people to listen to speeches, they said, but to get people to think for themselves.

Rather than expanding their group, the situationists worked to make it smaller, expelling careerist, backsliding, or art-as-politics (as opposed to politics-as-art) members almost from the day the group was formed. By the time of the May 1968 revolt, the Situationist International was composed mostly of Parisians hardly more numerous—perhaps less numerous—than those who walked the streets as the Lettrist International. Behind them they had eleven severely elegant numbers of their journal, more than a decade of fitting theory to fragments of practice, and the student scandals, university explosions set off by situationist readers, in Strasbourg and Nanterre, which gained the group a far wider audience than it had ever had before. And so, in May, they made a difference. They defined the mood and the spirit of the event: almost all of the most memorable graffiti from that explosion came, as inspiration or simply quotation, from situationist books and essays. "Those who talk about revolution and class struggle, without understanding what is subversive about love and positive in the refusal of constraints," ran one apparently spontaneous slogan, in fact a quote from Raoul Vaneigem, "such people have corpses in their mouths."

At the liberated Sorbonne and later in their own Council for Maintaining the Occupations, the situationists struggled against reformism, working to define the most radical possibilities of the May revolt—"[This] is now a revolutionary movement," read their "Address to All Workers" of May 30, 1968, "a movement which lacks nothing but *the consciousness of what it has already done* in order to triumph"—which meant, in the end, that the situationists would leave behind the most radical definition of the failure of that revolt. It was an event the situationists had constructed, in the pages of their journal, long before it took place. One can look back to January 1963 and read in *IS* no. 8: "*We will only organize the detonation.*"[27]

9

What to make of this strange mix of postsurrealist ideas about art, Marxian concepts of alienation, an attempt to recover a forgotten revolutionary tradition, millenarianism, and plain refusal of the world combined with a desire to smash it? Nothing, perhaps. The Situationist International cannot even be justified by piggybacking it onto official history, onto May 1968, not because that revolt failed, but because it disappeared. If three hundred books on May 1968 were published within a year of the event, as *IS* no. 12 trumpeted, how many were published in the years to follow? If the situationist idea of general contestation was realized in May 1968, the idea also realized its limits. The theory of the exemplary act—and May was one great, complex, momentarily controlling exemplary act—may have gone as far as such a theory or such an act can go. The group managed one more number of its journal, in 1969; it dissolved, moribund, in 1972.

What one can make of the material in *Internationale situationniste* is perhaps this: out of the goals and the perspectives the situationists defined for themselves came a critique so strong it forces one to try to understand its sources and its shape, no matter how much of it one might see through. In an attack on the Situationist International published in 1978, Jean Barrot wrote that it had wound up "being used as literature." This is undoubtedly true, and it is as well a rather bizarre dismissal of the way in which people might use literature. "An author who teaches a writer nothing," Walter Benjamin wrote in "The Author as Producer," "teaches nobody anything. The determining factor is the exemplary character of a production that enables it, first, to lead other producers to this production, and secondly to present them with an improved apparatus for their use. And this apparatus is better to the degree that it leads consumers to production, in short that it is capable of making co-workers out of readers or spectators." The fact is that the writing the situationists left behind makes almost all present-day political and aesthetic thinking seem cowardly, self-protecting, careerist, and satisfied. It remains a means to the recovery of ambition.

NOTES

Revised version of an essay that first appeared in the *Voice Literary Supplement* 7 (May 1982), 12–18.

1. "Notes éditoriales: Le bruit et la fureur," *Internationale situationniste* 1 (June 1958), 5; translated in Ken Knabb, ed. and trans., *Situationist International Anthology* (Berkeley: Bureau of Public Secrets, 1981), 41–42.

2. Gilles Ivain (pseudonym of Ivan Chtcheglov), "Formulaire pour un urbanisme nouveau," *Internationale situationniste* 1 (June 1958), 17–18; trans. in Knabb, ed., *Situationist International Anthology,* 2–3.

3. Guy Debord, *La société du spectacle* (Paris: Éditions Galllimard, Coll. "Folio," 1992), thesis 191.

4. Quoted from Debord's film *Sur le passage de quelques personnes* (1959); see Guy Debord, *Oeuvres cinématographiques complètes (1952–1978)* (Paris: Éditions Gallimard, 1994), 23–24; trans. in Knabb, ed., *Situationist International Anthology,* 30.

5. Ibid., 32–33; trans. in Knabb, ed., *Situationist International Anthology,* 32.

6. Ibid., 21; trans. in Knabb, ed., *Situationist International Anthology,* 29.

7. Guy Debord and Gil J. Wolman, "Pourquoi le lettrisme?," *Potlatch* 22 (September 9, 1955), n.p.; reprinted in *Potlatch 1954/1957* (Paris: Éditions Allia, 1996), 102.

8. Debord, *La société du spectacle,* thesis 1.

9. "Portrait de l'aliénation," *Internationale situationniste* 11 (October 1967), 5.

10. Debord, *La société du spectacle,* thesis 4.

11. Walter, Benjamin, "One-Way Street (Selection)," in *Reflections,* ed. Peter Demetz, trans. Edmund Jephcott (New York: Schocken Books, 1978), 73–74.

12. Raoul Vaneigem, *The Revolution of Everyday Life,* trans. Donald Nicholson-Smith (London: Left Bank Books and Rebel Press, 1983), 134.

13. Debord, *La société du spectacle,* thesis 30.

14. Ibid., thesis 23.

15. Ibid., thesis 12.

16. Ibid., thesis 30.

17. Ibid., thesis 17.

18. "Notes éditoriales: Domination de la nature, idéologies et classes," *Internationale situationniste* 8 (January 1963), 11; trans. in Knabb, ed., *Situationist International Anthology,* 106.

19. "Maintenant, l'I.S.," *Internationale situationniste* 9 (August 1964), 5; trans. in Knabb, ed., *Situationist International Anthology,* 138.

20. Debord, *La société du spectacle,* thesis 6.

21. *Internationale situationniste* 9 (August 1964), 29.

22. "Le déclin et la chute de l'économie spectaculaire-marchande," *Internationale situationniste* 10 (March 1966), 3; trans. in Knabb, ed., *Situationist International Anthology,* 153.

23. Ibid., 5, 7; trans. in Knabb, ed., *Situationist International Anthology,* 155, 157.

24. "Notes éditoriales: L'opération contre-situationniste dans divers pays," *Internationale situationniste* 8 (January 1963), 29; trans. in Knabb, ed., *Situationist International Anthology,* 113.

25. "Le point d'explosion de l'idéologie en Chine," *Internationale situationniste* 11 (October 1967), 7; trans. in Knabb, ed., *Situationist International Anthology,* 189.

26. "Deux guerres locales," *Internationale situationniste* 11 (October 1967), 21; trans. in Knabb, ed., *Situationist International Anthology,* 203–204.

27. "Notes éditoriales: L'opération contre-situationniste," 28; trans. in Knabb, ed., *Situationist International Anthology,* 113.

The Great Sleep and Its Clients

Guy Debord

TRANSLATED BY Tom McDonough

The other painters, whatever they think of it, instinctively keep
themselves at a distance from discussions about actual trade.

last letter of Vincent van Gogh

It is time to realize that we are capable as well of inventing feelings,
perhaps even feelings comparable in power to love or hate.

Paul Nougé, *Charleroi Conference*

The pitiful debates kept alive around a so-called experimental painting or piece of
music, the ludicrous respect accorded to every exported orientalism, even the
exhumation of "traditional" numerological theories are all the outcome of the
complete abdication of that avant-garde of bourgeois intellectual life that had,
until the past ten years, worked in concrete terms toward the wreck of the ideological superstructures of the society surrounding it, and toward their supersession.

The demands that the modern era allowed to be formulated have yet to be
synthesized, and that synthesis can only be situated at the level of a complete way
of life. The construction of life's setting and manner is an undertaking forbidden

to the isolated intellectuals of capitalist society (which accounts for the dream's long-standing fortune).

Artists whose renown was derived from their contempt for and destruction of art were not engaged in a contradictory practice, for their contempt was dictated by the course of social progress itself. But this phase of art's destruction remains merely a historically necessary social stage of artistic production, responding to given ends, and disappearing in turn with them. Having carried out this destruction, its instigators naturally find themselves incapable of realizing the least of their declared ambitions that lie outside the aesthetic disciplines. The contempt these aging discoverers then profess for the very values from which they make a living—that is, from productions contemporary with the decay of their arts—becomes such a tainted position, requiring submission to the indefinite prolongation of an aesthetic death composed merely of formal repetitions that win over no more than a backward part of college-aged youth. Their contempt moreover implies, in a contradictory way that is nevertheless explicable by class economic solidarity, the impassioned defense of the same aesthetic values against the meanness of, for example, socialist realist painting or politically engaged poetry. The generation of Freud and the dada movement contributed to the collapse of a psychiatry and a morality doomed by the contradictions of the time. They left nothing in their wake, other than forms that some nevertheless insist on believing absolute. To tell the truth, all worthwhile works of this generation and its predecessors lead us to think that the next revolution in sensibility can no longer be conceived of as a novel expression of known facts, but rather as the conscious construction of new emotional states.

We know that a higher order of desires, from its discovery, depreciates the value of lesser realizations, and leads necessarily to its own realization.

Faced with such a requirement, attachment to those creative forms permitted and valued in the economic milieu of the moment is difficult to justify. Voluntary blindness before the true prohibitions confining them leads the "revolutionaries of the mind" to formulate strange defenses: the accusation of bolshevism is the most typical of their indictments, which succeeds every time in placing their opponent outside the law in the eyes of civilized elites. It is common knowledge that so purely "North Atlantic" a conception of civilization is not without its infantile behavior: alchemy is discussed, séances are conducted, omens are observed.

In remembrance of surrealism, nineteen idiots thus recently published a collective tract against us, whose title described us as "Good Friends of the Great What's-Its-Name."[1] The Great What's-Its-Name, for these fellows, was obviously Marxism, the Moscow trials, money, the People's Republic of China, the Two Hundred Families, the late Stalin, and in the final analysis practically everything that is not automatic writing and Gnosticism. They, those Unaware of What's-Its-Name, live on in insignificance, in the high spirits of amusements already trite by 1930. They hold their stubbornness, and perhaps even their morals, in high esteem.

But opinions do not interest us, only systems. Certain comprehensive systems always seem to incur the anathema of individualists armed with their fragmentary theories, whether psychoanalytic or merely literary. These same Olympians, however, are happy to align their entire lives with other systems whose reign, and whose perishable nature, become more difficult to ignore by the day.

From Gaxotte to Breton, these laughable figures are content with denouncing—as if it were a sufficient argument—our rupture with their own views of the world, which are, when all is said and done, all too similar.

The watchdogs have gathered to bay at the moon.

NOTES

Potlatch 16 (January 26, 1955), n.p.

1. [This surrealist tract, published at the end of October 1954, took its title from a line in Rimbaud's poem, "Chant de guerre parisien." The pretext for their polemic was the expulsion of André-Franck Conord from the Lettrist International, on the grounds of "neo-buddhism, evangelism, and spiritualism." In response to this excommunication, Conord had written a parody of Stalinist autocritique, which was published as "Séismes et sismographes" in *Potlatch* 12 (September 28, 1954), n.p. Taking his contrition seriously, the surrealists accused the LI of being "Stalinist garbage" and of being engaged in their own version of the Moscow trials. The full text of their tract may be found in José Pierre, *Tracts surréalistes et déclarations collectives,* vol. 2 (*1940–1969*) (Paris: La Terrain vague, 1982). An account of the LI's ongoing diatribe with the surrealist group throughout 1954 may be found in Christophe Bourseiller, *Vie et mort de Guy Debord* (Paris: Plon, 1999), 82–87. Ed.]

One Step Back

G   D

     T   T   M D

The extreme point reached by the deterioration of all forms of modern culture, the public collapse of the system of repetition that has prevailed since the end of the war, the uniting of various artists and intellectuals on the basis of new perspectives of creation, still unevenly understood—all now beg the question of the foundation, by united avant-gardist trends, of a general revolutionary alternative to official cultural production, defined simultaneously by André Stil and Sagan-Drouet.

The broadening of our forces and the possibility (and necessity) of genuinely international action must lead us to profoundly change our tactics. We must no longer lead an external opposition based only on the future development of issues close to us, but seize hold of modern culture in order to use it for our own ends. We must act immediately to elaborate a critique and the formulation of complementary theses, toward, that is, a common experimental application of these theses. The faction around *Potlatch* must accept, if need be, a minority position within the new international organization, to permit its unification. But all concrete achievements of this movement will naturally lead to its alignment with the most advanced program.

We cannot exactly speak of a crisis of lettrism, since we have always (successfully) wished to foster an atmosphere of permanent crisis; and also because, if the very idea of lettrism is not lacking in all content, the values that interest us, while formed within the lettrist movement, were also formed against it. We might, however, note that a certain satisfied nihilism, in the majority in the LI until the expulsions of 1953,[1] objectively persisted under the guise of an extreme sectarianism that contributed to the distortion of many of our choices until 1956.[2] Such attitudes are not without a certain dishonesty. One of us proclaimed himself in the forefront of the renunciation of writing, valuing our isolation and our idle purity so much that he reached the decision to refuse collaboration with the journal that, of them all, is the closest to our positions. He had scarcely been expelled for five days when he entreated—in vain, naturally—the editorial board of this journal to pursue a literary collaboration "in a personal capacity." Had this comrade then been acting previously as an agitator? No: when the purely nominal alibi of "lettrism" had failed him, leaving only the void, he simply passed from one irresponsible behavior to another, opposite, one.[3]

The worn-out, worldly hoaxes that we are fighting can always, through some subterfuge, appear as something new, and thus hold us back. No label can shelter us from it. No seduction is sufficient. We have to find concrete techniques to revolutionize the setting of everyday life.

The first practical question we must face is the significant broadening of our economic base. In our present condition, it seems easier to invent new emotions than a new profession. The urgency with which we must attend the definition—and the justification through practice—of several new occupations, distinct for example from the social function of the artist, leads us to support the idea of a collective economic program, as called for by Piero Simondo and our Italian comrades.

Undoubtedly the decision to make use, from the economic as from the constructive viewpoint, of retrograde fragments of modernism entails serious risks of decomposition. To cite a specific case, friends worry about a sudden numerical predominance of painters, whose work they inevitably judge insignificant and indissolubly linked with artistic commerce.[4] However, we need to gather specialists from very varied fields, know the latest autonomous developments in those fields—without falling into the trap of ideological imperialism, whereby the reality of problems from a foreign discipline are ignored in favor of settling them from outside—and test out a unitary use of these presently dispersed means. We thus need to run the risk of regression, but we must also offer, as soon as possible, the means to supersede the contradictions of the present phase through a deepening of our general theory and through conducting experiments whose results are indisputable.

Although certain artistic activities might be more notoriously mortally wounded than others, we believe that the hanging of a painting in a gallery is a relic as inevitably uninteresting as a book of poetry. Any use of the current framework of intellectual commerce surrenders ground to ideological confusionism, and this includes us; but on the other hand we can do nothing without taking into account from the outset this ephemeral framework.

In the last instance, the politics we are now adopting will be judged on whether or not it is capable of assisting in the formation of a more progressive international group. Barring that, it will merely mark the beginning of a general reactionary trend within this movement. In that case, the formation of a revolutionary cultural avant-garde will depend upon the appearance of other forces.

NOTES

Potlatch 28 (May 22, 1957), n.p.

1. [Debord would seem here to refer to the first expulsions from the LI, which would include Jean-Michel Mension and François Dufrêne (1953), and Ivan Chtcheglov and Jean-Louis Brau (1954). Ed.]

2. [September 1956 marked the conference held in Alba, Italy, that began the process of the formation of the Situationist International and the end of the Lettrist International's intransigent isolation. See Guy Debord, "Report on the Construction of Situations . . . ," translated in this volume, 43. Ed.]

3. [The journal must be the Belgian *Les lèvres nues,* edited by Marcel Mariën; it was the only publication with which Debord and the LI collaborated at the time, and in which he published some of his most significant essays of the 1950s (notably, "Introduction to a Critique of Urban Geography" and, with Gil J. Wolman, "Methods of *Détournement*." The colleague in question, however, remains unidentified. Ed.]

4. [The "friends" referred to here must certainly include Constant; see his "Extracts from Letters to the Situationist International" from September 1958, translated in this volume, 75–76; and their reprise in his "Sur nos moyens et nos perspectives," *Internationale situationniste* 2 (December 1958), 23–26. Ed.]

Report on the Construction of Situations and on the Terms of Organization and Action of the International Situationist Tendency

GUY DEBORD

TRANSLATED BY TOM MCDONOUGH

REVOLUTION AND COUNTERREVOLUTION IN MODERN CULTURE

First, we believe that the world must be changed. We desire the most liberatory possible change of the society and the life in which we find ourselves confined. We know that such change is possible by means of pertinent actions.

Our concern is precisely the use of certain means of action, along with the discovery of new ones that may more easily be recognized in the sphere of culture and manners but that will be implemented with a view to interaction with global revolutionary change.

In a given society, what is termed culture is the reflection, but also the foreshadowing, of possibilities for life's planning. Our era is at heart characterized by the great distance at which revolutionary political action lags behind the development of the modern potentialities of production, which demands a superior organization of the world.

We are living through a fundamental historical crisis, in which the problem of the rational control of new productive forces, as well as the formulation of a civilization on a global scale, are each year expressed more clearly. Yet the action of the international workers' movement, on which depends the initial defeat of the exploitative economic infrastructure, has only achieved scattered half-successes. Capitalism is devising new forms of struggle (state intervention in the market, growth in the distribution sector, fascist governments); it is relying on the deterioration in workers' leadership; it is masking the nature of class oppositions by means of various reformist tactics. In this way, it has up to the present been able to preserve familiar social relations in the great majority of highly industrialized countries, thus depriving a socialist society of its essential material foundation. On the other hand, underdeveloped or colonized countries, which have been engaged en masse over the past decade in a more comprehensive battle against imperialism, are about to achieve a very important victory. Their successes are worsening the contradictions of the capitalist economy and, primarily in the case of the Chinese revolution, are furthering a revival of the entire revolutionary movement. This revival cannot be content with reforms in the capitalist or anticapitalist countries, but, on the contrary, must everywhere amplify conflicts that lead to the questioning of power.

The disintegration of modern culture is the result, on the level of ideological struggle, of the confused paroxysm of these conflicts. The new desires in the course of delineation are conceived in an awkward position: while the era's resources permit their realization, the obsolete economic structure is incapable of exploiting those resources. At the same time, the ruling class's ideology has lost all consistency thanks to the bankrupting of its successive conceptions of the world, a situation that inclines it to historical uncertainty; thanks as well to the coexistence of reactionary thoughts that have developed over time and that are, in principle, opposed to one another, like Christianity and social democracy; likewise, thanks to the fusion of contributions from several civilizations that are foreign to the contemporary West and whose value has only recently been recognized. The main goal of the ideology of the ruling class is thus to sow confusion.

In culture—and in using this word we are continually leaving aside its scientific or pedagogical aspects, even if ideological confusion makes them felt at the level of grand scientific theories or broad notions of education; culture for us refers rather to a compound of aesthetics, feelings, and manners, that is, to a period's reaction to everyday life—confusionist counterrevolutionary processes consist of, simultaneously, the partial annexation of new values and a deliberately anticultural production utilizing the means of large-scale industry (novels, cinema), the natural result of the mindlessness of youth trapped in schools and families. The ruling ideology arranges the trivialization of subversive discoveries, and widely circulates them after sterilization. It even succeeds in making use of subversive individuals: when dead, by doctoring their works; when alive, thanks to the general ideological confusion, by drugging them with one of the blind mystical beliefs in which it deals.

It so happens that one of the contradictions of the bourgeoisie in its stage of elimination is its respect for intellectual and artistic creation in principle, while at first opposing its creations and then making use of them. It needs to preserve the sense of critique and research among a minority, but only with the condition that this activity be directed toward strictly separated utilitarian disciplines, dismissing all comprehensive critique and research. In the cultural sphere, the bourgeoisie strives to divert the taste for the new, which has become dangerous for it, toward certain debased forms of novelty that are harmless and muddled. Through the commercial mechanisms that control cultural activity, avant-garde tendencies are cut off from the constituencies that might support them, constituencies that are already limited by the entirety of social conditions. People from these tendencies who have been noticed are generally admitted on an individual basis, at the price of a vital repudiation; the fundamental point of debate is always the renunciation of comprehensive demands and the acceptance of a fragmented work, open to multiple readings. This is what makes the very term *avant-garde,* which when all is said and done is wielded by the bourgeoisie, somewhat suspicious and ridiculous.

The very notion of a collective avant-garde, with the militant aspect that it entails, is a recent product of historical conditions that are leading simultaneously to the need for a consistent revolutionary cultural program, and to the need to struggle against the forces that are preventing the development of this program. Such groups are led to transpose a few of the organizational methods created by revolutionary politics into their sphere of activity, and in the future their actions will no longer be able to be conceived without a link to political critique. In this respect, there is a noticeable advance from futurism, dadaism, and surrealism to the movements formed after 1945. All the same, however, one discovers at each stage the same universal will for change, and the same quick breakup when the incapacity to change the real world profoundly enough leads to a defensive withdrawal into the very doctrinal positions whose inadequacy had just been revealed.

Futurism, whose influence was propagated from Italy in the period preceding the First World War, adopted a disruptive attitude toward literature and the arts, an attitude that did not fail to provide a large number of formal novelties but that was founded only on an exceedingly oversimplified use of the idea of technological progress. The childishness of the futurists' technological optimism evaporated along with the period of bourgeois euphoria that sustained it. Italian futurism plummeted from nationalism to fascism without ever achieving a more complete theoretical vision of its time.

Dadaism, contrived in Zurich and New York by refugees and deserters of the First World War, wished to be the refusal of all the values of bourgeois society, whose bankruptcy had just become so glaringly evident. Its drastic expressions in postwar France and Germany focused mainly on the destruction of art and writing and, to a lesser extent, on certain forms of behavior (intentionally idiotic shows, speeches, walks). Its historical role was to have dealt a mortal blow to the traditional conception of culture. The almost immediate breakup of dadaism was necessitated by its wholly negative definition. However, it is certain that the dadaist spirit has determined a part of all the movements succeeding it; and that an aspect of negation, historically associated with dadaism, must end up in every subsequent constructive position as long as those positions manage to resist being swept up by the force of social conditions that would impose the mere repetition of crumbling superstructures, whose intellectual verdict has long since been declared.

The creators of surrealism, who had participated in the dada movement in France, did their best to define the grounds for a constructive action starting from dada's emphasis on moral revolt and the extreme erosion of traditional means of communication. Arising from a poetic application of Freudian psychology, surrealism extended the methods it had discovered to painting, to film, and to some aspects of everyday life—and then, in a diffuse form, it extended them much further. Indeed, for an enterprise of this nature, it is not a question of being absolutely or relatively right, but of succeeding in catalyzing for a certain time the desires of an era. Surrealism's period of progress, marked by the liquidation of idealism and a momentary rallying to dialectical materialism, ceased soon after 1930, but its decay only became manifest at the end of the Second World War. Since that time, surrealism had spread to a rather large number of countries. It had, moreover, inaugurated a discipline whose severity must not be overestimated, moderated as it often was by commercial considerations, but which nevertheless remained an effective means of struggle against the confusionist mechanisms of the bourgeoisie.

The surrealist program, asserting the sovereignty of desire and surprise, offering a new practice of life, is much richer in constructive possibilities than is generally thought. Certainly, the lack of material means of realization seriously limited the scope of surrealism. But the spiritualistic outcome of its first agitators, and above all the mediocrity of its epigones, oblige us to search for the negation of the development of surrealist theory in its very origin.

The error that is at the root of surrealism is the idea of the infinite wealth of the unconscious imagination. The reason for the ideological failure of surrealism was its having wagered that the unconscious was the long-sought chief power of life. It was its having consequently revised the history of ideas, and its having stopped there. We now know that the unconscious imagination is poor, that automatic writing is monotonous, and that the whole genre of the "unusual," which the changeless surrealist trend ostentatiously parades, is extremely unsurprising. Strict fidelity to this style of imagination ends by reducing itself to the very opposite of the modern conditions of the imaginary, that is, to traditional occultism. The extent to which surrealism has remained dependent upon its hypothesis regarding the unconscious can be measured in the work of theoretical investigation attempted by the second-generation surrealists: Calas and Mabille link everything to the two successive viewpoints of the surrealist experience of the unconscious—the first to psychoanalysis, the second to cosmic influences. As a matter of fact, the discovery of the role of the unconscious had been a surprise, an innovation, and not the law of future surprises and innovations. Freud had also ended by discovering this as well when he wrote, "Everything conscious wears out. What is unconscious remains unvarying. But once it is set loose, does it not fall into ruins in its turn?"

Resisting an apparently irrational society in which the rupture between reality and still loudly proclaimed values was carried to ridiculous lengths, surrealism made use of the irrational to destroy that society's superficially logical values. The very success of surrealism played a big part in the fact that the former's ideology, in its most modern aspect, has renounced a strict hierarchy of artificial values, but makes open use, in its turn, of the irrational and of surrealist survivals at the same opportunity. The bourgeoisie must above all avert a new departure of revolutionary thought. It was conscious of the threatening nature of surrealism. It enjoys certifying, now that it has been able to disperse it into standard aesthetic commerce, that surrealism reached the furthest point of disorder. It thus cultivates a manner of nostalgia for surrealism, at the same time that it disparages all new enquiry by automatically reducing it to surrealist déjà-vu, i.e., to a failure that for it can no longer be questioned by anyone. Rejection of the alienation of the society of Christian morality led a few men to a respect for the fully irrational alienation of primitive societies; that's all. It is necessary to go further and rationalize the world more, the first condition for making it exciting.

DECOMPOSITION, THE ULTIMATE STAGE OF BOURGEOIS THOUGHT

Allegedly modern culture has its two chief centers in Paris and Moscow. Trends from Paris, which for the most part are not developed by the French themselves, influence Europe, America, and other advanced countries in the capitalist zone like Japan. Trends bureaucratically imposed by Moscow influence all the workers' states and, to a lesser extent, have an effect on Paris and its European zone of influence. Moscow's influence has a directly political origin, but in order to explain Paris's traditional influence, which it still maintains, we must take into account an established lead in the concentration of cultural professionals.

Bourgeois thought, lost in systematic confusion; Marxist thought, profoundly deformed in the workers' states—conservatism prevails in the East and the West, and above all in the sphere of culture and manners. It flaunts itself in Moscow by reviving the typical attitudes of the nineteenth-century petite bourgeoisie, while in Paris it disguises itself as anarchism, cynicism, or humor. Although the two dominant cultures would be fundamentally unfit to synthesize the genuine issues of our time, we might say that the experiment has been pushed further in the West, and that in this productive order Moscow's zone looks like an underdeveloped region.

In the bourgeois zone, where, by and large, an appearance of intellectual freedom has been tolerated, knowledge of the evolution of ideas or a muddled view of the numerous transformations of the environment encourage awareness of the upheaval under way, whose impulses are uncontrollable. The reigning sensibility tries to adapt while preventing new changes that are, in the final analysis, inevitably harmful to it. At the same time, the solutions put forward by reactionary trends ultimately boil down to three attitudes: a continuation of forms produced by the crisis of dadaism and surrealism (which is merely the developed cultural expression of a state of mind that spontaneously arises everywhere when past ways of life, the reasons for living accepted until then, collapse), a settling into the mental ruins, and finally the long look back.

As for tenacious forms, a diluted sort of surrealism is found everywhere. It has all the tastes of the surrealist era and none of its ideas. Its aesthetic is one of repetition. The remains of the orthodox surrealist movement at this senile-occultist stage are as incapable of having an ideological position as of thinking up anything at all: they support ever more vulgar charlatanisms and demand such support from others.

Settling into uselessness is the cultural solution that has most forcefully made itself known in the years following the Second World War. It leaves a choice between two possibilities, of which there have been abundant examples: dissembling nothingness by means of a suitable vocabulary, or its offhand affirmation.

The first option has been made famous, above all, by existentialist literature, which copies—under the shelter of a borrowed philosophy—the most mediocre aspects of the past thirty years of cultural development; this literature sustains its interest, whose origins lie in commercial promotion, through counterfeits of Marxism or psychoanalysis, or even through groping in the dark toward recurrent political commitments and resignations. This behavior has had a large number of followers, some of whom were swaggering, others sly. The continuing swarm of abstract painting, and of the theories explaining it, is a fact of the same nature and of comparable extent.

The joyous affirmation of a perfect mental nullity characterizes the phenomenon that in recent neoliterature is called "the cynicism of young novelists of the right." It extends far beyond people of the right, novelists, or their semi-youth.

Among the trends that call for a return to the past, the doctrine of socialist realism is proving to be the boldest, given that its claims of reliance upon the findings of a revolutionary movement allow it to support an indefensible position in the sphere of cultural creation. At the conference of Soviet musicians, in 1948, Andrei Zhdanov revealed the stakes of his theoretical repression: "Did we do the right thing in preserving the treasures of classical painting and in putting to rout the liquidators of painting? Would not the survival of such 'schools' mean the liquidation of painting?" In the presence of that liquidation of painting (and of many other liquidations) the enlightened Western bourgeoisie, taking note of the collapse of all its value systems, prepared total ideological decomposition by means of desperate reaction and political opportunism. On the other hand, Zhdanov—with the characteristic taste of an upstart—recognized himself in the petit bourgeois who is against the decomposition of the last century's cultural values and makes sure that nothing is attempted other than an authoritarian restoration of those values. It is unrealistic enough to believe that transient and localized political circumstances provide the power to evade the general problems of a period, never mind if one is required once again to take up superseded problems, after having dismissed a priori all the lessons that history has drawn from those problems in their time.

The traditional propaganda of religious organizations, and especially of Catholicism, is close in form and in several aspects of content to this socialist realism. Through an unvarying propaganda, Catholicism defends an overall ideological structure that it alone, of all the forces of the past, still possesses. However, in order to recapture the ever more numerous sectors that escape its influence, the Catholic church is attempting, parallel to its traditional propaganda, to incorporate modern cultural forms, chiefly among those that fall within the domain of torturous theoretical uselessness—so-called *informel* painting, for example.

The present outcome of this crisis of modern culture is ideological decomposition. Nothing new can be built any longer on these ruins, and the simple exercise of critical thought is becoming impossible, for any judgment comes up against others, and each makes reference to scraps of disused comprehensive systems or to personal, sentimental imperatives.

Decomposition has reached everything. We no longer see the massive use of commercial advertising to exert ever greater influence over judgments of cultural creation; this was an old process. Instead, we are reaching a point of ideological absence in which only the advertising acts, to the exclusion of all previous critical judgments—but not without dragging along a conditioned reflex of such judgment. The complex play of sales techniques is reduced to the automatic creation of pseudosubjects for cultural discussion, much to the surprise of the professionals. This is the sociological importance of the Sagan-Drouet phenomenon, an experience witnessed these last three years in France whose effect, prompting interest in the workers' states, has even surpassed the limits of the cultural zone centered on Paris. The professional judges of culture, in the presence of the Sagan-Drouet phenomenon, sense the unforeseeable result of mechanisms that elude them, and they generally explain it in terms of the methods of circus advertisement. But, owing to their occupation, they find themselves forced to contend, through critiques in name only, with the subject of these works in name only (a work whose significance is inexplicable constitutes, moreover, the richest subject for bourgeois confusionist criticism). They inevitably remain unaware of the fact that the intellectual mechanisms of criticism have eluded them long before external mechanisms came to exploit this vacuum. They refrain from recognizing in Sagan-Drouet the absurd reverse of the transformation of means of expression into means of action upon everyday life. This process of supersession has made the author's life more and more important in relation to his work. Then, the period of significant expressions having reached its ultimate reduction, the only remaining possibility of importance is the personage of the author who, rightly, could no longer have anything noteworthy other than his age, a fashionable vice, or an old, picturesque occupation.

The opposition that must now be united against ideological decomposition should not, furthermore, endeavor to critique the antics produced among doomed forms like poetry or the novel. Only activities important for the future, those that we need to use, must be critiqued. A most serious sign of today's ideological decomposition is functionalist architectural theory's basis in the most reactionary notions of society and ethics, i.e., that an excessively retrograde notion of life and its scope is smuggled into the imperfect yet temporarily beneficial contributions of the first Bauhaus or the school of Le Corbusier.

However, everything since 1956 indicates that we are entering into a new phase of struggle, and that an eruption of revolutionary forces, which on all fronts will come up against the most appalling obstacles, is beginning to change the conditions of the previous period. At the same time we can see socialist realism beginning to lose ground in the countries of the anticapitalist camp, along with the Stalinist reaction that had produced it; the culture of Sagan-Drouet most likely marking an impassable stage of bourgeois decadence; and finally a relative awareness, in the West, of the exhaustion of cultural expedients that have been of service since the end of the Second World War. The avant-garde minority can recover its positive import.

THE FUNCTION OF MINORITY TRENDS IN THE PERIOD OF REFLUX

The ebbing of the worldwide revolutionary movement, which became obvious a few years after 1920 and became ever more marked until the approach of 1950, was followed within five or six years by an ebbing of the movements that had tried to advance a liberatory new attitude in culture and everyday life. The ideological and material significance of such movements decreased continuously until they reached a point of complete social isolation. Their actions, which under more favorable conditions might have brought about an abrupt renewal of the affective climate, weakened until conservative trends managed to forbid them any direct access to the rigged game of official culture. These movements, dismissed from their role in the production of new values, would henceforth form a reserve army of intellectual labor from which the bourgeoisie could draw individuals who might add novel touches to its propaganda.

At this stage of decay, the experimental avant-garde's social significance is apparently inferior to that of pseudomodernist trends that in no way take the trouble to display a desire for change, but that represent—through drastic measures—the accepted face of modern culture. However, all those who have a place in the true production of modern culture and who discover their interests as producers of this culture (all the more keenly so as they are reduced to a negative position) are developing a consciousness based in these facts that is inevitably lacking among the modernist shams of a washed-up society. The poverty of recognized culture and its monopoly over the means of cultural production lead to a proportional poverty of the avant-garde's theory and expressions. But it is only within this avant-garde that a new revolutionary conception of culture is imperceptibly being formed. This new conception must assert itself at the moment when the ruling culture and the outlines of an oppositional culture reach the furthest point of their separation and their mutual powerlessness.

The history of modern culture during the ebb tide of revolution is thus the history of the theoretical and practical reduction of the movement for renewal, a history that reaches as far as the segregation of minority trends, and as far as the undivided domination of decomposition.

Between 1930 and the Second World War, we witnessed the continual decline of surrealism as a revolutionary force, at the same time as its influence extended far beyond its control. The postwar period brought about the quick liquidation of surrealism by the two elements that exhausted its development around 1930: first, the lack of possibilities for theoretical renewal, and the ebb of revolution, which found expression in the political and cultural reaction of the workers' movement. This second element is directly determinant, for example, in the disappearance of Romania's surrealist group. On the other hand, it was, above all, the first of these elements that sentenced the revolutionary-surrealist movement in France and Belgium to a quick breakup. Except in Belgium, where a group issuing from surrealism continued a valid experimental position, all the surrealist tendencies scattered around the world have rejoined the side of mystical idealism.

Assembling a part of the revolutionary-surrealism movement, an "International of Experimental Artists"—which published the journal *Cobra* (Copenhagen-Brussels-Amsterdam)—was set up between 1949 and 1951 in Denmark, Holland, and Belgium, and then extended to Germany. The merit of these groups was to have understood that such an organization is required by the complexity and extent of current problems. But the lack of ideological rigor, the limitation of their investigations chiefly to the plastic arts, and, above all, the absence of a general theory of the conditions and perspectives of their experiment provoked their breakup.

In France, lettrism had started from a complete opposition to all known aesthetic movements, whose continual decay it precisely analyzed. Intending the uninterrupted creation of new forms in all spheres, the lettrist group maintained a salutary agitation between 1946 and 1952. But, having generally accepted the idealist fallacy that aesthetic disciplines should take a new departure within a general framework similar to the former one, its productions were restricted to a few laughable experiments. In 1952 the lettrist left wing organized itself into a "Lettrist International" and expelled the backward group. In the Lettrist International, the search for new processes of intervention in everyday life was pursued, amid sharp struggles among different tendencies.

In Italy, with the exception of the antifunctionalist experimental group that in 1955 formed the soundest section of the International Movement for an Imaginist Bauhaus, the attempts at forming avant-gardes linked with old artistic viewpoints have not even succeeded in a theoretical expression.

In the meantime, the follow-the-leader attitude of Western culture has held sway from the United States to Japan, with all its triviality and popularizations (the avant-garde of the United States, which is in the habit of gathering in Paris's American colony, is there isolated from the ideological, social, and even topographical standpoints in the dullest conformism). The productions of peoples who are subject to cultural colonialism—often brought about by political oppression—play a reactionary role in advanced cultural centers, even if they are progressive in their country. Indeed, critics who have tied their entire careers to out-of-date references to the old systems of creation affect to find novelties after their own hearts in Greek cinema or the Guatemalan novel. Thus do they appeal to an exoticism that happens to be anti-exotic, since it is a question of the late reappearance in other nations of formerly employed approaches, but which certainly has the chief function of exoticism: the flight away from real conditions of life and creation.

In the worker's states, only the experiment led by Brecht in Berlin, in its questioning of the classical idea of theater, is close to the constructions that matter for us today. Only Brecht has succeeded in holding out against the stupidity of the reigning socialist realism.

Now that socialist realism is falling to pieces, we can expect everything from the revolutionary irruption of the intellectuals of the workers' states into the true problems of modern culture. If Zhdanovism has been the purest expression not merely of the cultural deterioration of the labor movement but also of the conservative cultural position of the bourgeois world, then those who are rising up against Zhdanovism at this moment in the East cannot be doing so, whatever their subjective intentions, in the name of a greater cultural freedom that is nothing more than that of, for example, Cocteau. It must truthfully be seen that the objective meaning of the negation of Zhdanovism lies in the negation of the Zhdanovist negation of "liquidation." The only possible supersession of Zhdanovism will be the practice of a genuine freedom, which is consciousness of present necessity.

Here, similarly, the years that have just passed have merely been, at the very most, a period of confused resistance to the confused reign of retrograde foolishness. We did not partake in this confusion. However, we must not linger over the tastes or the little discoveries of that era. The problems of cultural creation can no longer be resolved other than in relation to new progress in worldwide revolution.

———

Platform of a Provisional Opposition

A revolutionary action within culture cannot have as its aim to be the expression or analysis of life, but its expansion. Misery must be pushed back everywhere. Revolution does not only lie in the question of knowing what level of production heavy industry is attaining and who will be its master. Along with the exploitation of man, the passions, compensations, and habits that were its products must also wither away. Now, we must define desires appropriate to today's potentialities. Even at the height of struggle between present-day society and the forces that will destroy it, we must already find the initial components of a higher construction of the environment and of new conditions of behavior—the latter through experimentation and propaganda. All the rest belongs to the past and is its servant.

We must undertake an organized collective labor that will strive for a common usage of all the means of transforming everyday life. That is to say, we must first recognize the interdependence of those means from the viewpoint of a greater domination of nature, a greater freedom. We must build new settings that will be both the product and the instrument of new behaviors. To do this, at the outset, requires that we empirically use everyday approaches and cultural forms that presently exist, while questioning their value. The very criterion of novelty, of formal invention, has lost its meaning within the traditional limits of an art, i.e., within the limits of an inadequate, fragmentary medium whose partial renewals are already outdated, and hence unworkable.

We must not reject modern culture, but seize it in order to repudiate it. An intellectual cannot be revolutionary if he does not acknowledge the cultural revolution before us. A creative intellectual cannot be revolutionary simply by supporting the politics of a given party, even if he does so by original means, but must rather work, outside of parties, for the necessary change of all cultural superstructures. Similarly, the quality of a bourgeois intellectual is ultimately determined not by his social origin, nor by his cultural knowledge (the common starting point of criticism and of creation), but by his role in the production of historically bourgeois forms. Authors with revolutionary political opinions, when congratulated by bourgeois literary criticism, need to search for what mistakes they have made.

The union of several experimental trends into a revolutionary front within culture, begun at the conference held at Alba, Italy, at the close of 1956, assumes that we will not neglect three factors.

First of all, we require a complete agreement of persons and groups participating in this united action, and such an agreement must not be facilitated by allowing participants to close their eyes to certain consequences. We must distance ourselves from practical jokers or careerists whose lack of conviction leads them to wish to succeed by such a route.

Next, we need to remember that if every truly experimental attitude is useful, nevertheless the excessive use of this word has very often served as justification for an artistic act within a current structure, i.e., one discovered previously by others. The only valid experimental approach is one based on the uncompromising critique of existing conditions and their conscious supersession. Once and for all, it must be stated that we will not dignify with the term creation what is merely personal expression within the limits of means set up by others. Creation is not the arrangement of objects and forms, but the invention of new laws for such an arrangement.

Finally, we must eliminate sectarianism among ourselves, for it will stand in the way of acting toward defined ends in unity with potential allies, and it will prevent the infiltration of similar organizations. Between 1952 and 1955, the Lettrist International, after some necessary purges, moved continually toward a kind of uncompromising discipline that led to an equally uncompromising isolation and ineffectiveness, and that in the end favored a certain opposition to change, a decay of the spirit of critique and discovery. We must supersede such sectarian behavior once and for all in favor of genuine actions. On this lone criterion we must join or abandon our comrades. Of course, this does not mean that we have to renounce expulsions, as everyone invites us to do. On the contrary, we believe that we must go even further in banishing certain habits and people.

We must collectively define our program and carry it out in a disciplined manner, through all means—even artistic ones.

Toward a Situationist International

Our central purpose is the construction of situations, that is, the concrete construction of temporary settings of life and their transformation into a higher, passionate nature. We must develop an intervention directed by the complicated factors of two great components in perpetual interaction: the material setting of life and the behaviors that it incites and that overturn it.

Our prospects for action on the environment lead, in their latest development, to the idea of a unitary urbanism. Unitary urbanism first becomes clear in the use of the whole of arts and techniques as means cooperating in an integral composition of the environment. This whole must be considered infinitely more extensive than the old influence of architecture on the traditional arts, or the current occasional application to anarchic urbanism of specialized techniques or of scientific investigations such as ecology. Unitary urbanism must control, for example, the acoustic environment as well as the distribution of different varieties of drink or food. It must take up the creation of new forms and the *détournement* of known forms of architecture and urbanism—as well as the *détournement* of the old poetry and cinema. Integral art, about which so much has been said, can only materialize at the level of urbanism. But it can no longer correspond with any traditional definitions of the aesthetic. In each of its experimental cities, unitary urbanism will work through a certain number of force fields, which we can temporarily designate by the standard expression *district*. Each district will be able to lead to a precise harmony, broken off from neighboring harmonies; or rather will be able to play on a maximum breaking up of internal harmony.

Secondly, unitary urbanism is dynamic, i.e., in close touch with styles of behavior. The most reduced element of unitary urbanism is not the house but the architectural complex, which is the union of all the factors conditioning an environment, or a sequence of environments colliding at the scale of the constructed situation. Spatial development must take the affective realities that the experimental city will determine into account. One of our comrades has promoted a theory of states-of-mind districts, according to which each quarter of a city would tend to induce a single emotion, to which the subject will consciously expose herself or himself. It seems that such a project draws timely conclusions from an increasing depreciation of accidental primary emotions, and that its realization could contribute to accelerating this change. Comrades who call for a new architecture, a free architecture, must understand that this new architecture will not play at first on free, poetic lines and forms—in the sense that today's "lyrical abstract" painting uses these words—but rather on the atmospheric effects of rooms, corridors, streets, atmospheres linked to the behaviors they contain. Architecture must advance by taking as its subject emotionally moving situations, more than emotionally moving forms, as the material it works with. And the experiments drawn from this subject will lead to unknown forms. Psychogeographical research, "study of the exact laws and precise effects of the geographical environment, consciously organized or not, acting directly on the affective deportment of individuals," thus takes on its double meaning of active observation of today's urban areas and the establishment of hypotheses on the structure of a situationist city. Psychogeography's progress depends to a great extent on the statistical extension of its methods of observation, but principally on experimentation through concrete interventions in urbanism. Until this stage, the objective truth of even the first psychogeographical data cannot be ensured. But even if these data should turn out to be false, they would certainly be false solutions to a genuine problem.

Our action on deportment, in connection with other desirable aspects of a revolution in customs, can be defined summarily as the invention of a new species of games. The most general aim must be to broaden the nonmediocre portion of life, to reduce its empty moments as much as possible. It may thus be spoken of as an enterprise of human life's quantitative increase, more serious than the biological processes currently being studied. Even there, it implies a qualitative increase whose developments are unforeseeable. The situationist game stands out from the standard conception of the game by the radical negation of the ludic features of competition and of its separation from the stream of life. In contrast, the situationist game does not appear distinct from a moral choice, deciding what ensures the future reign of freedom and play. This is obviously linked to the certainty of the continual and rapid increase of leisure, at a level corresponding to that of our era's productive forces. It is equally linked to the recognition of the fact that a battle over leisure is taking place before our eyes whose importance in the class struggle has not been sufficiently analyzed. To this day, the ruling class is succeeding in making use of the leisure that the revolutionary proletariat extracted from it by developing a vast industrial sector of leisure that is an unrivaled instrument for bestializing the proletariat through by-products of mystifying ideology and bourgeois tastes. One of the reasons for the American working class's incapacity to become politicized should likely be sought amidst this abundance of televised baseness. By obtaining through collective pressure a slight rise in the price of its labor above the minimum necessary for the production of that labor, the proletariat not only enlarges its power of struggle but also widens the terrain of the struggle. New forms of this struggle then occur parallel with directly economic and political conflicts. Revolutionary propaganda can be said until now to have been constantly dominated in these forms of struggle in all countries where advanced industrial development has introduced them. That the necessary transformation of the base could be delayed by errors and weaknesses at the level of superstructures has unfortunately been proven by some of the twentieth century's experiences. New forces must be hurled into the battle over leisure, and we will take up our position there.

A first attempt at a new manner of deportment has already been achieved with what we have designated the *dérive,* which is the practice of a passionate uprooting through the hurried change of environments, as well as a means of studying psychogeography and situationist psychology. But the application of this will to ludic creation must be extended to all known forms of human relationships, and must, for example, influence the historical evolution of emotions like friendship and love. Everything leads to the belief that the main insight of our research lies in the hypothesis of constructions of situations.

A man's life is a sequence of chance situations, and if none of them is exactly similar to another, at the least these situations are, in their immense majority, so undifferentiated and so dull that they perfectly present the impression of similitude. The corollary of this state of affairs is that the singular, enchanting situations experienced in life strictly restrain and limit this life. We must try to con-

struct situations, i.e., collective environments, ensembles of impressions determining the quality of a moment. If we take the simple example of a gathering of
a group of individuals for a given time, and taking into account acquaintances
and material means at our disposal, we must study which arrangement of the site,
which selection of participants, and which incitement of events suit the desired
environment. Surely the powers of a situation will broaden considerably in time
and in space with the realizations of unitary urbanism or the education of a situationist generation. The construction of situations begins on the other side of the
modern collapse of the idea of the theater. It is easy to see to what extent the very
principle of the theater—nonintervention—is attached to the alienation of the
old world. Inversely, we see how the most valid of revolutionary cultural explorations have sought to break the spectator's psychological identification with the
hero, so as to incite this spectator into activity by provoking his capacities to revolutionize his own life. The situation is thus made to be lived by its constructors.
The role of the "public," if not passive at least a walk-on, must ever diminish,
while the share of those who cannot be called actors but, in a new meaning of
the term, "livers,"[1] will increase.

Let us say that we have to multiply poetic objects and subjects (unfortunately so rare at present that the most trifling of them assumes an exaggerated
emotional importance) and that we have to organize games of these poetic
subjects among these poetic objects. There is our entire program, which is essentially ephemeral. Our situations will be without a future; they will be places
where people are constantly coming and going. The unchanging nature of art,
or of anything else, does not enter into our considerations, which are in earnest.
The idea of eternity is the basest one a man could conceive of regarding his acts.

Situationist techniques have yet to be invented, but we know that a task
presents itself only where the material conditions necessary for its realization already exist, or are at least in the process of formation. We must begin with a
small-scale, experimental phase. Undoubtedly we must draw up blueprints for
situations, like scripts, despite their unavoidable inadequacy at the beginning.
Therefore, we will have to introduce a system of notation whose accuracy will
increase as experiments in construction teach us more. We will have to find or

confirm laws, like those that make situationist emotion dependent upon an extreme concentration or an extreme dispersion of acts (classical tragedy providing an approximate image of the first case, and the *dérive* of the second). Besides the direct means that will be used toward precise ends, the construction of situations will require, in its affirmative phase, a new implementation of reproductive technologies. We could imagine, for example, live televisual projections of some aspects of one situation into another, bringing about modifications and interferences. But, more simply, cinematic "news"-reels might finally deserve their name if we establish a new documentary school dedicated to fixing the most meaningful moments of a situation for our archives, before the development of these elements has led to a different situation. The systematic construction of situations having to generate previously nonexistent feelings, the cinema will discover its greatest pedagogical role in the diffusion of these new passions.

Situationist theory resolutely asserts a noncontinuous conception of life. The idea of consistency must be transferred from the perspective of the whole of a life—where it is a reactionary mystification founded on the belief in an immortal soul and, in the last analysis, on the division of labor—to the viewpoint of moments isolated from life, and of the construction of each moment by a unitary use of situationist means. In a classless society, it might be said, there will be no more painters, only situationists who, among other things, make paintings.

Life's chief emotional drama, after the never-ending conflict between desire and reality hostile to that desire, certainly appears to be the sensation of time's passage. The situationist attitude consists in counting on time's swift passing, unlike aesthetic processes which aim at the fixing of emotion. The situationist challenge to the passage of emotions and of time will be its wager on always gaining ground on change, on always going further in play and in the multiplication of moving periods. Obviously, it is not easy for us at this time to make such a wager; however, even were we to lose it a thousand times, there is no other progressive attitude to adopt.

The situationist minority was first formed as a trend within the lettrist left wing, then within the Lettrist International, which it eventually controlled. The same objective impulse is leading several contemporary avant-garde groups to similar conclusions. Together we must discard all the relics of the recent past. We deem that today an agreement on a unified action among the revolutionary cultural avant-garde must implement such a program. We do not have formulas nor final results in mind. We are merely proposing an experimental research that will collectively lead in a few directions that we are in the process of defining, and in others that have yet to be defined. The very difficulty of arriving at the first situationist achievements is proof of the newness of the realm we are entering. What alters the way we see the streets is more important than what alters the way we see painting. Our working hypotheses will be reconsidered at each future upheaval, wherever it may come from.

We will be told, chiefly by revolutionary intellectuals and artists who for reasons of taste put up with a certain powerlessness, that this "situationism" is quite disagreeable, that we have made nothing of beauty, that we would be better off speaking of Gide, and that no one sees any clear reason to be interested in us. People will shy away by reproaching us for repeating a number of viewpoints that have already caused too much scandal, and that express the simple desire to be noticed. They will become indignant about the conduct we have believed necessary to adopt on a few occasions in order to keep or to recover our distances. We reply: it is not a question of knowing whether this interests you, but rather of whether you yourself could become interesting under new conditions of cultural creation. Revolutionary artists and intellectuals, your role is not to shout that freedom is abused when we refuse to march with the enemies of freedom. You do not have to imitate bourgeois aesthetes who try to bring everything back to what has already been done, because the already-done does not make them uncomfortable. You know that creation is never pure. Your role is to search for what will give rise to the international avant-garde, to join in the constructive critique of its program, and to call for its support.

OUR IMMEDIATE TASKS

We must support, alongside the workers' parties or extremist tendencies existing within these parties, the necessity of considering a consistent ideological action for fighting, on the level of the passions, the influence of the propaganda methods of late capitalism: to concretely contrast, at every opportunity, other desirable ways of life with the reflections of the capitalist way of life; to destroy, by all hyperpolitical means, the bourgeois idea of happiness. At the same time, taking into account the existence among the ruling social class of elements who have always cooperated, through boredom and need of novelty, in that which finally entails the disappearance of these societies, we must urge persons who hold certain of the vast resources that we lack to give us the means to carry out our experiments, through an account analogous to what might be employed in scientific research and might be quite profitable as well.

We must introduce everywhere a revolutionary alternative to the ruling culture; coordinate all the enquiries that are happening at this moment without a general perspective; orchestrate, through criticism and propaganda, the most progressive artists and intellectuals of all countries to make contact with us with a view to a joint action.

We must declare ourselves ready to resume discussion on the basis of this platform with all those who, having taken part in a prior phase of our action, are again capable of rejoining us.

We must advance the keywords of unitary urbanism, of experimental behavior, of hyperpolitical propaganda, and of the construction of environments. The passions have been interpreted enough: the point now is to discover others.

NOTES

Presented by Guy Debord to the founding conference of the Situationist International at Cosio d'Arroscia (July 1957).

1. [In French, *viveurs,* a theatrical pun. Typically, the word means "rake" or "playboy," and was thus commonly linked with the dubious morality of the theatrical world; here, Debord assigns it a new meaning that recalls its roots in *vivre,* to live. Ed.]

One More Try If You Want to Be Situationists
(The SI *in* and *against* Decomposition)

Guy Debord

TRANSLATED BY John Shepley

to Mohamed Dahou

The collective task we have set ourselves is the creation of a new cultural *theater of operations,* placed hypothetically at the level of an eventual general construction of its surroundings through the preparation, depending on circumstances, of the terms of the environment/behavior dialectic. The depletion of modern forms of art and style is all too obvious; and analysis of this steady trend leads us to the conclusion that in order to overcome the general cultural picture, wherein we see a state of *decomposition* (for the definition of this term, cf. the "Report on the Construction of Situations")[1] that has arrived at its final historical stage, one must seek a higher organization of the means of action in this period of our culture. That is, we must foresee and experiment with what lies beyond the present atomization of worn-out traditional arts, with a new state of the world whose most consistent premise will be urbanism and the daily life of an emerging society—and

The images that appear on pages 54–84 were originally published in *Internationale situationniste* 2 (December 1958). They were meant to address the theme of "everyday life at the advent of the situationist movement."

not *go back* to some coherent unity or other. We can clearly see that the development of this task presupposes a revolution that has yet to take place, and that any research is restricted by the contradictions of the present. The Situationist International exists *in name,* but that means nothing but the beginning of an attempt to build beyond the decomposition in which we, like everyone else, are completely involved. Becoming aware of our real possibilities requires both the recognition of the presituationist—in the strict sense of the word—nature of whatever we can attempt, and the rupture, without looking back, with *the division of labor in the arts.* The main danger lies in these two errors: the pursuit of fragmentary works combined with simpleminded proclamations of an alleged new stage.

At this moment, decomposition shows nothing more than a slow *radicalization* of moderate innovators toward positions where outcast extremists had already found themselves eight or ten years ago. But far from drawing a lesson from those fruitless experiments, the "respectable" innovators further dilute their importance. I will take examples from France, which surely is undergoing the most advanced phenomena of the general cultural decomposition that, for various reasons, is being *manifested in its purest state* in western Europe.

Reading Alain Robbe-Grillet's first two columns in *France-Observateur* (October 10 and 17), one is struck by the fact that he is a *timid Isou* (in his arguments, as in the "daring" spirit of his novels), as when he claims "to belong to the History of forms, which in the final analysis is the best (and perhaps only) criterion for recognizing a work of art." With a banality of thought and expression that ends up being quite personal ("let me repeat, it is better to take risks than to settle for a sure error"), and much less invention and audacity, he hearkens back to the same *linear perception* of artistic evolution, a mechanistic idea whose function is to reassure: "Art goes on, or else it dies. We are among those who have chosen to go on." To go straight on. Who, in 1957, reminds him by direct analogy of Baudelaire? Claude Simon—"all the values of the past . . . would seem in any case to prove it." (This *appearance* of proof in claims for a direct lineage is due precisely to the denial of all dialectics, of any real change.) Indeed, everything that has been put forward since the last war, of any interest at all, naturally takes its place in the extreme decomposition, but with more or less of a desire to look beyond. This desire gets smothered by economic and cultural ostracism and also by the lack of ideas and proposals—these two aspects being *interdependent.* The *best-known* art appearing in our time is controlled by those who know "how far to go too far." (See the endless and profitable death throes of post-dadaist painting, which is usually presented as dadaism *in reverse,* and whereby they congratulate each other. Their aspirations and their enemies are cut to size.) Robbe-Grillet modestly renounces the title of avant-gardist (when one does not even have an authentic "avant-garde" view of the decomposition phase, one might as well reject its inconveniences—especially the noncommercial aspect). He will be content to be a "novelist of today," but, outside the little cohort of his fellows, it must be admitted that the others are quite simply a "rearguard." And he courageously takes issue with Michel de Saint-Pierre, which suggests that by talking about cinema he would bestow on himself the glory of insulting Gourguet, while hailing the present-day cinema of an Astruc. Actually, Robbe-Grillet is *up to date* for a certain social group, just as Michel de Saint-Pierre is up to date for a public made up of another class. Both are very much "of today" in relation to their audiences, and nothing more, to the extent to which they exploit, with different sensibilities, neighboring degrees of a traditional *mode of cultural action.* It is no big deal to be *up to date:* one is only more or less *part of the decomposition.* Originality now wholly depends on a leap to a higher level.

It is their timidity that keeps people from looking beyond decomposition. Unable to see anything after the present structures, and knowing them well enough to sense that they are doomed, they would like to *destroy them piecemeal,* while leaving something for the next generation. They are comparable to political reformers, impotent but just as harmful: living on the sale of false remedies. Anyone who cannot conceive a radical transformation is propping up the *arrangements* of the status quo—practiced with elegance—and is separated only by a few *chronological preferences* from those consistent reactionaries who (whether politically of the right or the left) would like to see a return to earlier (*more solid*) stages of the culture that is breaking down. Françoise Choay's naive art criticism is quite representative of the tastes of the "free intellectuals of the left" who constitute the chief social base of this timid cultural decomposition, and when she writes

We live subject to change, because, if you will allow me to say so, that is the law of the country we live in.

Bossuet

(*France-Observateur,* October 17) that "the path taken by Francken . . . is presently one of painting's chances for survival," she betrays concerns *fundamentally akin* to those of Zhdanov ("did we do the right thing . . . in putting to rout the liquidators of painting?").[2]

We are locked into relations of production that contradict the necessary development of productive forces, in the sphere of culture *as well.* We must breach these traditional relations, *the arguments and fashions they support.* We must direct ourselves *beyond* present-day culture, by a *clear-eyed critique of existing spheres* and their *integration* into a single space-time construction (the situation: a dynamic system in an environment and ludic behavior) that will bring about a *higher harmony of form and content.*

But these prospects, in themselves, cannot in any way validate current productions that naturally take on meaning in relation to the prevailing confusion, and this includes in our own minds as well. Among us, useful theoretical propositions may be contradicted by actual works limited to old sectors (on which it is necessary to act *first,* since for the moment they are alone in possessing a common reality). Or often other comrades, who have made interesting experiments on particular points, get sidetracked in outdated theories: thus W. Olmo, who is not lacking in good will, in order to connect his experiments in sound with the construction of environments, employs such defective formulations in a recent text submitted to the Situationist International ("For a Concept of Musical Experimentation") that the whole thing had to be refocused ("Remarks on the Concept of Experimental Art"), a discussion that, in my opinion, no longer offers even the memory of a reality.[3]

Just as there is no "situationism" as *doctrine,* one must not let certain earlier experiments—or everything to which our ideological and practical weakness now limits us—be called situationist achievements. But, on the other hand, we cannot concede even a temporary value to mystification. The abstract empirical fact that constitutes this or that manifestation of today's decayed culture only takes on concrete meaning by its connection with the overall vision of an end or a beginning of civilization. Which is to say that in the long run our seriousness can integrate and surpass mystification, as well as whatever promotes

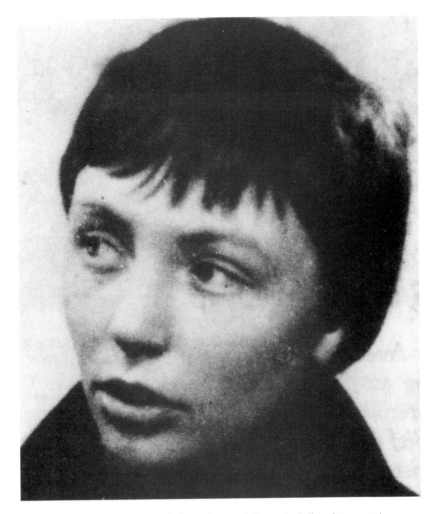

This medley of blue sashes, ladies, cuirasses, violins in the hall, and trumpets in the square provided a spectacle more often seen in novels than elsewhere.

Retz

I rose early above the chimeras of religion, perfectly convinced that the existence of the creator is a revolting absurdity that children no longer even believe in.

Sade

it as evidence of an actual historical state of decayed thought. Last June witnessed a scandal when a film I had made in 1952 was screened in London.[4] It was not a hoax and still less a situationist achievement, but one that depended on complex literary motivations of that time (works on the cinema of Isou, Marc'O, Wolman), and thus fully participated in the phase of decay, precisely in its most extreme form, without even having—except for a few programmatic allusions—the wish for positive developments that characterized the works to which I have just alluded. Afterward, the same London audience (Institute of Contemporary Arts) was treated to some paintings executed by chimpanzees, which bear comparison with respectable action painting. This proximity seems to me instructive. *Passive consumers* of culture (one can well understand why we count on the possibility of active participation in a world in which "aesthetes" will be forgotten) can love any manifestation of decomposition (they would be right in the sense that these manifestations are precisely those that best express their period of crisis and decline, but one can see that they *prefer* those that *slightly disguise* this state). I believe that in another five or six years they will come to *love* my film and the paintings of apes, just as they already love Robbe-Grillet. The only real difference between the paintings of apes and my complete cinematographic work to date is its possible threatening meaning for the culture around us, namely, a wager on certain formations of the future. And I wouldn't know on which side to put Robbe-Grillet, when you stop to think that at certain moments of rupture one is either aware or not of a qualitative turning point; and if not, the nuances don't matter.

But our wager always has to be renewed, and it is we ourselves who produce the various chances to respond. We wish to transform these times (to which everything we love, beginning with our experimental attitude, *also belongs*) and not to "write for it," as self-satisfied vulgarity intends: Robbe-Grillet and his times are made for each other. On the contrary, our ambitions are clearly megalomaniac, but perhaps not measurable by the prevailing criteria of success. I believe all my friends would be content to work anonymously at the Ministry of Leisure in a government that would finally undertake to change life, along with the salaries of qualified workers.

NOTES

Potlatch 29 (November 5, 1957), n.p.

1. [See Guy Debord, "Report on the Construction of Situations . . . ," translated in this volume, 34–38. Ed.]

2. [See ibid., 36. Ed.]

3. [Walter Olmo, a member of the Italian section of the SI, had presented his text to the group in September 1957. Debord's response was issued on October 15, 1957, and denounced Olmo and his supporters for their idealism and conservatism. When Olmo refused to retract the text, he was expelled from the group in January 1958. Cf. Stewart Home, *The Assault on Culture* (Stirling, Scotland: AK Press, 1991), 32. Ed.]

4. [For an account of the June 1957 screening of *Hurlements en faveur de Sade,* see Guy Atkins, *Asger Jorn: The Crucial Years, 1954–1964* (London: Lund Humphries, 1977), 57–58. Ed.]

Theses on Cultural Revolution

GUY DEBORD

TRANSLATED BY JOHN SHEPLEY

1

The traditional goal of aesthetics is to make one feel, in privation and absence, certain past elements of life that through the mediation of art would escape the confusion of appearances, since appearance is what suffers from the reign of time. The degree of aesthetic success is thus measured by a beauty inseparable from duration, and tending even to lay claim to eternity. The situationist goal is immediate participation in a passionate abundance of life, through the variation of fleeting moments resolutely arranged. The success of these moments can only be their passing effect. Situationists consider cultural activity, from the standpoint of totality, as an experimental method for constructing daily life, which can be permanently developed with the extension of leisure and the disappearance of the division of labor (beginning with the division of artistic labor).

2

Art can cease to be a report on sensations and become a direct organization of higher sensations. It is a matter of producing ourselves, and not things that enslave us.

3

Mascolo is right is saying (in *Le communisme*) that the reduction of the working day by the regime of the dictatorship of the proletariat is "the most certain assurance that it can give of its revolutionary authenticity." Indeed, "if a man is a commodity, if he is treated as a thing, if the general relations of men among themselves are the relations of thing to thing, it is because it is possible to buy his time from him." Mascolo, however, is too quick to conclude that "the time of a man freely employed" is always well spent, and that "the purchase of time is the sole evil." There is no freedom in the employment of time without the possession of modern instruments for the construction of daily life. The use of such instruments will mark the leap of a utopian revolutionary art to an experimental revolutionary art.

4

An international association of situationists can be seen as a union of workers in an advanced sector of culture, or more precisely as a union of all those who claim the right to a task now impeded by social conditions; hence as an attempt at an organization of professional revolutionaries in culture.

5

We are separated in practice from true control over the material powers accumulated by our time. The communist revolution has not occurred, and we still live within the framework of the decomposition of old cultural superstructures. Henri Lefebvre correctly sees that this contradiction is at the heart of a specifically modern discordance between the progressive individual and the world, and calls the cultural tendency based on this discordance revolutionary-romantic. The defect in Lefebvre's conception lies in making the simple expression of discordance a sufficient criterion for revolutionary action within culture. Lefebvre renounces beforehand all experiments toward profound cultural change, while

But I ask in utter and unexpected seriousness: what reproach does Charles
de Gaulle deserve in all this? What reasons does he give us not to trust him?

Mauriac (*L'Express*, 26 June 1958)

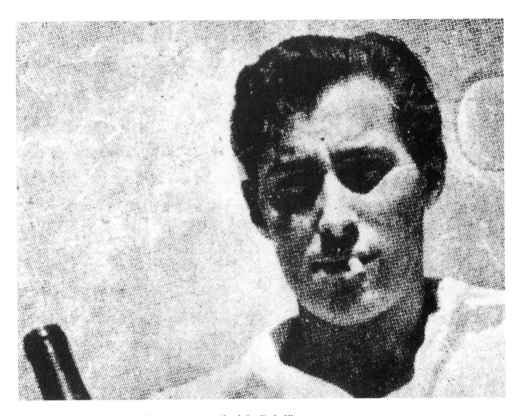

"Whom should I announce to milord the Duke?"

"The young man who picked a fight with him one evening on the Pont-Neuf, opposite the Samaritaine."

"Some recommendation!"

"You'll see it's as good as any other."

Dumas, *Les trois mousquetaires*

remaining satisfied with a content: awareness of the (still too remote) impossible-possible, which can be expressed no matter what form it takes within the framework of decomposition.

6

Those who want to overcome the old established order in all its aspects cannot attach themselves to the disorder of the present, even in the sphere of culture. One must struggle and not go on waiting, in culture as well, for the moving order of the future to make a concrete appearance. It is its possibility, already present in our midst, that devalues all expression in known cultural forms. One must lead all forms of pseudocommunication to their utter destruction, to arrive one day at real and direct communication (in our working hypothesis of higher cultural means: the constructed situation). Victory will be for those who will be able to create disorder without loving it.

7

In a world of cultural decomposition, we can test our strength but not employ it. The practical task of overcoming our discordance with the world, i.e., of surmounting decomposition by some higher constructions, is not romantic. We will be "revolutionary romantics," in Lefebvre's sense, precisely to the degree of our failure.

NOTE

Internationale situationniste 1 (June 1958), 20–21.

Contribution to the Debate "Is Surrealism Dead or Alive?"

GUY DEBORD

TRANSLATED BY TOM MCDONOUGH

Obviously, surrealism is alive. Its very creators have not yet died, and new members, although of an increasingly mediocre quality, adhere to it. The general public thinks of surrealism as the furthest extreme of modernism and, elsewhere, it has become the object of academic study. It is very much a matter of one of those things whose existence is contemporaneous with our own, like Catholicism and General de Gaulle.

Thus the real question is: what is the role of surrealism today? . . .

Since its very origin, there has been an antagonism in surrealism between attempts to assert a new way of life and a reactionary flight from reality.

At the outset, surrealism's progressive side lay in its demand for an unconditional freedom, and in a few attempts at intervening in everyday life. As an addition to art history, surrealism's existence in the realm of cultural production is like the shadow of an absent figure in a painting by de Chirico: it makes visible the lack of a much-needed future.

The reactionary side of surrealism appears straightaway in its overestimation of the unconscious and its monotonous artistic exploitation; in its dualistic idealism which tries to understand history as a simple contrast between forerunners of surrealist irrationality and the tyranny of Greco-Latinate logic; and in its participation in that bourgeois propaganda that presents love as the only possible adventure under modern conditions of existence. . . .

Surrealism today is thoroughly boring and reactionary. . . .

Surrealist dreams are mere bourgeois impotence, artistic nostalgia, and a refusal to envisage the liberating use of our era's superior technological means. Seizing such means for use in collective, concrete experimentation with new environments and behaviors is the start of a cultural revolution that cannot exist apart from these means.

It is in this direction that my comrades in the Situationist International are advancing. [This last sentence was followed by several minutes of loud applause, also previously recorded. Then a different voice announced: "You have been listening to Guy Debord, spokesman for the Situationist International. This intervention was brought to you by the Open Circle." A woman's voice joined in at the end, talking like a spokesperson in a radio advertisement: "But don't forget, your most urgent task remains the fight against dictatorship in France."]

NOTE

The question "Is surrealism dead or alive?" had been chosen as the theme of a debate by the "Open Circle" held on November 18, 1958. Debord's contribution was recorded on tape and was accompanied by guitar; this translation is based on the abridged version of the talk, which appeared as "Suprême levée des défenseurs du surréalisme à Paris et révélation de leur valeur effective," *Internationale situationniste* 2 (December 1958), 32–34.

In Praise of Pinot-Gallizio

MICHÈLE BERNSTEIN
TRANSLATED BY JOHN SHEPLEY

Italian painting occupies an exceptional place in the history of Western culture. Its fruits have not been lost. As always, social habits outlast the conditions of an historically outmoded artistic form, while maintaining material possibilities—economic privileges.

In today's Italy, which is incapable of resolving the problem of unemployment, there is at least one position to occupy: the social function of painter. The role of the painter and the importance of painting, both artificially maintained in a different society whose resources and problems are obviously those of the rest of the world in the twentieth century, have kept all their allure.

Which is why, anxious to prevail on this favored soil and assured of immortality by this geographical identity, some fine ambitions come to grief: what Giotto and Leonardo did in laying down the laws for the construction of painting, Fontana or Baj hope to imitate by providing the equivalent for its destruction. And the candidates do not stop to think that the invention of liquidation, in whatever branch of cultural activity, necessarily goes faster and is forgotten in less time than the invention of a culture. They keep trying.

Most often it is where confusion and decadence have been pushed to the extreme, where their social and economic importance is asserted the most, that one should expect to see the negation of this decadence emerge. Gallizio is accordingly Italian.

Aware of the problems that truly affect us, in this interregnum between civilizations in which we find ourselves caught, Gallizio foresakes painting—whether respectably figurative or abstract, or action painting, and in any case as modern as in 1930. He extends it into other realms, all the realms on which he touches with an extraordinarily inventive spirit. They follow one another in succession and are called chemical experiments, resins, resin painting, scented painting. In 1955, Gallizio was one of the founders of the Experimental Laboratory of the Imaginist Bauhaus.

It is then that he perfected, at the cost of unremitting labor and the lengthy patience of genius, the discovery we wish to speak of, one that will deliver the final blow to the little glories of the easel: industrial painting.

Gallizio produces painting by the meter.

Not a reproduction of the *Mona Lisa* stretched across fifty meters of wallpaper. No, his painting by the meter is original, its reproduction is forbidden, its process patented.

Its cost beats all competition. Its sale price too: Gallizio is honest.

His production is unlimited. No more speculators on canvases: if you have money to invest, be content to buy shares in the Suez Canal.

His sales take place preferably outdoors. Also in small shops and large department stores: Gallizio dislikes galleries.

It is hard to grasp all at once the myriad advantages of this astonishing invention. At random: no more problems of size—the canvas is cut before the eyes of the satisfied customer; no more bad periods—because of its shrewd mixture of chance and mechanics, the inspiration for industrial painting is never lacking; no more metaphysical themes—industrial painting will not sustain them; no more doubtful reproductions of eternal masterpieces; no more gala openings.

And of course, soon, no more painters, even in Italy.

Obviously one can laugh, and classify this phase of art as an inoffensive joke, or as bad taste. Or get indignant in the name of eternal values. One can pretend to believe that easel painting, which isn't doing so well these days, won't get any worse.

The progressive domination of nature is the history of the disappearance of certain problems, removed from "artistic"—occasional, unique—practice to

Mistress of her desires, she saw the world, and was seen by it.
Bossuet

massive diffusion in the public domain, until, finally, they tend even to lose any economic value.

Faced with this process, the reactionary inclination is always to restore value to old problems: the authentic Henry II sideboard, the fake Henry II sideboard, the forged canvas that isn't signed, the excessively numbered edition of something or other by Salvador Dalí, top quality in all realms. Revolutionary creation tries to define and spread new problems, new productions that alone can have value.

Considering the endowable buffooneries now after twenty years coming back to stay, the industrialization of painting thus appears as an example of technical progress to be taken up without further delay. It is Gallizio's greatness to have boldly pushed his tireless experiments to the point where nothing is left of the old pictorial world.

Anyone can see that previous procedures for overcoming and destroying the pictorial object, whether through abstraction carried to its extreme limits (in the vein opened by Malevich) or painting deliberately subjected to extraplastic concerns (Magritte's work, for example), have been unable, after decades, to emerge from the stage of repeating an artistic negation, within the framework imposed by the pictorial means themselves: an "inner" negation.

The problem thus raised can only drag on endlessly by repeating the same givens, in which elements of a solution have not been included. Meanwhile, all around us, the world keeps changing before our eyes.

We have now reached a stage of experimentation with new collective constructions and new syntheses, and there is no longer any point in combating the values of the old world by a neodadaist refusal. Whether these values be ideological, artistic, or even financial, the proper thing is to unleash inflation everywhere. Gallizio is in the forefront.

NOTE

Turin, 1958; published in *Pinot Gallizio* (Paris: Bibliothèque d'Alexandrie, 1960).

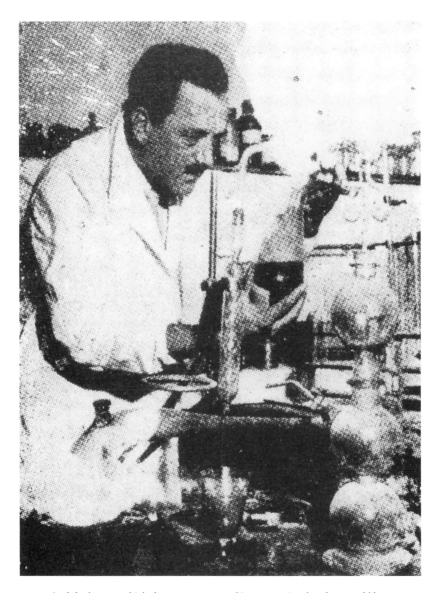

And the heat to which they are accustomed is so excessive that they would be chilled by the heat here in the depths of Africa.

Fontenelle

Extracts from Letters to the Situationist International

CONSTANT

TRANSLATED BY JOHN SHEPLEY

. . . I have as little taste for individualist primitivism in painting as for so-called cool architecture and abstraction, although people like to stress a quarrel between these two tendencies that is false and artificial.

Industrial and machine culture is an incontrovertible fact, and craft procedures, including the two tendencies in painting, are doomed (the concept of a "free" art is mistaken).

The machine is an indispensable tool for everyone, even artists, and industry is the sole means to provide for the needs, even the aesthetic ones, of humanity on the scale of the present world. These are no longer "problems" for artists; this is the reality that they cannot ignore with impunity.

Those who mistrust the machine and those who glorify it show the same incapacity to utilize it. Machine work and mass production offer unheard-of possibilities for creation, and those who are able to place these possibilities at the service of a daring imagination will be my creators of tomorrow.

Artists have the task of inventing new techniques and of using light, sound, movement, and in general all the inventions that can have an effect on environments.

Otherwise, the integration of art into the construction of the human habitat remains illusory. . . .

Ten years separate us from Cobra, and the history of so-called experimental art demonstrates its errors to us.

. . . For my part, I consider that the aggressive temperament required for the construction of environments excludes such traditional arts as painting and literature, now worn out and incapable of any revelation. Arts linked to a mystical and individualist attitude cannot be used by us.

We ought therefore to invent new techniques in all domains, visual, oral, and psychological, so as later to combine them in the complex activity that will produce unitary urbanism.

NOTE

September 1958; published in *Constant* (Paris: Bibliothèque d'Alexandrie, 1959).

Delegates from groups attending the SI meeting at the Alba congress.

It's no use for them to scribble, praise one another, wax enthusiastic, enlist women and fops in their cause; they will never be anything but insolent mediocrities.

Fréron, letter to Malesherbes about the Encyclopedists

Editorial Notes: Absence and Its Costumers

TRANSLATED BY JOHN SHEPLEY

Any creative effort that is not henceforth carried out in view of a new cultural theater of operations, of a direct creation of life's surroundings, is in one way or another a hoax. Within the context of the exhaustion of traditional aesthetic categories, some reach the point of making themselves known simply by signing a blank, which is the perfect result of the dadaist "readymade." A few years ago, the American composer John Cage obliged his audience to listen to a moment of silence. During the lettrist experiment of 1952, a twenty-four-minute dark sequence, with no sound track, was introduced into the film *Hurlements en faveur de Sade*. Yves Klein's recent monochrome paintings, inspired by Tinguely's machines, take the form of rapidly revolving blue disks, causing the critic for *Le Monde* (November 21, 1958) to remark:

> You might think that all this effort and so many detours do not lead very far. Even the protagonists do not take themselves too seriously. But their enterprise falls symptomatically within the present disarray. "They've run out of ideas" is heard on all sides. Is art, and especially painting, once and for all, "at the end of its rope"? This has been said of all periods, but it may, after all, have devolved on ours to coincide with the final impasse. This time the old surface of the canvas, where

impressionism and expressionism, fauvism and cubism, pointillism and abstract expressionism, geometric and lyrical abstraction have all been superimposed, is beginning to show its threads.

Actually, the artists' seriousness does not pose any sort of problem. The real question opposes an isolated artistic means with the unified use of several of these means. Immediately after the formation of the Situationist International, *Potlatch* no. 29 warned the situationists ("The SI *in* and *against* Decomposition"):

> Just as there is no "situationism" as *doctrine,* one must not let certain earlier experiments—or everything to which our ideological and practical weakness now limits us—be called situationist achievements. But, on the other hand, we cannot concede even a temporary value to mystification. The abstract empirical fact that constitutes this or that manifestation of today's decayed culture only takes on concrete meaning by its connection with the overall vision of an end or a beginning of civilization. Which is to say that in the long run our seriousness can integrate and surpass mystification, as well as whatever promotes it as evidence of an actual historical state of decayed thought.[1]

Indeed, these empty exercises seldom escape the temptation to rely on some kind of external justification, thereby to illustrate and serve a reactionary conception of the world. Klein's purpose, as we are told by the same article in *Le Monde,* "seems to be to transpose this purely plastic theme of color saturation into a sort of incantatory pictorial mystique. It involves being swallowed up in spellbinding blue uniformity like a Buddhist in Buddha." We know, alas, that John Cage participates in that Californian thought where the mental infirmity of American capitalist culture has enrolled in the school of Zen Buddhism. It is not by chance that Michel Tapié, the secret agent of the Vatican, pretends to believe in the existence of an American school of the Pacific Coast, and in its decisive importance: all kinds of spiritualists are closing ranks these days. Tapié's slimy procedure also aims, in parallel fashion, at destroying the theoretical vocabulary (in which he plays an artist's role, unacknowledged as such, but as a true contemporary of Cage and Klein). In a catalogue for the Galerie Stadler, on November 25, he thus decomposes language, using as a pretext a painter, naturally Japanese, named Imaï: "In recent months, Imaï has reached a new stage in a fruitful three-year pictorial development, which had progressed from a 'signifying Pacific' climate to a dramatic totalist graphism."

There is no need to point out how Klein and Tapié are spontaneously in the forefront of a fascist wave that is making headway in France. Others have been so more explicitly, if not perhaps more consciously—first of all, the putrid Hantaï, who proceeded directly from surrealist fanaticism to the royalism of Georges Mathieu. The simplicity of the recipe for dadaism in reverse, as well as Hantaï's obvious moral rot, have not stopped the worthy imbeciles of the Swiss orthodox neodadaist journal *Panderma* from giving him massive publicity, nor from admitting that they have not been able "to understand the slightest thing" about discussions of the show at the Galerie Kléber in March 1957, though it was clearly denounced—in the same way—by the surrealists and by us, in *Potlatch* no. 28.[2] It is true that the same journal, speaking for some reason of the SI, also reveals its perplexity: "What is it all about? No one knows." We would probably be amazed to be a current subject of conversation in Basel. Nevertheless, Laszlo, the editor of *Panderma,* has been seen making several vain attempts to meet situationists in Paris. It all goes to suggest that even Laszlo has read us. Except that his calling lies elsewhere: he is the mainspring of one of those vast gatherings where people who have no connection with each other put their signatures for a day to a manifesto that in itself has no content. Laszlo's great work, his simple but proud contribution to the sovereign nothingness of his time, is a "manifesto against avant-gardism," which, after some thirty lines of critical remarks, utterly acceptable because unfortunately quite trite, about the tiredness of modern art and the repetitions of what is called avant-gardism, suddenly turns into a profession of faith in a future of interest only to the signers. Since their chosen future is not otherwise defined, and is therefore probably awaited and accepted in its entirety and with enthusiasm—as by Hantaï—one of the signers, Edouard Roditi, has been careful to hold back, reserving for himself "the right to judge the future as uninteresting as the present." Roditi aside, all these thinkers (of whom the best known is the singer and composer Charles Estienne, a former art critic) are probably, for

Independence of Algeria.

> One day there will be no more parents
> In the gardens of youth . . .
> Violette dreamed of undoing
> And undid
> The frightful knot of serpents in the ties of blood.
>
> Eluard, "Violette Nozières"

the moment, interested in, and perhaps gratified by, the future that has necessarily followed the publication of their manifesto.

One can bet that a good number of these lovers of the future met again at that "rendezvous of the international avant-garde" held in September at the Palais des Expositions in Charleroi, of which nothing is known except the title, "Art of the Twenty-First Century," displayed on a modest advertising poster. One can also bet that the formula, which fell flat, will be repeated, and that all those who were so thoroughly incapable of discovering an art of 1958 will subscribe to that of the twenty-first century, nagged only by extremists trying to sell the same repetitions under a twenty-second-century label. The flight to the future, in its boastfulness, is thus the consolation of those who turn round and round in front of the wall that separates them from present-day culture.

NOTES

Internationale situationniste 2 (December 1958), 6–8.

1. [Guy Debord, "One More Try If You Want to Be Situationists (The SI *in* and *against* Decomposition)," translated in this volume, 55, 58. Ed.]

2. [In *Potlatch* 28 (May 22, 1957), the following notice appeared under the title "Testimonials": "The professional aristocrat Mathieu, with the help of one Hantaï, . . . has exploited as best he could his exhibition at the Galerie Kléber to force his contemporaries to recognize in him the originality of being the man about town who goes the furthest in retrograde thinking. But once again he strains his talent, he cheats on his origins. To find the inspirer of the manifestos of Mathieu-Hantaï, there is no need to go back to Thomas Aquinas or the Duke of Brunswick, as they would like you to think, but, much closer, to Marcel Aymé, who, in a short story entitled "En arrière!," not long ago amused himself by depicting the other side of the dada-surrealist coin: the scandal of a group of young people who call attention to themselves by a series of reactionary manifestos to the point of frenzy. The joke was funny for four pages: it so happens that someone has taken it seriously and reproduced it in his life.

"And the champions of our poor little world are so lacking in ideas that there is no piece of foolishness that cannot be used several times. Baron Hantaï enters the arena, and thus Paris already boasts two professional aristocrats."

Hantaï's mysticism was similarly denounced by the surrealists (who had hailed his first exhibition in 1953) in the tract "Coup de semonce" (Warning Shot). Ed.]

What often prevents us from giving ourselves over to a single vice is that we have several of them.

La Rochefoucauld

Editorial Notes: The Meaning of Decay in Art

TRANSLATED BY JOHN SHEPLEY

Bourgeois civilization, which has now spread all over the planet and has yet to be successfully overcome anywhere, is haunted by a specter: its culture, which appears in the modern dissolution of all its artistic means, is being called into question. This dissolution, first manifested at the starting point for the productive forces of modern society, i.e., Europe and later in America, has long been the prime truth of Western modernism. Everywhere, the liberation of artistic forms has signified their reduction to nothing. One can apply to the whole of modern expression what W. Weidlé, in 1947, wrote in the second issue of *Cahiers de la Pléiade* about *Finnegans Wake:* "This enormous *Summa* of the most enticing verbal contortions, this *Ars poetica* in ten thousand lessons, is not an artistic creation: it is the autopsy of its corpse."

Reactionary critics, to support their stupid dream of a return to the stylistic beauties of the past, never fail to point out that behind the inflationary flowering of novelties that can serve but once, the road of this liberation leads only to the void. For example, Emile Henriot (*Le Monde,* February 11, 1959) notes "the turn, many times signaled, that a certain literature of today has taken in the direction of the 'language of forms' for the use of literati specializing in the exercise of a 'literature for literati,' an object unto itself, just as there are experiments by painters for experimental painters and a music for musicians." Or Mauriac (*L'Express,* March 5, 1959): "The very philosophers whose lesson is that the end of a poem should be silence write articles to persuade us of it, and publish novels to prove to us that one shouldn't tell stories."

In the face of these jeers, those critics who have chosen to be modernists extol the beauties of dissolution, while hoping that it doesn't proceed too quickly. They are embarrassed, like Geneviève Bonnefoi taking note under the title "Death or Transfiguration?" of the ill-starred Paris Biennale (*Lettres nouvelles* no. 25). She concludes sadly: "Only the future will tell if this 'annihilation' of pictorial language, fairly similar to the one attempted on the literary plane by Beckett, Ionesco, and the best of the current young novelists, foreshadows a renewal of painting or its disappearance as a major art of our time. I have no space here to speak of sculpture, which seems to be in total disintegration." Or else, renouncing any sense of the comical, they loudly take the side of quasi-nothingness in formulas worthy to pass into history as the summing-up of the poverty of an era, like Françoise Choay, who *eulogistically* entitles an article on Tapiès: "Tapiès, Mystic of Almost Nothing" (*France-Observateur,* April 30, 1959).

The embarrassment of modernist critics is completed by the embarrassment of modern artists, on whom the accelerated decomposition in all sectors constantly imposes the need to examine and explain their working hypotheses. They bustle about in the same confusion and often in a comparable imbecility. Everywhere one can see the traces, among modern creators, of a consciousness traumatized by the shipwreck of expression as an autonomous sphere and absolute goal; and by the slow emergence of other dimensions of activity.

The fundamental work of a present avant-garde should be an attempt at general criticism of this moment, and a first attempt to respond to new requirements.

If the artist has passed, by a slow process, from the state of entertainer—pleasantly occupying people's spare time—to the ambition of a prophet, who raises questions and claims to impart the meaning of life, it is because, more and more, the question of how to spend our lives looms at the edge of the expanding freedom we have achieved by our appropriation of nature.

Thus the pretensions of the artist in bourgeois society go hand in hand with the practical reduction of his or her realm of real action to zero, and denial. All modern art is the revolutionary claim to other professions, once the current specialization in one-sided, canned expression has been relinquished.

The delays and distortions of the revolutionary project in our time are well known. The regression that has therein manifested itself has nowhere been so obvious as in art. This has been made easier by the fact that classical Marxism had not developed a real body of criticism in this area. In a famous letter to Mehring, written at the end of his life, Engels noted: "We all laid, and *were bound* to lay, the main emphasis, in the first place, on the *derivation* of political, juridical and other ideological notions, and of actions arising through the medium of these notions, from basic economic facts. But in so doing we neglected the formal side—the ways and means by which these notions, etc., come about—for the sake of the content." Moreover, at the time when Marxist thought was coming into its own, the formal movement in the dissolution of art was not yet apparent. Likewise, it can be said that it is solely in the presence of fascism that the workers' movement encountered in practical terms the problem of the formal "mode of appearance" of a political idea. It found itself poorly equipped to deal with it.

Independent revolutionary thinkers themselves show a certain reluctance to become involved in today's cultural problems. When we look at the endeavors, from more than one angle, of such intellectuals as Henri Lefebvre—in recent years—and Lucien Goldmann, we find in them the common trait of having amassed a number of positive contributions, important appeals to progressive truth at a moment when the ideology of the left is lost in a sense of confusion, to whose advantage it is all too clear, while at the same time being absent or insufficient when two kinds of questions come up: the organization of a political force, and the discovery of cultural means of action. These questions are indeed two essential and inseparable elements of the transitory action that would be needed from now on to lead to that enriched praxis usually offered to us as an external image, entirely separable from ourselves, instead of being linked to us by the slow movement of the future.

In an unpublished article of 1947 ("Le matérialisme dialectique, est-il une philosophie?"), included in his book *Recherches dialectiques,* Goldmann gives a good analysis of the future result of the cultural movement that lies before his eyes. "Like law, economics, or religion," he writes, "art as an independent phenomenon separated from other realms of social life will be led to disappear in a classless society. There will probably no longer be art separated from life because life will itself be a style, a form in which it will find its adequate expression." But Goldmann, who traces this very-long-term perspective on the basis of the overall forecasts of dialectical materialism, does not recognize its verification in the expression of his time. He judges the style of art or the art of his time in terms of the classical/romantic alternative, and in romanticism he sees only the expression of reification. Now, it is true that the destruction of language, after a century of poetry, has come about as a consequence of a deep-seated romantic, reified, petit-bourgeois tendency, and also—as Paulhan had shown in *Les fleurs de Tarbes*—by postulating that the inexpressible thought was worth more than the word. But the progressive aspect of this destruction, in poetry, fiction, or all the plastic arts, is that of being at the same time a testimony of a whole epoch on the insufficiency of artistic expression, of pseudocommunication. It is the practical destruction of the instruments of pseudocommunication that brings to the fore the question of inventing superior instruments.

Henri Lefebvre (*La somme et le reste*) wonders "if the crisis of philosophy does not mean its decline and end, as philosophy," while forgetting that this has been the basis of revolutionary thought since the eleventh of the *Theses on Feuerbach*. He has offered a more radical criticism in *Arguments* no. 15, considering human history as the successive traversal and abandoning of various spheres: the cosmic, the maternal, the divine, as well as philosophy, economics, and politics, and finally "art, which defines man by dazzling flashes and the human by exceptional moments, thus still external, alienating in the attempt at deliverance." But here we are back with the science fiction of revolutionary thought that is preached in *Arguments,* as daring in engaging thousands of years of history as it is incapable of proposing a single new element from now to the end of the century, and naturally bewitched in the present by the worst fumes of neoreformism. Lefebvre is well aware that each realm collapses in explicating itself, when it has reached the end of its possibilities and its imperialism, "when it has proclaimed

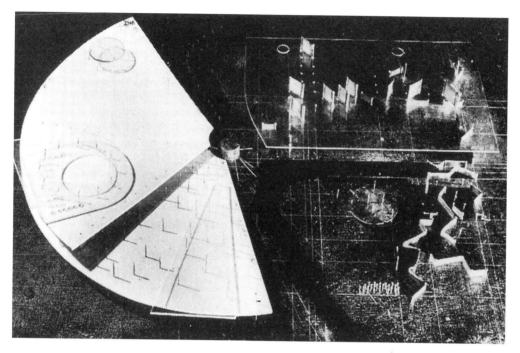

Constant, architectural maquette, 1958.

itself a totality on the human scale (thus complete). In the course of this development, and only after this illusory and extreme proclamation, the negativity already long contained in this world asserts itself, disowns it, corrodes it, dismantles it, casts it down. Only a finished totality can reveal that it is not totality." This scheme, which applies rather to philosophy after Hegel, perfectly defines the crisis of modern art, as can be easily verified by examining an extreme trend: for example, poetry from Mallarmé to surrealism. These conditions, already dominant beginning with Baudelaire, constitute what Paulhan calls the Terror, which he takes to be an accidental crisis of language, without considering the fact that they apply equally to all the other artistic means of expression. But the breadth of Lefebvre's views is of no avail to him when he writes about poems that are, as far as their date is concerned, on the historical model of 1925, and, as for the effective level attained by this formula, at the lowest. And when he proposes a conception of modern art (revolutionary-romantic), he advises artists to come back to this style of expression—or to others still older—to express the profound feeling of life, and the contradictions of men ahead of their time, i.e., both of their public and of themselves. Lefebvre would prefer not to see that this feeling and these contradictions have already been expressed by all modern art, and indeed *up to and including the destruction of expression itself.*

For revolutionaries, there can be no turning back. The world of artistic expression, whatever its content, has already lapsed. It repeats itself scandalously in order to keep going as long as the dominant society succeeds in preserving the privation and scarcity that are the anachronistic conditions of its reign. But the preservation or subversion of this society is not a utopian question: it is the most burning question of today, the one governing all others. Lefebvre should pursue the thought on the basis of a question he raised in the same article: "Has not every great period of art been a funeral rite in honor of a vanished moment?" This is also true on the individual scale, where every work is a funeral and memorial celebration of a vanished moment in one's life. The creations of the future should shape life directly, creating "exceptional moments" and making them ordinary. Goldmann weighs the difficulty of this leap when he remarks (in a note in *Recherches dialectiques,* p. 144): "We have no means of *direct* action on affects." It will be the task of the creators of a new culture to invent such means.

We need to find operative instruments midway between that global praxis in which every aspect of the total life of a classless society will one day dissolve and the present individual practice of "private" life with its poor artistic and other resources. What we mean by *situations* to be constructed is the search for a dialectical organization of partial and transitory realities, what André Frankin, in his *Critique du non-avenir,* has called a "planification of existence" on the individual level, not excluding chance but, on the contrary, "rediscovering" it.[1]

Situations are conceived as the opposite of works of art, which are attempts at absolute valorization and preservation of the present moment. That is the fancy aesthetic grocery store of a Malraux, of whom it might be remarked that the same "intellectuals of the left" who are indignant today at seeing him at the head of the most contemptible and imbecile political swindle once *took him seriously*—an admission that countersigns their bankruptcy. Every situation, as consciously constructed as can be, contains its own negation and moves inevitably toward its own reversal. In the conduct of an individual life, a situationist action is not based on the abstract idea of rationalist progress (which, according to Descartes, "makes us masters and possessors of nature"), but on the practice of arranging the environment that conditions us. Whoever constructs situations, to apply a statement by Marx, "by bringing his movements to bear on external nature and transforming it . . . transforms his own nature at the same time."

In conversations that led to the formation of the SI, Asger Jorn put forth a plan for ending the separation that had arisen around 1930 between avant-garde artists and the revolutionary left, who had once been allies. The root of the problem is that, since 1930, there has been neither a revolutionary movement nor an artistic avant-garde to respond to the possibilities of the time. A new departure, on both sides, will certainly have to be made to bring together problems and responses.

The obvious obstacles of the present have produced a certain ambiguity in the situationist movement as a magnet for artists ready to embark on a new

Constant, architectural maquette, 1958.

course. Like the proletarians, theoretically, before the nation, the situationists are encamped at the gates of culture. They do not want to establish themselves inside; they *decline* to inscribe themselves in modern art; they are the organizers of the absence of that aesthetic avant-garde that bourgeois critics are waiting for and which, forever disappointed, they are prepared to greet on the first occasion. This does not go without the risk of various retrograde interpretations, even within the SI. Decadent artists, for example at the last fair held in Venice, are already talking about "situations." Those who understand everything in terms of old-hat artistic ideas, as tame verbal formulas destined to assure the sale of still tamer little paintings, may see the SI as having already achieved a certain success, a certain recognition: that is because they have not understood that we have gathered at a great turning point *still to be taken*.

Of course, the decay of artistic forms, while indicated by the impossibility of their creative renewal, does not immediately involve their actual disappearance in practice. They can go on repeating themselves with various nuances. But everything shows "the upheaval of this world," as Hegel says in the preface to the *Phenomenology of Mind:* "The frivolity and boredom that are invading what still exists, and the vague presentiment of something unknown, are the preliminary signs of something else that is on its way."

We must keep moving ahead, without attaching ourselves to anything either in modern culture or its negation. We do not want to work toward the spectacle of the end of the world, but toward the end of the world of the spectacle.

NOTES

Internationale situationniste 3 (December 1959), 3–8.

1. [Published as André Frankin, "Esquisses programmatiques," *Internationale situationniste* 4 (June 1960), 16–18. Ed.]

A Different City for a Different Life

CONSTANT

TRANSLATED BY JOHN SHEPLEY

The crisis of urbanism is worsening. The construction of neighborhoods, old and new, is obviously at variance with established modes of behavior, and all the more so with the new ways of life we seek. As a result, we are surrounded by a dull and sterile environment.

In old neighborhoods, the streets have degenerated into highways, and leisure is commercialized and adulterated by tourism. Social relations there become impossible. Newly built neighborhoods have only two themes, which govern everything: traffic circulation and household comfort. They are the meager expressions of bourgeois happiness and lack any concern for play.

In response to the need to construct whole towns rapidly, cemeteries in reinforced concrete are being built where great masses of the population are condemned to die of boredom. For what is the use of the most astonishing technical inventions that the world now finds at its disposal if the conditions for deriving benefit from them are lacking, they contribute nothing to leisure, and the imagination defaults?

We require adventure. Not finding it any longer on earth, there are those who want to look for it on the moon. We opt first to create situations here, new situations. We intend to break the laws that prevent the development of meaningful activities in life and culture. We find ourselves at the dawn of a new era, and we are already trying to outline the image of a happier life and a unitary urbanism—urbanism made to please.

Our domain is thus the urban network, the natural expression of a collective creativity, capable of understanding the creative forces being released with the decline of a culture based on individualism. To our way of thinking, the traditional arts will no longer be able to play a role in the creation of the new environment in which we want to live.

We are in the process of inventing new techniques; we are examining the possibilities offered by existing cities, and making models and plans for future ones. We are aware of the need to take advantage of all the new technologies, and we know that the future constructions we envisage will have to be flexible enough to respond to the dynamic conception of life, creating our surroundings in direct relation to constantly changing modes of behavior.

Our concept of urbanism is thus a social one. We are opposed to the concept of a garden city, where spaced and isolated skyscrapers must necessarily reduce direct relations among people and their common action. For close relations between surroundings and behavior to be produced, agglomeration is indispensable. Those who think that the rapidity with which we move around and the possibility of telecommunications are going to dissolve the common life of agglomerations have little idea of humanity's true needs. Instead of the idea of a garden city, which most modern architects have adopted, we set up the image of the covered city, where the layout of thoroughfares and isolated buildings has given way to a continuous spatial construction, elevated above the ground, and which will include groups of dwellings as well as public spaces (permitting modifications of purpose depending on the needs of the moment). Since all traffic, in the functional sense, will pass underneath or on overhead terraces, streets can be done away with. The great number of different traversable spaces of which the city is composed form a vast and complex social space. Far from a return to nature—the notion of living in a park, as solitary aristocrats once did—we see in such immense constructions the possibility of overcoming nature and regulating at will the atmosphere, lighting, and sounds in these various spaces.

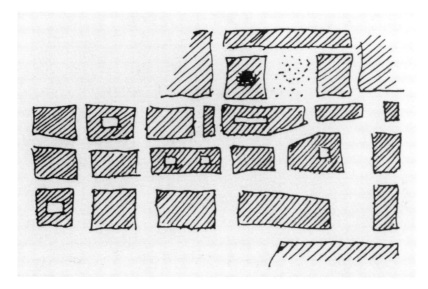

Quarter in a traditional city. Quasi-social space: the street. The streets, laid out logically for circulation, are *incidentally* used as a meeting place.

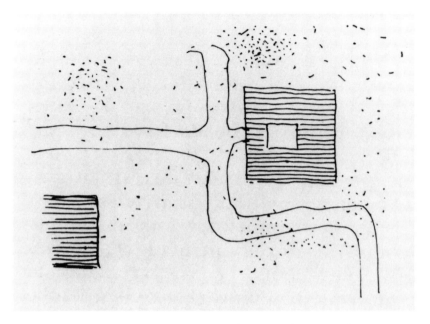

Garden city. Isolated dwelling units. Minimum social space: people meet only by chance and individually, in walkways or the park. Traffic circulation governs everything.

Do we mean by this a new functionalism that will put increased emphasis on the idealized utilitarian life? Let us not forget that once the functions are established, they are followed by play. For some time now, architecture has become a game of space and environment. The garden city lacks environments. We, on the contrary, want to take advantage of them more consciously; we want them to correspond to all our needs.

The future cities we envisage will offer an unusual variety of sensations in this realm, and unforeseen games will become possible through the inventive use of material conditions, such as air-conditioning and the control of sound and lighting. Urban planners are already studying how to harmonize the cacophony that reigns in present-day cities. Before long they should find there a new arena for creation, as with many other problems that will emerge. Space travel, which has been predicted, may influence this development, since bases established on other planets will immediately raise the problem of sheltered cities, which may provide the model for our study of future urbanism.

Above all, however, the decreased amount of work necessary for production due to extensive automation will create a need for leisure, for different behavior and a change in its nature, which will necessarily lead to a new conception of the collective habitat having the maximum of social space, contrary to the concept of a garden city, where social space is reduced to a minimum. The city of the future must be conceived as a continuous construction on pillars, or else as an extended system of different constructions, in which premises for living, pleasure, etc., are suspended, as well as those designed for production and distribution, leaving the ground free for circulation and public meetings. The use of ultralight and insulating materials, now being tried experimentally, will allow for light construction and broadly spaced supports. In this way it will be possible to build a multilayered city: underground, ground level, stories, terraces, of an expanse that may vary from a neighborhood to a metropolis. Note that in such a city the built surface will be 100 percent and the free surface 200 percent (parterre and terraces), whereas in traditional cities the figures are approximately 80 percent and 20 percent; in the garden city, this ratio can at most be reversed. The terraces form an outdoor terrain that extends over the whole surface of the city and can be used for sports, as landing pads for planes and helicopters, and for vegetation. They will be

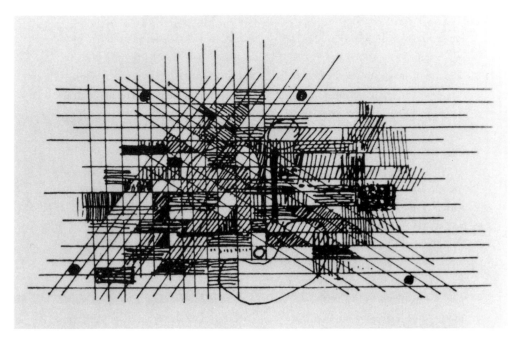

Principle of a covered city. Spatial "plan." Suspended collective dwellings are spread over the whole city and separated from traffic, which passes above or below.

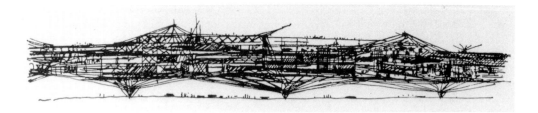

Section view of covered city.

accessible everywhere by stairways and elevators. The different levels will be divided into neighboring and communicating spaces, climate-controlled, which will make it possible to create an infinite variety of environments, facilitating the casual movements of the inhabitants and their frequent encounters. The environments will be regularly and consciously changed, with the help of all technological means, by teams of specialized creators, who will thus be professional situationists.

A study in depth of the means of creating environments and their psychological influence is one of the tasks we are presently undertaking. Studies involving the technical achievement of supporting structures and their aesthetics are the specific task of artist-architects and engineers. The contribution of the latter, above all, is an urgent necessity if we are to make progress in the preparatory work we are undertaking.

If the project we have just set forth in a few broad outlines risks being considered a fanciful dream, we insist on the fact that it is feasible from the technical standpoint, desirable from the human standpoint, and that from the social standpoint it will be indispensable. The growing dissatisfaction that grips all of humanity will reach a point where we will all be driven to carry out projects for which we possess the means, and that will contribute to the realization of a richer and more rewarding life.

NOTE

Internationale situationniste 3 (December 1959), 37–40.

Editorial Notes: Critique of Urbanism

TRANSLATED BY JOHN SHEPLEY

The situationists have always said that "unitary urbanism is not a doctrine of urbanism but a critique of urbanism" (*Internationale situationniste* no. 3). The project of a more modern, more progressive urbanism, conceived as a corrective to the present specialization in city planning, is as false as, for example, in the revolutionary project, the overestimation of the moment for seizing power, which is a specialist's idea that immediately involves forgetting, indeed repressing, all the revolutionary tasks posed, at each and every moment, by the whole inseparable combination of human activities. Until it merges with a general revolutionary praxis, urbanism is necessarily the first enemy of all possibilities for urban life in our time. It is one of those fragments of social power that claim to represent a coherent whole, and which tend to impose themselves as a total explanation and organization, while doing nothing except masking the real social totality that has produced them and which they preserve.

By accepting this specialization of urbanism, one puts oneself at the service of the prevailing social and urbanist lie of the State, in order to carry out one of the many possible "practical" urbanisms. But the only practical urbanism *for us,* the one we call unitary urbanism, is thereby abandoned, since it requires the creation of quite different conditions of life.

Over the past six or eight months, we have seen a number of moves, chiefly among West German architects and capitalists, to launch a "unitary urbanism" immediately, at least in the Ruhr. Some poorly informed entrepreneurs, carried away by thoughts of success, saw fit to announce, in February, the imminent opening of a Unitary Urbanism laboratory in Essen (as a conversion of the Van de Loo art gallery). They published a disgruntled denial only when faced with our threat to reveal publicly the watered-down nature of the plan. The former situationist Constant, whose Dutch collaborators had been excluded from the SI for having agreed to build a church, now himself shows *factory models* in his catalogue published in March by the Municipal Museum in Bochum. This shrewd operator frankly offers himself, along with two or three plagiarized and misconstrued situationist ideas, as public relations for the integration of the masses into capitalist technological civilization, and reproaches the SI for having abandoned his whole program for overturning the urban milieu, he himself being the only one still concerned with it. Under such conditions, yes! Moreover, one might do well to recall that in April 1959 this same group of former members of the Dutch section of the SI was firmly opposed to the adoption by the SI of an "Appeal to Revolutionary Artists and Intellectuals," and stated: "For us, these perspectives do not depend on a revolutionary overthrow of present-day society, for which the conditions are lacking" (for this debate, see *Internationale situationniste* no. 3, pp. 23 and 24). They have thus continued logically on their path. What is more curious is that there should be people who still try to seduce a few situationists in order to involve them in this kind of enterprise. Are they betting on the taste for glory or the lure of gain? On April 15, Attila Kotányi replied to a letter from the director of the Bochum museum proposing a collaboration with the Bureau d'Urbanisme Unitaire in Brussels: "If you know the original well enough, we do not think you can confuse our critical view with the apologetic view hidden behind a copy with the same label." And he cut off any further discussion.

It is not easy to know the situationist theses on unitary urbanism in their original version. In June, our German comrades published a special issue of their journal (*Spur,* no. 5), bringing together texts devoted to unitary urbanism over several years in the SI or the trends leading to its formation. Many of these texts were unpublished or had appeared in now-inaccessible publications, and none of them had ever been published in German. The measures taken in Germany against the situationists to prevent the appearance of these texts, or at least to have them altered, were immediately apparent: from a forced delay of three weeks for the whole edition at the printers to loud threats of prosecution for immorality, pornography, blasphemy, and incitement to riot. The German situationists have obviously weathered these various attempts at intimidation, and today the managers of respectable unitary urbanism in the Ruhr should begin to wonder if this label is a profitable way to launch their operation.

Confrontation with the whole of present-day society is the sole criterion for a genuine liberation in the field of urban architecture, and the same goes for any other aspect of human activity. Otherwise, "improvement" or "progress" will always be designed to lubricate the system and perfect the conditioning that we must overturn, in urbanism and everywhere else. Henri Lefebvre, in the *Revue française de sociologie* (no. 3, July–September 1961), criticizes a number of inadequacies in the plan that a team of architects and sociologists have just published in Zurich, *Die neue Stadt, eine Studie für das Fürttal.* But it seems to us that this criticism does not go far enough, precisely because it does not clearly challenge the actual role of this team of specialists in a social framework whose absurd imperatives it accepts without discussion. This means that Lefebvre's article still valorizes too many works that certainly have their utility and their merits, but in a perspective radically inimical to ours. The title of this article, "Experimental Utopia: For a New Urbanism," already contains the whole ambiguity. For the method of experimental utopia, if it is truly to correspond to its project, must obviously embrace the whole, and carrying it out would lead not to a "new urbanism" but to a new way of life, a new revolutionary praxis. It is also the lack of a connection between the project for an ardent overthrow of architecture and other forms of conditioning, and its rejection in terms of the whole society, that constitutes the weakness of Feuerstein's theses, published in the same issue of the journal of the German section of the SI, despite the interest of several points, in particular his notion of the erratic block, "representing chance and also the smallest organization of objects comprised by an event." Feuerstein's ideas, which follow the SI line on "accidental architecture," can only

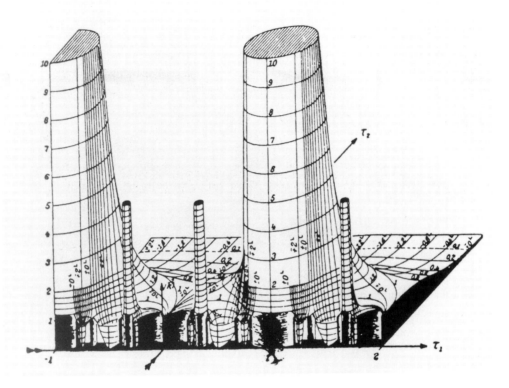

Representation in relief of the elliptical modular function.

The town of Mourenx. Its 12,000 inhabitants live in the horizontal blocks if they are married, in the towers if single. To the right of the picture lies the small middle-income quarter, consisting of identical houses, symmetrically divided between two families. Beyond, in the upper-income quarter, the houses are of another type, each entirely awarded to its occupant. Lacq CEOs live in Pau, Toulouse, and Paris.

be understood in all their consequences, and carried out, precisely by overcoming the separate problem of architecture and the solutions that would be reserved for it in the abstract.

Henceforth the crisis of urbanism is all the more concretely a social and political one, even though today no force born of traditional politics is any longer capable of dealing with it. Medico-sociological banalities on the "pathology of housing projects," the emotional isolation of people who must live in them, or the development of certain extreme reactions of denial, chiefly in young people, simply betray the fact that modern capitalism, the bureaucratic consumer society, *is here and there beginning to shape its own environment*. This society, with its new towns, is building the sites that accurately represent it, combining the conditions most suitable for its proper functioning, while at the same time translating into spatial terms, in the clear language of the organization of everyday life, its fundamental principle of alienation and constraint. It is likewise here that the new aspects of its crisis will be manifested with the greatest clarity.

In April, a Paris exhibition of urbanism entitled "Paris Tomorrow " offered in reality a defense of large housing complexes, those already built or planned for the far outskirts of the city. The future of Paris would lie entirely outside Paris. The first part of this didactic presentation sought to convince the public (mainly working people) that decisive statistics had shown Paris to be more unhealthy and unlivable than any other known capital. They would thus do well to transport themselves elsewhere, and indeed the happy solution was thereupon offered, failing only to mention the now necessary price for the construction of these regroupment zones: for instance, how many years of outright economic slavery the purchase of an apartment in these complexes entails, and what a lifetime of urban seclusion this acquired ownership will come to represent.

Still, the very necessity for this faked propaganda, the need to present this explanation to the interested parties after the administration had quite made up its mind, reveals an initial resistance by the masses. This resistance will need to be sustained and clarified by a revolutionary organization truly determined to know and combat all the conditions of modern capitalism. Sociological surveys, whose most stultifying defect is to present options only between the dismal variations of

DÉJEUNER	LUNDI	MARDI
	Salade de cervelas	Tomates en salade
	Côtelettes de porc	Steak grillé
	Pommes boulangère	Haricots verts
	Salade, fromage	Salade, yogourt
	Abricots	Fraises au sucre

DÎNER		
	Crêpes fourrées au fromage	Potage à l'oseille
	Petits pois au lard	Gratin de macaroni
	Œufs à la neige	Salade
		Fromage
		Tarte aux cerises

DÉJEUNER	MERCREDI	JEUDI
	Artichauts vinaigrette	Céleri rémoulade
	Ragoût de mouton	Paupiettes de veau braisées
	Flageolets	Pommes de terre frites
	Salade, fromage	Salade, fromage
	Pêches	Prunes

DÎNER		
	Sardines grillées	Omelette aux tomates
	Concombres à la crème	Gratin dauphinois
	Salade	Salade
	Charlotte aux fraises	Mousse aux framboises

DÉJEUNER	VENDREDI	SAMEDI
	Salade niçoise	Courgettes cuites en salade
	Colinot froid sauce fines herbes	Pot-au-feu
	Salade de pommes de terre	Fromage
	Groseilles au sucre	Glace à l'orange

DÎNER		
	Croquettes de poisson	Consommé froid
	sauce tomate	aux œufs pochés
	Carottes Vichy	Poivrons farcis au riz
	Fromage	Salade, fromage
	Compote panachée	Tarte aux pêches

DIMANCHE

DÉJEUNER		DÎNER	
	Salade d'été composée		Tarte au hachis de bœuf
	Curry de poulet		à la gelée
	Riz créole, fromage		Salade de haricots verts
	Framboises à la crème		Fromage
			Profiteroles glacées

Consumption and its spectacularization.

In the present framework of propaganda in favor of consumption, the fundamental hoax of advertising is to associate ideas of happiness with objects (television, or garden furniture, or cars, etc.), besides severing the natural tie these objects may have with others.

Editorial notes, *Internationale situationniste* 5 (December 1960) what already exists, indicate that 75 percent of the inhabitants of large housing projects dream of owning a house with a garden.

It is this mystic image of ownership, in the old-fashioned sense, that led Renault workers, for example, to buy the small houses that dropped in their laps in June, in a whole quarter of Clamart. It is not by returning to the archaic ideology of a discarded stage of capitalism that the living conditions of a society now becoming totalitarian can ever be truly replaced, but rather by freeing an instinct for construction presently repressed in everyone: a liberation that cannot go forward without the other elements in the conquest of an authentic life.

Debates in progressive inquiries today, on politics as well as art or urbanism, lag considerably behind the reality taking shape in all industrialized countries, namely, the concentration-camp organization of life.

The degree of conditioning imposed on working people in a suburb like Sarcelles, or still more clearly in a place like Mourenx (a company town in the petrochemical complex of Lacq), prefigures the conditions with which the revolutionary movement will everywhere have to struggle if it is to reestablish itself on a level with the real crises, the real demands of our time. In Brasília, functional architecture reveals itself to be, when fully developed, the architecture of functionaries, the instrument and microcosm of the bureaucratic Weltanschauung. One can already see that wherever bureaucratic capitalism has already planned and built its environment, the conditioning has been so perfected, the individual's margin of choice reduced to so little, that a practice as essential for it as advertising, which corresponded to a more anarchic stage of competition, tends to disappear in most of its forms and props. You might think that urbanism is capable of merging all former forms of advertising into a single advertisement for itself. The rest will be gotten for nothing. It is also likely that, under these conditions, the political propaganda that has been so strong in the first half of the twentieth century will almost totally disappear, to be replaced by an instinctive aversion to all political issues. Just as the revolutionary movement will have to shift the problem far away from the old field of politics scorned by everyone, the powers-that-be will rely more on the simple organization of the spectacle of

Decor and its uses. Four historians and several hundred million francs are said to have been provided this year to reconstruct part of the city of Alexandria on a heath in England, so that Elizabeth Taylor could play Cleopatra there. When the actress fell ill, the film could not be shot, nor could anything else be done with the set. In the end, Alexandria was burned down.

objects of consumption, which will only have consumable value illusorily *to the extent to which they will first of all have been objects of spectacle.* In Sarcelles or Mourenx, the showrooms of this new world are already being put to the test—atomized to the limit around each television screen, but at the same time extended to cover the whole town.

If unitary urbanism designates, as we would like it to, a useful hypothesis that would allow present humanity to construct life freely, beginning with its urban environment, it is absolutely pointless to enter into discussion with those who would ask us to what extent it is feasible, concrete, practical, or carved in stone, for the simple reason that nowhere does there exist any theory or practice concerning the creation of cities, or the kind of behavior that relates to it. No one "does urbanism," in the sense of constructing the milieu required by this doctrine. Nothing exists but a collection of techniques for integrating people (techniques that effectively resolve conflicts while creating others, at present less known but more serious). These techniques are wielded innocently by imbeciles or deliberately by the police. And all the discourses on urbanism are lies, just as obviously as the space organized by urbanism is the very space of the social lie and of fortified exploitation. Those who discourse on the powers of urbanism seek to make people forget that all they are creating is the urbanism of power. Urbanists, who present themselves as the educators of the population, have had to be educated themselves—by this world of alienation that they reproduce and perfect as best they can.

The notion of a center of attraction in the chatter of urbanists is quite the opposite of the reality, exactly as the sociological notion of participation turns out to be. The fact is that there are disciplines that come to terms with a society where participation can only be oriented toward "something in which it is impossible to participate" (point 2 of the *Programme élémentaire*)—a society that must impose the need for unappealing objects, and would be unable to tolerate any form of genuine attraction. To understand what sociology *never* understands, one need only envisage in terms of aggressivity what for sociology is neutral.

———

The "foundations" in preparation for an experimental life, of which the SI program of unitary urbanism speaks, are at the same time the places, the permanent elements of a new kind of revolutionary organization that we believe to be inscribed in the order of the day for the historical period we are entering. These foundations, when they come to exist, cannot be anything but subversive. And the future revolutionary organization will not be able to rely on instruments less complete.

NOTE

Internationale situationniste 6 (August 1961), 3–11.

Editorial Notes: Once Again, on Decomposition

TRANSLATED BY JOHN SHEPLEY

How goes cultural production? All our calculations are confirmed when one compares the phenomena of the last twelve months with the analysis of decomposition published a few years ago by the SI (cf. "Absence and Its Costumers," in *Internationale situationniste* no. 2, December 1958).[1] In Mexico, last year, Max Aub writes a thick book on the life of an imaginary cubist painter, Campalans, while demonstrating how well founded his praises are with the help of paintings whose importance is immediately established. In Munich, in January, a group of painters inspired by Max Strack arranges simultaneously for the biography, as sentimental as could be wished, and the exhibition of the complete oeuvre of Bolus Krim, a young abstract expressionist painter prematurely deceased—and just as imaginary. Television and the press, including almost all the German weeklies, express their enthusiasm for so representative a genius, until the hoax is proclaimed, leading some to call for legal proceedings against the tricksters. "I thought I had seen everything," the dance critic for *Paris-Presse* writes in November 1960, concerning *Bout de la nuit* by the German Harry Kramer, "ballets without subject and ballets without costumes, others without sets, finally others without music, and even ballets simultaneously devoid of all these elements. Well, I was wrong. Last night I saw the unheard-of, the unexpected, the unimaginable: a ballet without choreography. I mean it: without the slightest attempt at choreography, a motionless ballet." And the *Evening Standard,* of September 28 of the same year, reveals to the world one Jerry Brown, painter from Toronto, who means to demonstrate in both theory and practice "that in reality there is no difference between art and excrement." In Paris, this spring, a new gallery, founded on this Torontological aesthetic, exhibits the rubbish assembled by nine "new realist" artists, determined to redo Dada, but at "40° above," and who have nevertheless made the mistake of being too legibly introduced and justified by a sententious critic several degrees below, since he has found nothing better than to have them "consider the World as a Painting," calling even upon sociology "to aid consciousness and chance," in order stupidly to rediscover "emotion, sentiment, and finally, once more, poetry." Indeed. Niki de Saint-Phalle fortunately goes further, with her target-paintings painted with a carbine. In the courtyard of the Louvre, a Russian disciple of Gallizio executes, last January, a roll of painting seventy meters long, capable of being sold by the piece. But he spices things up by taking lessons from Mathieu, since he does it in only twenty-five minutes and with his feet.

Antonioni, whose recent mode has been confirmed, explains in October 1960 to the journal *Cinéma 60:* "In recent years, we have examined and studied the emotions as much as possible, to the point of exhaustion. That is all we've been able to do. . . . But we have not been able to find anything new, nor even glimpse a solution to this problem. . . . First of all, I'd say that one starts with a negative fact: the exhaustion of current techniques and means." Do they look for other cultural means, new forms of participation? Since March, special posters have been put up along the platforms of the New York subway for the sole purpose of being spray-painted by vandals. Moreover, the electronic gang, at least after this summer, will offer us, for the "Forme et Lumière" spectacle in Liège, a spatio-dynamic tower fifty-two meters high by the usual Nicolas Schoeffer, who this time will have at his disposal seventy "light brewers" to project abstract frescos in color on a giant screen 1,500 square meters in size, with musical accompaniment. Will this splendid effort be integrated, as he hopes, "with the life of the city"? To find out, we will have to wait for the next strike movement in Belgium, since the last time the workers had a chance to express themselves in Liège, on January 6, this Schoeffer Tower did not yet exist, and they had to vent their fury on the headquarters of the newspaper *La Meuse*.

Tinguely, more inspired, has unveiled, in full operation in the Museum of Modern Art in New York, a machine skillfully programmed to destroy itself. But it has been left to an American, Richard Grosser, to perfect, already several years ago, the prototype of a "useless machine," rigorously designed to serve no purpose whatsoever. "Built of aluminum, small in size, it includes neon lighting that goes on and off by chance." Grosser has sold more than five hundred of them, including one, it is said, to John Foster Dulles.

The truth is that even when they exhibit a certain sense of humor, all these inventors get quite excited, with an air of discovering the destruction of art, the reduction of a whole culture to onomatopoeia and silence like an unknown phenomenon, a new idea, one which was only waiting for them to come along. They all dig up corpses to kill them again, in a cultural no-man's-land beyond which they can imagine nothing. Yet they are precisely the artists of today, though without seeing how. They truly express our time of obsolete ideas solemnly proclaimed to be new, this time of planned incoherence, of isolation and deafness assured by the means of mass communication, of higher forms of illiteracy taught in the university, of scientifically guaranteed lies, and of overwhelming technical power at the disposal of ruling mental incompetence. The incomprehensible history that they incomprehensibly translate is indeed this planetary spectacle, as ludicrous as it is bloody, and whose program, in a crowded six months, has included: Kennedy hurling his cops into Cuba to find out whether the armed populace would spontaneously take their side; French shock troops embarking on a putsch and collapsing under the blow of a televised speech; de Gaulle resorting to gunboat diplomacy to reopen an African port to European influence; and Khrushchev coolly announcing that in another nineteen years communism will have essentially been achieved.

All this old stuff is of a piece, and all these mockeries cannot be overcome by a return to this or that form of "seriousness" or noble harmony of the past. This society is on its way to becoming, at all levels, more and more painfully ridiculous, until the time comes for its complete revolutionary reconstruction.

Notes

Internationale situationniste 6 (August 1961), 12–13.

1. [Translated in this volume, 79–83. Ed.]

Comments against Urbanism

RAOUL VANEIGEM
TRANSLATED BY JOHN SHEPLEY

In the opinion of an expert—Chombart de Lauwe—and after some precise experiments, the programs proposed by planners create in certain cases uneasiness and indignation, which might have been partly avoided had we had a deeper knowledge of real behavior, and especially of the motivations for such behavior.

Splendor and misery of urbanism. Once one has sniffed the urban planner with suspicious insistence, one turns away as one ought to before such a lack of respect, a similar breach of manners. Here it is not a question of impeaching the popular verdict. The people have long since pronounced themselves with the same incongruity: *"espèce d'architecte!"* has always been an explicit insult in Belgium. But when today such an expert sides with the opinion of the herd and also starts sniffing the planner, we are saved! Thus the urbanist is officially convicted of arousing uneasiness and indignation, arousing them "almost" like a primary instigator. One can only hope that the public authorities will react promptly; it is unthinkable that such centers of revolt should be openly maintained by the very people whose job it is to smother them. Here is a crime against social tranquillity that only a council of war can put a stop to. Will we see justice prevail among its own ranks? Unless the expert is, after all, merely a cunning urbanist.

If the planner is less able to understand the behavioral motivations of those he wants to house to the best of their nervous equilibrium than to incorporate urbanism without delay into the criminal investigation unit (to hunt down instigators—see above—and allow each to remain quietly in the hierarchy)—if he can really do it, then the science of crime fighting loses its raison d'être and changes its social purpose: urbanism is all that will be needed to preserve the status quo without recourse to the indelicacy of machine guns. Man assimilated to reinforced concrete—what a dream or happy nightmare for technocrats, wherein to lose whatever Higher Nervous Activity they have left, while trusting in the power and durability of reinforced concrete.

If the Nazis had known contemporary urbanists, they would have transformed their concentration camps into low-income housing. But this solution seems too brutal to M. Chombart de Lauwe. Ideal urbanism should urge everyone, without uneasiness or indignation, toward the final solution of the problem of humanity.

Urbanism is the most concrete and perfect fulfillment of a nightmare. A nightmare, according to the Littré dictionary, is "a state that ends when one awakens with a start after extreme anxiety." But a start against whom? Who has stuffed us to the point of somnolence? It would be as stupid to execute Eichmann as to hang the urbanists. It would be like getting mad at the targets when you're on a rifle range!

Planning is a big word, some say a dirty word. Specialists speak of economic planning and planned urbanism, then they wink with a knowing air, and everyone applauds so as to play the game. The chief attraction of the spectacle is the planning of happiness. The pollster is already conducting his inquiry; precise surveys establish the number of television viewers; it is a question of developing real estate around them, of building for them, without distracting them from the concerns that are being fed to them through their eyes and ears. It is a question of assuring equilibrium and a peaceful life to all, with that shrewd foresight expressed by comic-strip pirates in their maxim: "Dead men tell no tales." Urbanism and information are complementary in capitalist and "anticapitalist" societies—they organize silence.

To dwell is the "Drink Coca-Cola" of urbanism. You replace the necessity of drinking with that of drinking Coca-Cola. To dwell means to be at home everywhere, says Kiesler, but such a prophetic truth grabs nobody by the neck; it's a scarf against the encroaching cold, even if it evokes a flowing knot. We are dwelled-in; this is the necessary starting point.

As public relations, the ideal urbanism is the projection in space of a social hierarchy without conflict. Roads, lawns, natural flowers, and artificial forests lubricate the machinery of subjection and make it enjoyable. In a novel by Yves Touraine, the State even offers retired workers an electronic vibrator; happiness and the economy find it an advantage.

A certain urbanism of illusion is necessary, Chombart de Lauwe claims. The spectacle he offers us makes folklore out of Haussmann, who could arrange no illusion apart from a shooting gallery. This time, it is a matter of scenically organizing the spectacle across everyday life, letting each person live in the framework corresponding to the role that capitalist society imposes on him, and in the process further isolating him like a blind man trained to recognize himself illusorily in the materialization of his own alienation.

The capitalist training of space is nothing but training in a space where you lose your shadow, and end up losing yourself by dint of seeking yourself in what you are not. An excellent example of tenacity for all professors and other licensed organizers of ignorance.

The layout of a city, its streets, walls, and neighborhoods form that many signs of a strange conditioning. What sign should we recognize as our own? A few graffiti, words of rejection or forbidden gestures, hastily scrawled, in which cultured people only take an interest when they appear on the walls of some fossil city like Pompeii. But our cities are even more fossilized. We would like to live in lands of knowledge, amid living signs like familiar friends. The revolution will also be the perpetual creation of signs that belong to everyone.

There is an incredible dullness in everything having to do with urbanism. The word *build* sticks straight up out of the water where other possible words float on the surface. Wherever bureaucratic civilization has spread, the anarchy of individual construction has been officially sanctioned, and taken over by the authorized organisms of power, with the result that the building instinct has been extirpated like a vice and only barely survives in children and primitives (those not held accountable, in administrative parlance). And among all those who, unable to change their lives, spend them demolishing and rebuilding their shacks.

The art of reassurance—urbanism knows how to exercise it in its purest form: the ultimate civility of a power on the verge of asserting total mind control.

God and the City: No abstract and nonexistent force would be better able than urbanism to take over from God the post of doorkeeper left vacant by that death we've heard about. With its ubiquity, its immense goodness, perhaps someday its sovereign power, urbanism (or its project) would certainly have something to frighten the Church, were there the slightest doubt about the orthodoxy of power. But there is none, since the Church was "urbanism" long before power; what could it have to fear from a lay St. Augustine?

There is something admirable in causing thousands of human beings whom one deprives of even the hope of a last judgment to coexist in the word *dwell*. In this sense, the admirable crowns the inhuman.

Industrializing private life: "Make your life a business"—such will be the new slogan. To propose to each that he organize his vital milieu like a little factory to be managed like a miniature enterprise, with its substitute machinery, its illusory production, its fixed assets such as walls and furniture—isn't this the best way to make the concerns of those gentlemen who own a factory, a big and real one that must also produce, perfectly comprehensible?

Level the horizon: walls and unnatural patches of greenery set new limits to thought and dreaming, for it means poeticizing the desert rather than knowing where it ends.

New cities will wipe out the traces of the battles between traditional cities and the people they sought to oppress. To root out of everyone's memory the truth that each daily life has its history and, in the myth of participation, to contest the irreducible character of experience—these are the terms in which urbanists would express the goals they pursue if they deigned to suspend for a moment the air of seriousness that obstructs their thinking. Once the air of seriousness disappears, the sky lightens, everything becomes clearer, or almost; thus, as humorists well know, to destroy one's adversary with H-bombs is to condemn oneself to die in more protracted sufferings. How much longer will one have to go on mocking the urbanists before they grasp the fact that they're preparing the way for their own suicide?

Cemeteries are the most natural areas for greenery that exist, the only ones to be harmoniously integrated within the framework of future cities, like the last lost paradises.

Costs must cease to be an obstacle to the wish to build—so says the leftist builder. May he sleep in peace, for this will soon be the case, once the wish to build will have disappeared.

Procedures have been developed in France that turn construction into an erector set (J.-E. Havel). While making the best of things, a cafeteria is never anything but a place where you serve, in the sense that a fork serves for eating.

As it combines Machiavellianism with reinforced concrete, urbanism's conscience is clear. We are entering upon the reign of police refinement. Dignified enslavement.

To build in trust: even the reality of bay windows does not hide the fictive communication, even public settings show the despair and isolation of private consciences, even the frantic filling up of space is measured in intervals.

Project for a realistic urbanism: replace Piranesi's staircases with elevators, transform tombs into office buildings, line the sewers with plane trees, put trash cans in living rooms, stack up the hovels, and build all cities in the form of museums; make a profit out of everything, even out of nothing.

Alienation within easy reach: urbanism makes alienation tangible. The starving proletariat experienced alienation in the suffering of beasts. We will experience it in the blind suffering of things. To feel only by groping.

Honest and farsighted urbanists have the courage of stylites. Must we make our lives a desert so as to legitimize their aspirations?

It has taken the guardians of philosophic faith some twenty years to discover the existence of a working class. At a time when sociologists have come together to decree that the working class no longer exists, the urbanists them-

	FEMME Taille 1m59 Poids 54 k.	HOMME Taille 1m68 Poids 68 k.
A	0m200	0m240
B	0,550	0,600
C	0,660	0,720
D	1,100	1,350
E	1,370	1,550
F	0,200	0,240
G	0,300	0,335
H	0,480	0,550

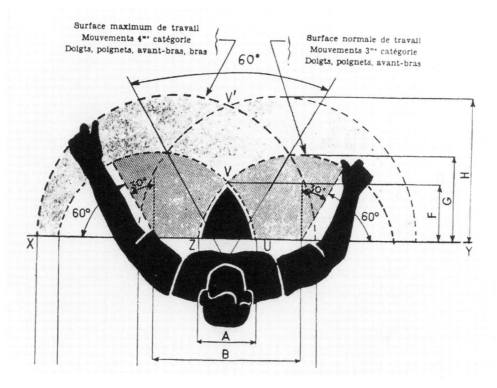

Maximum and normal work surfaces in the horizontal plane.

selves have invented the inhabitant without waiting for either philosophers or sociologists. One must give them credit for being among the first to discern the new dimensions of the proletariat. By a definition all the more precise and much less abstract, they have been able, using the most flexible training methods, to guide almost all of society toward a less brutal but radical proletarianization.

Advice to the builders of ruins: the urbanists will be succeeded by the last troglodytes of hovels and shantytowns. They will know how to build. The privileged residents of dormitory towns will only be able to destroy. We must wait a while for this encounter: it defines the revolution.

By being devalued, the sacred has become a mystery: urbanism is the final decadence of the Great Architect.

Behind the infatuation with technology a revealed truth lies hidden, and as such is unquestionable: we must "dwell." Concerning the nature of such a truth, the homeless know very well what to cling to. Probably better than anyone else, they are able to measure, amid the garbage cans where they are forced to live, how there is no difference between building their lives and building their dwellings on the only level of truth that exists—practice. But the exile to which our well-policed world consigns them makes their experience so laughable and difficult that the licensed builder could find there an excuse for self-justification—assuming, ridiculous idea, that the powers-that-be were to cease to guarantee his existence.

It looks like the working class no longer exists. Considerable quantities of former proletarians can today have access to the comfort formerly reserved for a minority—so goes the song. But isn't it rather that a growing quantity of comfort has access to their needs and gives them the itch to ask for it? It seems that a certain organization of comfort proletarianizes in epidemic fashion all those it contaminates by the force of things. Now, the force of things is exercised through the intervention of responsible authorities, priests of an abstract order whose sole prerogatives will sooner or later come together to reign over an administrative center surrounded by ghettoes. The last man will die of boredom as a spider dies of inanition in the middle of its web.

"Sure we know what guns are for . . . Where can you house us?"
"Come with me!"

We must build in haste, there are so many people to be lodged, say the humanists of reinforced concrete. We must dig trenches without delay, say the generals, if we are to save the whole fatherland. Isn't there some injustice in lauding the humanists and deriding the generals? In the era of missiles and conditioning, it is still in good taste to make jokes about generals. But to raise trenches in the air with the same pretext!

NOTE

Internationale situationniste 6 (August 1961), 33–37.

Editorial Notes: Priority Communication

TRANSLATED BY TOM McDONOUGH

Sociological and cultural theories so well hide the question of power that experts can write thousands of pages about communication or the means of mass communication in modern society without ever observing that this communication they speak of is unidirectional, that the *consumers of communication* have nothing to respond to. There is a rigorous division of tasks in so-called communication, which in the end confirms the more general division in industrial society (a society that integrates and shapes the whole of work and leisure) between those who organize time and those who consume it. Whoever is not bothered by the tyranny exercised over his life *at this level* understands nothing about society today, and is thus perfectly qualified to cover it with his sociological frescos. Anyone who is worried or awestruck before this mass culture, which, through a globally unified mass media, cultivates the masses and at the same time "massifies" "high culture," is forgetting that culture—even high culture, and including its expressions of revolt and self-destruction—is now buried in museums and that the masses—to whom, in the end, we all belong—are kept apart from life (from a participation in life), apart from free action: they are kept at a subsistence level, as defined by the spectacle. The law today dictates that everyone consume the greatest possible quantity of nothingness, including even the respectable nothingness of the old culture, which has been completely severed from its original meaning (progressive idiots will always be moved to see

Racine's drama televised, or Yakuts reading Balzac: they just do not plan for any other human progress).

The bombardment of information,[1] a revealing notion, must be understood in its broadest sense. Today, the population is subjected to a continuous bombardment of damned stupidities that are not in the least dependent on the mass media; and, above all, nothing would be more false, more worthy of the antediluvian left, than to imagine these mass media in competition with other spheres of modern life where people's true problems could be responsibly laid out. The university, the churches, traditional political conventions, or architecture all transmit the static of incoherent commonplaces just as strongly, and these commonplaces tend, anarchically but imperatively, to shape all the attitudes of everyday life (how to dress, whom to meet, how to deal with them). The first sociologist of "communication," whose bad joke is to contrast the alienation of the employee of the mass media with the satisfaction of the artist (which for him can be identified with the latter's work and be justified through it), does nothing but forever flaunt his joyous inability to conceive of artistic alienation itself.

Information theory straightaway ignores the chief power of language, which lies on its poetic level: to combat and to supersede. A writing that approaches emptiness, the complete neutrality of content and form, can only be deployed in accordance with a mathematical experimentation (like the "potential literature" that is the last period on the long white page written by Queneau). Despite the magnificent hypotheses of a "poetics of information" (Abraham Moles), despite the moving confidence of their misinterpretation of Schwitters or Tzara, the technologians of language will never understand anything but the language *of technology*. They do not know who will pass judgment on all this.

Considered in all its richness, considered in connection with the whole of human praxis and not in connection with the acceleration of the operation of checking accounts through the use of punched cards, communication is only ever found in action undertaken in common. And the most striking cases of massive misunderstanding are thus linked to massive nonintervention. No example could be clearer than the long and pitiful history of the French left's confrontation with Algeria's popular insurrection. Proof of the erstwhile policy's death in

France was provided not only by the abstention of almost all the workers, but doubtless even more by the political inanity of the minority who were determined to act: as in the extreme-left militants' illusions about the "popular front," illusions that can be described as existing in the second degree, seeing that, first, this phrase was strictly unfeasible in this period, and, second, that since 1936 it had been widely proven a quite reliable weapon of counterrevolution. If the collapse of the myths of the old political organizations was evident here, no new politics arose in their place. Indeed, the Algerian problem seemed like one of those French archaisms, insofar as the chief aim in this country is to attain the standing of a modern capitalist nation. The still unofficial, "wildcat" phenomena of workplace slowdown and sabotage that accompany this development do not in any way see themselves as linked with the struggle of underdeveloped Algerians. For those who cannot foresee a common protest, today's community with its apparently disparate interests is no longer founded on anything other than the dictates of memory (memories of what the old workers' movement did—or, more often, should have done—to support the exploited peoples of the colonies). This is so much the case that the only solidarity that could be conceived consisted of certain reflexes that have themselves become obsolete, and therefore abstract: we might have expected the ubiquitous, mythological French left of the PC-PSU-SFIO and the GPRA [Communist Party-Unified Socialist Party-French Section of the Workers' International and the Provisional Government of the Algerian Republic] to behave like the two sections of the Third International. Nevertheless, everything that has happened since 1920 seems to demonstrate that a fundamental critique of these solutions is everywhere inescapable; and such a solution was straightaway formulated by the Algerians, inevitably, in their current armed struggle. Internationalist solidarity, if it is not to be debased into the moralism of the Christian left, can only be a solidarity between revolutionaries of the two countries. This obviously assumes that they are to be found in France; and in Algeria, that one will opt for their interests when the current national front will have to decide the nature of its power.

The people who have tried to lead an avant-garde movement in France during this period have been divided between, on the one hand, their fear of completely cutting themselves off from the old political communities (despite their awareness of the latter's advanced state of glaciation), or in any case from their language; and, on the other hand, a certain scorn for the true emotion felt in some sectors—e.g., among the students—which are concerned with the struggle against colonialist extremism, a scorn that is owing to the latter's indulgence for a veritable anthology of political anachronisms (unified action against fascism, with none excluded, etc.).

Not a single group has been able to make an exemplary use of this opportunity by linking up the *maximum program* of potential revolt in capitalist society with a maximum program of the current revolt of colonized people; a situation that is, of course, explained by the weakness of such groups. But this very weakness must never be regarded as an excuse: on the contrary, it is simply a lack of work and rigor. It is inconceivable that an organization that represents people's real protest, and that can speak to them of it, should remain weak, even if its activities would be very severely curbed.

The complete separation of the workers of France and Algeria, which must be understood not primarily as a spatial distance but *as a temporal one,* has led to that frenzy of information, even "from the left," which was seen the day after February 8, when the police killed eight French demonstrators. The newspapers then spoke of the bloodiest clashes seen in Paris *since* 1934, without once recalling that less than four months earlier, the Algerian demonstrators of October 18 had been massacred by the dozens. That same frenzy allowed an "Antifascist Committee of Saint-Germain-des-Prés" to distribute a poster that began, "The people of France and Algeria have imposed negotiations . . . ," without keeling over at the absurdity of that list, in that order, of the two forces.

At a time when the reality of communication is so profoundly rotten, it is hardly surprising that sociology has developed the mineralogical study of petrified communication. Nor is it surprising that in art, the neodadaist rabble is rediscovering the importance of the dada movement as a formal positivity to be exploited *again,* after so many other modernist movements since the 1920s have already adopted what they could from it. They try their hardest to forget that the genuine dadaism was that of Germany, and to what extent it had been bound with the rise of the German revolution after the 1918 armistice. The need for such a link has not changed for whoever seeks to bring about a new cultural position today. Simply put, this new element must be discovered in art and politics *simultaneously*.

Simple anticommunication, borrowed today from dadaism by the most reactionary champions of the established lies, is worthless in an era when the urgent question is to create a new communication on all levels of practice, from the most simple to the most complex. Dadaism's most worthy sequel, its legitimate heir, must be recognized in the Congo during the summer of 1960. The spontaneous revolt of a people—held, more than anywhere else, in a state of childhood, and coming at a time when rationality has faltered, more than everywhere else in the world, from its very exploitation—knows how to immediately appropriate the foreign language of the masters as poetry and as a form of action. We should respectfully study the expression of the Congolese during this period in order to recognize in it the greatness and effectiveness (cf. the role of the poet Lumumba) of the only possible communication that, in all cases, accompanies intervention in events and the transformation of the world.

Although the public would be strongly encouraged to think otherwise, and not only by the mass media, the coherence of the Congolese's actions, as long as their avant-garde was not felled, and the excellent use they made of the few means that they had, contrast precisely with the basic incoherence of the social organization of all developed countries and with their dangerous inability to find a satisfactory use of their technological powers. Sartre, who is the perfect representative of his lost generation in his unique ability to be duped by *all* the myths among which his contemporaries chose, now decides, in a note to *Médiations* no. 2, that one cannot speak of a rotting artistic language that corresponds to a time of decay, for "an age builds more than it destroys." The grocer's scale thus tilts to the heavier side, but only because of a confusion between building and producing. Sartre must notice that today there is a greater tonnage of ships on the seas than before the war, despite all the torpedoes; that there are more buildings and more automobiles, despite all the fires and accidents. And that there are also more books, since Sartre has been alive. And yet society's reasons to go on have canceled each other out. Alternatives that demarcate illusory change have a tenure as short as that of a police chief, and then they too are relegated to the widespread decay of the old world. The only useful work that remains to be done is to rebuild society and life on an altogether different foundation. The diverse neophilosophies of those who have for too long ruled over the desert of supposedly modern and progressive thought do not provide this foundation. Their great men refuse even to go the museum, because this is a period too meaningless for museums. They were all alike, all identical products of the immense defeat of the movement for mankind's emancipation in the first third of this century. They accepted this defeat, and that acceptance exhausts their significance. To the last, the specialists of error will champion their specialization. But these dinosaurs of pseudocommunication, now that the climate is changing, no longer have anything to graze upon. The sleep of dialectical reason has produced monsters.

All unilateral ideas about communication have obviously been ideas about unilateral communication. They have corresponded to sociology's vision of the world and to its interests, as well as to those of the former domain of art, or to the administrative staff of political leaders. This is what will change. We are aware of "the incompatibility of our program, as expression, with the available means of expression and reception" (Kotányi).[2] It is a matter of simultaneously seeing what might be of use in communication and what communication might be used for. The communicative forms in existence, and their present crisis, are understood and justified from the viewpoint of their supersession. We must not exhibit such respect for art or writing that we would want to completely abandon them, and we must not hold modern art history or philosophy in such contempt that we would want to carry on with them as if nothing had happened. Our opinion is undeceived because it is *historical*. For us, every use of the permitted forms of communication has therefore to both be and not be a refusal of this communication: it must, that is, be a communication that contains its refusal and a refusal containing communication, i.e., the inversion of this refusal into a constructive project. All this must lead somewhere. Communication will now contain *its own critique.*

NOTES

Internationale situationniste 7 (April 1962), 20–24.

1. [This term was first used in the situationist context by Attila Kotányi in "Gangland et philosophie," *Internationale situationniste* 4 (June 1960), 33–35, who called for the SI to study "the *bombardment of information* that falls, during a given period, on present-day conurbations." Ed.]

2. [See Attila Kotányi, "L'étage suivant," *Internationale situationniste* 7 (April 1962), 47–48. Ed.]

Editorial Notes: The Avant-Garde of Presence

TRANSLATED BY JOHN SHEPLEY

In *Médiations* no. 4, Lucien Goldmann, recently turned critic specializing in the cultural avant-garde, speaks of an "avant-garde of absence," one that expresses in art and style a certain rejection of the reification of modern society, but which, in his opinion, expresses nothing else. He recognizes this negative role of avant-garde culture in our century about forty-five years after the event but, oddly enough, among his friends and contemporaries. Thus we find, disguised as resuscitated dadaists, none other than Ionesco, Beckett, Sarraute, Adamov, and Duras, not to mention Robbe-Grillet of *Marienbad* fame. This merry little crew, all present and accounted for, thereupon reenacts as farce the tragedy of the murder of artistic forms. Sarraute!—can you imagine? Adamov!—who would have believed it? Goldmann, an attentive audience, comments solemnly on what he sees: "Most of the great avant-garde writers express above all, not actual or possible values, but their *absence,* the impossibility of formulating or perceiving acceptable values in whose name they might criticize society." Here is precisely what is false, as is immediately apparent when one abandons the actors of Goldmann's comic novel to examine the historical reality of German dadaism, or of surrealism between the two wars. Goldmann seems literally unaware of them—which is curious: would he think that one is justified in rejecting the historical interpretation of his *Dieu caché,* while hinting that one has never read Pascal or Racine since the seventeenth century is complex and it's all one can do to get through Cotin's complete works? It is hard to see how he could have even a cursory knowledge of the original, and still find such freshness in the copy. Even his vocabulary is unsuited to the subject. He talks about "great writers" of the avant-garde, a notion that the avant-garde has long since rightly cast into ridicule once and for all. Later, mentioning the tasteful diversions agreeably mounted by Planchon with the bits and pieces of a dying theatrical tradition, Goldmann, still sniffing some avant-gardism there, says that all the same he does not find in it "a literary creation of equal importance, centered on the presence of humanist values and historical development." The notable quantity of insignificance that indelibly marks Goldmann's avant-garde nevertheless makes Planchon look good. But lastly Goldmann talks about literary creation. Doesn't he know that the rejection of literature, the very destruction of style, has been the prime tendency of twenty or thirty years of avant-garde experiments in Europe, that his circus clowns have looked only through the wrong end of the telescope, and cultivate with the parsimony of small stockholders? The avant-garde of the true self-destruction of art had expressed inseparably the absence and possible presence of quite another life. And does one have to plunge into the mystification of humanism so as not to follow Adamov into that absence that suits him so well that he stands a good chance of becoming its owner?

Let us be more serious than Goldmann. In the same article, he wonders whether there exist in present society, in this modern capitalism that is consolidating itself and developing in the regrettable ways we know, "social forces strong enough to overcome it or at least pointing in that direction." This is indeed a very important question. We will try to answer yes. A properly demystified study of *real* artistic or political avant-garde movements can, in any case, provide elements worth appreciating that are just as rare in Ionesco's work as in Garaudy's. What is socially *visible* in the world of the spectacle is more remote than ever from social reality. Even its avant-garde art and its challenging thought are henceforth cosmetically disguised in the illumination of this visual element. Those who refrain from entering this *son et lumière of the present* that so bedazzles Goldmann are precisely the ones, like the situationists for the moment, who are in the avant-garde of presence. What Goldmann calls the avant-garde of

Situationists between two sessions of the Antwerp conference.

Marxism being an error, one can see at what level to put the tenth-rate plagiarists of an ideology that they garble even more, and from which they extract a concept of cultural decomposition that even low-grade Marxists find completely insane.

Situationist critics, who hope to take over all the means of communication, having created none of them, at any level, and replace the whole, namely the various creations and trivialities that result from it, by their unique and enormous triviality, these morons, we say, represent excretions of the Hitlerite or Stalinist kind, in their extreme manifestations of present impotence, of which the most obvious and frenzied examples are the Nazi gangs in England and America.

Cahiers du lettrisme 1 (December 1962)

absence is nothing more than the *absence of the avant-garde.* We are confident that nothing of all this pretense and agitation will remain in the history and real problematics of this period. On this point as on others, *a hundred years will tell whether we were wrong.*

Moreover, Goldmann's avant-garde and its absenteeism are already behind the times (except for Robbe-Grillet, who bets on all the numbers in the roulette of avant-garde theater). The most recent tendency is to be integrated, to integrate several arts among themselves, and at all costs to integrate the spectator. First of all, ever since *Marienbad,* which for journalists is the obligatory reference point, there have been countless works that cannot exist without "the individual participation of the spectator, each of whom is destined to experience it differently" (Jacques Siclier in *Le Monde,* November 28, 1962, in connection with some televised ballet or other). Marc Saporta has just published a card game novel; one is supposed to shuffle the cards before reading in order to participate. Next to be integrated: experimental music with ceramics, which the visitor will be able to listen to at the Starczewski exhibition in Paris. Music by Stockhausen, but whose score becomes "mobile" at the whim of the performer, with an abstract film by the German Kirchgässer (Institute for Contemporary Music in Darmstadt). Nicolas Schoeffer has been integrated with the house of Philips in an audiovisual climate (the "creation wall"). Finally, countless integrations throughout Europe, which themselves get inter-integrated in biennales, which everywhere become Himalayas of integration. In the same journal, *Médiations,* one might point out the integration of a new profession: the criticism in "abstract" prose of the abstract work. It was common fifteen years ago in painting catalogues, where Michel Tapié performed wonders, and it makes its appearance in literature with Jean Ricardou, who simply transposes the sensible and childish forms of textual explication, but with the improvement that he paints black on black by commenting on the scarcely readable pages, deliberately poor in content, of the pure *nouveau roman,* in an abstract critical language worthy of its model for content and readability. You can also integrate whatever you like— thirty teaspoons, a hundred thousand bottles, a million Swiss—in "nouveau réalisme," such is its strength. The new figuration would like to integrate the past, present, and future of painting in anything that will pay off—no-fault insurance for lovers of the abstract and lovers of the figurative as well.

Our culture being what it is, all that gets integrated is one dissolution with another. And no one cares to point out that these dissolutions are themselves almost always repetitions of something older. (Saporta's card game novel is an echo of Paul Nougé's card game poem, *Le jeu des mots et du hasard,* dating back to before 1930 and reissued a few years ago. One could multiply such examples.) As for the integration of the spectator into these wonderful things, it is a poor little image of his integration into the new cities, into the banks of television monitors in the office or factory where he works. It pursues the same plan, but with infinitely less force, and even infinitely fewer guinea pigs. The old forms of the art of neodecadence are now, in themselves, far from the center of struggle for the control of modern culture. The change in the cultural terrain is not only the thesis of the revolutionary avant-garde in our culture, it is also unfortunately the opposite project, already widely achieved, of the present rulers. One ought not, however, to overlook the specialists of the "kinetic" movement. All they want is to integrate time into art. They've had no luck, since the program of our period is rather to dissolve art in the experience of time.

Already some researchers, to ensure themselves a less crowded specialty, have at several points ventured beyond these hasty integrations and their flimsy justifications. Some technicians would like to reform the spectacle. Le Parc, in a tract published in September 1962 by the "Groupe de Recherche d'Art Visuel," thinks it possible for the passive spectator to evolve into a "stimulated spectator" or even an "interpreter-spectator," but still within the framework of specialized old-hat ideas that would provide "some kinds of sculptures to be grappled with, dances to be painted, swordplay paintings." At most, Le Parc reaches the point of using a few para-situationist formulas: "In frankly admitting the reversal of the traditional situation of the passive spectator, one distorts the idea of the spectacle. . . ." This is an idea, however, that it is better not to distort, but properly to gauge its place in society. The futility of Le Parc's hopes for his spectator who will gratify him by achieving "real participation (the manipulation of elements)"— oh yes! and visual artists will certainly have their elements all ready—takes on more solidity when, at the end of his text, he extends a hand toward "the notion of programming," i.e., to the cyberneticians of power. There are those who go much further (cf. *France-Observateur,* December 27, 1962), like the "Service de la Recherche de la RTF," which wanted nothing less than to "*create a situation*" last December 21 by organizing a conference at UNESCO, with the participation of the well-known extraterrestrials who edit the journal *Planète.*

The dialectic of history is such that the victory of the Situationist International in matters of theory already obliges its adversaries to *disguise themselves* as situationists. From now on, there are two tendencies in the approaching struggle against us: those who proclaim themselves situationists without having any idea of what it's all about (the several varieties of Nashism),[1] and those who, on the contrary, decide to adopt a few ideas without the situationists, and without mentioning the SI. The growing probability that some of the simplest and least recent of our theses will be confirmed leads a number of people to adopt portions of one or the other *without saying so.* This is certainly not a matter of acknowledging antecedents or personal merits, etc. If there is any reason to point out this tendency, it is to denounce it on a single crucial point: in doing so, these people can speak of a new problem, so as to popularize it themselves after having rejected it as long as they could, and now extirpating only its violence, its connection with general subversion, thereby watering it down to an academic statement, or worse. With such intentions, it is necessary to conceal the SI.

Thus, the journal *Architecture d'aujourd'hui* (no. 102, June–July 1962) has finally got around to an account of "fantastic architecture," including certain former and present attempts that could be very interesting. But it so happens that only the SI holds the key to their interesting application. For the scribblers of *Architecture d'aujourd'hui,* they only serve to decorate the walls of passivity. The editor of this journal, for example, in his personal activity as an artist, if one may say so, has tried almost all the styles of fashionable sculptors, imitating them to the letter, which seems to have made him an expert on the subject of artistic conditioning. When such people take it into their heads that the surroundings ought to be improved, they act like all reformers, countering a stronger pressure by slowing it down. These authorities of today are quite prepared to reform the

Marilyn Monroe, August 5, 1962: the specialization of the mass spectacle constitutes, in the society of the spectacle, the epicenter of separation and noncommunication.

environment, but without touching the life that goes on within it. And they coolly give the name of "system" to investigations in these matters, so as to be shielded from any conclusions. It is not for nothing that in this issue they criticize the underdeveloped "technician" of unitary urbanism who had to leave the SI in 1960.[2] Even this extremely meager subtheory is too troubling for the eclecticism of converts from the old functionalism. We, however, rightly defend no system, and we see better than anyone, at all levels, the system that they themselves defend, and that defends them while maiming them so much. We want to destroy such a system.

We must make the same objection to those people who for six or ten months in some journals have been starting to rethink the problem of leisure time, or that of the new human relations that will be necessary within the future revolutionary organization. What is missing here? Actual experience, the oxygen of ruthless criticism of what exists, the total picture. The situationist point of view now seems as indispensable as yeast, without which the dough of the best themes raised by the SI falls again in a few years. Those who are entirely shaped by the *boredom* of current life and thought can only rejoice in the leisure of boredom. Those who have never accurately perceived either the present or the potential of the revolutionary movement can only search for a psychotechnical philosopher's stone. One that would retransmute modern depoliticized workers into devoted militants of leftist organizations, reproducing so well the model of established society that, like a factory, they could hire a few psychosociologists to apply a little oil to their microgroups. The methods of sociometry and psychodrama will not lead anyone very far ahead in the construction of situations.

To the degree that participation becomes more impossible, the second-class engineers of modernist art demand everyone's participation as their due. They distribute this invoice with the instruction booklet as the now explicit rule of the game, as if this participation had not always been the implicit rule of an art where it actually existed (within the limits of class and depth that have framed all art). They urge us insolently to "take part" in a spectacle, in an art that *so little* concerns us. Behind the comic aspect of this glorious beggary, one comes upon the sinister spheres of the cultural gendarmes who organize "participation in things where it is impossible to participate"—work or the leisure of private life—(cf. *Internationale situationniste* no. 6, p. 16).[3] In this light, one ought probably to take another look at the seeming naïveté of Le Parc's text, its peculiar unreality in relation to the public he would like to "stimulate." "In this concern for the spectators' violent participation," he writes, "one could even arrive at nonrealization, noncontemplation, nonaction. One might then be able to imagine, for example, a dozen nonaction spectators sitting motionless in the most complete darkness and saying nothing." It so happens that when people are placed in such a position, they cry out, as all those who participated in the real action of the negative avant-garde have fortunately been able to notice. Nowhere has there been, as Goldmann believes, an avant-garde of pure absence, but only the *staging of the scandal of absence* to appeal to a desired presence, "provocation to that game that is human presence" (manifesto in *Internationale situationniste* no. 4).[4] The pupils of the "Groupe de Recherche d'Art Visuel" have such a metaphysical idea of an abstract public that they certainly won't find it on the terrain of art—all these tendencies postulate with incredible impudence a totally besotted public, capable of the same weighty seriousness as these specialists for their little contrivances. But on the other hand, such a public shows signs of being created *at the level of global society.* It is the "lonely crowd" of the world of the spectacle, and here Le Parc is no longer so far ahead of reality as he thinks: in the organization of this alienation, there surely is no spectator free to remain purely passive. Even their passivity is organized, and Le Parc's "stimulated spectators" are already everywhere.

Furthermore, we note that the idea of constructing situations is a central one of our time. Its mirror image, its slavish symmetry, appears in all conditioning. The first psychosociologists—Max Pagès claims that only about fifty of them have emerged in the last twenty years—are about to multiply quickly; they are learning how to manipulate certain *given* but still crude situations, which would include the permanent collective situation that has been devised for the inhabitants of Sarcelles. The artists who align themselves in this camp to rescue a specialty of scene painters from cybernetic machination do not hide the fact that they've made their debut in the manipulation of integration. But with respect to the artistic negation that rebels against this integration, it appears that no one,

"Critique of Separation."

> Don't be so idiotic, she says, as to want to save the world—you can't do anything. This conspiracy is not on the earthly scale, nor even on that of the solar system. We are pawns in a game being played by star people.
>
> E. Van Vogt, *Le monde des Non-A*

unless he sticks to a position, can approach this minefield of situations without bumping into another dispute, coherent on all levels. And first of all on the political level, where no future revolutionary organization can seriously be conceived any longer without several "situationist" qualities.

We speak of recovering free play, when it is isolated on the sole terrain of familiar artistic dissolution. In the spring of 1962, the press began to take note of the practice of the *happening* among the artistic avant-garde of New York. This is a kind of theater dissolved to the extreme, an improvisation of gestures, of a dadaist bent, by people thrown together in an enclosed space. Drugs, alcohol, and sex all play a role. The gestures of the "actors" attempt a mixture of poetry, painting, dance, and jazz. One can regard this form of social encounter as a borderline case of the old artistic spectacle whose remnants get thrown into a common grave, or as an attempt at renewal—in that case, too overloaded with aesthetics—of an ordinary surprise party or classic orgy. One might even think that, by its naïve wish for "something to happen," the absence of outside spectators, and the wish to make some small innovations on the meager scale of human relations, the happening is an isolated attempt to construct a situation *on the basis of poverty* (material poverty, poverty of human contact, poverty inherited from the artistic spectacle, poverty of the specific philosophy driven to "ideologize" the reality of these moments). The situations that the SI has defined, on the other hand, can only be constructed on the basis of material and spiritual richness. Which is another way of saying that an outline for the construction of situations must be the game, the serious game, of the revolutionary avant-garde, and cannot exist for those who resign themselves on certain points to political passivity, metaphysical despair, or even the pure and experienced absence of artistic creativity. The construction of situations is the supreme goal and first model of a society where free and experimental modes of conduct will prevail. But the happening did not have to wait long to be imported into Europe (December at the Galerie Raymond Cordier in Paris) and turned completely upside down by its French imitators. The result was a mob of spectators frozen in the atmosphere of an École des Beaux-Arts ball, as pure and simple publicity for an opening of little surrealist-type things.

Whatever is constructed on the basis of poverty will always be reclaimed by the surrounding poverty, and will serve its perpetuators. Early in 1960 (cf. "Die Welt als Labyrinth," in *Internationale situationniste* no. 4),[5] the SI avoided the trap that the Stedelijk Museum's proposal had become, a proposal that called for the construction of a setting that would serve as a pretext for a series of urban *dérives* in Amsterdam and thus for some unitary urbanist projects. It turned out that the plan for a labyrinth submitted by the SI would be subjected to thirty-six kinds of restrictions and controls, thereby reducing it to something scarcely different from a product of traditional avant-garde art. We accordingly broke the agreement. This avant-gardist museum seems to have remained inconsolable for quite a while, since only in 1962 did it finally come forth with "its" labyrinth, more simply entrusted to the "nouveau réalisme" gang, which assembled something very photogenic with "dada in its heart," as Tzara used to say in the good old days.

We see that when we comply with the requests of those who urge us to exhibit usable and convincing detailed plans—why should we have to convince them?—they either turn them against us at once as proof of our utopianism, or else favor a watered-down version for the moment. The truth is that you can ask for detailed plans from almost all the others—you're the one who decides what number might be satisfactory—but certainly *not from us;* it is our thesis that there can be no fundamental cultural renewal in details, but only *in toto*. We are obviously well situated to discover, some years before others, all the possible tricks of the extreme cultural decay of our time. Since they can only be used in the spectacle of our enemies, we keep some notes about them in a drawer. After a while, someone really rediscovers a lot of them spontaneously and broadcasts them with great fanfare. Most of the ones we possess, however, have not yet been "overtaken by history." Several may never be. It is not even a game; it is one more experimental confirmation.

We think that modern art, wherever it has really found innovators and critics through the very conditions of its appearance, has well performed its role, which was a great one; and that it remains, despite speculation on its products, hated by the enemies of freedom. One needs only to look at the fear inspired at this moment in the leaders of homeopathic de-Stalinization by the slightest sign of its return to their homeland, where it had been caused to be forgotten. They denounce it as a leak in their ideology and confess that it is vital to their power to hold a monopoly in manipulating this ideology at every level. All the same, those who now make money in the West on the respectful extensions and artificial revivals of the stymied old cultural game are in reality the enemies of modern art. As for ourselves, we are its residuary legatees.

We are against the conventional form of culture, even in its most modern state, while obviously not preferring ignorance, the petit-bourgeois common sense of the local butcher, or neoprimitivism. There is an anticultural attitude that flows toward an impossible return to old myths. We place ourselves on the other side of culture. Not before it, but *after.* We say that one must *attain* it, while going beyond it as a separate sphere, not only as a domain reserved for specialists, but above all as the domain of a specialized production that does not directly affect the construction of life—including the very lives of its own specialists.

We are not wholly lacking in a sense of humor, but this very humor is of a somewhat different kind. If it is a matter of choosing quickly what attitude to adopt toward our ideas, without getting into the fine points or some more subtle understanding of nuances, the simplest and most correct one is to take us literally and with utter seriousness.

How are we going to bankrupt the prevailing culture? In two ways, at first gradually and then abruptly. We propose to use some concepts artistic in origin in a nonartistic way. We have begun with an artistic exigency, which did not resemble any former aestheticism since it was indeed the exigency of revolutionary modern art at its highest moments. We have thus brought this exigency into life, toward revolutionary politics, meaning its absence and the search for explanations of its absence. The total revolutionary politics that flows from it, and that is confirmed by the highest moments of the true revolutionary struggle of the last hundred years, then comes back to the beginning of this project (a wish for direct life), but now without there being any art or politics as independent forms, nor the recognition of any other separate domain. The objection to the world, and its reconstruction, live only in the undivided nature of such a project, in which the cultural struggle, in the conventional sense, is merely the pretext and cover for a deeper task.

It is easy to draw up an endless list of problems and difficulties in order of priority, as well as some short-term impossibilities that are saddening. It is probable that the excitement, for example, aroused among situationists by the project of a massive demonstration at the Paris headquarters of UNESCO testifies first of all to the taste, latent in the SI, to find a concrete *field of intervention,* where situationist activity would appear openly and positively as such, a kind of construction of the event here combined with the taking of a resounding position against the world center of bureaucratized culture. Complementary to this aspect of things, the views upheld by Alexander Trocchi, previously and at this moment, on the clandestine nature of a portion of situationist actions may lead us to augment our freedom of intervention. To the degree to which, as Vaneigem writes, "we cannot avoid making ourselves known up to a certain point in a spectacular way," these new forms of clandestinity would doubtless be useful in combatting our own spectacular image, which our enemies and disgraced followers are already forging. Like every source of attraction that can be constituted in the world (and though our "attraction" is really quite particular), we have begun to unleash the adverse forces of submission *to ourselves.* If we are not to yield to these forces, we will have to invent adequate defenses for ourselves, which in the past have been very little studied. Another worrisome subject for situationists is surely the kind of specialization required, in a society of highly specialized thought and practice, by the task of holding the fort of nonspecialization, besieged and breached on all sides, while raising the flag of totality. Still another is the obligation to judge people in terms of our actions and theirs, and to break off relations with several whom it would be pleasant to know in private life—an unacceptable frame of reference. Nevertheless, the quarrel with what exists, if it also involves daily life, is naturally translated into struggles *within* daily life. The list of these difficulties, we say, is a long one, but the arguments that flow from it are still extremely weak, since we are perfectly well aware of the alternative way of thinking at this crossroads of our time: namely, unconditional surrender on all points. We have founded our cause on *almost nothing:* irreducible dissatisfaction and desire with regard to life.

The SI is still far from having created situations, but it has already created situationists, and that is something. This power of liberated dispute, in addition to its first direct applications, shows that such liberation is not impossible. This is how from now on, in different areas, the task will be glimpsed.

NOTES

Internationale situationniste 8 (January 1963), 14–22.

1. ["On March 15, in Sweden, Jörgen Nash and Ansgar-Elde suddenly turned against the Situationist International, and have undertaken the transformation of the Scandinavian section into a 'Bauhaus'—yet another one—capable of quickly spreading about a few profitable artistic commodities, if possible marked by situationism. The unfolding of this conspiracy doubtless had been precipitated by the recent elimination of the SI's right wing, on which the Nashists expected to rely." From "Renseignements situationnistes," *Internationale situationniste* 7 (April 1962), 53. Ed.]

2. [I.e., Constant. Ed.]

3. [Attila Kotányi and Raoul Vaneigem, "Programme élémentaire du bureau d'urbanisme unitaire," *Internationale situationniste* 6 (August 1961), 16. Ed.]

4. ["Manifeste (17 mai 1960)," *Internationale situationniste* 4 (June 1960), 36. Ed.]

5. ["Notes éditoriales: Die Welt als Labyrinth," *Internationale situationniste* 4 (June 1960), 5–7. "Dylaby," or the "Labyrinthe dynamique," designed by Tinguely, Daniel Spoerri, and Pontus Hulten, Stedelijk Museum, Amsterdam, August 30–September 30, 1962. Ed.]

Editorial Notes: All the King's Men

TRANSLATED BY TOM MCDONOUGH

The problem of language is at the center of every struggle for the abolition or preservation of today's alienation; it is inseparable from the whole field of these struggles. We live in language as in polluted air. Contrary to what men of wit assume, words do not play. Nor do they make love, as Breton thought, except in dreams. Words *work* on behalf of the ruling organization of life. Yet nevertheless they have not become automatons; to the misfortune of the theorists of information, words themselves are not "informationist"; through them, forces are expressed that may frustrate calculations. Words coexist with power in a relationship similar to that which proletarians (in the classical as well as the modern meaning of this term) may maintain with power. Employed *almost* all the time, used full-time for their maximum sense and nonsense, they remain in some ways radically foreign.

Power only provides words with a forged identity card; it makes them carry a pass, fixes their place in production (where some clearly work overtime); and issues them their paysheet, as it were. Let us acknowledge the seriousness of Lewis Carroll's Humpty-Dumpty, who believes that, to determine the use of words, it is a question of "knowing who will be master, that's all there is to it." And he, a socially responsible employer in this matter, avers that he pays double those he employs a lot. Let us also understand the phenomenon of the *rebelliousness of words,* their retreat and their open resistance, which appears in all modern writing (from Baudelaire to the dadaists and Joyce) as the sign of the revolutionary crisis of the whole of society.

Under power's supervision, language always designates something other than authentic lived experience. It is precisely there that the possibility of a total opposition resides. The confusion in the organization of language has become so great that communication imposed by power is unveiled as an imposture and a deception. It is in vain that an embryonic cybernetic power endeavors to place language subordinate to machines that it controls, so that information henceforth would be the only possible communication. Even within this field resistances are appearing, and we have every right to consider electronic music an attempt—ambiguous and limited, of course—to reverse the relations of domination by appropriating machines in aid of language. But opposition is much more widespread and much more radical. It denounces all unilateral "communication," in the old art as in the modern reification of information. It calls for a communication that is the ruin of all separated power. Where there is communication, there is no State.

Power lives on stolen goods. It creates nothing; it recuperates. If it created the meaning of words, there would be no poetry, but solely useful "information." We could never confront one another within language, and every refusal would be outside it, would be purely lettrist. However, what is poetry if not language in revolution, and as such inseparable from revolutionary moments in world history as well as in the history of private life?

Power's capture of language is comparable to its capture of the totality. Only language that has lost all immediate reference to the totality can be at the origin of information. Information is power's poetry (the counterpoetry of the maintenance of law and order). It is the mediated faking of what is. Conversely, poetry must be understood as immediate communication in reality and real modification of that reality. It is nothing other than liberated language, language that wins back its richness and, breaking its significations, at once recovers words, music, cries, gestures, painting, mathematics, events. Poetry is thus dependent upon a standard of the greatest richness in which, at a given stage of socioeconomic development, life may be lived *and changed*. In which case it is pointless to specify that this relationship of poetry to its material basis in society is not a unilateral subordination, but an interaction.

Rediscovering poetry can merge with reinventing revolution, as certain stages of the Mexican, Cuban, or Congolese revolutions quite obviously prove. Between revolutionary periods when the masses accede to poetry through action, we might imagine that circles of poetic adventure remain the only places where the totality of revolution lives on, as an unfulfilled but immanent potentiality, as the shadow of an absent individual. This is so much the case that what is here called poetic adventure is difficult, dangerous, and in any case *never guaranteed* (in fact, it is a question of the sum total of an age's *almost impossible* courses of action). We may only be certain of what an age's poetic adventure no longer is: its accepted and sanctioned false poetry. So whereas surrealism, in the days of its attack on the oppressive order of culture and the everyday, could rightly specify its weapon as a "poetry if need be without poems," today for the SI it is a question of a poetry *necessarily* without poems. And all of our descriptions of poetry have nothing to do with reactionary, old-fashioned authors of a neoversification, even when they align themselves with the least ancient of formal modernisms. The program of fulfilled poetry is nothing less than the creation of events and their language at the same time, inseparably.

All clannish languages—those of informal youth gangs; those that current avant-gardes develop for their internal use as they search for an identity and define themselves; those which in the past, passed on as objective poetry writing for the outside world, were called *trobar clus* or *dolce stil nuovo*—all have for an aim and as actual result immediate transparency of a certain communication, of mutual recognition, and of agreement. But such endeavors are the accomplishment of limited groups, isolated on several accounts. The events that they were able to plan, the festivals to which they were able to devote themselves, had to remain within the most narrow limits. One of the problems facing the revolution consists in federating these manner of soviets, of *communication councils,* in order to open a direct communication everywhere, one that would no longer have to resort to the adversary's communication network (i.e., to the language of power), and could thus transform the world in accordance with its wishes.

It is not a question of putting poetry at the service of the revolution, but rather of putting revolution at the service of poetry. It is only thus that revolution does not betray its own project. We will not repeat the surrealists' mistake of taking up a position in its service exactly when it no longer existed. Bound to the memory of a partial, quickly exhausted revolution, surrealism quickly became a reformism of the spectacle, a criticism of a certain form of the reigning spectacle carried on within the ruling organization of this spectacle. The surrealists seem to have failed to grasp the fact that power imposed its own reading on any internal improvement or modernization of the spectacle, that it held the key to its deciphering.

Every revolution has originated in poetry, was first made through the force of poetry. This is a phenomenon that has escaped and continues to escape theorists of revolution—in fact, it cannot be understood if we cling to the old notion of revolution or of poetry—but has generally been sensed by counterrevolutionaries. Poetry, wherever it is to be found, frightens them; they try desperately to get rid of it through various exorcisms, from auto-da-fé to pure stylistic research. The moment of genuine poetry, which "has all of time before it," wishes time to redirect the whole of the world and the whole of the future according to its own ends. As long as it lasts, its claims can know of no compromise. It throws back into play the unsettled debts of history. Fourier and Pancho Villa, Lautréamont and the *dinamiteros* of the Asturias—whose successors are now inventing new forms of strikes—the sailors of Kronstadt or Kiel, and those throughout the world who with and without us are preparing to struggle for the long revolution, are just as easily emissaries of the new poetry.

Poetry as empty space is more and more clearly the antimatter of consumer society, because it is not a consumable substance (according to the modern criterion for the consumable object: something of equal value for passive multitudes of isolated consumers). Poetry is nothing when it is quoted; it can only be *appropriated*, thrown back into play. Knowledge of old poetry is otherwise mere academic exercise, assisting the overall duties of academic thought. The history of poetry is in this case only an evasion of the poetry of history, if we understand by that term not the spectacular history of the leaders, but rather that of everyday life and its potential liberation; the story of each individual life, and its fulfillment.

We must not leave any ambiguity here regarding the role of "conservators" of old poetry, those who increase its circulation while, for altogether different reasons, the State eliminates illiteracy. These people merely represent a special case of curators of all the art of museums. Reams of poetry are ordinarily preserved in the world, but there are nowhere the places, the times, the people to bring it back to life, to pass it on, and to make use of it. Admitting that this could only ever occur in the form of *détournement,* because understanding of the poetry of the past has changed through loss as well as through acquisition of knowledge, and because at any moment when the poetry of the past can actually be rescued, its being brought together with specific events gives it a largely new meaning. But, above all, a situation in which poetry is possible cannot restore any poetic failure of the past (this failure being what is left in the history of poetry, in inverted form, as success and poetic monument). It naturally moves toward the communication, and the possibilities for sovereignty, of *its own poetry.*

Strictly contemporaneous with the poetic archaeology that restores selections of the poetry of the past, by having specialists recite them on LPs for the new illiterate public constituted by the modern spectacle, the scientists of information have set about fighting all the "redundancies" of liberty in order to *simply convey orders.* Theorists of automation are explicitly aiming at an automatic theoretical thought, to be attained by fixing and eliminating variables in life as in language. They have not, however, finished finding bones in their cheese! Translation machines, for example, which are beginning to ensure the global standardization of information at the same time as the culture of the past is revised into information, are subject to their preestablished programs, which any new meaning of a word—along with its past dialectical ambivalences—must escape. Simultaneously, the life of language—which joins itself to each advance of theoretical understanding: "Ideas improve. The meaning of words contributes to this"—finds itself expelled from the mechanistic field of official information; but free thought may thereby organize itself in a secrecy uncontrollable by the techniques of the "informationist" police. The search for unequivocal signals and for instantaneous binary classification is moving so clearly in the direction of exist-ing power that it may come under the same criticism. Even in their most frenzied assertions, theorists of information behave like clumsy, diplomaed forerunners of the future they have chosen, and which, fittingly, the ruling forces of present-day society are fashioning: the strengthening of the cyberneticist State. They are the liegemen of all the suzerains of the technological feudalism which is being consolidated at present. There is no innocence in their clowning, for they are the king's jesters.

The alternative between the reification of information and poetry no longer concerns the poetry of the past, just as no variation on what the classic revolutionary movement has become can any longer, anywhere, be considered a true alternative in facing the reigning organization of life. From an identical opinion, we frame the denunciation of a total disappearance of poetry in the old forms in which it might have been produced and consumed, and the announce-ment of its return in unforeseen and effective forms. Our age no longer has *to write poetic orders,* but to carry them out.

NOTE

Internationale situationniste 8 (January 1963), 29–33.

The Situationists and the New Forms of Action in Politics or Art

Guy Debord

TRANSLATED BY Thomas Y. Levin

The situationist movement manifests itself simultaneously as an artistic avant-garde, as an experimental investigation of the free construction of daily life, and finally as a contribution to the theoretical and practical articulation of a new revolutionary contestation. From now on, all fundamental cultural creation as well as any qualitative transformation of society is indissolubly linked to the further development of this unitary approach.

Despite occasional differences in its ideological and juridical disguises, it is one and the same society—marked by alienation, totalitarian control, and passive spectacular consumption—that predominates everywhere. One cannot understand the coherence of this society without an all-encompassing critique informed by the opposing project of a liberated creativity, that is, the project of the dominion of all men over their own history at all levels.

To bring this project and this critique—which are *inseparable* since the one implies the other—into the present requires an immediate revival of all of the radicalism championed by the workers' movement, by modern poetry and art, and by the thought of the era of the surpassing of philosophy from Hegel to Nietzsche. This requires that one first acknowledge—without maintaining any comforting illusions—the full extent of the failure of the entire revolutionary project in the first three decades of this century and its official replacement in all parts of the world and in all domains by cheap and mendacious imitations that recuperate and reestablish the old social order.

Naturally, such a resuscitation of radicalism also involves a substantial and thorough study of all previous emancipatory endeavors. An understanding of how these endeavors failed due to isolation or have reverted into global mystification enables one to better grasp the coherence of the world that is to be changed. Through the rediscovery of this coherence one can, in turn, salvage the results of numerous partial explorations undertaken in the recent past, each of which thereby attains its own truth. The insight into this reversible coherence of the world—such as it is and such as it could be—unveils the fallaciousness of halfway measures. It also exposes the fact that such halfway measures are involved whenever a model of the functioning of the dominant society—with its categories of hierarchy and specialization and analogously its customs or its tastes—is resurrected within the very forces of negation.

Furthermore, the rate of the world's material development has increased. It is steadily amassing more and more virtual powers while the specialists that govern that society are forced, by the very fact of their role as guardians of passivity, to neglect to make use of them. This development produces simultaneously a generalized dissatisfaction and objective mortal dangers, neither of which can be controlled in a lasting manner by the specialized leaders.

Once it has been grasped that this is the perspective within which the situationists call for the surpassing of art, it will become clear that when we speak of a unified vision of art and politics this absolutely does not mean that we recommend any sort of subordination of art to politics whatsoever. For us and for all those who are beginning to view this epoch in a demystified manner, there has been no more modern art anywhere at all—in precisely the same way that there has been no further formation of revolutionary politics anywhere at all—since the end of the 1930s. The current revival of both modern art and revolutionary politics can only be their *surpassing*, which is to say precisely the realization of what was their most fundamental demand.

The new contestation that the situationists are talking about is already manifesting itself everywhere. In the large spaces of noncommunication and isolation organized by the current powers that be, indications are surfacing by way of new types of scandals from one country to another and from one continent to another: their exchange has begun.

The task of the avant-garde wherever it finds itself is to bring together these experiences and these people, that is, to simultaneously unify such groups and the coherent foundation of their project as well. We must make known, explain, and develop these initial gestures of the next revolutionary epoch. They are characterized by their concentration of new forms of struggle and a new—either manifest or latent—content: the critique of the existing world. In this way, the dominant society that is so proud of its permanent modernization will finds its match, as it has finally produced a modernized negation.

We have been rigorous in precluding ambitious intellectuals or artists incapable of really understanding us from participating in the situationist movement. We have also been equally rigorous in rejecting and denouncing various falsifications (of which the most recent example is the so-called Nashist "situationism"). However, we are also just as determined to acknowledge as situationists, to support, and never disavow the authors of these new radical gestures, even if many of these gestures are not yet entirely conscious but only on the track of the coherence of today's revolutionary program.

We will limit ourselves to a few examples of gestures that have our full approval. On January 16 some revolutionary students in Caracas made an armed attack on an exhibition of French art and carried off five paintings that they subsequently offered to return in exchange for the release of political prisoners. The forces of order recaptured the paintings after a gun battle with Winston Bermudes, Luis Monselve, and Gladys Troconis. A few days later, some other comrades threw two bombs at the police van transporting the recovered paintings. Unfortunately, they did not succeed in destroying it. This is clearly an exemplary way to treat the art of the past, to bring it back into play for what really matters in life. Since the death of Gauguin ("I tried to establish the right to dare everything") and of van Gogh, their work, recuperated by their enemies, has probably never received from the cultural world an homage so true to their spirit as the act of these Venezuelans. During the Dresden insurrection of 1849,

Bakunin proposed, unsuccessfully, that the insurgents take the paintings out of the museum and put them on a barricade at the entrance to the city, to see if this might prevent the attacking troops from continuing their fire. We can thus see how this skirmish in Caracas links up with one of the highest moments of revolutionary uprising in the last century and goes even further.

The action of Danish comrades during the last few weeks strikes us as no less motivated: on a number of occasions they have resorted to the use of incendiary bombs against travel agencies that organize tourist voyages to Spain, or they have made use of clandestine radio broadcasts as a means of alerting the public against the employment of atomic weapons. In the context of the comfortable and boring "socialized" capitalism of the Scandinavian countries, it is very encouraging to see the sudden appearance of people whose violence exposes certain aspects of the other violence that is at the foundation of this "humanized" order: its monopoly on information, for example, or the organized alienation of leisure or tourism. The horrible flip side of this comfortable boredom, which one must accept as part of the bargain, is not only a peace that is not life but also a peace built upon the threat of atomic death; not only is tourism merely a miserable spectacle that conceals the real countries through which one is traveling, but the reality of the country transformed in this manner into a neutral spectacle is the police of Franco.

Finally, the action of the English comrades who divulged in April the location and the plans of the "Regional Shelter of Government #6" has the immense merit of revealing the degree to which state power has already progressed in its organization of terrain, the highly advanced staging of a totalitarian operation of authority. This authority is not, however, tied solely to a military perspective. Rather, it is the omnipresent threat of thermonuclear war that serves now, in both the East and the West, to maintain the submissiveness of the masses, to organize the *shelters of power,* and to reinforce the psychological and material defenses of the power of the ruling classes. On the surface, the rest of modern urbanism complies with the same preoccupations. As early as April 1962, in the seventh issue of the French-language situationist journal *Internationale situation-*

niste, we wrote the following about the individual shelters constructed in the United States during the preceding year:

> But here, as in every racket, protection is only a pretext. The true use of the shelters is to measure—and thereby to reinforce—people's docility and to manipulate this docility in a manner advantageous to the ruling society. The shelters, considered as the creation of a new consumable good in the society of abundance, prove more than any preceding product that people can be made to work to satisfy highly artificial needs that most certainly "remain needs without ever having been desires" (cf. *Préliminaires du 20 juillet 1960*). . . . The new habitat now taking shape within the "large housing developments" is not really distinct from the architecture of the shelters; it merely represents a lower level of that architecture; of course, the two are closely related. . . . The concentration-camp organization of the surface of the earth is the normal state of a society in the process of development, whose condensed subterranean version merely represents that society's pathological excess. This sickness reveals all the better the real nature of its surface "health."[1]

The English have just made a decisive contribution to the study of this sickness, and thus also to the study of "normal" society. This study is itself inseparable from a struggle that is not afraid to violate the old national taboos of "treason" by breaking the *secrecy* that is vital to the smooth operation of power in modern society in so many matters behind the thick screen of its "information" glut. The sabotage was subsequently extended—despite the efforts of the police and numerous arrests—by surprise invasions of secret military headquarters isolated in the countryside (where some officials were photographed against their will) or by the systematic overloading of forty telephone lines belonging to British security centers through the continuous dialing of ultrasecret numbers that had also been discovered.

It is this first attack against the ruling organization of social space that we wanted to salute and further expand by organizing in Denmark the "Destruction of RSG-6" demonstration. In doing so we had envisaged not only the international expansion of this struggle, but equally its extension to yet another front of the same global struggle: the artistic domain.

The cultural activity that one could call situationist begins with the projects of unitary urbanism or of the construction of situations in life. The outcome of these projects, in turn, cannot be separated from the history of the movement engaged in the realization of the totality of revolutionary possibilities contained in the present society. However, as regards the immediate actions that must be undertaken within the framework that we want to destroy, critical art can be produced as of now using the existing means of cultural expression, that is, everything from the cinema to paintings. This is what the situationists summed up in their theory of *détournement*. Critical in its content, such art must also be critical of itself in its very form. Such work is a sort of communication that, recognizing the limitations of the specialized sphere of hegemonic communication, "will now contain *its own critique.*"[2]

For "RSG-6," we first of all created the atmosphere of an atomic fallout shelter as the first site meant to provoke one to think. Subsequently one encounters a zone that stages the rigorous negation of this sort of necessity. The medium here employed in a critical fashion is painting.

The revolutionary role of modern art that culminated in dadaism was the destruction of all conventions in art, language, or actions. Because, apparently, what has been destroyed in art or in philosophy is still not yet swept out of newspapers or churches, and because the critique of weapons had not followed at the time certain advances in the weaponry of critique, dadaism itself has become an acknowledged cultural style. Indeed, dada form was recently turned into reactionary advertisement by neodadaists making a career by taking up the style invented before 1920 and exploiting each detail in enormously exaggerated fashion, thereby making this style serve the acceptance and decoration of the present world.

Nevertheless, the negative truth contained by modern art has always been a *justified* negation of the society that surrounded it. When, in 1937 in Paris, the

Nazi ambassador Otto Abetz asked Picasso in front of his canvas *Guernica,* "Did you make that?" Picasso very rightly responded: "No. You did."

The negation and also the black humor that were so widespread in poetry and modern art in the wake of the experience of World War I surely deserve to reappear in light of the *spectacle of the third world war,* the spectacle in which we live. Whereas the neodadaists speak of recharging Marcel Duchamp's earlier plastic refusal with (aesthetic) positivity, we are sure that everything that the world offers us today as positive can only serve to recharge limitlessly the negativity of the currently sanctioned forms of expression and in this manner constitute *the only representative art of this time.* The situationists know that real positivity will come from elsewhere and that at the moment this negativity will help bring it about.

Above and beyond all pictorial preoccupations—and, we hope, even beyond anything that could recall subservience to a form of plastic beauty (which has been out of date for quite some time)—we have here traced a few perfectly clear signs.

The "directives" exhibited on empty canvases or on a "détourned" abstract painting should be understood as slogans that one could see written on walls. The titles of certain paintings in the form of political proclamations obviously also convey the same sense of derision and take up the academicism currently in fashion that attempts to base itself on a painting of "pure signs" that are incommunicable.

The "thermonuclear maps" are entirely beyond any of the laborious research toward "new figuration" in painting, because they unite the most liberated procedures of action painting with a representation *that can lay claim to perfect realism* of numerous regions of the world at different hours of the next world war.

The "victory series"—which here again blends the greatest, ultramodern lack of deference with a minute realism à la Horace Vernet—is involved in a revival of battle painting, but in a manner precisely opposite to that of Georges Mathieu and the retrograde ideological reversal on which he based his tiny publicity scandals. The reversal that we are here aiming at corrects the history of the past, rendering it better, more revolutionary, and more successful than it ever was. The "victories" continue the optimistic and absolute *détournement* by means of

which Lautréamont, quite audaciously, already disputed the validity of all manifestations of misfortune and its logic: "I do not accept evil. Man is perfect. The
soul does not fall. Progress exists. . . . Up to now, one has described misfortune
in order to inspire terror and pity. I will describe happiness in order to inspire the
contrary. . . . As long as my friends are not dying, I will not speak of death."

June 1963

NOTES

Guy Debord, "Les situationnistes et les nouvelles formes d'action dans la politique ou l'art," in
Destruktion af RSG-6: En kollektiv manifestation af Situationistisk International (Odense, Denmark:
Galerie EXI, 1963), 15–18.

1. ["Géopolitique de l'hibernation," *Internationale situationniste* 7 (April 1962), 6–7. A number
of elisions made without any indication in Debord's citation have been noted as such in the
present translation. Ed.]

2. ["Editorial Notes: Priority Communication," trans. Tom McDonough, in this volume, 134.
Ed.]

Perspectives for a Generation

Théo Frey

TRANSLATED BY JOHN SHEPLEY

An insane society proposes to manage its future by spreading the use of technically improved individual and collective straitjackets (houses, cities, real estate developments), which it imposes on us as a remedy for its ills. We are *invited* to accept and to recognize this prefabricated "nonorganic body" as our own; the Establishment intends to enclose the individual in another, radically different self. In order to accomplish this task, a vital one for itself as well as its flunkies (urbanists, real estate developers), it can count on the *misguided* souls currently working overtime in the so-called social sciences. Servants, in particular, of an "anthropology" that is no longer speculative but structural and operational, they busy themselves in extricating one more "human nature," but this time a directly usable one, like the police register, for various conditioning techniques. The final result of the process thus undertaken (assuming that the rising strength of the new opposition that everywhere accompanies it gives it enough *leisure*) henceforth appears as the modernized version of a solution that has proved itself, the concentration camp, here deconcentrated all over the planet. People in it will be absolutely free, especially to come and go, to *circulate,* while being total prisoners of that futile freedom to come and go in the byways of the Establishment.

The dominant society, which has nowhere been mastered (eliminated) by us, can only master itself by dominating us. The convergence of present forms of development for living space little by little makes this domination concrete. A room, an apartment, a house, a neighborhood, a town, a whole territory can and must be developed step by step or simultaneously: with no transition from "how to live happily in a large housing project" (*Elle*) to how "to make this society agreeable for everyone" (*Le Monde*). Present-day society, in its proclaimed desire—as sick as it is ingenuous—to *survive,* falls back entirely on a *growth* that can do nothing but develop in a dull way the ridiculous potentialities that are the only ones permitted by its own rationale, the *logic of the market*. Which means that political economy, as the "logical conclusion of the denial of humanity," pursues its destructive work. Everywhere there is a spectacular clash between divergent economic theories and policies, but nowhere are the absurd imperatives of political economy itself challenged and bourgeois economic categories abolished in practice for the benefit of a free (posteconomic) construction of situations, and therefore of all life, on the basis of the *currently* concentrated and squandered powers in "advanced" societies. This colonization of the future in the name of a past that deserves to be so utterly abandoned that the memory of it be lost presupposes the systematic reduction of any *possible radical alternative,* though such are quite *present* in all manifestations of our oppressive society, so much so that things seem to persist in "going off the tracks," *when they are forced to.*

This miserable feat of prestidigitation reveals its trademark from the start: ideology, albeit an upside-down, mutilated reflection of the real world and Praxis, but an ideology the practice of which makes what appears to be upside-down and distorted enter into reality, and not just in the heads of intellectuals and other ideologues: *the world upside-down in earnest.* This modern process of reducing the gap between life and its representation for the benefit of a *representation* that turns back on its assumptions is merely an artificial, caricatured, spectacular resolution of real problems posed by the widespread revolutionary crisis of the modern world, a simulacrum of resolution that will fall at the same time as the greater number of illusions that continue to foster it.

The Establishment lives by our incapacity to live, it maintains splits and *separations* infinitely multiplied, while at the same time planning occasions that are allowed to happen *almost* the way it likes. Its masterstroke is still its successful dissociation of everyday life as space-time, individual and social, from the presently possible indissolvable reconstruction of ourselves and the world, for the purpose of separately and jointly controlling time and space and ultimately reducing both one and the other, the one by the other. The progress of these operations *visibly* betrays the seriousness of an effort in which the sinister vies with the burlesque. The aim is the constitution of a "homogeneous," perfectly "integrated" space, formed by the addition of "homologous" functional blocks, structured hierarchically (the famous "hierarchical network of towns, innervating and coordinating a region of a given size, and common to industrial societies"), so that in the agglomerate thus achieved the gaps, segregations, and multiple conflicts born of separation and the division of labor will be buried in concrete: the conflict between classes, the conflict between city and countryside, the conflict between society and the State, classical ones since Marx, and to which one might add the many interregional "disparities" of which the current conflict between developed and underdeveloped countries is only the pathological exaggeration. The "ruse of history" is nevertheless such that the apparent early successes of this policing arrangement, an attenuation of the class struggle (in the former sense) and of the antagonism between city and countryside, disguise less and less the radical and hopeless proletarianization of the huge majority of the population, condemned to "live" in the uniform conditions that constitute the bastardized and spectacular "urban" milieu born of the breakup of the city, one that, combined with the antagonism between State and society, thereby reinforced and so alarming to the sociologists ("We must establish new channels of communication between the authorities and the population"—Chombart de Lauwe, *Le Monde,* July 13, 1965), betrays the literally "unreasonable" nature of the process of "rationalizing" the reification in progress, while assuring it all sorts of problems, perfectly "irrational" ones from its bureaucratic and alienated point of view, but no less well founded from the standpoint of the dialectical reasoning inherent in all living reality, all Praxis. As Hegel clearly saw, if only to congratulate himself on it, in the rule of modern States, the State allows the pseudofreedom of the individual to develop, while maintaining the coherence of the whole, and it *draws from this antagonism an infinite strength,* which normally turns out to be its Achilles' heel when a new coherence, radically antagonistic to such an order of things, is established and strengthened. Moreover, any coherent and "successful" arrangement must be imposed all over the planet in a *widespread urbanism* that means reducing the phenomenon of underdevelopment, as potentially disturbing to the impossible equilibrium being pursued. But, as though inadvertently, and in a fatal fidelity to itself, capitalism finds itself making war on underdeveloped countries instead of its touted war on underdevelopment, caught as it is in the trap of contradictory, but for it equally vital, demands, and thereby destroying its own claims to survival: all its technocratic-cybernetic "programmings." Such a dialectic promises a rude awakening to the rulers of the present prehistoric world who dreamed of putting themselves beyond reach while burying us under a wall of cement that *will surely end* by being their own tomb.

In this light, the arrangement should also be seen as the death throes of *communication* in the old limited but real sense, the residue of which is everywhere hunted down by the Establishment for the benefit of *information*. Henceforth a "universal communications network" radically suppresses the distance between things while indefinitely increasing the distance between people. Circulation in such a network ends by neutralizing itself, in such a way that the future solution will consist in making people circulate less and information circulate more. People will stay at home, transformed into mere audiovisual "receivers" of information: an attempt to perpetuate *in practice* the current—i.e., bourgeois—economic categories, in order to create the conditions for a permanent and automatic functioning of the present alienated society, "a more smoothly running machine" (*Le Monde,* June 4, 1964). The economists' "perfect market" is impossible, especially from the fact of distance: a perfectly rational economy would have to be concentrated *at a single point* (instantaneous Production and Consumption); if the market is not perfect, that would be due to the imperfection of the world itself, causing the developers to work hard to make the world perfect. Real estate development is a metaphysical enterprise in search of a neofeudal space. The planners' Great Work, their philosophers' stone, lies in the constitution of a space without surprises, where the map would be everything and the territory nothing, because it has been completely effaced and is no longer important, justifying too late all the "architecture" of those imbecile semanticists who claim to deliver you from the tyranny of Aristotle, from "A is not Not-A," as though it had not been established for centuries that "A *becomes* Not-A."

This is so true that today one no longer "consumes" space, which tends to become uniform, but time. The American who goes around the world from one Hilton hotel to another without ever seeing any variation in the setting, except superficially as imitation local color, thus integrated and reduced to a gimmick, clearly prefigures the itineraries of the multitude. The conquest of space, as an "adventure" reserved for an "elite" and resounding spectacularly all over the planet, will be the organized and foreseeable compensation. But, through the expedient of the colonization of space, the Establishment intends to "draw on the future," to "take a long-term view," which means emptying time of its substance (our achievements in the course of a History) in order to cut it up into perfectly inoffensive slices, devoid of any unforeseeable "future" not programmed by its machines. The aim is the constitution of a gigantic contrivance designed to "recycle" linear time for the benefit of an expurgated and "shrunken" time, the mechanical time of machines, without history, and which would combine the pseudocyclical time of the quotidian with a *universalized neocyclical time,* the time of passive acceptance and forced resignation to the permanence of the present order of things.

It must be said: "alienation and oppression in society cannot be arranged, according to any of their variations, but only rejected totally along with that society itself" (*IS* no. 4, p. 36).[1] The task of reunifying time and space in a free construction of individual and social time-space belongs to the *coming revolution:* the overthrow of the "developers" will coincide with a decisive transformation of everyday life, and it will be that transformation.

NOTES

Internationale situationniste 10 (March 1966), 33–35.

1. ["Manifeste (17 mai 1960)," *Internationale situationniste* 4 (June 1960), 36. Ed.]

Captive Words (Preface to a Situationist Dictionary)

MUSTAPHA KHAYATI

TRANSLATED BY TOM McDONOUGH

Platitudes, through what they hide, work for the prevailing organization of life. One such platitude is that language is not dialectical, a statement whose result is to prevent the use of all dialectical thought. However, nothing is more obviously subject to dialectics than language, insofar as it is a living reality. Thus all criticism of the old world has been made through that world's language and yet against it, hence automatically in a *different* language. All revolutionary theory must invent its own words, destroy the prevailing meaning of other words, and provide new positions in the "world of meanings" that correspond to the new reality under preparation, a reality that must be released from the prevailing muddle. The same reasons that prevent our adversary (the masters of the Dictionary) from fixing language today allow us to assert different positions, to deny existing meaning. Nevertheless, we know in advance that these very reasons do not in any way allow us to claim a permanent, legislated certainty; a definition is always open, it is never final, and ours are of value only historically, for a given period, while linked to a precise historical praxis.

It is impossible to get rid of a world without also getting rid of the language that both conceals and protects it, without stripping bare that language's truth. Just as power is ceaseless falsification and "social truth," so language is its constant safeguard and the Dictionary its all-purpose reference. All revolutionary praxis has sensed the need for a new semantic field and for the assertion of a new truth;

from the *encyclopédistes* to the "critique of the wooden language" of Stalin (by Polish intellectuals in 1956), this necessity has not ceased to be felt. *Power resides in language,* which is the refuge of its police violence. All dialogue with power is violence, whether suffered or instigated. When power husbands the use of its weapons, language is entrusted the task of protecting the oppressive order. Even more, the conjunction of the two is the most natural expression of all power.

There is only a fine line between words and ideas, a line that is always being crossed by power and its philosophers. All theories of language, from the ridiculous mysticism of being to the supreme(ly oppressive) rationality of the cybernetic machine, belong to one and the same world, that is to say, to the speech of power considered as the only possible domain of reference, the universal mediation. Just as the Christian god is the necessary mediation between two consciences and between the conscience and the self, so the speech of power becomes established in the heart of all communication, becomes the necessary mediation between self and self. So it manages to get its hands on protest, even now placing it under its own jurisdiction, controlling it, infiltrating it from the inside. Critique of the ruling language, its *détournement,* will become the continuous practice of new revolutionary theory.

Because every new meaning is termed *misinterpretation* by the *authorities,* situationists will establish the legitimacy of misinterpretation, and indict the fraud of meaning as guaranteed and provided by power. Because the dictionary is the warden of *current* meaning, we propose to systematically destroy it. The *replacement* of the dictionary, of the speech (and thought) instructor, of all inherited and domesticated language, will find its pertinent expression in the revolutionary infiltration of language, in *détournement* as widely used by Marx, systematized by Lautréamont, and which the SI places within everybody's reach.

Détournement, what Lautréamont called plagiarism, bears out that thesis long affirmed by modern art, namely the insubordination of words, the impossibility of power *completely harnessing* created meanings, fixing current meaning once and for all—in short, the objective impossibility of a "newspeak." New revolutionary theory cannot proceed without a redefinition of the main concepts that sustain it. "Ideas improve," Lautréamont says; "the meaning of words has a part in the improvement. Plagiarism is necessary. Progress demands it. Staying close to an author's phrasing, plagiarism exploits his expressions, erases false ideas, replaces them with correct ideas." To salvage Marx's thought, it must continually be clarified, corrected, and reformulated in the light of one hundred years of the intensification of alienation and of the opportunities for its negation. Marx needs to be appropriated by those who are upholding that historical trajectory and not be idiotically quoted by all the thousand varieties of recuperator. Moreover, in our hands the thought of power itself becomes a weapon against it. From its advent, the triumphant bourgeoisie has dreamed of a universal language, which cyberneticists are today trying to achieve via technology. Descartes dreamed of a language (a forerunner of newspeak) in which thoughts occurred one after the other with a mathematical rigor, like numbers: "mathesis universalis" or the permanence of bourgeois categories. The *encyclopédistes,* who dreamed (under feudal power) of "definitions so rigorous that tyranny would not know how to accommodate them," prepared the eternity of future power, as the world's—and history's—ultima ratio.

From Rimbaud to the surrealists, the insubordination of words has revealed—at an experimental level—that the theoretical critique of power is inseparable from a practice bent on destroying it: the harnessing of all modern art by power and its conversion into the oppressive categories of its prevailing spectacle is the depressing confirmation of this fact. "What does not extinguish power is extinguished by power." The dadaists were the first to inform words of their mistrust, a suspicion inseparable from their will to "change life." Following Sade, they asserted the right to *say everything,* to liberate words and to "replace the alchemy of words with a true chemistry" (Breton). *The innocence* of words was henceforth consciously attacked, and language was declared "the worst of conventions," something to be destroyed, demystified, freed. Dada's contemporaries made sure to emphasize its will to total destruction (an "operation of destruction," worried Gide) and the danger that it represented to ruling meanings. With dada, belief that a word was forever linked to an idea became nonsensical: dada achieved everything within the powers of *speech,* and forever closed the door on art as a specialty. It definitively posed the problem of art's fulfillment. Surrealism was only valuable as an extension of this demand: it provided a *response* through its literary productions. However, art's fulfillment, poetry (in the situationist sense), means that one cannot find fulfillment in an individual "work," but rather must find fulfillment *tout court*. "Saying everything," whose commencement was marked by Sade, already meant the abolition of a separate literary sphere (in which only what is deemed literature may be spoken). But that abolition, consciously affirmed by the dadaists after Rimbaud and Lautréamont, was not a *supersession*. There is no supersession without fulfillment, and art cannot be superseded without fulfilling it. In practice, there was not even a true abolition, for after Joyce, Duchamp, and dada a new spectacular literature continues to proliferate. "Saying everything" cannot exist without the freedom to do everything. Dada had a chance of fulfillment in Spartakus, in the revolutionary practice of the German proletariat. The latter's failure made the former's inevitable. In subsequent artistic schools (and without excluding nearly all of its own protagonists), it became the literary expression of the emptiness of making poetics, the art of expressing the emptiness of everyday freedom. The ultimate expression of this art of "saying everything" deprived of doing is the blank page . . . Modern (experimental, permutational, spatialized, surrealist, or neodadaist) poetry is the opposite of poetry; it is the artistic project as reclaimed by power. It abolishes poetry without fulfilling it; it lives on its continuous self-destruction. "What is the point of saving language," Max Bense admits pitifully, "when there is no longer anything to say?" The admission of a specialist! Parrotry or silence are the only alternatives offered by the specialists of permutation. Philosophy and modern art, protected by power and in turn protecting it, are thus driven into what Hegel called "the language of flattery." Both add their voices to the praise of power and its products, perfecting reification and making it commonplace. By declaring that "reality lies within language" or that language "can only be considered in itself and for itself," language specialists conclude with the "language-object," with "word-things," and delight in the praise of their own reification. The model of the thing becomes dominant, and the commodity yet again finds its fulfillment, its poets. The theory of the state, of the economy, of law, of philosophy, of art, all now have this quality of flattering circumspection.

Wherever separate power replaces the independent action of the masses, hence wherever bureaucracy seizes the administration of all aspects of social life, it attacks language and reduces its poetry to the ordinary prose of its information. It takes language for its own use, like everything else, and imposes it on the masses. Language is then supposed to pass on its messages and accommodate its thought; it is the material support of its ideology. That language is above all a means of communication between men is ignored by bureaucracy. Since all communication passes through it, men no longer even need to speak of it: above all, they must accept their role as *receivers,* that is, receivers of orders to be carried out in the information-based communication network to which all of society is being reduced.

Bureaucracy is this language's way of life, and bureaucratization its future. The Bolshevik order that resulted from the failure of the Soviet revolution imposed a series of more or less magical, impersonal expressions (and in those ways just like the bureaucracy in power). "Politburo," "Komintern," "Cavarmy," "agit-prop" are so many mysterious names of specialized bodies, which are themselves truly mysterious, moving in the shadowy sphere of the State (or Party leadership), whose only connection to the masses was to institute and reinforce domination. Language when colonized by bureaucracy is reduced to a series of clear-cut, inflexible expressions in which even nouns always appear accompanied by the same adjectives and participles; they are governed by the noun, and each time it appears they automatically follow at the opportune place. This "bringing to heel" of words is the expression of a more profound militarization of the entire society, its division into two main categories: the managerial caste and the great mass of those who carry out their orders. But these same words are called upon to play other roles as well; they are imbued with the magic power to uphold stifling reality, to mask it, and to present it as the truth, the only possible truth. Thus one is no longer a "Trotskyist," but a "Hitlero-Trotskyist"; there is no longer Marxism, but "Marxism-Leninism"; and opposition is automatically "reactionary" in the "Soviet regime." The rigidity with which ritual expressions are made sacred has as its goal the preservation of the purity of that "substance" when faced with facts that apparently contradict it. The language of the masters is thus everything, and reality

---

nothing, or at the very most the mere shell of this language. People must, in their acts, in their thoughts and their feelings, pretend as if their State was that reason, that justice, that freedom proclaimed by ideology; ritual (and the police) are there to see that this behavior is maintained (cf. Marcuse, *Soviet Marxism*).

The deterioration of radical thought considerably increases the power of words, the words of power. "Power creates nothing, it recuperates" (cf. *IS* no. 8).[1] Words molded by revolutionary critique are like the weapons of partisans that have been abandoned on the field of battle: they are passed on to be used by the counterrevolution; and like prisoners of war, they are subjected to a regime of hard labor. Our most immediate enemies are those who espouse spurious critique, its officially recognized employees. The divorce between theory and practice provides the central basis of recuperation, of the hardening of revolutionary theory into ideology that transforms real practical demands (whose signs of fulfillment already exist in society today) into systems of ideas and demands of reason. Ideologists of all stripes, watchdogs of the reigning spectacle, are the agents of this task; and the most corrosive concepts are thus emptied of their content, placed back into circulation in the service of maintaining alienation: dadaism in reverse. They become advertising slogans (cf. the new brochure from Club Méditerranée). The concepts of radical critique share the lot of the proletariat: they are stripped of their history, cut off from their roots; they are made fit for the thought-machines of power.

Our project of the liberation of words is historically comparable to the undertaking of the *encyclopédistes*. The conscious historical dimension was lacking to the language of the *Aufklärung*'s "severing" (to continue with the Hegelian imagery); it was all well and good to critique the decrepit old world of feudalism, but it was utterly unaware of what would come from it—none of the *encyclopédistes* was republican. Rather it expressed the bourgeois thinker's own severing; ours above all aims at the practice that will rend the world, starting with rending the veils that hide it. Whereas the *encyclopédistes* sought quantitative enumeration, the enthusiastic description of a world of objects in which the already-present victory of the bourgeoisie and the commodity was unfolding, our dictionary is the expression of the *qualitative* and of the still-absent potential

---

victory, the repressed of modern history (the Proletariat) and *the return of the repressed*. We are proposing the true liberation of language, for we propose to put it into practice free of all fetters. We reject *all authority,* linguistic or otherwise: only real life *allows for* a meaning, and only praxis for truth. The debate over the truth or falsity of the meaning of a word, isolated from practice, is a purely scholastic question. We place our dictionary in that libertarian region that still eludes power but is its sole possible universal inheritor.

Language still remains the necessary mediation of awareness of the world of alienation (Hegel said: necessary alienation), the instrument of radical theory that will eventually seize the masses, because it is theirs; and only thus will it discover its truth. Therefore it is essential that we mold our own language, the language of real life, against the ideological language of power, where all the categories of the old world are justified. From this moment on, we must prevent the adulteration of our theories, their potential recuperation. We are employing specific concepts that are already employed by specialists, but we give them a new content, turning them on the specializations they are meant to uphold, and on the waged thinkers of the future who (as Claudel did for Rimbaud and Klossowski for Sade) are tempted to project their own rottenness onto situationist theory. Future revolutions must themselves invent their own language. To regain their truth, the concepts of radical critique will be reconsidered one by one: the word *alienation,* for example, one of the key concepts for understanding modern society, must be disinfected after having passed through the mouth of someone like Axelos. All words, all servants of power, whoever they are, share the same relation to the latter as the proletariat and, like it, they are instrument and agent of future liberation. Poor Revel! There are no forbidden words; in language, as it will soon be everywhere else, *everything is permitted.* To forbid the use of a word is to relinquish a weapon that our opponents will use.

Our dictionary will be a sort of grid with which one could decipher pieces of information and tear off the ideological veil covering reality. We will provide potential translations that will allow the apprehension of different aspects of the society of the spectacle, and will show how the smallest clues (the smallest signs) contribute to its maintenance. It is in a way a bilingual dictionary, for each word possesses an "ideological" meaning from power and a real meaning, what we consider to correspond to real life in the present historical stage. We could also establish at every step the various positions of words in the social war. If the problem of ideology is knowing how to descend from the heaven of ideas to the real world, our dictionary will be a contribution to the development of the new revolutionary theory, in which the problem is knowing how to pass from language to life. The genuine appropriation of words that *work* cannot be achieved apart from the appropriation of work itself. The institution of liberated creative activity will simultaneously be the institution of genuine, finally liberated communication, and the transparency of human relations will replace the poverty of words under the old regime of opacity. Words will not stop *working* so long as men have not.

NOTES

Internationale situationniste 10 (March 1966), 50–55.
1. ["Notes éditoriales: All the King's Men," *Internationale situationniste* 8 (January 1963), 30; translated here as "Editorial Notes: All the King's Men," 154. Ed.]

The Situationists and the New Forms of Action against Politics and Art

RENÉ VIÉNET

TRANSLATED BY TOM McDONOUGH

Up to this point we have chiefly endeavored to accomplish our subversion through the use of forms or categories inherited from revolutionary struggles that for the most part derive from the previous century. I suggest that we supplement these expressions of our protest with means that dispense with any reference to the past. This is not to say that we should give up the forms through which we have fought on the traditional terrain of the supersession of philosophy and the fulfillment of art, as well as of the abolition of politics; rather it is a matter of perfecting the work of this journal wherever it has not yet become effective.

Many proletarians have realized that they have no power to determine the use made of their lives, but do not express this insight in the language of socialism and of earlier revolutions.

So let us spit as we pass by those students-turned-grassroots-militants, with their "groupuscules" that intend to become mass parties, who on occasion have dared to claim that workers find the *IS* unreadable, that its paper is too glossy for their lunch bags, and that it is too expensive for those making only minimum wage. The most logically consistent of them thus spend their time distributing the cheaply mimeographed image they hold of the consciousness of a class among which they feverishly search for their Ouvrier Albert. They are forgetting, among other things, that workers have sometimes had to pay quite a high price for reading revolutionary writing, a price comparatively higher than that of a seat at the

TNP [National Popular Theater], and that, when seized by the desire, they will not balk at spending two or three times what it costs to buy *Planète*. But what these critics of our typography fail to grasp above all is that the few individuals who deign to take one of their bulletins are precisely those who possess the few references that would allow them to immediately understand us, and that what they write is utterly unreadable for all the others. Some of them, who cannot even appreciate the complexity of thought in bathroom graffiti (particularly that found in cafés), have almost convinced themselves that, thanks to a parody of elementary-school-level writing printed on sheets that they paste to drainpipes like advertisements for apartment rentals, they can get the signifier and the signified of their slogans to coincide. Here is precisely the measure of what is not to be done.

For us it is a question of linking the theoretical critique of modern society with its critique in acts. By appropriating the very suggestions of the spectacle, we may at once provide the reasons for present and future rebellions.

I propose that we should endeavor:

1. *to experiment with the* détournement *of photo love stories* and so-called pornographic photographs, and that we should deliver their truth in plain language by restoring true dialogue to them. This operation will make the subversive speech *bubbles,* which spontaneously if largely unconsciously form among those who look at them only to be immediately dissolved, burst to the surface. In the same spirit, it is equally possible to appropriate *all* advertising posters—especially those in the corridors of the Métro, which form such striking sequences—by pasting on new speech bubbles.

2. *to promote guerilla warfare in the mass media,* an important form of protest not only at the stage of urban guerilla warfare but even beforehand. The way has been pioneered by those Argentinians who will besiege the headquarters of some reputable newspaper and in this way use it to issue their own orders and slogans. We still have some time to take advantage of the fact that radio and television stations are not yet guarded by the army. On a more modest level, we know that any radio ham can inexpensively transmit to the neighborhood, and that the small size of the necessary equip-

ment allows for a high level of mobility and thus for evading attempts at tracing the broadcast location. A few years ago a band of Danish dissidents from the CP was able to set up its own pirate radio station. False editions of a given periodical can work to increase the enemy's confusion. For obvious reasons this list of examples is vague and limited.

The illegality of such acts precludes any organization that has not gone underground from following such a program, for it requires the formation in its very heart of a *specific organization;* such an organization cannot be conceived (or be effective) without compartmentalization and hence hierarchy, etc.—in a word, without leading back down the slippery slope to terrorism. So it is preferable instead to refer to the idea of propaganda of the deed, which is a very different method. Everyone shares our ideas—it is a well-known fact—and any group with no necessary ties to us, just a few individuals who get together on the occasion, can improvise on and improve the formulas tested out elsewhere by others. This type of uncoordinated action cannot suppose as its aim any definitive upheaval, but it may usefully punctuate the dawning consciousness of the time. But in any case it is not a matter of obsessing over the word *illegality.* The majority of actions in this domain have no need to break existing laws. The fear of such crimes, however, will lead the directors of newspapers to distrust their typographers, the heads of radio stations to distrust their technicians, and so forth, until the specific repressive laws are finalized.

3. *to perfect situationist comics.* Comic strips are the only genuinely popular literature of our century. Idiots who have been indelibly marked by their years in high school may not be able to stop discussing them, but reading and collecting ours will annoy them. Doubtless they will buy them only in order to burn them. Who cannot immediately sense how easy it would be, in our task of "making shame more shameful still," to change *13, rue de l'Espoir* into *1, bd du Désespoir* by integrating into the background a few additional elements, or simply by changing the speech balloons? This method, as you can see, is the exact opposite of pop art, which breaks comics into pieces. This, on the contrary, aims at restoring to the comics their greatness and meaning.

4. *to produce situationist films.* Cinema, which is the newest and without doubt most useful means of expression of our epoch, has made no progress for close to three-quarters of a century. To summarize, let us say that it has effectively become the "seventh art" so dear to film buffs, film societies, and parents' associations. For our purposes let us note that the cycle (Ince, Stroheim, the unique *Âge d'Or, Citizen Kane* and *Mr. Arkadin,* lettrist films) has ended, even if some masterpiece (of, however, a classic and narrative construction) still remains to be discovered among foreign distributors or in the film archives. Let us appropriate the stammerings of this new form of writing; let us, above all, appropriate its most accomplished and modern examples, those that have escaped the ideology of art to an even greater extent than American B-movies: I mean, of course, newsreels, trailers, and most of all filmed advertisements.

Made in the service of the commodity and the spectacle, indeed, but when freed from that support, filmed advertisements can lay the foundations for what Eisenstein foresaw when he spoke of filming *The Critique of Political Economy* or *The German Ideology.*

I am quite sure that I could film "The Decline and Fall of the Spectacle-Commodity Economy"[1] in a way that would be immediately understandable to the proletarians of Watts, even though they are not aware of the concerns implied in that title. And this translation into a new form will, without any doubt, reciprocally contribute to the deepening and exacerbating of the "written" expression of the same issues; we could confirm this, for example, by shooting the film *Incitement to Murder and Debauchery* before writing its equivalent in the journal, "Correctives to the Consciousness of a Class Which Will Be the Last." Among other possibilities, cinema lends itself particularly well to studying the present as a historical problem, to dismantling processes of reification. Historical reality can, of course, be apprehended, known, and filmed only in the course of a complicated process of mediations that allow consciousness to recognize one moment immanent within another, to recognize its aim and its action in its destiny, its destiny in its aim and action, and its own essence in this necessity. This mediation would be difficult if the empirical existence of facts themselves was not already a mediated existence, which only takes on an appearance of immediateness because and to the extent that, on the one hand, consciousness of the mediation is lacking and, on the other hand, the facts have been uprooted from the network of their determinations, placed in an artificial isolation, and poorly linked together again by the montage of classical cinema. It is precisely this mediation that has been lacking, and inevitably so, in pre-situationist cinema, which has limited itself to so-called objective forms or re-presenting politico-moral concepts, whenever it has not been a merely academic type of narrative with all its hypocrisies. All this explanation is more torturous to read than to see filmed, as all commonplaces are. But Godard, the most famous of pro-Chinese Swiss, could never understand it. He may well harness what has been done before, as is his wont—that is, from all that has been done before he may pick up a word or an idea, like that of appropriating advertising films—but he could never do anything but brandish such little novelties that he took from elsewhere, images or keywords of the time that definitely have a resonance, but one that he cannot grasp (Bonnot, worker, Marx, Made in USA, Pierrot le Fou, Debord, poetry, etc.). He is in fact nothing more than the child of Mao and Coca-Cola.

Anything can be expressed in the cinema that can be expressed in an article, a book, a pamphlet, or a poster. This is why from now on we must require that each situationist be as able to shoot a film as write an article (cf. "Anti-Public Relations," no. 8, p. 59).[2] Nothing is too beautiful for the negroes of Watts.

NOTES

Internationale situationniste 11 (October 1967), 32–36.

1. [See "Le déclin et la chute de l'économie spectaculaire-marchande," *Internationale situationniste* 10 (March 1966), 3–11. Ed.]

2. ["Situationist International: Anti-public relations service/Internationale situationniste: service des anti-public-relations," *Internationale situationniste* 8 (January 1963), 59. Ed.]

The Practice of Theory: Cinema and Revolution

TRANSLATED BY TOM McDONOUGH

In *Le Monde* of July 8, 1969, J.-P. Picaper, correspondent to the Berlin Film Festival, marvels that from this moment forward, "Godard is carrying on with his salutary self-criticism in *Le gai savoir* (banned in France), a coproduction of the ORTF and Radio-Stuttgart, which goes so far as to project sequences filmed in darkness or even leave the spectator before an empty screen for what is a barely tolerable length of time." Without trying to determine what this critic calls "a barely tolerable length of time," we see that Godard's work, always in the forefront, reaches its zenith in a destructive style that is as belatedly plagiarized and as pointless as all the rest. For this negation was formulated in the cinema even before Godard had begun his long series of pretentious false innovations that aroused so much enthusiasm among that distant era's students. The same journalist reports that the same Godard, in a short film entitled *L'amour,* uses one of his characters to confess that we cannot "portray revolution" because "cinema is the art of illusion." The cinema has no more been an "art of illusion" than all the rest of art, which was dead in its entirety long before Godard, who has *not even* been a modern artist, i.e., someone capable of even the slightest personal originality. The pro-Chinese liar then concludes his bluff by encouraging admiration for his discovery of a cinema that will not be one, all the while denouncing a kind of ontological lie in which he participated like all the others, but will no more. In fact, Godard was immediately outmoded by the movement of May 1968, relegated, as the spectacular manufacturer of a pseudocritique of *recuperated* art and for his makeshift solutions, to the ashcan of the past (cf. "Godard's Role," in *IS* no. 10).[1] At this moment, Godard has basically vanished as a filmmaker, just as he has been personally insulted and ridiculed on several occasions by revolutionaries who found him in their way. Cinema as a means of revolutionary communication is not intrinsically deceitful because Godard or Jacopetti have touched it, just as all political analysis is not doomed to falseness because Stalinists wrote it. At present, in different countries, several young filmmakers are trying to use films as instruments of revolutionary critique, and some of them will partially achieve their ends. In our opinion, the only thing that will still continue to prevent them from going as far as needs be is the limits to their acknowledgment of revolutionary truth as well as to their aesthetic means. We deem that at this time only situationist positions and methods, following the arguments set out by René Viénet in our last issue,[2] have direct access to a revolutionary use of cinema today—while acknowledging that politico-economic conditions are, of course, still able to pose problems.

We know that Eisenstein hoped to film *Capital*. We might wonder, however, given that filmmaker's formal ideas and political submissiveness, whether his film would have been faithful to Marx's text. As for us, we have no doubt that we will do better. For example, as soon as it is possible, Guy Debord will himself produce a film adaptation of *The Society of the Spectacle* that will certainly not fall short of his book.

NOTES

Internationale situationniste 12 (September 1969), 104–105.

1. ["De l'aliénation, examen de plusieurs aspects concrets: Le rôle de Godard," *Internationale situationniste* 10 (March 1966), 58–59. Ed.]

2. [René Viénet, "Les situationnistes et les nouvelles formes d'action contre la politique et l'art," *Internationale situationniste* 11 (October 1967), 32–36; translated here as "The Situationists and the New Forms of Action against Politics and Art," 181–185. Ed.]

Asger Jorn's Avant-Garde Archives

CLAIRE GILMAN

Throughout his writings, Guy Debord made his stance on dada clear. Statements like "dadaism . . . has become an acknowledged cultural style,"[1] and his assertion that "since the negation of the bourgeois conception of art and artistic genius has become pretty much old hat, [Duchamp's] drawing of a mustache on the *Mona Lisa* is no more interesting than the original version of that painting,"[2] position the Situationist International as a distinctly postdada movement. But if Debord's rejection of his radical predecessors is this emphatic, why don't critics accept him at his word?

Sadie Plant's recent critical history is a case in point. Although Plant explicitly claims the situationists for a "postmodern age," likening the group's radical artistic strategy to pastiche and deconstruction, her analysis ends up tracing old ground. Equating these methods with "subversive violence" and critical negation, Plant concludes that SI tactics represent a "reworking . . . of those strategies employed by the dadaists and surrealists, extended by the Situationists to every area of social and discursive life."[3] In the same way, even the excellent catalogue from the major ICA Boston exhibition positions the group squarely in line with their dada and surrealist precursors, with the result that the situationists seem bound to prewar avant-garde methods albeit in wider spheres and to greater extremes.[4]

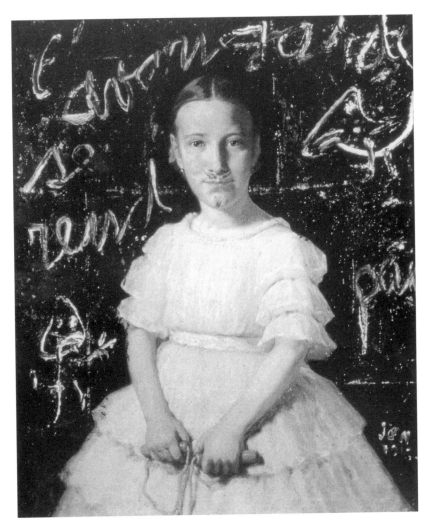

Asger Jorn, *The Avant-Garde Doesn't Give Up,* 1962.

Asger Jorn's *Modification* paintings assume particular significance in relation to Debord's rhetoric. Take, for example, *The Avant-Garde Doesn't Give Up* from 1962.[5] The found painting of a young girl inscribed with mustache and beard immediately recalls Duchamp's *L.H.O.O.Q.* as well as Debord's statement that Duchamp's gesture is now "pretty much old hat." It is possible to accept Jorn's painting at its word, in which case it becomes a simplistic reinscription of Duchampian negation, although, in light of Debord's statement, it could equally be that the title (also scrawled across the surface of the canvas) is an ironic commentary on the pathetic mutilation of an already valueless kitsch painting.

Yet there is a third way to view the work, one that does not fundamentally depend on the relationship between image and text. It is crucial to recognize that Jorn's defacement of the girl is, as a reference to Duchamp, less an instance of mutilation than an unmanipulated appropriation. If Duchamp's act is primary— overturning the stable icon that is further undone by its status as photoreproduction—Jorn's mark is necessarily secondary—a received rather than a productive gesture. Duchamp's work makes us laugh—regardless of anything else, it is indisputably comic. When confronted with Jorn's painting, we are also tempted to laugh, but for other reasons. Our laughter is tinged with embarrassment—for ourselves as viewers but, more importantly, for Jorn. "What is going on here?" we ask. "What can be the point?" Where Duchamp's line visibly (and texturally) mars the flat photoreproduction, Jorn's painterly defacement enters the work only to merge with its surface. Moreover, on closer look, the girl proves to be merely one motif among others that include Jorn's scrawled title and his childlike forms painted on the black ground. This work is not a reference to Duchamp so much as a reflection on several previous styles that come together with no apparent rhyme or reason.

If the appropriationist method typical of Jorn's paintings relates to montage/collage tactics, it does not find its parallel in Duchamp's parodic maneuvers or, alternatively, in the propagandistic interventions of someone like John Heartfield. Instead, Jorn's works differ from traditional collage aesthetics by their express departure from previous structures of visuality and spatiality. With their painterly marks that collect in abstract equivalence like mindless traces on a windowpane, Jorn's "paratactic" surfaces reject dada's "syntactic" organization in which disjunction and fragmentation, shock and simultaneity, ultimately combine in new, synthetic configurations.[6] In other words, instead of employing internal fragmentation and rupture to critically provide meaning, Jorn's works function as a sort of neutral collection from which meaning has not been overturned but evacuated. Jorn's paintings (and Debord's statements regarding Duchamp) do not suggest an elaboration of earlier, critical efforts, but rather a view from a place where such gestures are no longer considered possible. In this light, Jorn's banal image quotations find a certain purpose.

Executed in 1959, Jorn's *Modifications* were first displayed in May of that year at the Galerie Rive Gauche in Paris. Jorn made approximately twenty-three of these paintings, all second-rate canvases that the artist found in flea markets and decorated with Pollock-like drips or Dubuffet-inspired childlike forms. Needless to say, an initial look at these paintings is a discouraging one. To interrupt second-rate canvases with painterly scrawls hardly seems a relevant critical strategy for the late fifties. Indeed, if we confine such moves to "playful irreverence" and active, critical vandalism, then Jorn's paintings would seem to render that strategy hopelessly naive. Must these paintings be seen to depict, as Peter Wollen would have it, "objective beings . . . broken open, vandalized, and mutilated to release the 'becoming' latent within them," transformed through "magical actions" into "living signs"?[7] Although interpretations like Wollen's are consistent with Jorn's early paintings from his CoBrA period—fields of anonymous, magical encounters and wondrous, festive beings—they do not adequately account for the *Modifications*, which instead constitute a relatively isolated moment in Jorn's career.

An offhand remark made by Guy Atkins, the author of the "official" multi-volume work on Jorn's career, suggests another way to read these works. Atkins notes that in the kitsch, rural images where fishermen fish and shepherds tend their flocks, the people and main event are always protected from "the rampaging hordes that he [Jorn] unleashes on the scene."[8] Put another way, these painterly creatures that Wollen describes as "mutilating" the forms on which they are overlaid precisely do *not* interrupt the original image. The central figures and composition remain intact and the mood undisturbed.

An excellent example is *Paris by Night* (1959), a found painting (of a man leaning over a balcony looking down on the streets—or river?—of Paris, which Jorn has overlaid with paint in the bottom right and upper left-hand corners. At the top, a schematic, ovoid face is discernible, while at the bottom, attempts at figuration have degenerated into a web of tangled lines and isolated drops of paint. The dusky blue tones create a heavy stillness that Jorn's additions, despite their valiant efforts, cannot enliven. Rather than encroaching on the man's contemplative solitude, or disrupting the pictorial space in any significant way, these forms read as what they literally are: impotent paint splotches encrusted on the canvas. Instead of "vandalizing" or "breaking open" the picture plane, Jorn's *non*-alterations testify to the impenetrability of the mute canvas and the failure of immanent deconstructive strategies.

This work begs comparison with a typical pre-Situ painting like *Untitled* (1954), in which a monstrous, swirling face emerges amidst pools of paint. Jorn's thick strokes are here deeply impressed as though attacked by clawing fingers, their violent motions still registered in the dizzying eddies that both compose and dissolve the central face. Is this figure bursting forth from or being sucked back into the hot, viscous lava that oozes around it? The painting is a volatile space indeed. Five years later a similar ovoid face appears, but this time it is limp and colorless, a mere ghost of its former self. What had read as incisions in the earlier painting now look like stains. Thick and pulsing paint has given way to thin, white dribbles that settle on the surface like milk skim.

Paris by Night can also be productively compared with an untitled modification performed by Jorn and his CoBrA peers Constant, Appel, and Corneille in 1949. In this case, the original painting has been completely eradicated as bright, playful forms dance triumphantly over its surface. These figures assert their brute authority, whereas in *Paris by Night* Jorn's motifs are relegated to the sides. It is all too easy to ignore these invaders and conclude that the man at his balcony remains alone.

Asger Jorn, *Paris by Night,* 1959.

Asger Jorn, *Untitled*, 1954.

The year 1959 falls in the middle of Jorn's involvement with the SI, which lasted from 1957 to his resignation in April 1961, and concludes an intense period of collaboration with Debord (the second of two joint book projects, *Mémoires,* was published in early 1959). Although the *Modifications* are not the only works that Jorn executed during his involvement with the SI (in fact, many of his works from these years recall his CoBrA period), nor the only time that Jorn experimented with modifying old canvases, they are the paintings that situationist texts and contemporary critics hold up as the quintessential manifestation of situationist art practice. As reused canvases, they are a primary example of the artistic strategy of *détournement,* literally defined in SI essays and manifestos as "the integration of present or past artistic production into a superior construction of a milieu."

For critics like Plant, *détournement* is easily understood as a form of critical sabotage, parallel, once again, to dada and surrealist collage tactics. Taken in isolation, many situationist statements would seem to support this view. For instance, the article "Détournement as Negation and Prelude," published in *Internationale situationniste,* explains: "*détournement* is a game made possible by the capacity of 'devaluation' . . . all the elements of the cultural past must be 'reinvested' or disappear." However, the author's next point is somewhat more surprising and suggests a dimension that has been all but ignored by critics, one that takes on particular significance when applied to Jorn's work. Quoting "Methods of Détournement" (1956), the authors conclude: "'it is necessary . . . to conceive of a parodic-serious stage where the accumulation of detourned elements, far from aiming at arousing indignation or laughter by alluding to some original work, will express our *indifference* toward a meaningless and forgotten original, and concern itself with rendering a certain sublimity.'"[9]

Debord and Gil Wolman provide an instructive illustration of this idea using D. W. Griffith's *Birth of a Nation.* They explain that "it would be better to detourn it as a whole, without necessarily even altering the montage, by adding a soundtrack that made a powerful denunciation of the horrors of imperialist wars and of the activities of the Ku Klux Klan, which are continuing in the United States even now." This method is common, but the authors' conclusion is not:

"Such a detournement—a very moderate one—is in the final analysis nothing more than the moral equivalent of the restoration of old paintings in museums."[10] In short, instead of dismantling the original work of art to make an effective political statement, appropriation *preserves* the work, albeit as inert artifact. The work is not superseded by a new, enlightened meaning, but reconfirmed as a mere object suitable for the museum. Such a recontextualization exposes the very fallacy of radical claims for reinvestment or "indignation," and ultimately positions the film as an object of "indifference." The work of art, it seems, permits neither free expression nor dadaist negation. In *The Society of the Spectacle*, Debord suggests as much:

> The fact that the language of real communication has been lost is what the modern movement of art's decay expresses *positively*. What it expresses *negatively* is that a new common language has yet to be found . . . in a praxis embodying both an unmediated activity and a language commensurate with it.[11]

Or in a text of 1961:

> When a newly independent art paints its world in brilliant colors, then a moment of life has grown old. By art's brilliant colors it cannot be rejuvenated but only called to mind. The greatness of art makes its appearance only as dusk begins to fall over life.[12]

The art object is capable only of reflecting life, a life grown old as soon as it is registered on the work's surface. It cannot produce or activate—it does not speak a viable critical language—but only solidifies with its "brilliant," impotent forms. And yet, in this alone it possesses some value. In Debord's thinking, the only positive thing about modern culture is that its very inertia testifies to its own disintegration, to "its withering away, its witness against itself."[13]

By registering their own impotence, Jorn's painterly marks testify to the end of the artwork as a critical arena—to its failure to speak as a revolutionary tool. Treating the original canvas with "indifference," Jorn's mute scribbles collect like so many colored traces. As such, they represent the antithesis of avant-garde rupture and penetration embodied succinctly in Walter Benjamin's cinemateur/surgeon who "operates" on reality and the filmic surface through effects like cutting and splicing, who "greatly diminishes the distance between himself and the patient by penetrating into the patient's body, and increases it but little by the caution with which his hand moves among the organs."[14] Benjamin's description finds an apt parallel in a photomontage by John Heartfield that shows the artist preparing to cut off the head of Zorgiebel, the Berlin Chief of Police. Brows furrowed in intense concentration, he wields an enormous pair of scissors. Heartfield is here the surgeon, and although what Heartfield dismantles in the image is not undone in reality, there remains nonetheless the suggestion that the picture surface is a valid place for criticism to begin. Internal rupture can at least be *compared* to real, revolutionary action.

Heartfield also modified old paintings, and the difference between his and Jorn's works is illuminating. One such picture is *War: A Painting by Franz v. Stuck Brought Up to Date by John Heartfield* (1933). Several alterations to the original are immediately apparent, most notably the photograph of Hitler inserted on the horse's back behind the victorious warrior and the gas mask placed over the face of the prostrate victim in the bottom right corner. The final image takes on a variety of connotations. At a most basic level, it likens Hitler to the brute warrior, and the masked figure to his potential victims. Stiffly positioned and with head bowed, Hitler appears ridiculous as he takes backseat on the horse's rump. Equally interesting is the way in which the original painting, a typical example of the mythical images promoted by Hitler, is transformed into the degenerate art he despised, precisely through the insertion of his own image. In this way, each individual element is undermined and yet brought together to form a new, startling composite. The photo slices through the painted surface in such a way that it both combines with it illusionistically—as a logical part of the scene—and speaks its own alienation.

This kind of "breaking open," this dismantling of two different realities and their recombination into a new, meaningful whole, is exactly what is *not* achieved

John Heartfield, *War: A Painting by Franz v. Stuck Brought Up to Date by John Heartfield,* 1933.

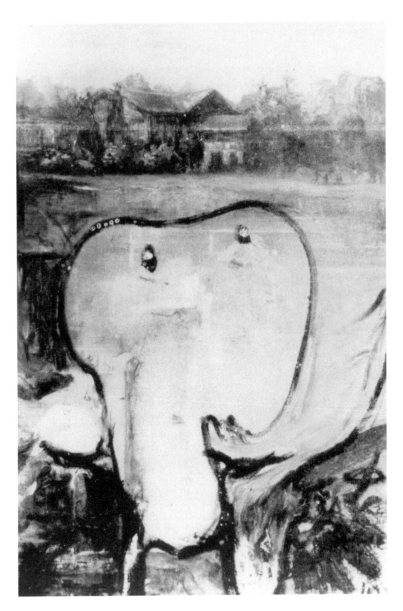

Asger Jorn, *Story of the North*, 1959.

in works like *Paris by Night* or, alternately, *Story of the North,* in which an abstract, ghostlike face is traced over the lower portion of the painting to stop just below the horizon line on which the house and foliage sit. Gliding over the water below the house, this figure is a passive observer. Its eyes look out (or in) blankly, but it has no mouth with which to speak or protest. The compact layers exclude penetration and fragmentation, presenting an amalgam of images that do not interrelate in any significant way.

If Heartfield's strategy recalls Benjamin's surgeon, then Jorn and Debord's degradation of the art object to a position of "self-liquidation" finds a surprising parallel in the writing of Theodor Adorno, that champion of the radical, autonomous artwork. In his *Aesthetic Theory,* Adorno lauds Baudelaire for being the first to acknowledge that art in a mature commodity society is powerless to do anything but look on as that society takes its course. Art can transcend capitalist society's reign only by integrating its own autonomy with society's images. "The modernity of art lies in its mimetic relation to a petrified and alienated reality. This, and not the denial of that mute reality is what makes art speak."[15] Like Debord, Adorno holds that the work of art can no longer justify itself through strategies such as montage, for "now that shock has lost its punch, the products of montage revert to being indifferent stuff or substance."[16] In plagiarizing images, themes, and ideologies, the situationist work does not negate these forms but rather presents them as "surplus," revealing prior avant-garde strategies to be "indifferent stuff and substance," undone by their own irrelevance within contemporary culture. Jorn's paintings reveal previous critical gestures to be mere crust on the canvas.

According to Adorno, art's very repulsiveness carries a certain "catastrophic potential" that conjures up the possibility of "the unutterable, which is Utopia."[17] It is with Adorno's utopian view of the art object that he and the SI part. Whereas Adorno holds that the "realist" work can "transcend" reification precisely through its honest self-criticism, the SI reaches an opposite conclusion. For the situationists, this authentic possibility can be realized only by transcending the work of art, which, as mere mimetic object, is itself mired in alienation. This is the sentiment of the situationists' father figure Jean-Paul Sartre,[18] who, despite his recognition that the self is rooted in the world, claims that the liberated subject is realized in an active negation of societal forms and relationships, in withdrawing itself from these ties and positing them "as if they were painted objects."[19] *Détournement* acts like Sartrian prose by which "I transfix [a situation], I display it in full view; at present I dispose of it," and through which, in conjunction with social praxis, "I involve myself a little more in the world, and by the same token I emerge from it a little more, since I go beyond it towards the future."[20] By bracketing reality in the mute, congealed artwork, the Sartrian subject is able to bypass worldly claims for unfettered motion into the world.

If Jorn's paintings are mute, mimetic artifacts, they are also archives. With their dense planes that "preserve" and collect bankrupt gestures (including both the kitsch paintings and the painterly marks that overlay them), they parallel that classificatory system that looks on past moments from an external vantage point, avoiding all interpretation or the belief that originary, intimate meaning can be rediscovered or reapplied to the present. In likening these works to archives, I am thinking not of methods of hierarchical ordering so much as of the way in which Jorn's works function as memory tableaus that, nonetheless, do not provide intimate, internal access to past moments.[21] In this way, we are reminded of Foucault's archaeological method whose function "is not to awaken texts from their present sleep, and, by reciting the marks still legible on their surface, to rediscover the flash of their birth; on the contrary, its function is to follow them through their sleep" to discover in what mode of existence "they are preserved, in which they are reactivated, and used, in which they are also—but this was not their original destiny—forgotten, and possibly even destroyed."[22]

Debord and Jorn's second book, *Mémoires,* assumes particular significance in relation to this archival strategy.[23] Approximately fifty pages long, the book is divided into three sections labeled June 1952, December 1952, and September 1953 respectively—roughly the time frame of the first two years of Debord's radical, pre-Situ group, the Lettrist International (1952–1957). Within each section, the white pages are strewn with photo reproductions, anonymous texts clipped from a variety of sources, and Jorn's overlapping swirls ranging from bright reds and blues to hot pink and acid green. Greil Marcus has likened the rivulets of paint and print that seem to form routes and passages on the book's pages to the situationist *dérive,* and the book in general to a blueprint or map of these routes through everyday life and space.[24] And yet, at the same time as it is a map, laying the ground for an active course, it is also a memoir—specifically, the story of the Lettrist International. This conflation of map and memoir is significant, for as a means of describing, recording, and translating the external features of a path or place, a map would seem to preclude access to the intimate, internal arena of memory. Composed entirely of borrowed phrases, *Mémoires* acknowledges this tension between a desire to record and remember and the fact that, once solidified on the pages of a book or artwork, the relevance of these moments is long gone. In this vein, the quotations seem to alternate between utopian optimism— "the grand affair of this night, which for all nights and days to come assures us a sovereign autocracy and absolute empire"—and a melancholic sense of failure— "the solicitations of a past that can only be revived in remembrance, or in a repetition where, whatever one does, it degrades itself."[25] More than describing events and desires, *Mémoires* tells of the external conditions surrounding the formulation of past moments: "on the deserted streets," "in the quarter," *Mémoires* gives us where, when, and how, but not what. It translates the past, as it were, "through secondary details." Admitting the impossibility of intimately appropriating one's own words and actions, *Mémoires* enters the domain of the already said: "Ours is a singular profession: enormous labor, fatigue beyond words, never respite, a destiny on the fringes of others."[26]

Alienated from the originary sites that it translates, the book becomes its own structural space with specific material conditions. As *Mémoires* recognizes, "the passion to speak and remember rests on a material base." In this vein, the book becomes a leveling surface on which Jorn's painted swirls, printed text, and photo-reproductions collect in banal equivalence. The reference to Pollock is unmistakable in Jorn's splatterings of color, and yet the photolithographed drips and splatters undermine the rhetoric of gestural authenticity surrounding Pollock's work. However, in contrast to Heartfield's photo, which ruptures the thick, painted plane into which it is inserted, *Mémoires* reduces everything—including the painted

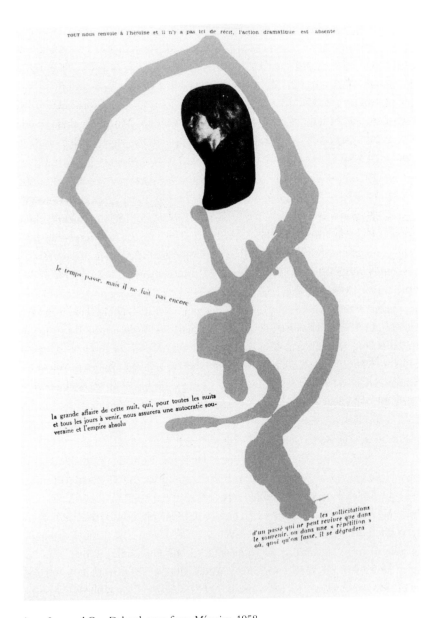

TOUT nous renvoie à l'héroïne et il n'y a pas ici de récit, l'action dramatique est absente

le temps passe, mais il ne fuit pas encore

la grande affaire de cette nuit, qui, pour toutes les nuits et tous les jours à venir, nous assurera une autocratie souveraine et l'empire absolu

les sollicitations d'un passé qui ne peut revivre que dans le souvenir, ou dans une « répétition » où, quoi qu'on fasse, il se dégradera

Asger Jorn and Guy Debord, page from *Mémoires*, 1958.

marks—to the state of the photographic. As reproductions, word and image confront no primary model. Rather, they participate in a space of rootless exchange in which there can be no criticism precisely because there is no way to differentiate one gesture from another. The failure to dismantle or disrupt is poignantly underscored by the frenetic splotches that overlay but which, as with Jorn's détourned paintings, do not hide or erase the typed text beneath. Moreover, these frantic jumbles of color, words, and photos are followed by more static, gridded pages, in which the colored lines serve the sole function of scoring the text. In this way, they parallel the mechanistic diagrams of rooms and houses that run throughout the book—tautological word/image illustrations. Toward the end of *Mémoires,* a washy blue/green splotch that seems to hover almost magically on its page is followed on the next page by a bubble-shaped, hot pink, cartoonlike alter ego. The text underneath the figure reads: "the mess goes away!" Attempts at spontaneous expression in the manner of dada collage poems or futurist *parole in libertà* are replaced by the codified, graphic signs that characterize the book's structure.

Mémoires is predicated on the alienating effect of language, specifically as it enters the domain of the aesthetic object. As archival recollection, the book conjures up "the epoch [that] itself is the frame of the whole work,"[27] at the same time as it relegates those moments to mere shadows. The anguished voice that speaks through anonymous phrases calls to mind Foucault's fictitious interlocutor from *The Archaeology of Knowledge:*

> What! All those words, piled up one after another, all those marks made on all that paper . . . all that and nothing remaining of the poor hand that traced them, of the anxiety that sought appeasement in them, of that completed life that has nothing but them to survive in? . . . . Must I suppose . . . that in speaking I am not banishing my death, but actually establishing it?[28]

Foucault's image of words piled up one after another recalls not only *Mémoires* but Jorn's détourned paintings as well, and none more so than *The Avant-Garde Doesn't Give Up.*[29] Taking Jorn's Duchampian gesture in conjunction with the scrawled words, the childlike, primitive figures overpainted on the black ground, and the red, yellow, and blue paint splotches that turn this field into a kind of action painting, the entire image reads as a recollection of earlier artistic forays, a kind of archive of the avant-garde. Registered on the painting's surface—"one after the other"—each motif becomes a distinct, borrowed style, made equivalent with all other artistic interventions, and preserved—albeit as a mere trace—for posterity. Like the book, the painted surface becomes its own discursive space— grounding Duchamp's strategy in precisely that arena that the dadaists sought to destroy. These paintings admit the paradox of modernism whereby avant-garde movements ultimately succumb to their own aestheticism. The avant-garde may not have given up but, as a result, it has become a received gesture indistinguishable (both literally and figuratively) from Jorn's kitsch paintings.

For Debord, "the very fact that such 'recollections' of the history of art have become possible amounts to the *end of the world of art*." He writes:

> Only in this era of museums, when no artistic communication remains possible, can each and every earlier moment of art be accepted —and be accepted as *equal in value*—for none, in view of the disappearance of the prerequisites of communication *in general,* suffers any longer from the disappearance of its own *particular* ability to communicate.[30]

This ability to recollect, which is complicit with art's failure to signify, is not to be lamented. Rather, in Debord's thinking, such a testament to art's dissolution is necessary in that it promotes recognition of the current need to supersede the work of art entirely. The museum, as an institution that kills any authentic relation between art and society once and for all, is therefore the final catalyst. It is only in this age of the museum and the archive that, according to Debord, any obstructive illusions about the revolutionary potential of art will finally be put to rest and real, communal praxis can begin.

In the catalogue essay to his 1959 show, Jorn writes: "Be modern, collectors, museums. If you have old paintings do not despair. Retain your memories

---

but detourn them so that they correspond with your era. . . . Painting is over. You might as well finish it off. Detourn. Long live painting."[31] The détourned work functions both as a form of preservation and, as such, as a recognition of the death of painting (and the artwork in general) as a vital field for critical investigation. It is significant that these works remain paintings, not only because, as such, they reinforce the naiveté of mechanical strategies like photography that once carried such utopian potential, but also because through their inert opacity they become ciphers of their own demise. Jorn notes: "It is impossible to establish a future without a past. The future is made through relinquishing or sacrificing the past." He concludes: "In this exhibition I erect a monument in honor of bad painting. Personally I like it better than good painting. But above all, this monument is indispensable, both for me and for everyone else. It is painting sacrificed." Jorn is not the cinemateur/surgeon who "moves among the patient's organs." Instead, Jorn stands back as his paintings self-destruct before his eyes: "I solemnly tip my hat and let the blood of my victims flow while intoning Baudelaire's hymn to beauty."[32]

What sort of beauty is Jorn referring to here? Is he speaking of that ephemeral quality that mirrors the age it typifies and, in this way, comes to parallel Adorno's autonomous artwork, or is he instead referencing Baudelaire's other beauty—the eternal and immutable—and implying that this kind of rigidity must ultimately be rejected? It is this second appeal that speaks to the paradox at the heart of Jorn's *Modifications* and Debord's writing. For it is important to emphasize that utopian aspirations do not disappear from situationist theory even if they can no longer be located within the domain of the art object. In fact, in their very bounded materiality, Jorn's paintings suggest that avant-garde failures can be contained and so disposed, that one should transcend the spectacle and reified art forms for a space that resembles Sartrian negativity: pure creative spirit unencumbered by obstacles. Gradually the situationists came to reject artistic structures altogether as, one by one, artists affiliated with the SI were either excluded or, like Jorn, chose to resign. As Debord concluded in 1972 after the disbanding of the SI, it was now necessary to go into hiding: "And now when we can flatter ourselves that we have achieved the most shocking notoriety . . . we will become even less accessible, we will go even further underground. The more famous our theses become, the more obscure we ourselves will be."[33]

This rhetoric manifests a certain idealism. For all their radicalism, the situationists maintain a strangely limited view of art, one that holds that the relevance of the artwork ends with the death of its critical/creative function. In fact, in this respect, the situationist scorn for neo-avant-garde "repetitions" recalls Peter Bürger's condemnation of postwar movements as pathetic, repetitive failures.[34] In the end, "bad painting" is just that. Jorn's painterly carcasses cannot conceive of an art that would offer a provocative analysis of the way in which we come to meaning *within* discursive frameworks and *without* complete subjective control. Responding to a desperate need to escape from reified objects and relationships, the situationists looked to rediscover a utopian space of free, creative subjects.

The garden/building complex that Jorn constructed in Albisola, Italy, was such a place. In "On Wild Architecture,"[35] Debord contrasts contemporary architecture, "a form that to this day is like oil stains on 'the frozen waters of egotistical calculation,'" with Jorn's "concrete . . . appropriation of space, demonstrating that everyone could undertake to reconstruct around themselves the earth which badly needs it. The painted and sculpted sections . . . the trees . . . a cistern, vines, the most varied sorts of always welcomed debris, all thrown together in a perfect disorder, compose one of the most complicated and ultimately, one of the best unified landscapes that one can traverse." Whereas the spectacular space of "accumulation" is characterized by inert surfaces like "oil stains on 'the frozen waters,'" which we can only look on from a position of passive contemplation, Jorn's landscape is one in which objects bow to a creative will. The result is rich, traversable ambiances. If the work of art fails as internal critical intervention and comes to resemble the spectacular surface, it can be reused, as such, as building blocks of alternative, imaginative environments. Nonetheless, Jorn's world remains a fantasy. It is the realm of kings and castles situated far away "on a hill overlooking the Ligurian coast." It is, essentially, as Debord puts it, a "private property," demonstrating what one can do "'with a little time, luck, health, money, thought (and also) good mood,'"[36] a utopian oasis within which one can shut the door on reality for a time.

Ultimately, it seems, it is in the world of the imagination, as manifest in Jorn's fantastical garden and Debord's place of "underground" retreat, that the situationists find a home. Beyond the spectacle's domains, "we wander around in a circle in the night and are consumed by fire."[37] A noble pursuit, a heroic endeavor, and yet one that can only take place in far-off realms.

Notes

Originally published in *October* 79 (Winter 1997), 33–48.

1. Guy Debord, "Les situationnistes et les nouvelles formes d'action dans la politique ou l'art," in *Destruktion af RSG-6: En kollectiv manifestation af Situationistisk International* (Odense, Denmark: Galerie EXI, 1963), 15–18; translated as "The Situationists and the New Forms of Action in Politics or Art," in this volume, 164.

2. Guy Debord and Gil Wolman, "Mode d'emploi du détournement," *Les lèvres nues* 8 (May 1956); trans. as "Methods of Detournement," in Ken Knabb, ed. and trans., *Situationist International Anthology* (Berkeley: Bureau of Public Secrets, 1981), 9.

3. Sadie Plant, *The Most Radical Gesture: The Situationist International in a Postmodern Age* (London: Routledge, 1992), 6.

4. See Elisabeth Sussman, ed., *On the Passage of a Few People through a Rather Brief Moment in Time: The Situationist International, 1957–1972* (Boston: Institute of Contemporary Art; Cambridge, Mass: MIT Press, 1989).

5. This work does not belong to the original *Modifications* series from 1959, but rather to a group entitled *New Disfigurations*. See note 29.

6. I am indebted here to Benjamin Buchloh's contrast between Marcel Broodthaers's photo vitrines and dada and surrealist collage tactics. See Buchloh, "Contemplating Publicity: Marcel Broodthaers's Section Publicité," in *Marcel Broodthaers: Musée d'Art Moderne, Département des Aigles, Section Publicité,* ed. Maria Gilissen and Benjamin H. D. Buchloh (New York: Marian Goodman Gallery, 1995), 96–97.

7. Peter Wollen, "Bitter Victory: The Art and Politics of the Situationist International," in Sussman, ed., *On the Passage of a Few People,* 47–48.

8. Guy Atkins, *Asger Jorn: The Crucial Years, 1954–1964* (New York: Wittenborn Art Books, 1977), 60.

9. Italics mine. "Le détournement comme négation et comme prélude," *Internationale situationniste* 3 (1959); translated as "Detournement as Negation and Prelude," in Knabb, ed., *Situationist International Anthology,* 55–56. Sublimity must be understood here in line with Debord's statements about "art's brilliant colors" (see below) as manifesting the artwork's reified impotence. This idea recalls Jean-Paul Sartre's concept of the "sacred" and its thickening of life and consciousness.

10. Debord and Wolman, "Methods of Detournement," 12.

11. Guy Debord, *The Society of the Spectacle,* trans. Donald Nicholson-Smith (New York: Zone Books, 1994), 133.

12. Debord, "For a Revolutionary Judgment of Art" (1961), in Knabb, ed., *Situationist International Anthology.*

13. Ibid., 310.

14. Walter Benjamin, "The Work of Art in the Age of Mechanical Reproduction" (1936), in *Illuminations,* ed. Hannah Arendt, trans. Harry Zohn (New York: Schocken Books, 1985), 233.

15. Theodor Adorno, *Aesthetic Theory* (London: International Library of Phenomenology and Moral Sciences; Boston: Routledge & K. Paul, 1984), 31.

16. Ibid., 223.

17. Ibid., 48.

18. Sartre and his philosophy of the situation are fundamental to the SI's notion of everyday life authentically experienced. For an excellent clarification of this relationship, see Wollen, "Bitter Victory," 30.

19. Jean-Paul Sartre, *Saint-Genet,* quoted in Bernd Jäger, "Sartre's Anthropology," in Paul Arthur Schilpp, ed., *The Philosophy of Jean-Paul Sartre* (La Salle, Illinois: Open Court, 1981), 481.

20. Jean-Paul Sartre, *"What Is Literature?" and Other Essays* (Cambridge: Harvard University Press, 1988), 37.

21. Once again my analysis is inspired by Buchloh's discussion of Broodthaers's photo arrangements and their relation to archival ordering systems. However, as pointed out above, my use of the term differs from Buchloh's emphasis on the archive as a site of administrative, programmatic display.

22. Michel Foucault, *The Archaeology of Knowledge,* trans. A. M. Sheridan Smith (New York: Pantheon Books, 1972), 122. This pairing of the situationists and Foucault may seem surprising considering that they represent manifestly different philosophical positions, particularly as regards the role of the subject. In citing Foucault, I am drawing a parallel between the situa-

tionist/Debordian art object and the impotence that grounds Foucault's "self." I do not mean to diminish the discrepancy between the situationists' Lukács- and Sartre-inspired quest for free, unalienated subjectivity and Foucault's all-pervasive, insurmountable economy of "power."

23. *Fin de Copenhague,* Jorn and Debord's first book from 1957, is equally interesting and deserves consideration in its own right. However, for lack of space I have decided to limit my remarks to *Mémoires.* The general format of the two books is very similar and much of my discussion of *Mémoires* can be applied to the earlier book. One crucial difference is that *Fin de Copenhague,* with its interspliced cartoons and advertising slogans, must be seen as a commentary on consumer society associated, in this way, with pop gestures. This is not, I would argue, the way that *Mémoires* should be read.

24. Greil Marcus, "Guy Debord's *Mémoires:* A Situationist Primer," in Sussman, ed., *On the Passage of a Few People,* 128.

25. All translations from *Mémoires,* unless otherwise specified, are my own.

26. Translated in Marcus, "Guy Debord's *Mémoires,*" 125.

27. Ibid.

28. Foucault, *The Archaeology of Knowledge,* 210.

29. This painting (part of a series entitled *New Disfigurations*) was executed after the *Modifications* and, for that matter, after Jorn's resignation from the SI in 1961. Atkins notes the difference between these works' "more serious intention" and the earlier paintings. The title of the series alone—most fully applicable to a work like *Sugar Tart* in which a woman's face has been replaced by the head of a pig—suggests its departure from the *Modifications* as I have discussed them. Nevertheless, many of these paintings read as similarly tired gestures. Paintings like *The Avant-Garde Doesn't Give Up* or *The Two Penguins* bear particular affinity with the earlier works.

30. Debord, *The Society of the Spectacle,* 135.

31. Asger Jorn, "Peinture détourné," in *Vingt peintures modifiées par Asger Jorn* (Paris: Galerie Rive Gauche, 1959). Translated as "Detourned Painting" in Sussman, ed., *On the Passage of a Few People,* 140.

32. Ibid., 142.

33. Debord, *La véritable scission dans l'Internationale* (Paris: Éditions Champ Libre, 1972); quoted in Roberto Ohrt, "If I Wasn't Alexander I Would Like to Be Diogenes," *Durch* 3–4 (November 1987), 37.

34. Peter Bürger, *Theory of the Avant-Garde,* trans. Michael Shaw (Minneapolis: University of Minnesota Press, 1984).

35. Debord, "De l'architecture sauvage," in *Jardin d'Albisola,* text by Ezio Gribaudo, Alberico Sala, and Guy Debord (Turin: Edizioni d'Arte Fratelli Pozzo, 1974); trans. as "On Wild Architecture," in Sussman, ed., *On the Passage of a Few People,* 174–175.

36. Greil Marcus has helpfully suggested that this word should instead be translated as "high spirits."

37. This is the accepted translation of the title of Debord's final film, *In girum imus nocte et consumimur igni* (1978).

Architecture and Play

Libero Andreotti

> After all, it was modern poetry, for the last hundred years, that had
> led us there. We were a handful who thought that it was necessary to
> carry out its program in reality, and in any case to do nothing else.

Guy Debord, *Panegyric* (1989)

In girum imus nocte et consumimur igni—We Go Round and Round in the Night
and Are Consumed by Fire—the long Latin palindrome used by Guy Debord as
the title for one of his last films, can also serve to characterize the urban play tactics of the Situationist International.[1] As the great Dutch historian Johan
Huizinga noted in a book that was a key source for this group, but whose role is
all but completely ignored in recent historical writings, the palindrome is in fact
an ancient play form that, like the riddle and the conundrum, "cuts clean across
any possible distinction between play and seriousness."[2] Debord seems aware of
this when he notes, somewhat cryptically, that his title is "constructed letter by
letter like a labyrinth that you cannot find the way out of, in such a manner that
it renders perfectly the form and content of perdition"—a remark that can be interpreted in many ways but that recalls the phenomenon of "losing oneself in the
game" described so well by Huizinga himself.[3] Certainly, of all the *détournements*
for which Debord is justly famous, this one seems best suited to convey the

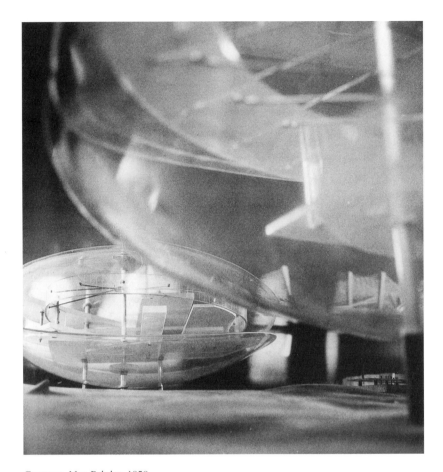

Constant, *New Babylon*, 1958.

iconoclastic spirit of the SI, a movement of great ambition and influence, whose reflections on the city, the spectacle, and everyday life have ensured it a vital place in the art and politics of the last forty years.

In what follows, I would like to explore the play element in the activities of three key protagonists around the time of the group's founding in 1957, namely Debord himself, the Italian environmental artist Giuseppe Gallizio, and the Dutch painter Constant Nieuwenhuys, whose models for a future city called New Babylon vividly expressed the principles of unitary urbanism underlying the group.[4] More specifically, and in the spirit of the palindrome, I would like to show how each of them radicalized Huizinga's theory of play into a revolutionary ethics that effectively abolished any distinction between play and seriousness, or between art and everyday life.

One of the favorite play forms engaged in by the SI and its predecessor organization, the Lettrist International, was the *dérive,* the art of wandering through urban space whose special mood is well conveyed in the palindrome's darkly romantic meaning. The *dérive*'s closest cultural precedents would have been the dadaist and surrealist excursions organized by Breton in 1925, such as the one to the church of Saint-Julien-le-Pauvre. However, Debord was careful to distinguish the *dérive* from such precedents, emphasizing its active character as "a mode of experimental behavior" that ultimately reached back to romanticism, the baroque, and the age of chivalry, with its tradition of the long voyage undertaken in a spirit of adventure and discovery. In Paris this kind of urban roaming was characteristic of Left Bank bohemianism, where the art of drifting was a favorite way of cultivating that feeling of being "apart together" that Huizinga described as characteristic of play.[5] A vivid record of this time and place is Ed Van der Elsken's book of photographs, which recorded some of the favorite haunts of the lettrists.[6] Later some of these images would find their way into Debord's poetry and films.

Central to the *dérive* was the awareness of exploring forms of life radically beyond the capitalist work ethic, as seen in the famous graffiti incitement, "Ne travaillez jamais" (Never work), made by Debord in 1953 and reproduced in the SI's journal with the caption "minimum program of the situationist movement."

Ed Van der Elsken, page from *Love on the Left Bank,* 1957.

Another fine example of such street philosophy is the lettrist flier showing Debord and his friends next to the revolutionary slogan of Saint-Just, "La guerre de la liberté doit être faite avec colère" (The war for freedom must be waged angrily). Both recall Huizinga's lively description of the itinerant sophists of ancient Rome, whose seditious propaganda would lead to Emperor Vespasian's banishing all philosophers from the city.[7]

A key source of information on the *dérives* is a book of poetry entitled *Mémoires,* composed by Debord and the painter Asger Jorn in 1957, which evoked the activities of the Lettrist International.[8] The dominant technique, consisting of Jorn's drippings and splashes of color, over which Debord scattered his own literary and visual fragments, was evidently intended to minimize the amount of labor and handicraft characteristic of a "serious" work. In this sense, *Mémoires* is a radically antiproductivist work, or, more precisely, an antiwork, whose discursive antiphonal form reflected the *dérive*'s emphasis on collective play. (Jorn, it should be noted, had already experimented with similar techniques in his word paintings with Christian Dotremont in the late 1940s, and somewhat similar letter poetry could be found in the works of the lettrists Gil Wolman and Isidore Isou.) The eloquent improvisation of textual fragments that makes up the first page—where allusions to some of Debord's favorite themes, such as time passing, love, war, and drinking,[9] are all underlined with the witty ceremonial statement, "je vais quand même agiter des évènements et émettre des considérations" (I will anyway discuss some facts and put forward some considerations)—is typical of the lyrical tone constantly hovering between farce and seriousness that Huizinga described as characteristic of the play spirit.

In their use of recycled images, the following pages of *Mémoires* exemplified a second play tactic theorized by Debord in the early 1950s: *détournement,* or the creative pillaging of preexisting elements.[10] About halfway into the book, beginning in the fall of 1953, fragments of city plans begin to appear. On one page, the various parts of the plan of Paris are most likely related to the written account of a *dérive* that appeared in the Belgian journal *Les lèvres nues.*[11] On another, the focus is on the Contrescarpe region, celebrated by the lettrists for its "aptitude for play and forgetting."[12] Both pages exemplify the mythmaking turns described

Lettrist International leaflet, 1954.

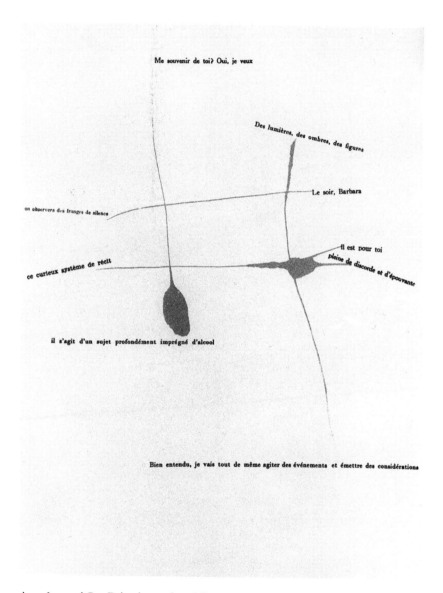

Asger Jorn and Guy Debord, page from *Mémoires,* 1958.

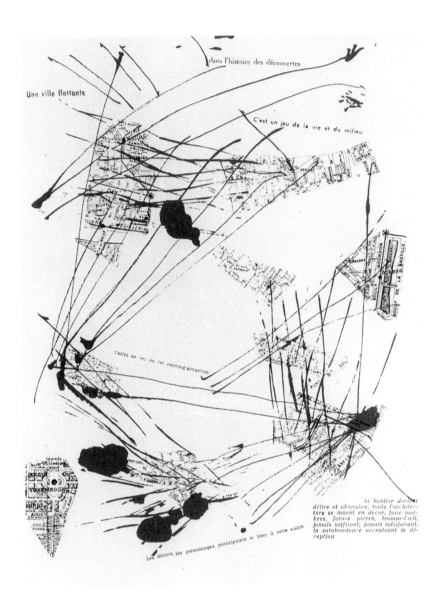

Asger Jorn and Guy Debord, page from *Mémoires,* 1958.

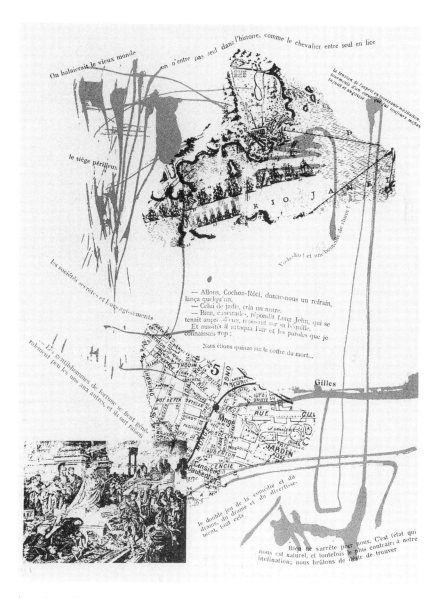

Asger Jorn and Guy Debord, page from *Mémoires*, 1958.

by Huizinga as typical of play.[13] Among these is the tendency to exaggerate and embellish actual experience and invest surroundings with personality, as seen in the phrase "une ville flottante" (a floating city), possibly alluding to the Île de la Cité.[14] Also characteristic is the tendency toward extravagant self-praise, as in the phrase "Rien ne s'arrête pour nous. C'est l'état qui nous est naturel . . . nous brûlons de désir de trouver" (Nothing ever stops for us. It is our natural state . . . we burn with the desire to find), and the playing at being heroes and warriors. Indeed, one of the most remarkable features of these pages is the agonistic tone, as seen on the same page, where a plan of the Contrescarpe region is juxtaposed against an identical surface in reverse representing a battle scene in the Americas, the literary fragments including "le siège périlleux"(the perilous siege) and "On balayerait le vieux monde"(We would wipe away the old world), with other comments probably referring to the urban renewal projects denounced by the lettrists in this district.[15] This warlike tone is in fact a recurring mode of address throughout *Mémoires*.[16]

Debord's best-known and widely reproduced psychogeographies of Paris, also dating from this period, belong in the same family as *Mémoires* and should be read in a similar vein. Both enact a fluctuation between spatial and temporal registers: the isolated fragments form complete and self-enclosed entities, while the red vectors, much like Jorn's drippings, suggest forces of movement and "passional" attraction. This sort of temporalization of space was a key situationist tactic and a distinctive quality of the *dérive,* which aimed to resist the reifying tendency to spatialize physical surroundings by means of the player's anti-objectifying stance.[17] The erotic overtones of the two titles, of which the second, *Discours sur les passions de l'amour,* was appropriated from a famous essay by Pascal, underscored the irreducibility of the *dérive,* and of pleasure in general, to the productivist imperatives of bourgeois living.

One source offered by Debord for the *dérive* was the *Carte du pays de Tendre,* an imaginary representation of the Land of Love devised as an aristocratic pastime by the seventeenth-century noblewoman Madeleine de Scudéry. Like *The Naked City,* it also charted a "passional terrain"—the erotic theme suggested also by its strange resemblance to the female reproductive organs.[18] In Debord's case,

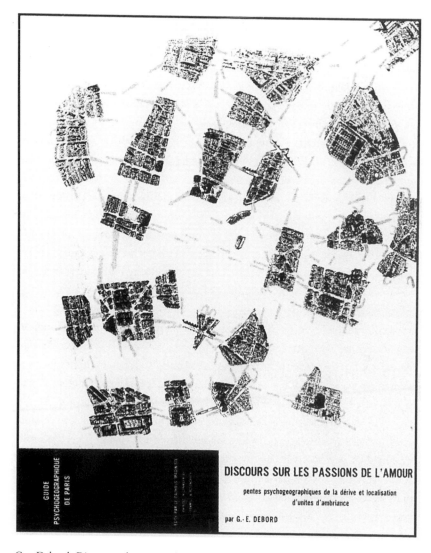

Guy Debord, *Discours sur les passions de l'amour*, 1956.

however, the elaborate narrative that accompanies the *Carte du pays de Tendre* is replaced by a much more realistic urge to map actual urban sites, including, as he would say, "their principal points of passage, their exits and defenses."[19]

This revolutionary idea of pleasure was a constituent feature of the psychogeographical "research" that these maps were supposed to exemplify, and which, as Kristin Ross notes, entailed a "careful survey of the residual and interstitial spaces of the city in a systematic search for elements that might be salvaged from the dominant culture, and, once isolated, put to new use in a utopian reconstruction of social space."[20] The understanding of city space as a contested terrain in which new forms of life had no proper place but could only assert themselves in a provisional way can also be seen in the flier announcing "A New Theater of Operations in Culture," which juxtaposed new methods of military aerial survey against an array of programmatic terms related to the higher goal of "constructing situations." It is necessary at this point to mention the sociopolitical transformations of Paris during these years, which witnessed an increased policing of city space under de Gaulle and the wider phenomenon known as "internal colonization" as seen in the massive displacement of poor populations into new belts of grimly functionalist housing projects at a safe distance from the city center. It is not by chance that many of the areas included in Debord's psychogeographies were sites of political battle, including the overwhelmingly North African neighborhood of La Huchette, where the SI was headquartered.

The first attempt actually to construct a situation was Gallizio's *Cavern of Anti-Matter.* Made entirely of his so-called industrial paintings—long rolls of painted cloth made collectively with the help of rudimentary "painting machines" and sold by the meter on the market square—this complete microenvironment was designed in close collaboration with Debord, who played a much greater role than is generally assumed (in fact, the event was orchestrated by Debord with Gallizio a sometimes uncomprehending bystander). The goal of the *Cavern* was to merge art with everyday life in a move complementary to the *dérive*'s elevation of the quotidian realities of city space. The source of this idea was again Huizinga's description of the "overvaluation" of art, which he saw as the main cause for its increasing remoteness from everyday concerns.[21]

Pinot Gallizio showing his industrial paintings in Alba, Italy, 1960.

The *Cavern* proposed an opposite process of "devaluation," an immersion of art in the everyday, which was symbolized by the use of painting as clothing and urban decor. The fact that Gallizio was an amateur who dabbled equally well in archaeology and chemistry only served to intensify the *Cavern*'s attack on professionalism and the institution of the art gallery.

The opening event recalled an early scientific demonstration, complete with staged explosions showing off the pyrotechnic possibilities of Gallizio's newly invented resins. The ludic tone of the whole proceeding could also be seen in the invitation card, which promised to illustrate "the encounter between matter and anti-matter," and whose mock-scientific tone recalls Huizinga's definition of the ludic element of science as the tendency toward "perilous" theorizings.[22] The reference in this case was to the theories of anti-matter developed by the English physicist Paul Adrien Maurice Dirac and the Italian mathematician Enrico Severi. The *Cavern*'s neofuturist tone was also apparent in the use of sound machines that would rise to a high pitch as one approached the walls of the room, as well as the deployment of perfumes and moving lights. The ludic reconversion of technology, suggested by the very idea of industrial painting, reflected a positive faith in industry's liberating potential, quite similar in fact to Benjamin's description of the loss of aura resulting from mechanical reproduction. In both cases, the power and destiny of technology to become an instrument for human emancipation was asserted against its actual use for opposite ends. As Debord put it, "this society is moved by absurd forces that tend unconsciously to satisfy its true needs."[23]

The *Cavern*'s challenge to the institution of the art gallery would have gone further, and perhaps taken an unpredictable turn, if the SI had been allowed to mount a group exhibition planned for the Stedelijk Museum in Amsterdam a few months later. The installation, as seen in a diagrammatic plan that is its only surviving evidence, would have turned a wing of the museum into a two-mile-long obstacle course culminating in a tunnel of industrial painting. At the same time, a series of real operational *dérives* were to take place in downtown Amsterdam, where teams of situationists would have drifted for three days communicating with each other and the museum space with radio transmitters.[24]

Pinot Gallizio, *La caverne de l'anti-matter*, Galerie René Drouin, Paris, 1959. Gallizio is second from the right.

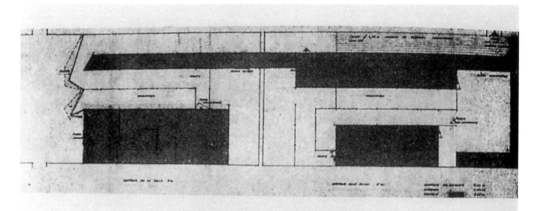

Plan des structures du labyrinthe non-aménagé.

Plan for an exhibition at the Stedelijk Museum, Amsterdam, 1960. From *Internationale situationniste* 4 (June 1960).

Nowhere was the mirage of a civilization liberated from work more evident, however, than in Constant's *New Babylon,* whose title, attributed to Debord, evoked the material abundance made possible by automation as well as the anti-Christian morality that animated the group.[25] This single attempt to work out the technical, structural, and sociopolitical outline of a situationist architecture had its origins in Constant's own evolution from painter to sculptor. This process began with the large and impressive *Ambiance de jeu* (1954), which for the first time moved to the horizontal plane and began to address issues of three-dimensional space; continued with a series of geometric explorations like *Structure with Curved Planes* (1954), which already indicates a search for lightness and dynamism in its displaced corner supports; and culminated in the series of dynamic neoconstructivist works such as *Suspended Spiral* (1958) and *Nébuleuse mécanique* (1958), whose tensile system of cables and steel elements provided the basic syntax for Constant's first practical application in *Nomadic Encampment.* This latter was a flexible shelter whose lightweight and transportable elements were supposed to serve a Gypsy community that Constant befriended during a stay in northern Italy. From here, Constant moved directly into the development of his large steel-and-Plexiglas structures, lifted off the ground and offering a multilayered and potentially extensible system of construction. The first was called *Yellow Sector,* a title that reflects Constant's aversion to the more homelike and bourgeois connotations of "neighborhood." Like most of the other models, it was organized around fields of movable prefabricated elements arranged randomly to emphasize their dependence on changing needs. The guiding idea was what Constant called "the principle of disorientation"—a deliberate confusion of spatial hierarchy through obstacles, incomplete geometries, and translucent elements. Aside from designating certain areas as especially suitable for ludic activities, the absence of any functional zoning or separation of public and private space reflected a desire to multiply the variability of the space—somewhat as Cedric Price would do a few years later with his *Fun Palace* (1964), where not only the walls but also the floor and roof elements were to be fully movable.[26]

The exotic *Oriental Sector* that followed shortly after, along with the *Ambiance de départ,* explored the range of atmospheric effects that could be achieved

Constant, *Ambiance de jeu*, 1954.

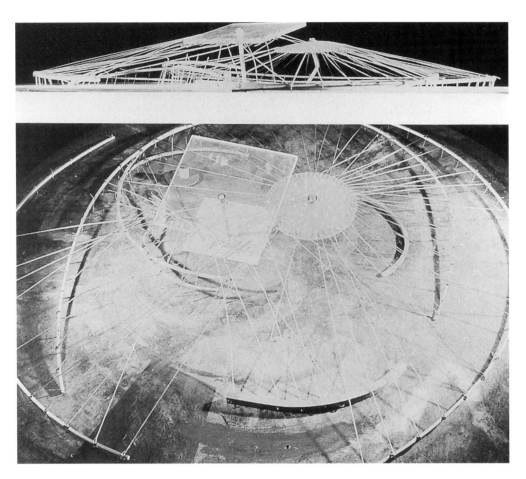

Constant, *Nomadic Encampment,* 1958.

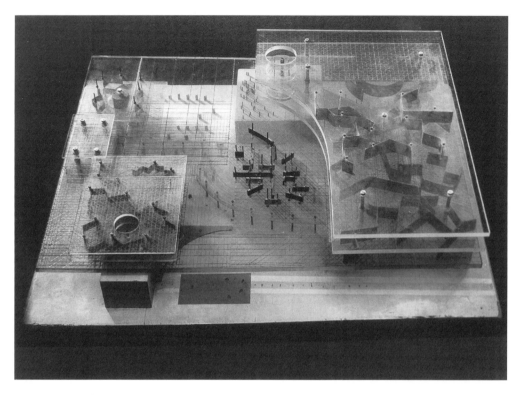

Constant, *Oriental Sector,* 1959.

within this basic formal syntax. Both works recall the hedonistic vision of a situationist city advanced by Gilles Ivain (Ivan Chtcheglov) as early as 1952: a series of city quarters designated according to different moods, and in which the principal activity of the inhabitants would be a continuous *dérive*.[27] Constant described these models as examples of an "urbanism intended to bring pleasure." In an essay significantly entitled "A Different City for a Different Life," he noted:

> We require adventure. Not finding it any longer on earth, there are those who want to look for it on the moon. We opt first to create situations here, new situations. We intend to break the laws that prevent the development of meaningful activities in life and culture. We find ourselves at the dawn of a new era, and we are already trying to outline the image of a happier life.[28]

The science fiction theme implied here is best seen in the series of oyster-like space units called *Spatiovore,* which vividly express the uprooted and nomadic life of the "New Babylonians," free to roam and alter their surroundings at will. Liberated from work, no longer tied to fixed places of habitation, relieved of the oppressions of the family structure, the citizens of this new community would be free to abandon themselves to the *dérive* and the play spirit.[29]

On a larger scale, New Babylon presented itself as a wide-mesh, decentered network of connecting sectors, superimposed over a system of rapid transportation routes. As Ohrt notes, the most likely precedent for such a scheme would have been Alison and Peter Smithson's 1958 competition entry for central Berlin, which offered a similar arrangement of elevated pedestrian platforms and walkways. At the same time, New Babylon gave form to the notion of the *tissu urbain* developed by the philosopher Henri Lefebvre in his utopian descriptions of an urban civilization beyond the old distinction between city and countryside.

The similarities between New Babylon and other megastructural fantasies of the 1960s, such as those of Archigram and Metabolism, are worth pursuing. Certainly New Babylon shared with them a fascination with technology and a positive faith in the power of architecture to stimulate new behavior—two

Constant, *New Babylon*, 1958.

aspects that made it an easy target for criticism, especially in view of the eventual assimilation of the megastructural theme within the commercial real estate speculations of the 1970s and 1980s. Moreover, as several other situationists were quick to point out, its own nature as a romantic prefiguration meant that it was sure to be "recuperated" and turned into a mere "compensation" for society's shortcomings.[30]

Against this eventuality, the so-called second phase of the SI, following Constant's resignation in May 1960, showed that another direction lay open for the extension of play tactics into highly politicized behavior, as seen in the urban poetry of the graffiti, the wild architecture of the barricades, and the *détournement* of entire city streets in May '68.[31] While the role of the SI in these events is still disputed, it is clear that many of them were inspired by its play spirit and its capacity, in Huizinga's terms, to "express a formidable seriousness through play."[32]

To conclude, three general remarks. First, Huizinga's ludic philosophy was only one of many elements that fed into the SI's urban practices; one must also consider its critique of postwar consumer culture and its multiple connections with other cultural and political manifestations in France and elsewhere—a subject developed by Simon Sadler, among others, in his recent book *The Situationist City*. Second, it is no less important to elucidate the SI's complex relations with Marxist theory, especially Debord's readings of Lukács's critique of reification.[33] A theorization of the phenomenological structure of play, in this sense, might help to bridge the gap between the SI's so-called first and second phases, a division still strongly reflected, unfortunately, in the exclusive focus of recent historical writings on either the artistic or the political dimensions of the movement.[34]

Third, and finally, it is essential to stress the agonistic drive that animated the urban theories and practices of the SI. This suggests a more general reading of the Latin palindrome with which I began this essay, in addition to its function as a literary play form and poetic figure of the *dérive*. "We go round and round in the night and are consumed by fire" recalls, in fact, Renato Poggioli's classic description of the agonistic moment of the avant-garde, the point of self-immolation reached when, as he put it, "in its febrile anxiety to go always further," it reaches a point where it ignores even its own "catastrophe and perdition," welcoming this

Rue Gay-Lussac, May 10, 1968.

self-ruin as "an obscure sacrifice to the success of future movements."[35] The point could not have been made better than by Debord himself, who, in another statement recalling the palindrome's cyclical form, wrote: "All revolutions enter history and history rejects none of them; and the rivers of revolution go back to where they originated, in order to flow once again."[36]

NOTES

Originally published in *October* 91 (Winter 2000), 37–58.

1. A version of this paper was delivered at the conference "Reconceptualizing the Modern: Architectural Culture, 1945–1968," Harvard Graduate School of Design, April 24–25, 1998. Research for this paper was made possible by a grant from the French Ministry of Culture, Délégation aux Arts Plastiques. A special thanks to Jean-Paul Flamand, Daniel Dobbels, Alice Debord, Sarah Williams Ksiazek, and Diane de Ravel for their helpful comments and assistance. The palindrome is commonly attributed to the Roman orator Sidonius Apollinare, who used it to describe the arabesques formed in the air by those notoriously blind insects, moths, circling around a lit candle at night. Recent writings on the Situationist International are too numerous to be listed here, but see Libero Andreotti and Xavier Costa, eds., *Situationists: Art, Politics, Urbanism* (Barcelona: ACTAR, 1996); *October* 79 (Winter 1997), special issue on Guy Debord and the SI, edited by Thomas McDonough; and Gianfranco Marelli, *L'amara vittoria del situazionismo* (Pisa, Italy: BFS Edizioni, 1996). Most recently, see Simon Sadler, *The Situationist City* (Cambridge: MIT Press, 1998), and Mark Wigley, *Constant's New Babylon: The Hyper-Architecture of Desire* (Rotterdam: 010 Publishers, 1998). The best general reference text in English is still Ken Knabb, ed. and trans., *Situationist International Anthology* (Berkeley: Bureau of Public Secrets, 1990). On the SI's urban practices, see Thomas Levin, "Geopolitics of Hibernation," in *Situationists: Art, Politics, Urbanism*.

2. Johan Huizinga, *Homo Ludens: A Study of the Play Element in Culture* (Boston: Beacon Press, 1990), 110. While the importance of Huizinga's writings for the SI is often noted, no effort has yet been made to examine it in detail. Two recent books on the SI, Sadie Plant's *The Most Radical Gesture: The Situationist International in a Postmodern Age* (London: Routledge, 1992) and Anselm Jappe's *Debord* (Pescara, Italy: Edizioni Tracce, 1992), for example, contain no mention of Huizinga, one of the few acknowledged sources of the SI. See in particular Guy Debord, "Architecture and Play," reprinted in Libero Andreotti and Xavier Costa, eds., *Theory of the Dérive and Other Situationist Writings on the City* (Barcelona: ACTAR, 1996), 53–54. According

to Debord, Huizinga's "latent idealism and narrowly sociological understanding of the higher forms of play do not diminish his work's basic worth." In fact, "it would be futile to want to find any other motive behind our theories of architecture and drifting than a passion for play," adding that "what we must do now is change the rules of the game from arbitrary conventions to ones with a moral basis." A year before this article appeared in *Potlatch* 20 (May 1955), André Breton praised Huizinga's work in *Medium* 2 and 3 (February and May 1954) and linked it to various surrealist games. See Mirella Bandini, *La vertigine del moderno: percorsi surrealisti* (Rome: Officina Edizioni, 1986), 152ff.

3. Huizinga, *Homo Ludens,* 12 and passim. A suggestive discussion of the player's anti-objectifying stance and play's "total mediation of form and content" is Hans Georg Gadamer's in *Truth and Method* (New York: Crossroad, 1986), 91–113. See also Roger Caillois, *Les jeux et les hommes—le masque et le vertige* (Paris: Gallimard, 1967), and Giorgio Agamben, "In Playland: Reflections on History and Play," in *Infancy and History: Essays on the Destruction of Experience* (London: Verso, 1993), 65–88.

4. Gallizio is often incorrectly referred to as "Giuseppe Pinot Gallizio." Pinot is short for Giuseppe.

5. Huizinga, *Homo Ludens,* 12.

6. Ed Van der Elsken and André Deutsch, *Love on the Left Bank* (Haarlem: Verenigde Drukkerijen, n.d.). See also the recollections of an LI member in Jean-Michel Mension, *La tribu* (Paris: Allia, 1999).

7. Huizinga, *Homo Ludens,* 153.

8. Guy Debord and Asger Jorn, *Mémoires* (1957; Paris: Jean-Jacques Pauvert aux Belles Lettres, 1993).

9. "Me souvenir de toi? oui, je veux," "Le soir, Barbara," "pleine de discorde et d'épouvante," "il s'agit d'un sujet profondément imprégné d'alcool."

10. See Guy Debord and Gil Wolman, "Methods of Détournement," in Knabb, ed., *Situationist International Anthology,* 8, and "Détournement as Negation and Prelude," in ibid., 55–56.

11. This was a weeklong drift around Christmas of 1953. All the places mentioned in the account (including the Île de la Cité, Les Halles, the Samaritaine department store, and the Contrescarpe district) are shown on this page of *Mémoires.* See Guy Debord, "Two Accounts of the Dérive," in Andreotti and Costa, ed., *Theory of the Dérive,* 28–32.

12. "Position du Continent Contrescarpe," in *Les lèvres nues* 9 (November 1956), 40.

13. See especially "The Elements of Mythopoiesis," in Huizinga, *Homo Ludens,* 136–146.

14. *Une ville flottante* is also the title of a book by Jules Verne on the steamboat used to lay the telegraph cable across the Atlantic in 1867.

15. "Position du Continent Contrescarpe," 40.

16. Debord also designed a board game entitled *Le jeu de la guerre* (Paris: Société des Jeux Stratégiques et Historiques, 1977). See also his reflections on war in *Commentaires sur la société du spectacle* (Paris: Editions Gérard Lebovici, 1988).

17. See Joseph Gabel, *False Consciousness: An Essay on Reification* (Bristol, UK: Blackwell, 1975), 148 and passim.

18. In *Les lèvres nues* 5 (June 1955), 28, an anonymous writer notes the similarity, which would have been consistent with Madeleine de Scudéry's naturalist philosophy. In the *Carte du pays de Tendre,* the River of Inclination leads from the town of Budding Friendship toward the uncharted territories of Love above. It divides the Land of Reason on the right, dominated by the Lake of Indifference, from the Land of Passion on the left, stretching out toward the Forest of Madness. On *The Naked City,* see also Tom McDonough's perceptive comments in "Situationist Space," reprinted in this volume, 241–265. Another likely source for *The Naked City* would have been the erotic novel of Jens August Schade, *Des êtres se rencontrent et une douce musique s'élève dans leurs coeurs* (Paris: Editions Gérard Lebovici, 1991), describing the aimless wanderings of the libertine, constantly falling in and out of love and unable to keep a fixed course. Schade's novel was first published in French in 1947 and was widely read in Debord's circle.

19. Guy Debord, "Theory of the Dérive," in Andreotti and Costa, eds., *Theory of the Dérive,* 26.

20. Kristin Ross, "French Quotidien," in Lynn Gumpert, ed., *The Art of the Everyday: The Quotidian in Postwar French Culture* (New York: New York University Press, 1997), 22.

21. Huizinga, *Homo Ludens,* 158–172.

22. Ibid., 203–204. See also Mirella Bandini, *L'estetico e il politico: da Cobra all'Internazionale Situazionista 1948–1957* (Rome: Officina Edizioni, 1977), 170–181, and the many letters from Debord to Gallizio in the Gallizio archive, Museo Civico di Torino.

23. Debord, "Architecture and Play," 53.

24. See "Die Welt als labyrinth" in *Internationale situationniste* 4 (June 1960), 5–7.

25. On New Babylon, see Jean-Clarence Lambert, ed., *Constant, New Babylon: art et utopie* (Paris: Cercle d'Art, 1997), and now Mark Wigley, *Constant's New Babylon: The Hyperarchitecture of Desire.* As Roberto Ohrt notes in *Phantomavantgarde: Eine Geschichte der Situationistischen Internationale und der modernen Kunst* (Hamburg: Edition Nautilus, 1990), the title was also a likely reference to the 1929 film by Kosinzev and Trauberg, *Nowi Wawilon,* on the

Paris Commune, that moment of utopian transformation presented by the SI as "the only realization of a revolutionary urbanism to date." See *Internationale situationniste* 12 (September 1969), 110.

26. See Levin, "Geopolitics of Hibernation," 128.

27. Gilles Ivain, "Formulary for a New Urbanism," in Andreotti and Costa, eds., *Theory of the Dérive,* 14–17.

28. Constant, "A Different City for a Different Life," translated in this volume, 95–96.

29. See Constant, "La révolte de l'Homo ludens," in Lambert, ed., *Constant, New Babylon,* 127–158.

30. See, in particular, "Critique de l'urbanisme," *Internationale situationniste* 6 (August 1961), 6, translated in this volume as "Editorial Notes: Critique of Urbanism," 104; "Now, the SI," *Internationale situationniste* 9 (August 1964), reprinted in Knabb, ed., *Situationist International Anthology,* 135–136. Other critiques of Constant are in "Révolte et récupération en Hollande," *Internationale situationniste* 11 (October 1967), 66, and "L'avant-garde de la présence," *Internationale situationniste* 8 (January 1963), 17, translated in this volume as "The Avant-Garde of Presence," 142, 144.

31. On the SI and May '68, see René Viénet, *Enragés et situationnistes dans le mouvement des occupations* (Paris: Gallimard, 1968), and Pascal Dumontier, *Les situationnistes et mai 68: théorie et pratique de la révolution (1966–1972)* (Paris: Editions Gérard Lebovici, 1990).

32. Huizinga, *Homo Ludens,* 145.

33. See Jappe, *Debord,* 30–48.

34. See my "Leaving the Twentieth Century: The Internationale Situationniste," *Journal of Architectural Education* (February 1996).

35. Renato Poggioli, *The Theory of the Avant-Garde* (Cambridge: Harvard University Press, 1968), 26.

36. Guy Debord, *Panegyric* (London: Verso, 1991), 25.

Situationist Space

Tom McDonough

I The Naked City

In the summer of 1957, the International Movement for an Imaginist Bauhaus, an avant-garde group composed of various ex-CoBrA artists and their Italian counterparts,[1] published a singularly odd map of Paris entitled *The Naked City,* the creation of which was credited to G[uy]-E[rnest] Debord. The publication of this map was in fact one of the last actions taken by this group, as it had recently decided to join with the French Lettrist International—of which Debord was the most significant member—and the English Psychogeographical Society of London in order to form the Situationist International.[2] The map served both as a summary of many of the concerns shared by the three organizations, particularly around the question of the construction and perception of urban space, and as a demonstration of the directions to be explored by the SI in the following years. Surprisingly little attention has been accorded this document, despite the fact that it has become an almost iconic image of the early years of the group, appearing on dust jackets and as an illustration in several major books and articles devoted to its history.

The Naked City is composed of nineteen cut-out sections of a map of Paris, printed in black ink, which are linked by directional arrows printed in red. Its

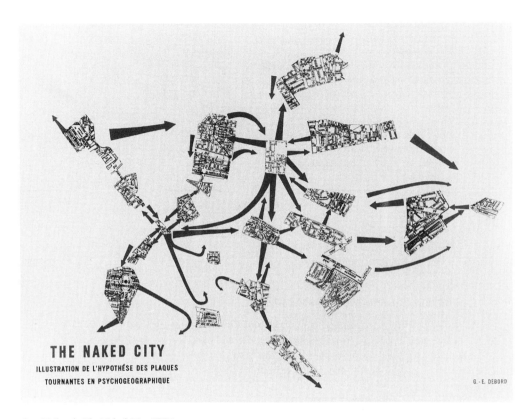

Guy Debord, *The Naked City,* 1957.

subtitle describes the map as an "illustration of the hypothesis of psychogeographical turntables." Appropriated by Debord, the term *plaque tournante,* which usually denotes a railway turntable (a circular revolving platform with a track running along its diameter, used for turning locomotives), here describes the function of the arrows linking the segments of the psychogeographical map. Each segment has a different "unity of atmosphere." The arrows describe "the spontaneous turns of direction taken by a subject moving through these surroundings in disregard of the useful connections that ordinarily govern his conduct."[3] Linking various "unities of atmosphere" and dictating the path taken by the given subject, these turns correspond to the action of the turntable, which links various segments of track and dictates the orientation of the locomotive. The implications of analogizing the subject to a locomotive are, of course, founded on a certain ambiguity: although self-propelled, the locomotive's path is determined within strict boundaries, just as, for the situationists, the subject's freedom of movement is restricted by the instrumentalized image of the city propagated under the reign of capital.

It is immediately apparent that *The Naked City* did not function like an ordinary map. This observation is confirmed when its antecedents in the *Carte du Tendre* of Madeleine de Scudéry are examined. Cited in a 1959 article in the journal *Internationale situationniste,* the *Carte* had been created three hundred years earlier in 1653 by Scudéry and the members of her salon and used the metaphor of the spatial journey to trace possible histories of a love affair.[4] Key geographical features, through pathetic fallacy, mark significant moments or emotions (e.g., the "lac d'indifférence"). Positing this aristocratic diversion as an antecedent of *The Naked City* is another instance of appropriation, but despite its very different origins, the *Carte* did illustrate the key principle of the psychogeographic map: its figuration as narrative rather than as tool of "universal knowledge." The users of these maps were asked to choose a directionality and to overcome obstacles, although there was no "proper" reading. The reading chosen was a performance of one among many possibilities (of the course of the love affair in the *Carte du Tendre;* of the crossing of the urban environment in *The Naked City*) and

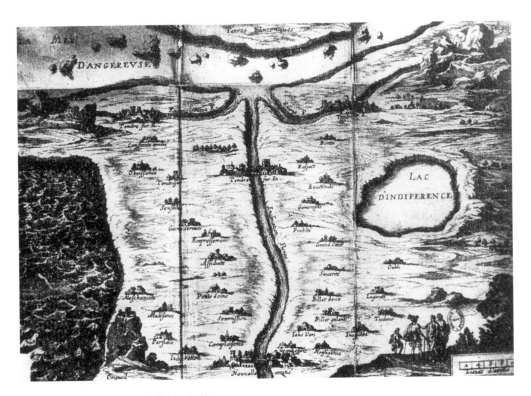

Madeleine de Scudéry, *Carte de Tendre*, 1653.

would remain contingent. The subject's achievement of a position of mastery, the goal of narrative's resolution, was thereby problematized.

The odd title, rendered in bright red capitals, was also an appropriation, taken from the name of an American film noir of 1948: *The Naked City,* a detective story set in New York and noted for its documentary style.[5] (The title of the film, however, is itself an appropriation: originally entitled *Homicide,* the movie's name was changed to match the title of a famous book of crime photographs by Weegee, published in 1945.)[6] Although the reference to this Hollywood film of the previous decade may at first seem arbitrary, its purpose becomes clear when one examines the structure of the movie. As Parker Tyler explains in *The Three Faces of the Film:*

> In *Naked City* it is Manhattan Island and its streets and landmarks that are starred. The social body is thus, through architectural symbol, laid bare ("naked"). . . . The fact that the vastly complex structure of a great city, in one sense, is a supreme obstacle to the police detectives at the same time that it provides tiny clues as important as certain obscure physical symptoms are to the trained eye of a doctor.[7]

Just as the term *turntable* serves as a useful analogy for the "spontaneous turns of direction" indicated on the map, so the title *The Naked City* serves as an analogy for the function of the map as a whole. It is no longer the streets and landmarks of Manhattan but those of Paris that are "starred": one quickly recognizes, in the cutout fragments, parts of the Jardin du Luxembourg, Les Halles, the Gare de Lyon, the Panthéon, and so forth. The act of "laying bare" the social body through the city's architectural symbols is implicit in the very structure of the map. Freed from the "useful connections that ordinarily govern their conduct," the users could experience "the sudden change of atmosphere in a street, the sharp division of a city into one of distinct psychological climates; the path of least resistance—wholly unrelated to the unevenness of the terrain—to be followed by the casual stroller; the character, attractive or repellant, of certain places."[8] So wrote Debord in his "Introduction to a Critique of Urban Geography" of 1955, two years before the publication of his map. For Debord the structure of Paris, like that of New York in the movie, was also a "great obstacle" that simultaneously offered "tiny clues"—only they were no longer clues to the solution of a crime, but to a future organization of life in its presentation of a "*sum of possibilities.*"

Visually, *The Naked City* is a collage based on the use of an already-existing document, composed of nineteen fragments of a map of Paris. It is significant in this light that in the "Introduction to a Critique of Urban Geography" Debord had discussed "a renovated cartography": "the production of psychogeographical maps may help to clarify certain movements of a sort that, while surely not gratuitous, are wholly insubordinate to the usual directives."[9] These influences or attractions determine the habitual patterns through which residents negotiate the city. The complete "insubordination" of such influences is realized in *The Naked City* by the fragmenting of the most popular map of Paris, the *Plan de Paris,* into a state of near-illegibility. *The Naked City* subverts the structure of that canonical map. The latter is structured in a way analogous to the mode of discourse called "description," which acts to "mask its successive nature and present it as redundant repetition, as if all were present at the same time. It is as if the object [here, the city of Paris] were always already visually present, fully offered to full view."[10] The Paris of the *Plan* exists in a timeless present; this timelessness is imaged spatially in the map's (illusory) total revelation of its object. Users of the map see the entire city laid out before their eyes; however, such an omnipresent view is seen from nowhere: "it is in fact impossible to occupy this space. It is a point of space where no man can see: a no place not outside space but nowhere, utopic."[11]

If the *Plan de Paris* is structured by description, which is predicated on a model of seeing that constitutes an exhibition of "the knowledge of an order of places,"[12] then a very different mode of discourse structures *The Naked City*. It is predicated on a model of moving, on "spatializing actions," known to the situationists as *dérives;* rather than presenting the city from a totalizing point of view, it organizes movements metaphorically around psychogeographic hubs. These movements constitute narratives that are openly diachronic, unlike description's false "timelessness."[13] *The Naked City* makes it clear, in its fragmenting of the conventional, descriptive representation of urban space, that the city is only ex-

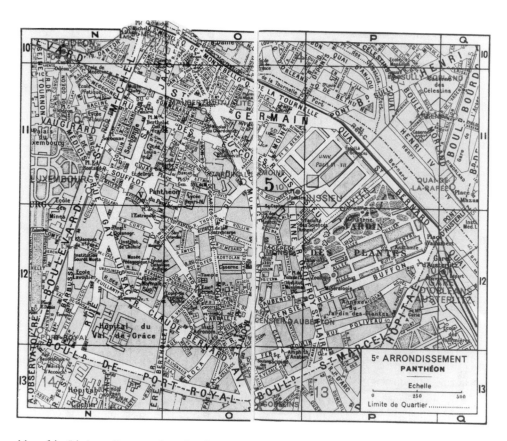

Map of the 5th Arrondissement, from the *Plan de Paris*.

perienced in time by a concrete, situated subject, as a passage from one "unity of atmosphere" to another, not as the object of a totalized perception.

II THE NAKED CITY AND SOCIAL GEOGRAPHY

But the narrative mode does not fully account for the appearance of Debord's map. First, *The Naked City* does not cover all of Paris, as would be expected of any "good" map. Second, the fragments have no logical relation to one another; they are not properly oriented according to north-south or east-west axes, and the distance between them does not correspond to the actual distance separating the various locales. (Consider, for instance, the distance separating the Jardin des Plantes from its annex, which are contiguous in the *Plan de Paris*.) Debord explains these features in his article of 1956, "Theory of the Dérive." The fragments only represent certain areas of Paris because the map's goal is "the discovery of unities of atmosphere, of their main components and of their spatial localization."[14] Presumably, not all areas in the city lend themselves to such spatial localization; *The Naked City* names parts of the city (certain "unities of atmosphere") instead of the whole ("Paris") that includes them. Through this synecdochic procedure, totalities like the Paris of the *Plan de Paris* are replaced by fragments like the components of Debord's map.[15] But beyond the "discovery" of such unities of atmosphere, the map also describes "their chief axes of passage, their exits and their defenses." The psychogeographical turntables of the map's subtitle allow one to assert "distances that may be quite out of scale with what one might conclude from a map's approximations."[16] Such distances become blank areas in *The Naked City*, gaps that separate the various fragments. The suppression of the linkages between various "unities of atmosphere," except for schematic directional arrows, corresponds to the procedure called "asyndeton"—a process of "opening gaps in the spatial continuum" and "retaining only selected parts of it."[17]

Structuring *The Naked City* through synecdoche and asyndeton disrupts the false continuity of the *Plan de Paris*. The city map is revealed as a representation: the production of a discourse about the city. This discourse is predicated on the appearance of optical coherence, on what Henri Lefebvre called the reduction of the city to "the undifferentiated state of the visible-readable realm."[18] This abstract space homogenizes the conflicts that produce capitalist space; the terrain of the *Plan de Paris* is that of Haussmannized Paris, where modernization had evicted the working class from its traditional quarters and then segregated the city along class lines. But abstract space is riddled with contradictions; it not only conceals difference, but its acts of division and exclusion are themselves productive of difference. Distinctions and differences are not eradicated; they are only hidden in the homogeneous space of the *Plan. The Naked City* brings these distinctions and differences out into the open, the violence of its fragmentation suggesting the real violence involved in constructing the former's homogeneity.

In this manner *The Naked City* engages the discourse of geography. In France, academic geography was a product of the 1870s; in the wake of the defeat suffered in the Franco-Prussian War, a number of historians around Paul Vidal de la Blanche founded what may be called a "spatial history." Vidalian geography considered itself a "science of landscape" whose goal was taxonomic description; but, as in the *Plan de Paris,* "description" cannot be considered an ideologically neutral term. By presuming an already "given" object of study (country, region, city), this geography hypostatized as transhistorical concepts that were actually the products of particular historical relations. Moreover, the geographer's interest in description privileges visual criteria that depend on the illusion of an object "fully offered to full view," a view that is gendered as masculine, from which a feminized space is perceived. (Vidal for example spoke of the eye "embracing" the landscape, which "offers itself up" to view.)[19] But there is a curious contradiction in Vidal's methodology of description: despite his reliance on the visual presence of the object of study, his landscapes cannot actually be seen. That is, he is not so much concerned with an observable, concrete space, but with a typical, abstract space that is constructed from a "synthetic and derivative mobilization of cliché" in the form of various exoticisms, references to literature, and enumerations of local flora and fauna.[20] The abstract space of academic geography is the source of the homogeneous, abstract space of the *Plan de Paris.*

In making *The Naked City,* however, Debord was not simply refuting an eighty-year-old tradition of academic geography; he was also, unconsciously, reasserting the goals of a social geography. "Social geography" was a term first used by Elisée Reclus, a communard, socialist, and geographer for whom geography would become "history in space." Unlike Vidal's "geography of permanences," geography for Reclus is "not an immutable thing. It is made, it is remade, every day; at each instant, it is modified by men's actions."[21] Rather than explaining spatial organization, like Vidal, as the consequence of inevitable social processes (mediated by deterministic metaphors, as in the "individuality" or "personality" of a region), Reclus theorized space as a social product and thus as inseparable from the functioning of society. Two dissimilar concepts of society are being proposed in these geographies. On the one hand, Vidal desocializes the social, employing an "environmental determinism" in which "forms of metropolitan social life" are the adaptations of "human populations to environments in which certain processes tend to remain constant and invariable." On the other hand, Reclus understands space as a socially produced category—as an arena "where social relations are reproduced" and as a social relation itself.[22] Debord, developing similar ideas, would also comprehend this indivisibility of urban space and social relations; but with the experience of psychogeographic exploration, space could also be the arena for the contestation of these relations through an active construction of new "unities of atmosphere."

Debord was most likely unaware of Elisée Reclus, but he did know of a French sociologist whose work of the early 1950s was concerned with such "social space" and with urbanism: Paul-Henry Chombart de Lauwe. Debord quotes Chombart de Lauwe's "Paris and the Parisian Agglomeration" (1952) in his "Theory of the Dérive."[23] Even more significant, *The Naked City* adapts the form of a map that appears in Chombart de Lauwe's report. This map, made by Louis Couvreur (a researcher working along with Chombart de Lauwe), depicts "the residential units of the 'Wattignies' district in the 12th Arrondissement of Paris."[24] In the 1952 report, Chombart de Lauwe defines the elementary unit of the city as the residential unit or, as its inhabitants call it, the *quartier:* "a group of streets, or even of houses, with more or less clearly defined borders, including a commercial center of variable size and, usually, other sorts of points of attraction. The borders of a neighborhood are usually marginal (dangerous) frontier

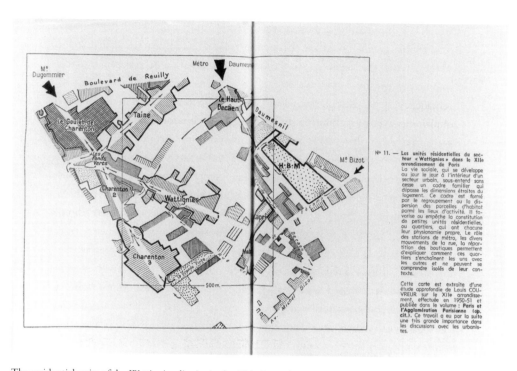

The residential units of the Wattignies district in the 12th Arrondissement, from Chombart de Lauwe, *Paris and the Parisian Agglomeration.*

areas."[25] It is important that these *quartiers* are not "given" urban districts, clearly defined and logically linked one to the other. Rather, Chombart de Lauwe states that they "reveal themselves . . . to the attentive observer" in "the behavior of the inhabitants, their turns of phrase."[26]

Clearly dependent on these ideas, Debord also altered them in the fabrication of the psychogeographic map. For example, the notion of the *quartier* as the basic unit of urban structure is held in common by both Debord and Chombart de Lauwe; for both, it is the site of social life and possesses a distinct character. (Chombart de Lauwe, in a telling naturalizing metaphor, writes that each *quartier* has its own "physiognomy.") However, Chombart de Lauwe defines this space as a "residential unit," giving it a preeminently functional role, whereas Debord defines it as a "unity of atmosphere," which proves to be a much less empirical idea. Chombart de Lauwe ultimately relies on the notion that *quartiers* can be "discovered," their existence proven, through more or less traditional research methods. Space is thought of here as a context or container for social relations— an idea that hypostatizes both space and the social. But space does not simply reflect social relations; it is constitutive of and is constituted by them. That is, the *quartier* is not only the expression of the needs of its inhabitants, the spatial form of their social relations; as Rosalyn Deutsche has written, it is also "an arena for the reproduction of social relations and is itself such a relation."[27] Debord's psychogeography and its graphic representation in *The Naked City* take this into account, constructing "unities of atmosphere" rather than "discovering" them like physical, geographical phenomena that exist in a spatial context. *The Naked City* denies space as context and instead incorporates space as an element of social practice. Rather than a container suitable for description, space becomes part of a process: the process of "inhabiting" enacted by social groups.

In this respect Debord takes up a position some distance from Chombart de Lauwe, but one that is quite close to certain ideas developed by Henri Lefebvre later in the 1960s. Lefebvre was also interested in the *quartier* as the essential unit of social life. Like Debord, he chose to study "not the ossified socioecological forms (which are, by definition, inapprehensible), but the tendencies of the urban units, their inertia, their explosion, their reorganization, in a word, the practice of 'inhabiting,' rather than the ecology of the habitat."[28] Although Lefebvre here refers to the Chicago School of urban ecology, his distance from Chombart de Lauwe's functionalist model of urban sociology is clear enough. Against such a model he posits the notion of "inhabiting"—what the situationists called "experimental behavior"—a practice, as will be seen, mapped in *The Naked City.*

III The Naked City and Cognitive Mapping

Debord's map images a fragmented city that is both the result of multiple restructurings of a capitalist society and the very form of a radical critique of this society. Its figuration of a type of inhabiting is simultaneously related to and distinct from Fredric Jameson's "aesthetic of cognitive mapping," a concept most succinctly described in his classic article "Postmodernism, or the Cultural Logic of Late Capitalism." Jameson concludes that fragmentations of urban space and the social body create the need for maps that would "enable a situational representation on the part of the individual subject to that vaster and properly unrepresentable totality which is the ensemble of the city's structure as a whole."[29] These maps would allow their users to "again begin to grasp our positioning as individual and collective subjects and regain a capacity to act and struggle which is at present neutralized by our spatial as well as our social confusion."[30] Certainly Debord also saw the "spatial confusion" of the modern city as symptomatic of the violence inherent in capitalism's configuration of the space of the production and reproduction of its social relations. *The Naked City,* however, adamantly refuses the status of a regulative ideal, which is the goal of the cognitive map. If the latter is a means toward "a capacity to act and struggle," the former is a site of struggle itself. In its very form it contests a dominant construction of urban space as homogeneous, appropriating pieces of the *Plan de Paris* and making them speak of the radical discontinuities and divisions of the public realm. The cognitive map's normative function relies on the production of a spatial imagability that desires to assume what Rosalyn Deutsche has called "a commanding position on the battleground of representation."[31] The danger in this position is that the positionality of the viewer and relations of representation are sacrificed in order to obtain a "coherent," "logical" view of the city. Debord's map, on the other hand, foregrounds its contingency by structuring itself as a narrative open to numerous readings. It openly acknowledges itself as the trace of practices of inhabiting rather than an imaginary resolution of real contradictions. Likewise, its representation of the city only exists as a series of relationships, as in those between *The Naked City* and the *Plan de Paris,* or between fragmentation and unity, or between narrative and description.

IV THE *DÉRIVE* AND SOCIAL SPACE

Debord wrote in *The Society of the Spectacle* that under advanced capitalism "everything that was directly lived has moved away into a representation."[32] As formulated by Lefebvre, the corollary to this in spatial discourse was that directly lived space ("representational space") had moved away into the space of the conceived and the perceived ("representations of space"). Social, concrete space was denied in favor of mental, abstract space—"*the free space of the commodity.*"[33] However, this thoroughly dominated capitalist space was not seamless; in fact, it was full of contradictions, hidden only by a homogenizing ideology. These contradictions made possible the struggle formulated by the situationist project: the exploration of psychogeography and the construction of spaces that accommodated difference. Situationist "experimental behavior," their practice of "inhabiting," was an operation in dominated space meant to contest the retreat of the directly lived into the realm of representation, and thereby to contest the organization of the society of the spectacle itself.

The move from abstract space to social space can be seen in condensed form in the different attitudes taken toward aerial photographs by Chombart de Lauwe and the situationists. In Chombart de Lauwe's 1952 report, he reproduces an aerial photograph of the city center of Paris along with its immediate suburbs. He writes that such photographs permit a better understanding of certain structures and the contrasts between "the different kinds of urban fabric." He cites the different fabrics of the bourgeois districts on the one hand (the 7th and

17th arrondissements), and on the other hand the "popular" *quartiers* (Belleville and Menilmontant), the former characterized by regularity, the latter by disorder. From these visual characteristics, he asserts, one may deduce the respective conditions of life and social practices of each *quartier*.[34] Chombart de Lauwe's praise of the aerial photograph as a research tool raises the question posed by Michel de Certeau in *The Practice of Everyday Life:* "Is the immense texturology spread out before one's eyes anything more than a representation, an optical artifact?" The elevation provided by "the overflight at high altitude" transforms the sociologist into a voyeur of sorts, who not only enjoys the erotics of seeing all from his hidden vantage point, but who also enjoys the erotics of knowing all. The scopic and epistemophilic drives unite in their mutual search for pleasure taken in the totality of the city as seen in the "vue verticale" of the aerial photograph (or of the *Plan de Paris,* for that matter). But this whole is imaginary, a fiction, and "the voyeur-god created by this fiction . . . must disentangle himself from the murky intertwining daily behaviors and make himself alien to them."[35]

It is precisely this disentanglement, this alienation, that the situationists refused by locating cultural struggle within the city. In contrast to Chombart de Lauwe's faith in the knowledge provided by the spectacularized image of the city as seen in the aerial photograph, they refuted this voyeuristic viewpoint. The first issue of *Internationale situationniste* reprinted an aerial photograph very similar to that discussed by Chombart de Lauwe, but this photograph was not used for ascertaining the structure of the city. Instead it bore the caption "New Theater of Operations in Culture." The military term indicated the refusal to take up the disengaged position implied in Chombart de Lauwe's interest in the aerial photograph. Rejecting this viewpoint, the situationists opted precisely for the "murky intertwining behaviors" that the sociologist placed at a distance. With the city as their "theater of operations" their primary tactic was the *dérive,* which reflected the pedestrian's experience, that of the everyday user of the city. The *dérive* took place literally below the threshold of visibility of that aerial overview, beyond what is visible to the sociologist-voyeur's gaze. As Debord describes it, the *dérive* replaced the figure of the voyeur with that of the walker: "One or more persons committed to the *dérive* abandon, for an undefined period of time, the

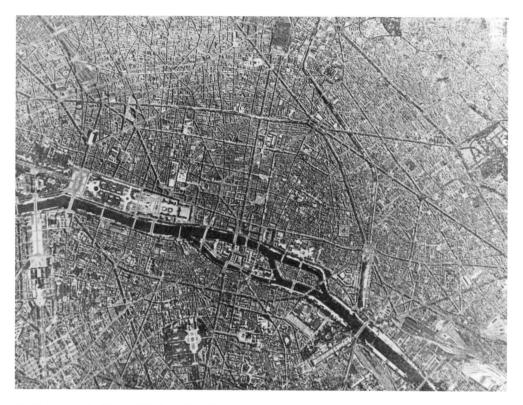

Aerial photograph of Paris, 1950, from Chombart de Lauwe, *Paris and the Parisian Agglomeration*.

motives generally admitted for action and movement, their relations, their labor and leisure activities, abandoning themselves to the attractions of the terrain and the encounters proper to it."[36] In allowing themselves "to be drawn by the solicitations of the terrain," persons on the *dérive* escaped the imaginary totalizations of the eye and instead chose a kind of blindness.[37]

Operating in the realm of everyday life, the *dérive* constitutes an urban practice that must be distinguished, first, from "classic notions of the journey and the walk," as Debord noted in "Theory of the Dérive." The *dérive* was not simply an updating of nineteenth-century *flânerie*, the Baudelairean strolling of the "man in the crowd." This is not to say that they do not share some characteristics: both the *flâneur* and the person on the *dérive* move among the crowd without being one with it. They are both "already out of place," neither bourgeois nor working-class.[38] But whereas the *flâneur's* ambiguous class position represents a kind of aristocratic holdover (a position that is ultimately recuperated by the bourgeoisie), the person on the *dérive* consciously attempts to suspend class allegiances for some time. This serves a dual purpose: it allows for a heightened receptivity to the "psychogeographical relief" of the city as well as contributing to the sense of "dépaysement,"[39] a characteristic of the ludic sphere. For the situationists, however, the *dérive* was distinguished from *flânerie* primarily by its critical attitude toward the hegemonic scopic regime of modernity. As Griselda Pollock describes him (the *flâneur*, unlike the participant of the *dérive*, was an exclusively masculine type), the *flâneur* is characterized by a detached, observing gaze: "The *flâneur* symbolizes the privilege or freedom to move about the public arenas of the city observing but never interacting, consuming the sights through a controlling but rarely acknowledged gaze. . . . The *flâneur* embodies the gaze of modernity which is both covetous and erotic."[40] It is precisely these class- and gender-specific privileges that the *dérive* critiques in its refusal of the controlling gaze. The city and its quarters are no longer conceived of as "spontaneously visible objects" but are posited as social constructions through which the *dérive* negotiates while simultaneously fragmenting and disrupting them.

The situationists also located the *dérive* in relation to surrealist experiments in space. In his article on the *dérive*, Debord cited "the celebrated aimless stroll"

NOUVEAU THÉATRE D'OPÉRATIONS
DANS LA CULTURE

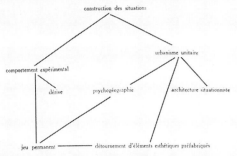

LA DISSOLUTION DES IDEES ANCIENNES VA DE PAIR AVEC LA DISSOLUTION DES ANCIENNES
CONDITIONS D'EXISTENCE :

INTERNATIONALE SITUATIONNISTE

From *International situationniste* 1 (June 1958).

undertaken in May 1924 by Aragon, Breton, Morise, and Vitrac, whose course was determined by chance procedures. The surrealists had embraced chance as the encounter with the totally heterogeneous, an emblem of freedom in an otherwise reified society. Clearly this type of journey was resonant for the situationists; for example, in 1955 Debord discussed a similar trip that a friend took "through the Hartz region in Germany, with the help of a map of the city of London from which he blindly followed the directions."[41] However, Debord would go on to critique the surrealist experiments for an "insufficient mistrust of chance." Perhaps, paralleling Peter Bürger's argument, Debord felt that these diversions had degenerated from protests against bourgeois society's instrumentalization to protests against means-end rationality as such. Without such rationality, however, no meaning can be derived from chance occurrences, and the individual is placed in a position of a "passive attitude of expectation."[42] Given that the situationists were interested not only in the discovery of the uncanny, or the making strange of familiar urban terrain, but in the transformation of urban space, their mistrust of surrealist chance is understandable.

The blindness of the people on the *dérive* was a tactical practice, dependent neither upon spectacular consumption of the city nor upon factors of chance. This blindness, characteristic of the everyday user of the city who confronts the environment as opaque, was consciously adopted in order to subvert the rational city of pure visuality. The *dérive* was a tactic in the classic military sense of the term, "a calculated action determined by the absence of a proper locus."[43] Or, in the words of Clausewitz, a military theorist Debord greatly admired, the *dérive* as a tactic was an "art of the weak."[44] It is a game (Debord writes that the *dérive* entailed "a ludic-constructive behavior")[45] that takes place in the strategic space of the city: "it must play on and with a terrain imposed on it and organized by the law of a foreign power. It does not have the means to *keep to itself,* at a distance, in a position of withdrawal, foresight, and self-collection: it is a maneuver 'within the enemy's field of vision,' as von Bulow put it, and within enemy territory."[46] The *dérive,* therefore, does not possess a space of its own, but takes place in a space that is imposed by capitalism in the form of urban planning.

The *dérive* appropriates this urban space in the context of what may be called a "pedestrian speech act," in that "the act of walking is to the urban system what the speech act is to language."[47] Through the conscious appropriation of the city, the situationists force it to speak of the divisions and fragmentations masked by abstract space, the contradictions that enable political struggle over the production of space to exist at all. The fragmented space of the city, as actualized in the *dérive,* is precisely what is imaged in *The Naked City,* with its invention of *quartiers,* its shifting about of spatial relations, and its large white blanks of non-actualized space—whole segments of Paris that are made to disappear, or rather that never even existed in the first place. The *dérive* as a pedestrian speech act is a reinstatement of the "use value of space" in a society that privileges the "exchange value of space"—its existence as property. In this manner, the *dérive* is a political use of space, constructing new social relations through its "ludic-constructive behavior."

V The *Dérive* and Representations of Public Space

This contestation over the signification of public space leaves unaddressed the question of the very status of this space in the postwar period. It has been argued that with the increasingly rapid growth of mass media through the 1950s, the formerly contested realm of the streets was evacuated. It was, after all, precisely technologies of the home—first radio, then television—that were the conduits for spectacular society's attempts to domesticate fantasy. In this view, the *dérive* was doomed to being an anachronism. Indeed, some texts on the *dérive* and urban space seem curiously sentimental. For example, in the bulletin *Potlatch* in 1954 an article mourns the destruction of the rue Sauvage in the 13th arrondissement: "we lament the disappearance of a thoroughfare little known, and yet more *alive* than the Champs-Elysées and its lights." Despite the qualification that "we were not interested in the charms of ruins,"[48] it is easy to agree with Benjamin Buchloh that, with the rise of technologies for controlling the domestic interior, the street "would increasingly qualify as an artistic attraction, in the manner that all evacuated locations (ruins) and obsolete technologies appearing to be exempt from or abandoned by the logic of the commodity and the instrumentality of engineered desire had so qualified."[49] The city, however, has *not* been fully evacuated; the street is not left uncontaminated simply because spectacle culture has come to be administered primarily in the home—quite the opposite. The "evacuated" city was not so much "exempt from . . . the logic of the commodity" as it was made into the site of mythic discourse, a discourse wholly contingent upon spectacle culture.

Its meaning does not disappear; rather, it is put at a distance, held in reserve. If the public realm is no longer "hypersignificant"[50] or "filled," as it was before the advent of spectacle culture, it nonetheless must be acknowledged that its aesthetic role as "ruin" reproduces power. The "hyposignificant" city of myth is appropriated to various ends: its history is put back into play in harmless form as entertainment in, for example, tourist attractions where "public" space is commodified for very "private" consumption. (In his "Introduction to a Critique of Urban Geography," Debord cites tourism as that "popular drug as repugnant as sports or buying on credit.")[51] The "museumization" of Paris is one obvious example of this process. As stated earlier, these representations have a very definite ideological character: "the city is submitted to the norms of an abstract space which corresponds fairly precisely to the constitution of a political organization—the State—external to the daily activity of the citizens and to their attachment to the places they live in."[52] The situationists' antipathy toward the "charms of ruins" was precisely an acknowledgment that these "norms of abstract space" that construct the public domain as evacuated were not "charming" at all. But these representations were not impervious to contestation; in fact, the coherence of the city's signification was constantly threatening to break down. This was due to the fact that, despite the spectacle's hegemonic power, the production of the city remained a social practice, one that could not be fully instrumentalized. Contrary to the projections of spectacular society, which posited the city as a natural, timeless form, it existed only as "an environment formed by the interaction and the integration of different practices."[53] The *dérive* as a practice of the city reappropriated public space from the realm of myth, restoring it to its fullness, its richness, and its history. As an important tool in the situationists' struggle over who would speak through the city during the 1950s, the *dérive* was an attempt to change the meaning of the city through changing the way it was inhabited. And this struggle was conducted not in the name of a new cognitive map but in order to construct a more concrete collective space, a space whose potentialities remained open-ended for all participants in the "ludic-constructive" narrative of a new urban terrain.

Notes

Originally published in *October* 67 (Winter 1994), 59–77.

1. On the International Movement for an Imaginist Bauhaus, see Peter Wollen, "The Situationist International," *New Left Review* 174 (1989), 87–90.

2. The official history of the founding is told in Jean-François Martos, *Histoire de l'Internationale situationniste* (Paris: Editions Gérard Lebovici, 1989), 9–65. See Wollen, "The Situationist International," 87–90.

3. From a text printed on the reverse side of *The Naked City:* Asger Jorn, "Quatrième expérience du MIBI (Plans psychogéographiques de Guy Debord)," reprinted in Gérard Berreby, ed., *Documents relatifs à la fondation de l'Internationale situationniste: 1948–1957* (Paris: Editions Allia, 1985), 535.

4. The map was published in 1654 in her *Clélie: histoire romaine* (Geneva: Slatkine Reprints, 1973). It is cited in "L'urbanisme unitaire à la fin des années 50," *Internationale situationniste* 3 (December 1959), 11–16. On the map, see Claude Filteau, "Tendre," in *Cartes et figures de la terre* (Paris: Centre Georges Pompidou, 1980), 205–207.

5. Albert Maltz and Malvin Wald, *The Naked City* (Carbondale and Edwardsville: Southern Illinois University Press, 1979). Maltz, born in Brooklyn in 1908, was a mainstay of the American literary left throughout the 1930s; in 1941 he moved to Los Angeles, where he worked on several movies—generally either detective films (e.g., *This Gun for Hire,* 1942) or wartime propaganda movies (e.g., *Pride of the Marines,* 1945). In 1947 he was called before the House Committee on Un-American Activities for his involvement with the Communist Party in the 1930s; his refusal to testify led to his being named one of the "Hollywood Ten." *The Naked City* was his last film before being committed to federal prison in 1950. See Jack Salzman, *Albert Maltz* (Boston: G. K. Hall, 1978) for a full biography, which, however, slights Maltz's years in Hollywood.

6. Arthur Fellig (Weegee), *Naked City* (New York: Da Capo Press, 1975).

7. Parker Tyler, *The Three Faces of the Film: The Art, the Dream, the Cult,* rev. ed. (South Brunswick, N.J.: A. S. Barnes, 1967), 97.

8. Guy-Ernest Debord, "Introduction to a Critique of Urban Geography," in Ken Knabb, ed. and trans., *Situationist International Anthology* (Berkeley: Bureau of Public Secrets, 1981), 5–8.

9. Ibid., 7.

10. Louis Marin, *Utopics: Spatial Play,* trans. Robert A. Vollrath (Atlantic Highlands, N.J.: Humanities Press, 1984), 202.

11. Ibid., 207.

12. Michel de Certeau, *The Practice of Everyday Life,* trans. Steven Rendall (Berkeley: University of California Press, 1984), 119.

13. Marin, *Utopics,* 201–202. Although "narrative" may not be the ideal term to describe the structure of *The Naked City,* it does convey the sense that the map is a representation of an event—or more properly, a sum of events, i.e., the spatializing actions of the *dérive.*

14. Guy-Ernest Debord, "Theory of the Dérive," in Knabb, ed., *Situationist International Anthology,* 53.

15. De Certeau, *The Practice of Everyday Life,* 101.

16. Debord, "Theory of the Dérive," 53.

17. De Certeau, *The Practice of Everyday Life,* 101.

18. Henri Lefebvre, *The Production of Space,* trans. Donald Nicholson-Smith (Oxford and Cambridge, Mass.: Blackwell, 1991), 355–356.

19. This discussion of academic and social geography is indebted to the work of Kristin Ross in *The Emergence of Social Space: Rimbaud and the Paris Commune* (Minneapolis: University of Minnesota Press, 1988), 85–97. The space of narrative (e.g., of concealment and discovery in film noir) is also gendered; see Teresa de Lauretis, *Alice Doesn't: Feminism, Semiotics, Cinema* (Bloomington: Indiana University Press, 1984), and Laura Mulvey, "Visual Pleasure and Narrative Cinema," *Screen* 16, no. 3 (1975), 6–18. To the extent that Debord's *Naked City* may be compared with the narrative of film noir (as the map's title indicates), its point of view must be problematized; however, there are obviously significant differences in the subjects constructed by these respective "narratives." (Perhaps this is where the limits of the usefulness of this term for describing Debord's map are reached.)

20. Ross, *Emergence of Social Space,* 86–87.

21. Quoted in ibid., 91. For more on Elisée Reclus, see Gary S. Dunbar, *Elisée Reclus: Historian of Nature* (Hamden, Conn.: Archon Books, 1978), and Marie Fleming, *The Geography of Freedom: The Odyssey of Elisée Reclus* (Montreal: Black Rose Books, 1988).

22. See Rosalyn Deutsche, "Uneven Development: Public Art in New York City," *October* 47 (Winter 1988), 24. See also Manuel Castells, *The Urban Question: A Marxist Approach,* trans.

Alan Sheridan (Cambridge: MIT Press, 1977), and Peter R. Saunders, *Social Theory and the Urban Question* (New York: Holmes & Meier, 1981).

23. Paul-Henry Chombart de Lauwe, "Paris et l'agglomération parisienne" (1952), in *Paris: Essais de sociologie, 1952–1964* (Paris: Les éditions ouvriéres, 1965), 19–101. For Debord, see "Theory of the Dérive," 50. This dependence is noted in passing by Wollen in "The Situationist International," 80 n. 40.

24. Chombart de Lauwe, "Paris et l'agglomération parisienne," 60–61.

25. Ibid., 67.

26. Ibid.

27. Rosalyn Deutsche, "Alternative Space," in *If You Lived Here: A Project by Martha Rosler,* ed. Brian Wallis (Seattle: Bay Press, 1991), 55.

28. Henri Lefebvre, "Quartier et vie de quartier, Paris," *Cahiers de l'IAURP* 7 (1967).

29. Fredric Jameson, "Postmodernism, or the Cultural Logic of Late Capitalism," *New Left Review* 146 (1984), 90. See his more developed argument in "Cognitive Mapping," in Cary Nelson and Lawrence Grossberg, ed., *Marxism and the Interpretation of Culture* (Urbana: University of Illinois Press, 1988), 347–357.

30. Jameson, "Postmodernism, or the Cultural Logic of Late Capitalism," 92.

31. Rosalyn Deutsche, "Men in Space," *Artforum* 28, no. 6 (February 1990), 21–23. An expanded version of this article appeared as "Boys Town," *Society and Space* 9 (1991), 5–30.

32. Guy Debord, *Society of the Spectacle* (Detroit: Black & Red, 1977), 1.

33. Ibid., 166.

34. Chombart de Lauwe, "Paris et l'agglomération parisienne," 33–34.

35. De Certeau, *The Practice of Everyday Life,* 92–93.

36. Debord, "Theory of the Dérive," 50.

37. This use of the term "blindness" is to be distinguished from the paradoxical blindness of totalization that de Certeau discusses. Here it is meant to indicate the situationists' problematization of the scopic regime of modernity as formulated in the nineteenth century.

38. See Walter Benjamin, "On Some Motifs in Baudelaire," in *Illuminations,* ed. Hannah Arendt, trans. Harry Zohn (New York: Schocken Books, 1968), 172–173.

39. *Dépaysement* is a term often found in early situationist writings on the *dérive*. Literally it means the condition of being "taken out of one's element" or "misled." The situationists seem to use the term in the same sense that Lévi-Strauss calls anthropology a "technique du dépaysement," in his essay "The Concept of Archaism in Anthropology" (in *Structural Anthropology,* trans. Claire Jacobson and Brooke Grundfest Schoepf [New York: Basic Books, 1963], 117,

118 n. 23). As the translators of this essay note, the term refers to "the conscious cultivation by the anthropologist of an attitude of marginality toward all cultures, including his [sic] own." The same attitude is cultivated by persons on the *dérive*.

40. Griselda Pollock, *Vision and Difference* (London: Routledge, 1988), 67.

41. Guy-Ernest Debord, "Introduction to a Critique of Urban Geography," trans. in Knabb, ed., *Situationist International Anthology,* 7.

42. Peter Bürger, *Theory of the Avant-Garde,* trans. Michael Shaw (Minneapolis: University of Minnesota Press, 1984), 66.

43. De Certeau, *The Practice of Everyday Life,* 36–37.

44. See Karl von Clausewitz, *On War,* trans. M. Howard and P. Paret (Princeton: Princeton University Press, 1976).

45. Debord, "Theory of the Dérive," 50. The ludic nature of the *dérive* is indebted to Johan Huizinga's *Homo Ludens: A Study of the Play-Element in Culture* (Boston: Beacon Press, 1950), a text originally published in 1937 and translated into French in 1951. Huizinga argued that humans are defined not merely by their functional or utilitarian behavior but also by their need for play; his ideas were of great interest to northern European situationists Constant and Asger Jorn, who were in close contact with Debord. On Huizinga and the situationists, see Wollen, "The Situationist International," 89.

46. De Certeau, *The Practice of Everyday Life,* 37.

47. Ibid., 97–99.

48. "On détruit la rue Sauvage," *Potlatch* 7 (3 August 1954), reprinted in Berreby, ed., *Documents relatifs à la fondation de l'Internationale situationniste,* 176. This article was followed up in "La forme d'une ville change plus vite," *Potlatch* 25 (26 January 1956), reprinted in *Documents relatifs,* 234–235.

49. Benjamin H. D. Buchloh, "From Detail to Fragment: Décollage Affichiste," *October* 56 (Spring 1991), 100.

50. A term adopted from Françoise Choay; cf. her "Sémiologie et urbanisme," *L'architecture d'aujourd'hui* 132 (1967).

51. Debord, "Introduction to a Critique of Urban Geography," 7.

52. Raymond Ledrut, "Speech and the Silence of the City," in M. Gottdiener and Alexandros Ph. Lagopoulos, eds., *The City and the Sign: An Introduction to Urban Semiotics* (New York: Columbia University Press, 1986), 125.

53. Ibid., 122.

Lefebvre on the Situationists: An Interview

KRISTIN ROSS

TRANSCRIBED BY MARIE-FRANCE NIZET-SANGRONES

TRANSLATED BY KRISTIN ROSS

In the introduction to a recent anthology of Henri Lefebvre's writings on the city, the editors of the volume comment that the relationship between Lefebvrian and situationist concepts awaits a serious study.[1] What follows is less a serious study than an at times playful conversation in which Lefebvre recalls his relationship with Guy Debord and the Situationist International. The interview, if we may call it that, took place in 1983 at the University of California at Santa Cruz, where Lefebvre was, on the invitation of Fredric Jameson, a visiting scholar in residence. I had then just begun my own reading of Lefebvre and the situationists—research that would result in a book on Rimbaud and an issue of *Yale French Studies,* coedited with Alice Kaplan, on "everyday life."[2] From the outset of the conversation, it was evident that Lefebvre, then in his eighties, had very clear ideas of the directions he wanted to pursue.

HL Are you going to ask me questions about the situationists? Because I have something I'd like to talk about . . .
KR Fine, go ahead.
HL The situationists . . . It's a delicate subject, one I care deeply about. It touches me in some ways very intimately because I knew them very well. I was close friends with them. The friendship lasted from 1957 to 1961 or '62, which is to say about five years. And then we had a quarrel that got worse and worse in

conditions I don't understand too well myself but which I could describe to you. In the end it was a love story that ended badly, very badly. There are love stories that begin well and end badly. And this was one of them.

I remember a whole night spent talking at Guy Debord's place, where he was living with Michèle Bernstein in a kind of studio near the place I was living on the rue Saint Martin, in a dark room, no lights at all, a veritable . . . a miserable place, but, at the same time, a place where there was a great deal of strength and radiance in the thinking and the research.

KR They had no money?

HL No . . .

KR How did they live?

HL No one could figure out how they got by. One day, one of my friends (someone to whom I had introduced Debord) asked him: "What do you live on?" And Guy Debord answered very proudly, "I live off my wits" [*je vie d'expédients*]. [*Laughter*] Actually, he must have had some money; I think that his family wasn't poor. His parents lived on the Côte d'Azur. I don't think I really know the answer. And also Michèle Bernstein had come up with a very clever way to make money, or at least a bit of money. Or at least this is what she told me. She said that she did horoscopes for horses, which were published in racing magazines. It was extremely funny. She determined the date of birth of the horses and did their horoscopes in order to predict the outcome of the race. And I think there were racing magazines that published them and paid her.

KR So the situationist slogan "Never work" didn't apply to women?

HL Yes, it did, because this wasn't work. They didn't work; they managed to live without working to quite a large extent—of course, they had to do something. To do horoscopes for race horses, I suppose, wasn't really work; in any case, I think it was fun to do it, and they didn't really work.

But I'd like to go farther back in time, because everything started much earlier. It started with the CoBrA group. They were the intermediaries: the group made up of architects, with Constant in particular (the architect from Amsterdam), and Asger Jorn (the painter), and people from Brussels—it was a Nordic group, a group with considerable ambitions. They wanted to renew art, renew the action of art on life. It was an extremely interesting and active group that came together in the 1950s, and one of the books that inspired the founding of the group was my book *Critique de la vie quotidienne*.[3] That's why I got involved with them from such an early date. And the pivotal figure was Constant Nieuwenhuys, the utopian architect who designed a utopian city, New Babylon—a provocative name since in the Protestant tradition "Babylon" is a figure of evil. New Babylon was to be the figure of good that took the name of the cursed city and transformed itself into the city of the future. The design for New Babylon dates from 1950. And in 1953 Constant published a text called "Pour une architecture de situation." This was a fundamental text based on the idea that architecture would allow a transformation of daily reality. This was the connection with *Critique de la vie quotidienne*: to create an architecture that would itself instigate the creation of new situations. So this text was the beginning of a whole new research that developed in the following years. Especially since Constant was very close to popular movements; he was one of the instigators of the Provos, the Provo movement.

KR So there was a direct relationship between Constant and the Provos?

HL Oh yes, he was recognized by them as their thinker, their leader, the one who wanted to transform life and the city. The relation was direct; he spurred them on.

It's important to understand the periodization of the times. Politically, 1956 was an important year because of the end of Stalinism. There was Khrushchev's famous report to the Twentieth Congress of the Communist Party in the USSR, where he demolished the figure of Stalin—a report that was much discussed, argued about. In France people claimed that it was false, that it had been invented by the American secret service. In fact it was entirely the work of the one who succeeded Stalin, Nikita Khrushchev—and who demolished the figure of his predecessor. We have to keep the periodization in mind. During the postwar years, the figure of Stalin was dominant. And the Communist movement was *the* revolutionary movement. Then, after '56 or '57, revolutionary movements moved outside the organized parties, especially with Fidel Castro. In this sense, situationism wasn't at all isolated. Its point of origin was Holland, Paris too, but Holland especially, and it was linked to many events on the world scale, especially the fact that Fidel Castro succeeded in a revolutionary victory completely outside of the Communist movement and the workers' movement. This was an event. And I remember that in 1957 I published a kind of manifesto, "Le romantisme révolutionnaire," which was linked to the Castro story and to all the movements happening a little bit everywhere that were outside of the parties. This was when I left the Communist Party myself. I felt that there were going to be a lot of things happening outside the established parties and organized movements like unions.

There was going to be a spontaneity outside of organizations and institutions: that's what this text from 1957 was about. It was this text that put me into contact with the situationists, because they attached a certain importance to it—before attacking it later on. They had their critiques to make, of course; we were never completely in agreement, but the article was the basis for a certain understanding that lasted for four or five years—we kept coming back to it.

KR And at this point you were working on the second volume of the *Critique de la vie quotidienne*?

HL Yes, and also on a book about the Paris Commune . . .

KR You were working on both at once?

HL Yes, at the same time, in a state of confusion. It was the moment when I left the Party, the moment of the Algerian War. There was a lot going on . . . I was almost fired. I went before commissions for having . . . I wasn't in the university, I was a research director at the CNRS [Centre Nationale de la Recherche Scientifique] and I was almost dismissed for having signed manifestos for the Algerians and for having offered support—a feeble support, of course—to the Algerian cause. It was a moment of intense fermentation. But in France support for the Algerians didn't happen through the Party, nor through the official organizations within the Party or through the unions; it went on outside the institutions. The Communist Party only supported the Algerians grudgingly, in appearance only. In fact, they hardly helped them at all, and afterward the Algerians were very angry with the Party. An oppositional group within the Party, and also the movement outside of the Party: these were the only ones that supported the Algerians, and that played a role in this story, since we have to situate it within the context of the times and the political context.

And then there were the rather extremist movements like that of Isidore Isou and the lettrists. They also had ambitions on an international scale. But that was all a joke. It was evident in the way that Isidore Isou would recite his dadaist poetry made up of meaningless syllables and fragments of words. He would recite it in cafés. I remember very well having met him several times in Paris.

But even that showed a certain fermentation in French life, which was crystallized in the return of de Gaulle to power in 1958. The Communist Party showed a deep incapacity by not understanding Stalinism, by doing nothing for the Algerians, and by opposing de Gaulle's return to power very ineffectively, limiting itself to calling de Gaulle a fascist, which wasn't exactly the case. de Gaulle wanted to bring order to the Algerian question. He was the only one who could. We realized that later on. But, throughout, the period was one of a great fermentation, comparable to 1936.

KR Did the situationist theory of constructing situations have a direct relationship with your theory of "moments"?

HL Yes, that was the basis of our understanding. They more or less said to me during discussions—discussions that lasted whole nights—"What you call 'moments,' we call 'situations,' but we're taking it farther than you. You accept as 'moments' everything that has occurred in the course of history: love, poetry, thought. We want to create new moments."

KR How did they propose to make the transition from a "moment" to a conscious construction?

HL The idea of a new moment, of a new situation, was already there in Constant's text from 1953, "Pour une architecture de situation." Because the architecture of situation is a utopian architecture that supposes a new society, Constant's idea was that society must be transformed not in order to continue a boring, uneventful life, but in order to create something absolutely new: situations.

KR And how did the city figure into this?

HL Well, "new situations" was never very clear. When we talked about it, I always gave as an example—and they would have nothing to do with my example—love. I said to them: in antiquity, passionate love was known, but not individual love, love for an individual. The poets of antiquity write of a kind of cosmic, physical, physiological passion. But love for an individual only appears in the Middle Ages within a mixture of Islamic and Christian traditions, especially in the south of France. Individual love is Dante's love for Beatrice: *La vita nova,* new life. It's the love between Tristan and Yseult, tragic love: courtly love in the south of France. Where I come from near Navarrenx, there is the tower of Prince Gaston Phébus, who was the first prince-troubadour to sing songs about individual love: "When I sing, I do not sing for me, but I sing for my friend who is close to me." This is already individual love, the tragedy of individual love that endures throughout the centuries, in *La princesse de Clèves,* in novels, theaters, in Racine's *Bérénice,* through all of literature . . .

KR But didn't constructing "new situations" for the situationists involve urbanism?

HL Yes. We agreed. I said to them: individual love created new situations, there was a creation of situations. But it didn't happen in a day; it developed. Their idea (and this was also related to Constant's experiments) was that in the city one could create new situations by, for example, linking up parts of the city, neighborhoods that were separated spatially. And that was the first meaning of the *dérive.* It was done first in Amsterdam, using walkie-talkies. There was one group who went to one part of the city and could communicate with people in another area.

KR Did the situationists use this technique too?

HL Oh, I think so. In any case, Constant did. But there were situationist experiments in unitary urbanism. Unitary urbanism consisted of making different parts of the city communicate with each other. They did their experiments; I didn't participate. They used all kinds of means of communication—I don't know when exactly they were using walkie-talkies. But I know they were used in Amsterdam and in Strasbourg.

KR Did you know people in Strasbourg then?

HL They were my students. But relations with them were also very strained. When I arrived in Strasbourg in 1958 or '59, it was right in the middle of the Algerian War, and I had only been in Strasbourg for about three weeks, maybe, when a group of guys came up to me. They were the future situationists of Strasbourg—or maybe they were already a little bit situationist. They said to me, "We need your support; we're going to set up a maquis in the Vosges. We're going to make a military base in the Vosges, and from there spread out over the whole country. We're going to derail trains." I replied: "But the army and the police . . . you aren't sure of having the support of the population . . . you're precipitating a catastrophe." So they began to insult me and call me a traitor. And after a little while, a few weeks, they came back to see me and told me: "You were right, it's impossible. It's impossible to set up a military base in the Vosges . . . we're going to work on something else."

So I found myself getting along with them, and afterward they became situationists, the same group that wanted to support the Algerians by starting up military activity in France; it was crazy . . . But, you know, my relations with them were always very difficult. They got angry over nothing. I was living at the time with a young woman from Strasbourg; I was the scandal of the university: she was pregnant, she had a daughter (my daughter Armelle), and it was the town scandal: a horror, an abomination. Strasbourg was a very bourgeois city. And the university wasn't outside the city; it was right in the middle. But at the same time, I was giving lectures that were very successful, on music, for example, music and society. I taught a whole course one year on "music and society"; many people attended, so I could only be attacked with difficulty. Armelle's mother, Nicole, was friends with the situationists; she was always with them; she invited them over. They came to eat at our place and we played music: this was a scandal in Strasbourg. So that's how I came to have close relations, organic relations, with them, not only because I taught Marxism at the university, but through Nicole, who was an intermediary. Guy came to my place to see Nicole, to eat dinner. But relations were difficult; they got angry over tiny things . . . Mustapha Khayati, author of the brochure, was in the group.

KR What was the effect of the brochure [*De la misère en milieu étudiant*]?[4] How many copies were given out?

HL Oh, it was very successful. But in the beginning it was only distributed in Strasbourg; then Debord and others distributed it in Paris. Thousands and thousands were given out, certainly tens of thousands of copies to students. It's a very good brochure, without a doubt. Its author, Mustapha Khayati, was Tunisian. There were several Tunisians in the group, many foreigners who were less talked about afterward, and even Mustapha Khayati didn't show himself very often at the time because he might have had problems because of his nationality. He didn't have dual citizenship; he stayed a Tunisian, and he could have had real troubles . . . But anyway, in Paris, after 1957, I saw a lot of them, and I was also spending time with Constant in Amsterdam. This was the moment when the Provo movement became very powerful in Amsterdam, with their idea of keeping urban life intact, preventing the city from being eviscerated by autoroutes and being opened up to automobile traffic . . . they wanted the city to be conserved and transformed instead of being given over to traffic; they also wanted drugs, they seemed to count on drugs to create new situations: imagination sparked by LSD. It was LSD in those days.

KR Among the Parisian situationists too?

HL No. Very little. They drank. At Guy Debord's place, we drank tequila with a little mezcal added. But never . . . Mescaline, a little, but many of them took nothing at all. That wasn't the way they wanted to create new situations.

KR To return to unitary urbanism, this way of linking *quartiers* together without creating homogeneity. Each *quartier* retained its distinct aspects, right?

HL Yes, they didn't merge together; they're already a whole, but a whole that is in some sense fragmented and is only in a virtual state. The idea is to make of the city a whole, but a whole in movement, a whole in transformation.

KR Was Constant's project predicated on the end of work?

HL Yes, to a certain extent. Yes, that's the beginning: complete mechanization, the complete automatization of productive work, which left people free to do other things. He was one of the ones who considered the problem.

KR And the situationists too?

HL Yes.

KR Do you also situate your work in that lineage? From Lafargue to . . . ?

HL Yes, but not from Lafargue. I think my starting point was a science fiction novel called *City*. It's an American novel by [Clifford] Simak in which work is performed by robots. Humans can't stand the situation; they die because they are so used to working. They die, and the dogs that are left take advantage of the situation. The robots work for them, feed them, and so forth. And the dogs are perfectly happy because they aren't deformed by the work habit. I remember the role played by this novel in our discussions. I don't remember when it came out in the United States, but I think it's one of the first science fiction novels that was acclaimed and had influence, but it was maybe only in those years. In any case, that was Constant's starting point: a society liberated from work. And it was in the orientation of Lafargue's *Droit à la paresse,* but renewed by the perspective of automation which began in those years.

And so, a complete change in revolutionary movements beginning in 1956–1957, movements that leave behind classic organizations . . . What's beautiful is the voice of small groups having influence . . .

KR So the very existence of microsocieties or groupuscules like the situationists was itself a new situation?

HL Yes, to a certain extent. But then again, we musn't exaggerate either. For how many of them were there? You know that the Situationist International never had more than ten members. There were two or three Belgians, two or three Dutch, like Constant. But they were all expelled immediately. Guy Debord followed André Breton's example. People were expelled. I was never a part of the group. I could have been, but I was careful, since I knew Guy Debord's character and his manner, and the way he had of imitating André Breton, by expelling everyone in order to get at a pure and hard little core. In the end, the members of the Situationist International were Guy Debord, Raoul Vaneigem, and Michèle Bernstein. There were some outer groupuscules, satellite groups, where I was, and where Asger Jorn was too. Asger Jorn had been expelled; poor Constant was expelled as well. For what reason? Well, Constant didn't build anything, he never built anything—he was an architect who didn't build, a utopian architect. But he was expelled because a guy who worked with him built a church, in Germany: expulsion for reason of disastrous influence. It's rubbish. It was really about keeping oneself in a pure state, like a crystal. Debord's dogmatism was exactly like Breton's. And, what's more, it was a dogmatism without a dogma, since the theory of situations, of the creation of situations, disappeared very quickly, leaving behind only the critique of the existing world, which is where it all started, with the *Critique de la vie quotidienne.*

KR How did your association with the situationists change or inspire your thinking about the city? Did it change your thinking or not?

HL It was all corollary, parallel. My thinking about the city had completely different sources. Where I come from—an agricultural region—I had been studying agricultural questions for a long time. One bright day, in my region, bulldozers arrived and started leveling the trees: they had discovered oil there. There are oil wells in my region, not very many, but still a significant number; one of the biggest refineries in Europe was at Mourenx, Lacq-Mourenx.

So then I saw a new city being built where before there were only fields and oak forests. This began in 1953–1954. Little by little I left the agricultural questions behind, saying to myself: now here's something new, something important. I didn't expect the very brutal urbanization that followed. That new city was called Lacq-Mourenx, "ville nouvelle." Since I was at the CNRS, I sent some people there right away to watch the development. I even wanted to write a book—which I never did, like so many projects—entitled *Birth of a City*. That was the starting point. But at the same time I met Guy Debord, I met Constant, I knew that the Provos in Amsterdam were interested in the city, and I went there to see what was going on, maybe ten times. Just to see the form that the movement was taking, if it took a political form. There were Provos elected to the city council in Amsterdam. I forget which year, but they pulled off a big victory in the municipal elections. Then, after that, it all fell apart. All this was part and parcel of the same thing. And after 1960 there was the great movement in urbanization. They abandoned the theory of unitary urbanism, since unitary urbanism only had a precise meaning for historic cities like Amsterdam that had to be renewed, transformed. But from the moment that the historic city exploded into peripheries, suburbs—like what happened in Paris, and in all sorts of place, Los Angeles, San Francisco, wild extensions of the city—the theory of unitary urbanism lost any meaning. I remember very sharp, pointed discussions with Guy Debord, when he said that urbanism was becoming an ideology. He was absolutely right, from the moment that there was an official doctrine on urbanism.

I think the urbanism code dates from 1961 in France—that's the moment that urbanism becomes an ideology. That doesn't mean that the problem of the city was resolved—far from it. But at that point they abandoned the theory of unitary urbanism. And then I think that even the *dérive,* the *dérive* experiments, were little by little abandoned around then too. I'm not sure how that happened, because that was the moment I broke with them.

After all, there's the political context in France, and there are also personal relations, very complicated stories. The most complicated story arose when they came to my place in the Pyrenees. And we took a wonderful trip: we left Paris in a car, and stopped at the Lascaux caves which were closed not long after that. We were very taken up with the problem of the Lascaux caves: they are buried very deep, with even a well that was inaccessible—and all this filled with paintings. How were these paintings made, who were they made for, since they weren't painted in order to be seen? The idea was that painting started as a critique . . . All the more so in that all the churches in the region have crypts. We stopped at Saint-Savin, where there are frescos on the church's vaulted dome and a crypt full of paintings, a crypt whose depths are difficult to reach because it is so dark. What are paintings that were not destined to be seen? And how were they made? So we made our way south; we had a fabulous feast in Sarlat and I could hardly drive— I was the one driving. I got a ticket; we were almost arrested because I crossed a village going 120 kilometers per hour. They stayed several days at my place, and, working together, we wrote a programmatic text. At the end of the week they spent at Navarrenx, they kept the text. I said to them, "You type it" (it was handwritten), and afterward they accused me of plagiarism. In reality, this was complete bad faith. The text that was used in writing the book about the Commune was a joint text, by them and by me, and only one small part of the Commune book was taken from the joint text . . .

I had this idea about the Commune as a festival, and I threw it out into debate, after consulting an unpublished document about the Commune, which is at the Feltrinelli Foundation in Milan. It's a diary about the Commune. The person who kept the diary, who was deported, by the way, and who brought back his diary from deportation several years later, around 1880, recounts how on

March 28, 1871, Thiers's soldiers came to look for the cannons that were in Montmartre and on the hills of Belleville, how the women who got up very early in the morning heard the noise and all ran out in the streets and surrounded the soldiers, laughing, having fun, greeting them in a friendly way. Then they went off to get coffee and offered it to the soldiers, and these soldiers who had come to get the cannons were more or less carried away by the people. First the women, then the men, everyone came out, in an atmosphere of popular festival. The Commune cannon incident was not at all a situation of armed heroes arriving and combating the soldiers taking the cannons. It didn't happen at all like that. It was the people who came out of their houses, who were enjoying themselves. The weather was beautiful, March 28 was the first day of spring, it was sunny: the women kiss the soldiers, they're relaxed, and the soldiers are absorbed into all of that, a Parisian popular festival. But this diary is an exception. And afterward the theorists of the heroes of the Commune said to me, "This is a testimonial; you can't write history from a testimonial." The situationists said more or less the same thing. I didn't read what they said; I did my work. There were ideas that were batted around in conversation, and then worked up in common texts. And then afterward, I wrote my study on the Commune. I worked for weeks in Milan, at the Feltrinelli Institute; I found unpublished documentation, I used it, and that's completely my right. Listen, I don't care at all about these accusations of plagiarism. And I never took the time to read what they wrote about it in their journal. I know that I was dragged through the dirt.

And then, as for how I broke with them, it happened after an extremely complicated story concerning the journal *Arguments*. The idea had come up to stop publishing *Arguments* because several of the collaborators in the journal, such as my friend Kostas Axelos, thought that its role was over; they thought they had nothing more to say. In fact, I have the text by Axelos where he talks about the dissolution of the group and of the journal; they thought it was finished and that it would be better to end it rather than let it drag along. I was kept informed of these discussions. During discussions with Guy Debord, we talked about it, and Debord said to me, "Our journal, the *Internationale situationniste,* has to replace

Arguments." And so *Argument*'s editor, and all the people there, had to agree. Everything depended on a certain man who was very powerful at the time in publishing; he did a literary chronicle for *L'Express,* he was also in with the *Nouvelle revue française* and the Editions de Minuit. He was extremely powerful, and everything depended on him.

Well, at that moment I had broken up with a woman—very bitterly. She left me, and she took my address book with her. This meant I no longer had Herval's address. I telephoned Debord and told him I was perfectly willing to continue negotiations with Herval, but that I no longer had his address, his phone number—nothing. Debord began insulting me over the phone. He was furious and said, "I'm used to people like you who become traitors at the decisive moment." That's how the rupture between us began . . . but there was a time when it was a real, very warm friendship.

KR You even wrote an article entitled "You Will All Be Situationists."

HL Oh yes, I did that to help bring about the replacement of *Arguments* by the *Internationale situationniste* . . . Guy Debord accused me of having done nothing to get it published.

KR Let's talk a bit about the *dérive* in general. Do you think it brought anything new to spatial theory or to urban theory? In the way that it emphasized experimental games and practices, do you think it was more productive than a purely theoretical approach to the city?

HL Yes, as I perceived it, the *dérive* was more of a practice than a theory. It revealed the growing fragmentation of the city. In the course of its history the city was once a powerful organic unity; for some time, however, that unity was becoming undone, was fragmenting, and they were recording examples of what we all had been talking about, like the place where the new Bastille Opera is going to be built. The Place de la Bastille is the end of historic Paris—beyond that, it's the Paris of the first industrialization of the nineteenth century. The Place des Vosges is still aristocratic Paris of the seventeenth century—when you get to the Bastille, another Paris begins, which is of the nineteenth century, but it's the Paris of the bourgeoisie, of commercial, industrial expansion, at the same time that the commercial and industrial bourgeoisie takes hold of the Marais, the center of Paris—it spreads out beyond the Bastille, the rue de la Roquette, the rue du Faubourg Saint-Antoine, etc. So already the city is becoming fragmented. We had a vision of a city that was more and more fragmented without its organic unity being completely shattered. Afterward, of course, the peripheries and the suburbs highlighted the problem. But back then it wasn't yet obvious, and we thought that the practice of the *dérive* revealed the idea of the fragmented city. But it was mostly done in Amsterdam . . . The experiment consisted of rendering different aspects or fragments of the city simultaneous, fragments that can only be seen successively, in the same way that there exist people who have never seen certain parts of the city.

KR While the *dérive* took the form of a narrative.

HL That's it; one goes along in any direction and recounts what one sees.

KR But the recounting can't be done simultaneously.

HL Yes, it can, if you have a walkie-talkie; the goal was to attain a certain simultaneity. That was the goal—it didn't always work.

KR So, a kind of synchronic history.

HL Yes, that's it, a synchronic history. That was the meaning of unitary urbanism: unify what has a certain unity, but a lost unity, a disappearing unity.

KR And it was during the time when you knew the situationists that the idea of unitary urbanism began to lose its force?

HL At the moment when urbanization became truly massive, that is, after 1960, and when the city, Paris, completely exploded. You know that there were very few suburbs in Paris; there were some, but very few. And then suddenly the whole area was filled, covered with little houses, with new cities, Sarcelles and the rest. Sarcelles became a kind of myth. There was even a disease that people called the "sarcellitis." And around then Guy Debord's attitude changed; he went from unitary urbanism to the thesis of urbanistic ideology.

KR And what was that transition, exactly?

HL It was more than a transition, it was the abandonment of one position in order to adopt the exact opposite one. Between the idea of elaborating an urbanism and the thesis that all urbanism is an ideology is a profound modification. In fact, by saying that all urbanism was a bourgeois ideology, they abandoned the problem of the city. They left it behind. They thought that the problem no longer interested them. While I, on the other hand, continued to be interested; I thought that the explosion of the historic city was precisely the occasion for finding a larger theory of the city, and not a pretext for abandoning the problem . . .

The theory of situations was itself abandoned, little by little. And the journal itself became a political organ. They began to insult everyone. That was part of Debord's attitude, or it might have been part of his difficulties: he split up with Michèle Bernstein. I don't know, there were all kinds of circumstances that might have made him more polemical, more bitter, more violent. In the end, everything became oriented toward a kind of polemical violence. I think they ended up insulting just about everyone. And they also greatly exaggerated their role in May '68, after the fact.

The '68 movement didn't come from the situationists. At Nanterre there was a little groupuscule known as *les enragés*. They were insulting everyone too. But they were the ones who made the movement. The movement of March 22 was made by students, among them Daniel Cohn-Bendit, who was not a situationist.

It was an energetic group that took form as the events developed, with no program, no project: an informal group, with whom the situationists linked up, but it wasn't they who constituted the group; the group took shape apart from them—Trotskyists joined up with the March 22 group; everybody ended up joining with them little by little. We called it "getting aboard a moving train." So even though the situationists at Nanterre may have joined up with the group from the outset, they weren't the animators, the creative element . . . In fact, the movement began in a big, crowded amphitheater where I was giving a course, and where students whom I knew well asked me if we could name some delegates to go to the administration to protest the blacklist. (The administration was insisting on establishing a list of the most disruptive students in order to sanction them.) "Of course," I said. So it was on that podium that the election took place of delegates to protest the blacklist business. And all sorts of people participated in that election: Trotskyists as well as situationists.

The group of March 22 was formed after these negotiations and arguments with the administration, and then the group occupied the administration building. The stimulus was this business about the blacklist, and I was the one who concocted the blacklist. What actually happened was that the administration phoned my office and asked for a list of the most politically disruptive students. I told them to get lost; I frequently had to say to the dean in those days, "Sir, I am not a cop." So the blacklist never existed, in black and white. But they were trying to do it, and I told the students to defend themselves; I stirred things up a bit. One has one's little perversities, after all . . .

I always tell the story. On Friday evening, May 13, we were all at the Place Denfert-Rochereau. Around the Belfort lion, there were maybe seventy or eighty thousand students discussing what to do next. The Maoists wanted to go out to the suburbs, toward Ivry; the anarchos and the situationists wanted to go make noise in the bourgeois quarters. The Trotskyists were in favor of heading for the proletarian districts, the 11th Arrondissement, while the students from Nanterre wanted to go to the Latin Quarter. Then some people cried out, "We've got friends in the Prison de la Santé—let's go see them!" and then the whole crowd started off down the Boulevard Arago toward the Prison de la Santé. We saw hands at the windows, we yelled things, and then we headed off toward the Latin Quarter. It was chance. Or maybe it wasn't chance at all. There must have been a desire to go back to the Latin Quarter, to not get too far away from the center of student life. There must have been some obscure feeling of attachment to the Latin Quarter . . . It was curious; after that hour of floating around, not knowing which way to go. And then, in the Latin Quarter, the television was there, until midnight, that is. Then there was just the radio, Europe No. 1. And at about three in the morning—in complete bedlam, there was noise from all directions—a radio guy handed the microphone to Daniel Cohn-Bendit who had the brilliant idea of simply saying: "General strike, general strike, general strike." And that was the decisive moment; it was then that there was action. That was what took the police by surprise. That students were making trouble, that there was a little violence, some wounded, tear gas, paving stones, barricades, and bombs: that was all just the children of the bourgeoisie having a good time. But a general strike, well, that was no laughing matter.

NOTES

Originally published in *October* 79 (Winter 1997), 69–83.

1. Henri Lefebvre, *Writings on Cities,* ed. and trans. Eleonore Kofman and Elizabeth Lebas (Oxford: Blackwell, 1996), 13.

2. *Yale French Studies* 73, special issue on "Everyday Life" (1987), ed. Alice Kaplan and Kristin Ross.

3. Henri Lefebvre, *Critique de la vie quotidienne,* 3 vols. (Paris: L'Arche, 1947–1981); English translation of volume 1, *Critique of Everyday Life* (London: Verso, 1991).

4. L'Internationale situationniste, *De la misère en milieu étudiant considérée sous ses aspects économique, politique, psychologique, sexuel et notamment intellectuel et de quelques moyens pour y remédier* (1966; Paris: Editions Champ Libre, 1976). An English translation appears in Ken Knabb, ed. and trans., *Situationist International Anthology* (Berkeley: Bureau of Public Secrets, 1981).

Angels of Purity

Vincent Kauffman

translated by John Goodman

1 Black Art

The fact that the language of real communication has been lost is
what the modern movement of art's decay, and ultimately of its formal annihilation, expresses *positively*. What it expresses *negatively* is
that a new common language has yet to be found—not, this time, in
the form of unilaterally arrived-at conclusions like those which, from
the viewpoint of historical art, *always came on the scene too late,* speaking *to others* of what had been experienced without any real dialogue,
and accepting this shortfall of life as inevitable—but rather in a praxis
embodying both an unmediated activity and a language commensurate with it. The point is to take effective possession of the community of dialogue and the playful relationship to time, which the works
of the poets and artists have heretofore merely *represented*.[1]

The merit of modern artists, Guy Debord writes in *The Society of the Spectacle,* is to expose artistic communication to the uncommunicable, and thus to be
a critical reflection of the "society of the spectacle," characterized by an absence
of all authentic communication. But this passion for decomposition—as attributed to Mallarmé, for example, or to Joyce—is also what condemns modern art

to a definitive aporia requiring its transcendence. Situationism is intent on succeeding precisely where dadaism and surrealism remained unfinished projects: "Dadaism sought *to abolish art without realizing it,* and Surrealism sought *to realize art without abolishing it.* The critical position since worked out by the situationists demonstrates that the abolition and the realization of art are inseparable aspects of a single transcendence of art."[2] Genuine community will lead to an absence of that art which had failed it by becoming increasingly detached from the religious and mythic ground that held it together. To regain vitality or be transcended, art must stop being a language of address, a "speaking to," and transform itself into a "speaking with" that, like the Mallarméan Book, is no longer identified exclusively with either the author or the reader-spectator but becomes the work of everyone.

"We are artists precisely insofar as we are no longer artists: we come to realize art," one reads in the *Internationale situationniste.*[3] An art transcending art, situationism is characterized by its invisibility, by its irreducible opposition to all forms of representation, of spectacle. The situationists mustered some enthusiasm for a newly established situationist library in Jutland, but this was primarily because it included a "copy section" denouncing everyone who had seen and imitated the real situationists, themselves determined to remain out of sight: "Finally, and this is probably its most interesting initiative, this library has opened a *copy section* for the preservation of works imitating any of the realizations of our friends whose strange role, due to their very membership in the SI, is not voluntarily acknowledged" (*IS* 5, 11). Situationist art functions as an invisible model: any (re)presentation of it constitutes treason, even when it is the work of real situationists, always vulnerable to being raked through the coals when they expose (themselves) to the light of day. It exists only for those who have eyes not to see, for those who are not blind victims of the society of the spectacle, anesthetized by the barrage of images. It is alive for those capable of recognizing the evidence of the invisible, evoked one last time by the situationists at the moment of the movement's self-dissolution (in 1972): "Never have we been seen mixing in affairs, rivalries, and frequentations, mingling with the most extreme leftist politicians or the most advanced members of the intelligentsia. And now that we can flatter ourselves with having acquired among this rabble the most revolting celebrity, we are going to become *still more inaccessible,* still more clandestine. The more famous our theses become, the more obscure we ourselves will become."[4] As Flaubert might have put it, if situationism is to flourish, I must diminish myself, I must make myself even more obscure, at least as obscure as Mallarmé, unreadable on the ground of the invisible Book.

The situationists' commitment to obscurity does not date from 1972. In fact, their attempt to transcend art was always coincident with a gesture toward dissolution and disappearance, with a will to secrecy. As early as 1962, the message was clear: the situationists are fish soluble in the water of the people:

> We are totally popular. We take into consideration only those problems that are already in suspension in the entire population. Situationist theory is in the people as fish are in water. To those who believe the SI is building castles of speculation, we affirm the contrary: we are going to dissolve ourselves in the population that lives our project at every moment, living it first, of course, as lack and repression (*IS* 7, 17).

Situationism tends toward invisibility due to its popular character: it is invisible because popular and popular because invisible. It realizes itself in the people, all the more so because the latter, like Mallarmé's crowd, is slow to speak its mind: the people lacks situationism but lives it in the form of something it lacks, but needs to make its will known. Not only does the situationist Book revel in the disappearance of the poet's voice and obscurity; it comes to pass only with its own dissolution, it realizes itself as a popular lack (as we speak of the popular front), it is coincident with an invisible community whose visible reverse will be revolution, the crowd making its will known. It is the culmination of a certain history of the avant-garde: raising the stakes behind the situationists' backs is impossible, because they are no longer visible, from the front, the back, or head-on. They have become more transparent, more incontestably authentic than Breton would ever have imagined possible.

Situationism thus represents the most Mallarméan version of the adventure of realizing art in life, for the most exemplary thing about the situationists is their gift for obscurity, or what might be called their autobiographical discretion. From the situationist perspective, everything visible is false, impure. I see or, worse, I present for viewing, I self-present for viewing, thus I am blind to the illness of my own life. The source of infection is the image: hence the startling therapeutic strength of Debord's film *Hurlements en faveur de Sade* (Howls for Sade), celebrated for its final twenty-four minutes of darkness and silence. To reestablish communication and recreate community, the subject must be purged of what it sees, its eyes must be opened by a dark screen, and simultaneously it must be purged of anything that it itself might present to view. The originality of situationism consists in its stripping the subject not only of its passion for the visible but also of its own visibility. Debord's exemplarity is that of a dark screen, of a subject reduced to a blind stain, thereby avoiding the loss of authenticity and the fall into representation. Autobiography, a genre dear to both the surrealists and Artaud, is genuine only when it is not written, when it remains virtual; it should be impersonal and collective, dreaming of itself as autobiography without a subject. To avoid the errors and compromises of its predecessors, to liberate the subject from its tainted allegiance to the seductions of the image (or the imaginary), situationism decrees a blackout. Open season is declared on fantasy and self-love.

The situationist ego is detestable, and the use of "I" is permissible only when certain requirements are met. It must be emptied of all desire for self-representation and all singular qualities, which are to be replaced by the "radical theory" of situationist theses. This is apparent in what might be called situationism's lyrical tendency, exemplified by the *Traité de savoir-vivre à l'usage des jeunes générations* (The Revolution of Everyday Life) by Raoul Vaneigem, published in 1967.[5] At the outset, Vaneigem warns his readers: "I have no intention of rendering what there is of lived experience in this book palpable to readers not prepared to relive it fully for themselves, in full consciousness. I expect them to lose and rediscover themselves in a general movement of minds, just as I am so bold as to think that present conditions will erase themselves from human memory."[6] This is not autobiography, or, to be more precise, whatever in the book is autobiographical is not visible because it is not meant to be read but rather experienced firsthand by readers who are no longer readers. I write to separate myself from my book, to disappear as a speaking subject, to be forgotten in the general movement of the revolution to come. The knowledge that I propose be lived as opposed to read about is exemplary because it is anonymous and anyone can experience it: "That is why there is nothing in the following notes which is not subject to trial and correction in light of anyone's immediate experience."[7] No autobiography: Vaneigem is exemplary because he doesn't represent himself, because he writes himself off, disqualifying in advance what he has written, something he emphasizes again in a "Toast aux ouvriers révolutionnaires" (Toast to Revolutionary Workers), added in 1972: "Evidence supporting the principal theses of the *Traité* should now manifest itself in the hands of its anti-readers in the form of concrete results. No longer in student agitation but in total revolution."[8]

True poetry results when the subject renounces self-representation, when, precipitated by a kind of certitude of its own transparence, it dissolves, by anticipation, in an anonymous and collective life to come, in accordance with the logic "I am where they will be, where there is no 'I'": "However, men also use words and signs in attempts to perfect their interrupted gestures. And because they do this, a poetic language exists that, for me, is indistinguishable from radical theory, from theory penetrating the masses and becoming a material force."[9] True poetry is indistinguishable from the realization of situationist theory by the masses. As long as there is something to write and someone to write for, the subject itself remains theoretical, virtual, advancing only under the dark cloak of theory, which, in sum, constitutes the provisional form of a supreme language, of a total communication reinvented in and through the revolution to come.

Under a situationist regime, as under an *oulipiste* one, true communication entails the disappearance not only of the speaking subject but also of the poet-as-writer. It is not encompassed by any book, unless it be a situationist dictionary in which language is explained exclusive of any subject, of any speech, one whose project would be to liberate words from the meaning—or the absence of meaning and force—imposed on them by power. Realization of the supreme situationist language would require completion of a dictionary to take its place, one that would also be a kind of total book, a depository of the incorruptible transparence of a new symbolic order to come, announced in the following terms in "Les mots captifs (Préface à un dictionnaire situationniste)" (Captive Words (Preface to a Situationist Dictionary)):

> Our dictionary will be a sort of grid with which one could decipher pieces of information and tear off the ideological veil covering reality. We will provide potential translations that will allow the apprehension of different aspects of the society of the spectacle, and will show how the smallest clues (the smallest signs) contribute to its maintenance. It is in a way a bilingual dictionary, for each word possesses an "ideological" meaning from power and a real meaning (*IS* 10, 55; translation in this volume, 179–180).

Reinvention of communication entails a lexicographical operation, a reappropriation of the meaning and work of words. To give purer meanings to the words of the tribe, to make them more immediate, such would be the situationist project: "The institution of liberated creative activity will simultaneously be the institution of genuine, finally liberated communication, and the transparency of human relations will replace the poverty of words under the old regime of opacity" (ibid.). The restoration of purer meanings to the words of the tribe, and especially the totality of those meanings, which power contrives to forfeit in order to produce its own discourse: "Power's capture of language is comparable to its capture of the totality. Only language that has lost all immediate reference to the totality can be at the origin of information. Information is power's poetry . . . the mediated faking of what is" (*IS* 8, 30–31; translation in this volume, 154). The Book is lacking? That is the result of power's recycling of it in the form of news and information. Language deprived of totality and hence of authenticity constitutes the poetry of a power responsible for the degradation of language into coarse speech, a currency intended only to be passed silently from one hand to the next. True poetry, by contrast, is essential speech; it is totality recovered, communication that is authentic and immediately efficient, supported by a language all of whose qualities have been newly liberated—a language again made perfect: "Conversely, poetry must be understood as immediate communication in reality and real modification of that reality. It is nothing other than liberated language, language that wins back its richness and, breaking its significations, at once recovers words, music, cries, gestures, painting, mathematics, events" (ibid.). True poetry begins where it casts off the defects of language (for which power is responsible) to make itself a perfect, total language in phase with the real. A supreme language in which meaning, image, sound, gesture, and number function as one. One that is no longer lacking and is on the verge of being very beautiful.

But perhaps we must still summon up our patience. The status of this situationist supreme language remains profoundly equivocal. The situationists do not really believe in the possibility of a Book that is the repository of a universal or mathematical language, one purified of subjectivity's throws of the dice, any more than Mallarmé did. On the contrary: they recognize in such a language— glimmers of which are perceptible in cybernetics and computer science—the desubjectivizing project of the society of the spectacle: "From its advent, the triumphant bourgeoisie has dreamed of a universal language, which cyberneticists are today trying to achieve via technology. Descartes dreamed of a language (a forerunner of newspeak) in which thoughts occurred one after the other with a mathematical rigor, like numbers: 'mathesis universalis' or the permanence of bourgeois categories" (*IS* 10, 51; translation in this volume, 175). In fact, the situationist dictionary was to implement an operation of *diversion (détournement)*, an alleged response to the first diversion or confiscation effected by power: "Critique of the ruling language, its *détournement,* will become the continuous practice of new revolutionary theory" (ibid., 50; this volume, 174). The permanent revolution will be lexicographical or it will be nothing. It is not a matter simply of opposing the language of power with another language encompassable by a dictionary, but of destabilizing language in order to liberate its virtualities. Of necessity, the situationist dictionary will never get beyond its preface, for it is an affirmation of the linguistic imaginary *détourné* by power (later echoed by certain "lexicographical" passages in Debord's *Commentaires sur la société du spectacle* [Commentaries on the Society of the Spectacle]).[10]

The notion of *détournement,* which the situationists apply to texts and images as well as to words, is doubtless the best known feature of their "aesthetic," and this has led inevitably to its banalization. Its prominence in the project for a "Preface to a Situationist Dictionary" makes it possible to reach a more precise understanding of what is at stake in the idea. It should be noted first of all that, insofar as the dictionary is to be limited to its preface, such *détournements* do not serve the work but effect an "unworking" (*désoeuvrement*) of it. Preface to a dictionary, preface to a Book: doubtless this would be very beautiful. Next, it should be emphasized that these *détournements* blur the boundary between the personal and the impersonal: who is the author of a text that has been *détourné* in this way; who signs it? *Détournement* is a poetry produced by several individuals and theoretically by everyone, given that in principle it is within anyone's reach, like automatic writing and oulipian inventions (which the situationists reject vigorously because they reduce the diverting subject to a pure mathematical contrivance, for situationism requires a subject who diverts out of revolutionary conviction, a subject constituting itself through confrontation with the language of power). Finally, the prominence of *détournement* in the dictionary project underscores the degree to which it should be understood not in terms of play but as the key component in a politics of communication. The situationist community is constituted by *détournement,* precisely because of its character as an act: it institutes a pragmatics at the heart of poetic language. Declaring his support for anarchists accused of planning to plant bombs, Mallarmé referred to them as "angels of purity" who had failed to understand that books, too, produce effective explosions ("The only bombs I know are books").[11] With the situationists, angels of purity born in the age of the cathode tube, angelic messengers of communication regained, the book no longer explodes: it implodes as a result of *détournement,* the contemporary equivalent of the restrained form of intervention dear to their ancestor and accomplice.

2 How to Do Everything with Words

In an article published in the *Internationale situationniste* (one crediting dadaism with having affirmed, after Sade, the right to say all), one reads the following lines pertaining to the failure of dadaism: "'Saying everything' cannot exist without the freedom to do everything. Dada had a chance of fulfillment in Spartakus, in the revolutionary practice of the German proletariat. The latter's failure made the former's inevitable" (*IS* 10, 51–52; translation in this volume, 176). Such is almost the consensus view today, when the immediate postwar period in Germany, like the Paris Commune, is widely regarded as one of those paradisal moments for revolutionary art premised on the bitter defeat of a workers' movement. On the other hand, the "theoretical" dimension of such a statement merits careful examination, for saying all is possible only when reinforced by a readiness to do all. If one is to say all, one must become an agent; the word must be immediately convertible into action. The authenticity, the totality in question cannot be solely a matter of speech: acts must follow, acts that deprive the prior utterances of all reason for being.

The only authentic communication is the one presenting itself from the outset as a form of common action, of everyday life collectively reinvented, in an immediacy dispensing with all representation (if not linguistic, then at least artistic). The situationist is an essentially impatient being. Not only is he averse to making himself visible, he also is at no pains to make himself heard; he speaks only to those who no longer need to hear him because they have proceeded to action: "To those who follow one step behind us, we prefer those who reject us with impatience because our language is not yet authentic poetry, which is to say the free construction of everyday life" (*IS* 8, 38). Situationism is a communicative project intolerant of delay. Resolutely avant-gardiste, it is not for those who linger, who follow a step behind, but for those who are ahead of it, those situated where statements give way to realizing deeds, those who have already made themselves the subjects of political action.

From this perspective, one might also say that, as a matter of principle, situationism brooks no delay in the realization of desire. No sooner desired than realized: such is its watchword. Desire must not be given the time to become caught in images or fantasies, which are open doors to the society of the spectacle. Situationist desire is itself quite literally avant-garde; it anticipates every possible representation of a desired object, it tries to situate itself beyond such objects, thereby making their conversion into images useless. A hunt for the imaginary, a struggle for the invisibility (obscurity?) of the object of desire, it is psychoanalysis become absolutely efficient (at the risk of total inversion of its meaning). It dispenses with desire for the labyrinthine dramaturgy characteristic of the talking cure (even in the shortest of sessions), it unloads all phantasmatic weight to dedicate itself from the outset to the angelic purity of the unrepresentable:

> Hence it is necessary to envision a kind of psychoanalysis for situationist ends, each participant in this adventure being obliged to find precise ambient desires *in order to realize them,* contrary to the aims pursued by the currents issuing from Freudianism. Everyone must search for what he likes, what attracts him (and here again, contrary to certain modern literary endeavors—that of Leiris for example—, what matters to us is not the individual structure of our minds, nor the explanation of their formation, but their possible application in constructed situations). (*IS* 1, 11)

No more dreaming: the new agenda calls for the invention of situations favorable to the realization of desires that in turn generate new situations. Situationism purges desire of its phantasmatic indolence and politicizes it, attempting to make its realization coincide with a moment of pure consciousness of this desire, made possible by the uprooting of representation, and more generally of the society of the spectacle: "Consciousness of desire and the desire for consciousness together and indissolubly constitute that project which in its negative form has as its goal the abolition of classes and the direct possession by the workers of every aspect of their activity. The opposite of this project is the society of the spectacle, where the commodity contemplates itself in a world of its own making."[12] In other words, no subjectivity is possible without a break with the order of merchandise, without destruction of the class society. Situationism is Freud diverted and politicized: "Where economic id was, there ego shall be. The *subject* can only emerge out of society—that is, out of the struggle that society embodies. The possibility of a subject's existing depends on the outcome of the class struggle."[13] This makes it easier to understand the situationist prohibition against all forms of subjective expression, against all self-representation. The advent of the subject—and thus of a form of expression distinct from that of power—depends on the existence of the class struggle, whose aim is nothing other than the realization of art, against a background of the obliteration or oblivion of the degraded art of the spectacle: "Situationists will place themselves in the service of the necessity of *oblivion*. The only force from which they can expect something is the proletariat, theoretically without a past and obliged to permanently reinvent itself, of which Marx said that it 'is revolutionary or it is nothing.' Will it be in our time, or not? The question is important for our purpose: the proletariat should realize art" (*IS* 1, 8).

Marx also affirmed that art, as a complementary and ideal world, can only be transcended by its realization in a classless society. The situationists take up this assertion but with a difference, imperceptibly reversing means and ends. It is as though realizing art through situationist transcendence would make the classless society possible. "Communism realized will be the work of art transformed into the totality of everyday life," writes Asger Jorn.[14] Communism, then, is the work of art become totality, the total oeuvre realized, the Book made by everyone and integrated into everyday life, and situationism is but the implementation of such a Book: a fish dreaming itself in the water of the people-become-artist. Revolution is a precondition for realization of the Book, and vice versa. Paraphrasing the surrealist dictum of Lautréamont, Vaneigem suggests that revolution is poetry made not by an individual but collectively, in everyday life.[15] Thus, situationism has the advantage of taking into account the political equivocations characteristic of the twentieth-century avant-garde, whose revolutionary pretensions have never prevented literature from following its course. If there is a point at which making revolution and realizing the Book are one and the same, it is only logical that, pursuant to the first of these goals, and despite itself, the avant-garde so often frequented the rue Sébastien-Bottin.

By means of its performative becoming, poetry simultaneously reinvents itself and makes itself revolution: "Rediscovering poetry can merge with reinventing revolution, as certain stages of the Mexican, Cuban, or Congolese revolutions quite obviously prove" (*IS* 8, 30; translation in this volume, 155). And in the same article one reads the following: "The program of fulfilled poetry is nothing less than the creation of events and their language at the same time, inseparably" (ibid.). Poetry is by definition productive of revolution, or to be more precise, it is already revolution, but in a virtual state. It is a summons to the real revolution that should somehow place itself at its disposal, something the surrealists dared not say: "It is not a question of putting poetry at the service of the revolution, but rather of putting revolution at the service of poetry" (ibid.). At the very least, poetry is always a figure for revolution. It is revolution in absentia, become its phantom; it tries to ward off its absence by reiterating its promise: "Between revolutionary periods when the masses accede to poetry through action, we might imagine that circles of poetic adventure remain the only places where the totality of revolution lives on, as an unfulfilled but immanent potentiality, as the shadow of an absent individual" (ibid.). The circles of poetic adventure are the circles of the revolution provisionally out of view, communities that nurture and celebrate the possibility of the Book, incarnating the "absent individual" of the revolution all the better insofar as they themselves tend toward disappearance, making themselves invisible to the gaze of the spectacle of which they are the virtual interruption. Never were the situationists simultaneously so close and so distant from Mallarmé, a determined adept of obscurity in all its forms, as well as of subterranean depths and scarcely visible circles, absent a present, absent the crowd's speaking its mind.

The circles of poetic adventure are the depositories of revolution because it is in them, and in them only, that authentic communication is reinvented: "All have for an aim and as actual result immediate transparency of a certain communication, of mutual recognition, and of agreement" (ibid.). Communal desire coincides with revolutionary desire, because true poetry is communication in action, impersonal and hence collective. Thus the greatest *poetic* event of the century was May '68 (a status held in the previous century by the Paris Commune).

Everything in the situationist world came to fruition in the streets of May '68: in poetry become graffiti, in the endless deliberations in the Odéon and the Sorbonne, in the workers' occupations, described as "a *generalized critique* of all alienation, of all ideology, and of the entirety of old organizations of real life . . . an *acknowledged desire* for dialogue, for integrally free speech, a taste for true community" (*IS* 12, 3).

3 INVISIBLE GAMES

Putting the psychoanalytic couch in the street, transforming the city into an immense divan, a site for applying and realizing the slightest desire, for making the fabulist and weaver of confidences disappear behind a new kind of architect or urbanist who undertakes to give body, in the very fabric of the city, to the vain dreams of mortals, to render visible their most secret fantasies, to build and even improve upon their dreams, with no need to purify them of the unavowable. Such remained the terms of the situationist project some thirty or forty years later, as evidenced by the following pronouncement, which I have already cited: "Hence it is necessary to envision a kind of psychoanalysis for situationist ends, each participant in this adventure being obliged to find precise ambient desires *in order to realize them,* contrary to the aims pursued by the currents issuing from Freudianism" (*IS* 1, 11).

To transform into realty that which on the couch remains fantasy, to move from a reclining position to the construction of lived situations, to allot desire its time and space. There is an urbanist-architectural phase of the situationist experiment that represents a radicalization—doubtless the last—of the surrealist project, of which it constitutes a kind of vanishing point, a horizon beyond which there can be no return through swinging doors. With the situationists, all the doors are resolutely open, everything happens outside, there is no longer room for either interior or interiority: henceforth subjectivity is lived or expresses itself externally, it is collective or it is nothing, it is detached from all individual representation, and consequently from all literary practice. Bedrooms and sleep are off-limits for the situationists. Poetry will be made by everyone, but outside.

This radicalization also can be understood as a determination to transcend everything aesthetic, all formal and figural production, and replace it with the ludic requirement to "construct lived situations." Passage must be effected from the white page and the blank canvas—*détourné* or not—to a place favoring the concrete realization of desires, to a place where life, all of it, is *play*. The communal promise represented by art will be kept in concrete terms, through spatial investments. Situationist man lives not by bread alone but also through the recasting of space. Where the white page was, there the ideal city shall be. From signifying networks, whose attractions were becoming a matter for concern, one passes to resolutely urban networks, to writing on the ground. The death of individualized diction assumes a spatial dimension, and thanatography becomes "psychogeography." Realization of the Book entails a conquest of space, even the totality of space, because the construction of situations is meant to infiltrate all of life. The game will not be a discreet activity limited in time and space but a wholesale reinvention of life, or if one prefers, poetry realized, poetry liberating itself from subjugation to the society of the spectacle:

> The construction of situations begins on the other side of the modern collapse of the idea of the theater. It is easy to see to what extent the very principle of the theater—nonintervention—is attached to the alienation of the old world. Inversely, we see how the most valid of revolutionary cultural explorations have sought to break the spectator's psychological identification with the hero, so as to incite this spectator into activity by provoking his capacities to revolutionize his own life. The situation is thus made to be lived by its constructors.[16]

The same text goes on to specify that situations, while made to be lived individually, are at the same time necessarily collective. It could even be said that the construction of situations is nothing other than a stimulus to community, an art of sharing and participation—if, that is, the term "art" were not a portal through which the spectacular regime might reassert itself. For if the construction of situations proceeds by means of theatrical effects, and even through a director (or *opérateur,* as Mallarmé would say), it is nonetheless quite distinct from the theater. It is an experience as opposed to a performance or representation, because, ideally, everyone takes part in it and no one assumes the passive role of spectator:

> Against a unilateral art, situationist culture will be an art of dialogue, of interaction. Artists—along with all of visible culture—have become totally separate from society, just as they are isolated from one another by competition. Even before the impasse of capitalism art was essentially one-sided, without replies. It will transcend this hermetic primitivist era to become a complete communication.
>
> Because everyone will become an artist at a superior stage, that is to say, inseparably both producer and consumer of a total cultural creation, we will witness a rapid dissolution of the linear criterion of novelty. . . . We are now inaugurating what will be, historically, the last of the *métiers,* or crafts. Even the role of situationist, of professional amateur, of antispecialist will remain a specialization until the moment of economic and mental abundance when everyone becomes an "artist," in a sense that artists have never before attained: the construction of their own lives. (*IS* 4, 37–38)

Such clarification brings comfort. If it is possible to confuse the construction of situations with theater, if unsympathetic critics even connect such construction with the contemporary happenings and performance art toward which the situationists were in fact quite hostile, that is because everyone is not yet a situationist or an artist. When the Book is realized, when poetry has infiltrated everyone's everyday life, this ambiguity will disappear of its own accord, because all passive desire for spectacle will have disappeared. There will be no parasitic third parties to mitigate communicative authenticity. Everyone will be occupied with living and "playing" their lives. But the idea of playing the voyeur to one's neighbor will occur to no one, for poetry realized in the everyday lives of all, and in a space restored to all, precludes spectatorship.

In the meantime, the situationists make considerable efforts to maintain the distinction between the construction of situations and parodic spectacular performances. Situationist constructions are typified by their exemplary invisibility, proof simultaneously of their existence and of their revolutionary character. Unlike surrealist frolics, their own ludic actions [*jeux*] remain clandestine; they are made neither for visual consumption nor for publication, only being made visible when presented in a theoretical and obscure way. Their presentation is always restrained: their texts never propose anything more than conditions of possibility. The desired outcome is indeed a stage, but one from which the actors who set out to build it have disappeared into the wings, leaving it indefinitely empty.

This becomes clear with the mythic *dérives* (drifts or driftings), the most practical phase of the situationists' spatial investigations. Relating to "psychogeography" much as textual analysis does to literature, these are exercises in territorial reconnaissance or interpretation of the urban text, exploratory forays into singular surroundings. At a moment when drifting at the mercy of the signifier was becoming ubiquitous, the situationists oppose the *dérive* to space itself, as different from the classical practice of strolling and *flânerie* as fire is from water: "The concept of *dérive* is indissolubly linked to the recognition of effects that are psychogeographical in nature, and to the affirmation of a ludic-constructive behavior, something which opposes it in all respects to the classical notions of travel and promenade" (*IS* 2, 19). To be an artist is to take psychogeographic bearings, to make oneself a theorist of space as others are of text, and the artistic enterprise, again like that of textual theorists, is a collective one: "One can *dériver* alone, but everything indicates that the most fruitful numerical distribution consists of several small groups of two or three persons who have reached a similar state of consciousness, for comparing the impressions of these different groups makes it possible to reach objective conclusions" (ibid., 20).

In the history of the French avant-garde, walking is decidedly a must. But with the situationists, the subjective impressionism of a Breton, who strolled only to know and (above all) to show who he was, and the *flâneries* of an Aragon, who explored Parisian *passages* with a voyeur's eye, give way to promenades whose goal is to attain an impersonal objectivity of impression through the regulated use of chance:

> One or several persons delivering themselves to the *dérive* renounce, for a more or less extended period of time, their customary rationales for moving and acting, the relations, work, and leisure proper to them, abandoning themselves to the solicitations of the terrain and the encounters corresponding to it. The part of chance is less determinant here than one might think: from the point of view of the *dérive,* cities have a psychogeographical relief with running currents, stable points, and whirlpools that make entering and exiting certain zones very uncomfortable. (ibid., 19)

Thus, walking changes from a subjective activity to an objective one. Impersonal, it obliges the subject to renounce his or her customary practices in the interest of obtaining a kind of cure on the urban couch: to listen attentively to the city, like others listen to language, the Other having shifted. By the same token, the modalities for describing the "promenade" must also change. It might even be said that the *dérive* is walking purged of autobiographical representation, that it is a practice requiring the enunciatory and ambulatory disappearance of the walker. Where the *flâneries* of Breton and Aragon were, there shall be the impersonal theory of the *dérive,* which makes potential sites for this activity shimmer furtively but precludes the display of the "I" in any of them:

> Slipping by night into a house undergoing demolition, traversing Paris ceaselessly during a transport strike by hitchhiking, on the pretext of aggravating the confusion by having oneself taken anywhere and everywhere, wandering through underground passages of the catacombs off-limits to the public, such actions would take the bearings of a more general feeling that would be nothing other than the feeling of the *dérive.* Whatever one might write would be worthwhile only as passwords to this grand game. (ibid., 22)

The real game—the grand game—begins where descriptions cease, being mere passwords granting access to an initiation to take place on different terrain. Surrealist street adventures are replaced by impersonal psychogeographic surveys, and photographic illustrations of *Nadja* by Boiffard and Man Ray give way to plans of Parisian neighborhoods, which are to the situationists as railroad timetables were to Mallarmé and Proust: so many *cartes du Tendre* over which to dream or desire, but as if in the absence of all dreamers and all images (in no. 3 of the *Internationale situationniste,* a reproduction of the *Carte du Tendre* is juxtaposed with an aerial view of the center of Amsterdam [deemed a potential subject for psychogeographic investigation], as if situationism were a reincarnation of the preciosity of the French classical age).

As for the players, they remain invisible, literally blending into the landscape. Their preference runs, if not to secret places, then to deserted ones, like the forementioned catacombs and houses slated for demolition—or the Métro, which should be opened at night after the trains have stopped running, its corridors only dimly illuminated. Also noteworthy from this perspective is the frequency of the figure of a labyrinth from which the situationists have no intention of exiting, a kind of ultimate refuge from the society of the spectacle. The world is to culminate in a beautiful labyrinth in which little situationist monsters can hide to outwit the formidable beast that is the society of the spectacle, which is too large to follow them inside, or, should it manage to gain access, would summarily be devoured by them.[17] That the role formerly assumed by the *ventre de Paris* would fall to the labyrinth, such is the implication of the "Essai de description psychogéographique des Halles" (Attempt at a Psychogeographic Description of Les Halles):

> The first architectural measure obviously would be to replace the present pavilions [in the Paris central market] by autonomous series of small situationist architectural complexes. In the vicinity of these new structures . . . , there should rise labyrinths that are perpetually changing with the aid of objects more adequate than the crates of fruit and vegetables that provide the material for the only barricades of today. (*IS* 2, 17)

Contrary to their mythic predecessor, the new labyrinths will change constantly. Like all architectural projects complicit with utopian instability, a notion prevalent since the nineteenth century, that of the situationists had little chance of being realized. But in this case the impossibility of realization is essential, for the situationists regard mobility as fundamental. They are builders of movement; they interest themselves only in buildings earmarked for demolition or endlessly transformable into new labyrinths, sites constantly productive of desire in which one can lose one's way:

> In architecture itself, a taste for the *dérive* tends to sanction all kinds of new forms of labyrinth, which are facilitated by modern architectural possibilities. Thus in March of 1955 the press announced the construction in New York of a building in which might be seen the first signs of applicability of the *dérive* to apartment interiors: "The rooms in the helicoidal house will be like slices of cake. They can be made larger or smaller at will by shifting movable partitions. . . . This system makes it possible to transform three four-room apartments into a single apartment with twelve or more rooms in six hours." (*IS* 2, 23)

Project for New York: the world is to culminate in a beautiful cake with slices that can be reshaped, renewed, multiplied each day. Such is the solution proposed by the situationists: a being together, a desiring together in which desire would lose none of its essential mobility, none of its resistance to structural permanence and stability in any form. The situationist labyrinth is at the service of movement and the *dérive: cartes du Tendre* for invisible monsters. How could one resist the temptation to become lost in them?

4 ELEVATIONS

Unlike his surrealist ancestor, the situationist walker is sometimes equipped with a walkie-talkie, a device still rare during the interwar period. As for signs of destiny, he occasionally influences chance with the aid of a little modern technology. He walks, he deciphers the surrounding environment, but at the same time he communicates with other *dériveurs,* and together they transform the urban space into a clandestine communications network devised to elude power. The same holds for the projected psychogeographic investigations of Amsterdam: "The *dérives* to be undertaken by the Situationist International in Amsterdam in the spring of 1960, with considerable transportation and communication resources, are envisioned both as an objective study of the city and as a communicative game" (*IS* 3, 14–15). In more general terms, one would say that the goal of "unitary urbanism," which is to say situationist urbanism (whose "unitary" character seems to echo the "organic" urbanism of the Saint-Simonians), is reestablishment of the same communication that official urbanism contrives to interrupt, notably by confiscating the street, by doing everything possible to prevent its becoming once more the communal space it supposedly was when large cities first developed—in other words, immediately prior to the dehumanizing interventions of Haussmannization. The *dérive* is, simultaneously, the street reclaimed and communication reestablished. In the end, the only authentic communication takes place in and through the street, which is the bête noire of the society of the spectacle:

> Urbanism is the modern way of tackling the ongoing need to safe-
> guard class power by ensuring the atomization of the workers dan-
> gerously *massed together* by the conditions of urban production. The
> unremitting struggle that has had to be waged against the possibility
> of workers coming together in whatever manner has found a perfect
> field of action in urbanism. The effect of all established powers, since
> the experience of the French revolution, to augment their means of
> keeping order in the street has eventually culminated in the suppres-
> sion of the street itself.[18]

The more boulevards, railways, and expressways pierce the city, the smaller the chances for encounter and assembly. The development of means of communication is actually intended to suppress communication, and the multiplication of modes of transportation (especially public ones) is at odds with genuine transport, with flights of passion. Too much street, and especially too much speed in the street, effectively makes the street disappear, while the situationists, by contrast, dream—even more systematically than Breton with his glass house—of introducing the street even into places of residence. Breton occasionally risked leaving the door of his hotel rooms open to the street. The situationists imagine houses constantly open to circulation in which everything would be communication, or at least communicative. We have already had a glimpse of this in the New York helicoidal house, and further verification is provided by the "Description de la zone jaune" (Description of the Yellow Zone), which includes a description of a model housing block:

> Everything else is interconnected and constitutes a large common space. . . . By means of movable partitions, each floor is broken into many rooms accessible to one another—horizontally as well as vertically, by means of stairways—whose various environments are changed continually by situationist teams in collaboration with a technical support staff. They are used primarily for intellectual games. (*IS* 4, 24–25)

In another part of the same block, there will of course be labyrinths for random wanderings. The idea of opening the roofs of Paris to promenades by outfitting them with emergency stairs and connecting footbridges is proposed elsewhere.[19] Which amounts to saying that insofar as a unitary urbanism takes hold, the street will be delivered to one's doorstep, key in hand. And a good thing, too, for "Description de la zone jaune" figures in a vast project for a "covered" city, or more precisely a hanging city, one premised on the complete suppression of the street as a communal space. Unlike official urbanism, which uses the imperative for circulation to impede communication, the situationist hanging city gives over the entirety of its ground level to functional transport. Circulation is to take place *below* the space of everyday life, which by the same token reclaims its communicative essence. Real life ascends one floor to unfold in an infinity of communicating spaces that no boulevard can interrupt or pollute. The street is relieved of its functionality and restored to desire by an elevation effect. It is divided into a ground floor of need, surrendered to individualizing automobiles and spurious communal transportation (Sartre saw buses as the emblem par excellence of the serial, alienated group), and a first floor reserved for real transport and real mobility: that of a desire allergic to all circulation but its own. Finally, there would be yet another floor of Edenic gardens conducive to still more extraordinary transports—and increasingly aerial ones, for unitary urbanism foresaw the imminent development of private helicopters that would make traffic jams a thing of the past. To change life, to recover community, it is sufficient to raise the standard of living. We are much more "situationist" than we think.

Like his surrealist ancestor, situationist man tends toward elevation, toward disburdenment. He is weightless, like an angel. The resistance of things, their weight and tendency to fall, their downward inclination, their putrefaction, their reversion to earth—such are not his strong points. Angels never age, being beautiful children who never become corpses. Situationist man, too, is forever young. The games he imagines often resemble those of children for whom the world is a kind of continuous Luna Park, as conceived by the situationist Pinot Gallizio: "The world will be the stage and parterre of a never-ending performance. The planet will be transformed into a boundless Luna Park producing new passions and emotions" (*IS* 3, 32).

In a sense, the boundless games of the situationists are meant to be played out not in urban space but in the sky, as suggested later in the same article: "Thus we should paint the routes of the future with unknowable material, stake out the great way of the heavens with signals of a kind commensurate with our grandiose enterprises. Where today there are sodium flares, tomorrow there will be rainbows, fata morganas, aurora borealises constructed by ourselves" (ibid.). Not only the world but also the sky exists to become the *Gesamtkunstwerk* of Pinot Gallizio, who certainly knows how to take the long view when it comes to "the total work." What became of the situationists when they decided to become even more obscure, even more clandestine? They went to heaven. By dint of elevation and *angélisme,* they dissolved in interstellar space, whence they play the invisible redeemers of the society of the spectacle. Perhaps from that altitude they intend to be for the capitalist spectacle what the FTC is for planet earth and its poor ozone layer.

The situationist city ascends to heaven because it has been unburdened of its weight and resistant capacity, having been lightened of all matter, that of stones as well as that of bodies, especially when the latter fall asleep, age, or become corpses. According to the situationist ideal, even death's ward will be made for life—for living in peace: "Ward of death, not for dying but for *living there in peace*" (*IS* 1, 19). At its worst, situationist death is a kind of unjustly slandered mishap, but it comes across more often as a form of serenity. In any event, it never really occurs because there is never any lack of time in the situationist world—except, that is, when it has been confiscated by power, like the rest. Situationist life is a tragedy that ends happily, or, more precisely, one that never ends: "The *construction of situations* will be the continuous realization of a grand game resolutely chosen, the passage between decors and conflicts like those that would dispatch the characters in a tragedy within twenty-four hours. But time for living will no longer be lacking."[20] In the situationist ideal city, time is accomplice to a life impervious to death. It is a city with no place for the phantoms and vampires of the society of the spectacle, so keen on messages and gestures suitable for interception and *détournement* into representation. It is a city of gods, or at least of invisible mortals, installed between a planetary Luna Park and Never-Never Land. Only the dead bury the dead.

There is no place for tombs in the situationist city. Consequently, the dead themselves must move about, becoming if not angels then at least phantoms, and requiring transformable tombs with movable walls, sliding doors, and even footbridges (they, too, must have their communications network). But the dead generally move little; they want not so much to live in peace as to rest in peace; they prefer immobility, even stonelike rigidity (corpselike or not). That is why there is really no place for them in the land of the situationists, so hostile to stone, to buildings made of stone, to the edifying and immobilizing powers of stone. Some situationists call for the outright demolition of religious edifices, while others advocate their transformation into fun houses (effectively combining Notre-Dame with Disneyland), but all agree, following Stendhal, that aesthetic objections to such destruction or transformation should be rejected: "Beauty, *when it is not a promise of happiness,* should be destroyed."[21]

The beauty of the beyond, the beauty of death, the beauty captured in stone has no currency in the Land of Situationism. It is only one short step from contemplation of the portal of Chartres to faith, but the situationists carefully avoid taking it, despite their penchant for the *dérive:* art indeed "derives" from religion, but it also provides the surest means of returning to it. More generally, the situationist project to realize or transcend art implies a relentless struggle against all things religious, an openly adversarial stance against them: from the situationist perspective, art is but the spectacular degradation of old religious practices that fostered community. By contrast, situationist *angélisme* is to be resolutely profane, compulsorily secular. It has nothing to do with the perverse defiance of a Bataille; it is an outright attempt to suppress religion and replace it with a sovereign community purged of all forms of transcendence, whether philosophical or religious. The priest will give way to the architect, the constructor of situations, who measures himself against the theater as well as against religion: "One might say that the construction of situations will replace the theater only in the sense that the real construction of life has increasingly replaced religion" (*IS* 1, 12). In sum, what is in question is a reappropriation of the life coefficient that was lost to art when it became distinct from religion: a dream of immanence, of community without transcendence.

Situationist man is to take up what is good about religion to realize it in its integrity, in its sovereignty. Hence the necessity of replacing the religious buildings that were the glory of ancient architecture with new symbolic structures figuring communal desires, with "personal cathedrals" emptied of all transcendence:

The new vision that is to serve as the theoretical basis for the constructions to come is not yet fully developed, and it won't be until urban experiments are conducted that systematically combine facilities indispensable for a minimum of comfort and security with symbolic edifices figuring desires, forces, and events of the past, the present, and the future. The need for rational expansion of old religious systems, of old tales, and above all of psychoanalysis in the interest of architecture becomes more urgent every day, as the reasons for becoming impassioned disappear. In some way, everyone will inhabit his personal "cathedral." There will be rooms that stimulate dreams better than drugs, and houses in which love will be impossible to resist. Others will exert an irresistible attraction over travelers. (*IS* 1, 18–19)

To personalize cathedrals, to expand religious systems, but rationally, without the imposture of transcendence or belief, to reinvent places charged with mythic or symbolic force, and capable of reinvigorating passion and making it generally accessible: such are the goals of the architect-therapists, in heated competition not only with priests (who have the considerable advantage of the indulgence conferred by faith) but also with psychoanalysts, licensed specialists in the nonrealization of desire: where desire was that of the Other rather than my own, there shall be the mobile houses of a universal community of angelic lovers, or labyrinths for passionate *dériveurs* determined to cede nothing in the matter of desire.

But sometimes the competition is so intense that one cannot help but suspect a kind of complicity, or at least a mimetic rivalry, between the situationists and those they wish to replace. The situationists are implacable when it comes to the vestiges of religion, but in the context of a society that, as they themselves emphasize, is governed by a spectacular regime whose sole divinity is merchandise, which makes all authentically transcendent experience impossible. Are the cathedrals to be destroyed because they serve a purpose or because they do not? Will new cathedrals be necessary, or are they to be replaced by personalized cathedrals, and what exactly is the difference between the two? These questions become especially pressing when the situationist critique of functionalist architecture takes on something that ought not to concern it, namely church construction:

The functionalists, who express the technical utilitarianism of an era, cannot manage to build a single successful church, in the sense that cathedrals with the unitary success of a society that must be called primitive, being much more deeply entrenched than we are in the miserable prehistory of humanity. In a period when technical developments have made functionalism possible, situationist architects seek to create new frameworks for behavior delivered from banality as well as from old taboos, and are absolutely opposed to the edification, and even to the conservation of religious buildings, with which they find themselves in direct competition. The interests of unitary urbanism are objectively consistent with those of general subversion. (*IS* 3, 12)

Situationist architects want to destroy the churches that functionalist architects are incapable of building. "Do not construct the churches that we alone know how to build," they tell them. They aim to replace religious edifices with secular temples of communication whose construction requires some kind of "general subversion," which effectively postpones their becoming visible to the advent of utopia, to which situationism is so closely related through its attempts to produce divinity rationally. The situationist city remains utopian, mythic, a pure promise of community. In the end, it is nothing but a figure given to myth, something that might realize art and by the same token bring art to an end, something that constitutes its perpetually evanescent horizon, something that coincides with the Book. Something that doubtless would be very beautiful.

NOTES

Originally published in *October* 79 (Winter 1997), 49–68.

1. Guy Debord, *The Society of the Spectacle,* trans. Donald Nicholson-Smith (1967; New York: Zone Books, 1994), 133.

2. Ibid., 136.

3. *Internationale situationniste, 1958–69* (Paris: Champ Libre, 1975), vol. 9, 25. All citations from the twelve issues of this journal are from this edition and are hereafter cited in the text by volume and page number.

4. *La véritable scission dans l'Internationale* (Paris: Champ Libre, 1981), 79–80.

5. Raoul Vaneigem, *Traité de savoir-vivre à l'usage des jeunes générations* (Paris: Gallimard, 1968; new edition 1989).

6. Ibid., 7.

7. Ibid., 17.

8. Ibid., 289.

9. Ibid., 103.

10. Guy Debord, *Commentaires sur la société du spectacle* (Paris: Gérard Lebovici, 1988).

11. Cited by Henri Mondor, *Vie de Mallarmé* (Paris: Gallimard, 1941), 687.

12. Debord, *The Society of the Spectacle,* 34.

13. Ibid.

14. Asger Jorn, *Critique de la politique économique* (Brussels, 1960), cited by Jean-François Martos, *Histoire de l'Internationale situationniste* (Paris: Gérard Lebovici, 1989), 103.

15. Vaneigem, *Traité de savoir-vivre,* 207.

16. Guy Debord, "Rapport sur la construction des situations"; translated as "Report on the Construction of Situations and on the Terms of Organization and Action of the International Situatinist Tendency," in this volume, 47.

17. Such a labyrinth would itself be an image of a recent work by Guy Debord entitled *"Cette mauvaise réputation . . ."* (Paris: Gallimard, 1993). In addition to refuting the quasi-totality of criticism leveled against situationism over the last several decades, it is also meant to devour, in effect, all those who dared to penetrate the labyrinth so cunningly arranged by Debord. *"Cette mauvaise réputation"* consists largely of extended citations from contemporary assessments of Debord's work, which makes it a situationist version of the Mallarméan Book: a work produced not individually but collectively, one that verifies the disappearance of the isolated poetic voice in the name of objectivity, of impersonality, something Mallarmé often attempted in his *Tombeaux* and his sepulchral correspondence.

18. Debord, *The Society of the Spectacle,* 121–122.

19. *Potlatch,* October 23, 1955.

20. *Potlatch,* August 7, 1954.

21. *Potlatch,* October 23, 1955.

Difference and Repetition: On Guy Debord's Films

Giorgio Agamben

translated by Brian Holmes

My aim here is to define certain aspects of Debord's poetics, or rather of his compositional technique, in the area of cinema. I will purposefully avoid the notion of "cinematographic work" with respect to Debord, because he himself declared it inapplicable. "Considering the history of my life," he wrote, "I see clearly that I could not make what is called a cinematographic work" (*In girum imus nocte et consumimur igni*). Indeed, not only do I find the concept of work to be useless in Debord's case, but more importantly I wonder if it isn't necessary today, whenever one seeks to analyze what is called a work—literary, cinematographic, or otherwise—to call into question its very status as a work. Rather than inquiring into the work as such, I think we should ask about the relation between what could be done and what actually was done. Once, when I was tempted (as I still am) to consider Guy Debord a philosopher, he told me: "I'm not a philosopher, I'm a strategist." Debord saw his time as an incessant war that engaged his entire life in a strategy. That's why I think that where Debord is concerned, we should ask about the meaning that cinema could have in this strategy. Why cinema, for example, and not poetry, as was the case for Isou, who was very important for the situationists, or why not painting, as for another of Debord's friends, Asger Jorn?

What is at stake here, I believe, is the close tie between cinema and history. Where does the tie come from and what is the history involved?

What is at stake is the specific function of the image and its eminently historical character. There are a couple of important details here. First, man is the only being who is interested in images as such. Animals are very interested in images, but only to the extent that they are fooled. You can show a male fish the image of a female fish and the male will eject his sperm; you can fool a bird with the image of another bird, in order to trap it. But when the animal realizes it's dealing with an image, it loses interest completely. Now, man is an animal who is interested in images when he has recognized them as such. That's why he is interested in painting and why he goes to the cinema. A definition of man from our specific point of view could be that man is a moviegoing animal. He is interested in images after he has recognized that they are not real beings. The other point is that, as Gilles Deleuze has shown, the image in cinema—and not only in cinema, but in modern times generally—is no longer something immobile. It is not an archetype, but nor is it something outside history: rather, it is a cut which itself is mobile, an image-movement, charged as such with a dynamic tension. This dynamic charge can be clearly seen in the photos of Etienne-Jules Marey and Eadweard Muybridge which are at the origins of cinema, images charged with movement. It was a force of this kind that Benjamin saw in what he called the "dialectical image," which he conceived as the very element of historical experience. Historical experience is obtained by the image, and the images themselves are charged with history. One could consider our relation to painting in a similar way: paintings are not immobile images, but stills charged with movement, stills from a film that is missing. They would have to be restored to this film. (You will have recognized the project of Aby Warburg.)

But what is the history involved? Here it must be stressed that it is not a matter of a chronological history in the strict sense, but of a messianic history. Messianic history is defined by two major characteristics. First, it is a history of salvation: something must be saved. But it is also a final history, an eschatological history, in which something must be completed, judged. It must happen here, but in another time; it must leave chronology behind, but without entering some other world. This is the reason why messianic history is incalculable. In the Jewish tradition, there is a tremendous irony surrounding calculations to predict the day of the Messiah's arrival, but without ceasing to repeat that these were forbidden calculations, because the Messiah's arrival is incalculable. Yet at the same time, each historical moment is the time of his arrival. The Messiah has always already arrived, he is always already there. Each moment, each image is charged with history because it is the door through which the Messiah enters. This messianic situation of cinema is what Debord shares with the Godard of *Histoire(s) du cinéma*. Despite their old rivalry—you may recall that in 1968 Debord said Godard was the stupidest of the pro-Chinese Swiss—Godard finally adopted the same paradigm that Debord had been the first to sketch. What is this paradigm, what is this compositional technique? Serge Daney, writing about Godard's *Histoire(s)*, explained that it is montage: "Cinema was looking for one thing, montage, and this was the thing twentieth-century man so terribly needed." This is what Godard shows in *Histoire(s) du cinéma*.

The specific character of cinema stems from montage, but what is montage, or rather, what are the conditions of possibility for montage? In philosophy since Kant, the conditions of possibility for something are called transcendentals. What are the transcendentals of montage?

There are two transcendental conditions of montage: *repetition* and *stoppage*. Debord did not invent them, but he brought them to light; he exhibited the transcendentals as such. And Godard went on to do the same in his *Histoire(s)*. There's no need to shoot film anymore, just to repeat and stop. That's an epoch-making innovation in cinema. I was very much struck by this phenomenon in Locarno. The compositional technique has not changed, it is still montage, but now montage comes to the forefront and is shown as such. That's why one can consider that cinema enters a zone of indifference where all genres tend to coincide, documentary and narrative, reality and fiction. Cinema will now be made on the basis of images from cinema.

But let's return to cinema's conditions of possibility, *repetition* and *stoppage*. What is repetition? There are four great thinkers of repetition in modernity: Kierkegaard, Nietzsche, Heidegger, and Gilles Deleuze. All four have shown us that repetition is not the return of the identical; it is not the same as such that returns. The force and the grace of repetition, the novelty it brings us, is the return as the possibility of what was. Repetition restores the possibility of what was, renders it possible anew; it's almost a paradox. To repeat something is to make it possible anew. Here lies the proximity of repetition and memory. Memory cannot give us back what was, as such: that would be hell. Instead, memory restores possibility to the past. This is the meaning of the theological experience that Benjamin saw in memory, when he said that memory makes the unfulfilled into the fulfilled, and the fulfilled into the unfulfilled. Memory is, so to speak, the organ of reality's modalization; it is that which can transform the real into the possible and the possible into the real. If you think about it, that's also the definition of cinema. Doesn't cinema always do just that, transform the real into the possible and the possible into the real? One can define the already-seen as the fact of perceiving something present as though it had already been, and its converse as the fact of perceiving something that has already been as present. Cinema takes place in this zone of indifference. We then understand why work with images can have such a historical and messianic importance, because they are a way of projecting power and possibility toward that which is impossible by definition, toward the past. Thus cinema does the opposite of the media. What is always given in the media is the fact, what was, without its possibility, its power: we are given a fact before which we are powerless. The media prefer a citizen who is indignant, but powerless. That's exactly the goal of the TV news. It's the bad form of memory, the kind of memory that produces the man of *ressentiment*.

By placing repetition at the center of his compositional technique, Debord makes what he shows us possible again, or rather he opens up a zone of undecidability between the real and the possible. When he shows an excerpt of a TV news broadcast, the force of the repetition is to cease being an accomplished fact and to become possible again, so to speak. You ask, "How was that possible?"—first reaction—but at the same time you understand that yes, everything is possible. Hannah Arendt once defined the ultimate experience of the camps as the principle of "everything is possible," even the horror we are now being shown. It is in this extreme sense that repetition restores possibility.

The second element, the second transcendental, is stoppage. It is the power to interrupt, the "revolutionary interruption" of which Benjamin spoke. It is very important in cinema, but once again, not only in cinema. This is where the difference lies between cinema and narrative, the prose narrative with which cinema tends to be compared. On the contrary, stoppage shows us that cinema is closer to poetry than to prose. The theorists of literature have always had a great deal of trouble defining the difference between poetry and prose. Many elements that characterize poetry can also pass over into prose (from the viewpoint of the number of syllables, for example, prose can contain verse). The only things that can be done in poetry and not in prose are the caesura and the enjambment (that is, the carryover to a following line). The poet can counter a syntactic limit with an acoustic and metrical limit. This limit is not only a pause; it is a noncoincidence, a disjunction between sound and meaning. This is what Paul Valéry meant in his very beautiful definition of the poem: "the poem, a prolonged hesitation between sound and meaning." This is also why Hölderlin could say that by stopping the rhythmic unfolding of words and representations, the caesura causes the word and the representation to appear as such. To bring the word to a stop is to pull it out of the flux of meaning, to exhibit it as such. The same could be said of the stoppage practiced by Debord, stoppage as constitutive of a transcendental condition of montage. One could return to Valéry's definition of poetry and say that cinema, or at least a certain kind of cinema, is a prolonged hesitation between image and meaning. It is not merely a matter of a chronological pause, but rather a power of stoppage that works on the image itself, that pulls it away from the narrative power to exhibit it as such. It is in this sense that Debord in his films and Godard in his *Histoire(s)* both work with the power of stoppage.

These two transcendental conditions can never be separated, they form a single system. In Debord's last film there is a very important sentence right at the beginning: "I have shown that the cinema can be reduced to this white screen, then this black screen." What Debord refers to is precisely repetition and stoppage, which are indissoluble as transcendental conditions of montage. Black and white, the ground where the images are so present that they can no longer be seen, and the void where there is no image. There are analogies here with Debord's theoretical work. Take, for example, the concept of "constructed situation," which gave its name to situationism. A situation is a zone of undecidability, of indifference between a uniqueness and a repetition. When Debord says we should construct situations, he is always referring to something that can be repeated and yet is also unique.

Debord says the same thing at the close of *In girum imus nocte et consumimur igni,* where instead of the traditional word "End" there appears the sentence "To be taken up again from the beginning." The same principle is at work in the very title of the film, which is a palindrome that can be read both ways. A sentence that curls back into itself. In this sense, there is a kind of essential palindromy in Debord's cinema.

Together, repetition and stoppage carry out the messianic task of cinema I have described. This task essentially involves creation. But it is not a new creation after the first. One cannot consider the artist's work uniquely in terms of creation; on the contrary, at the heart of every creative act there is an act of decreation. Deleuze once said of cinema that every act of creation is also an act of resistance. What does it mean to resist? Above all it means de-creating what exists, de-creating the real, being stronger than the fact in front of you. Every act of creation is also an act of thought, and an act of thought is a creative act, because it is defined above all by its capacity to de-create the real.

If such is the task of cinema, what is an image that has been worked on in this way, by repetition and stoppage? What is it that changes in the status of the image? We will have to rethink entirely our traditional conception of expression. The current concept of expression is dominated by the Hegelian model, in which all expression is realized by a *medium*—an image, a word, or a color— which in the end must disappear in the fully realized expression. The expressive act is fulfilled when the means, the medium, is no longer perceived as such. The medium must disappear in that which it gives us to see, in the absolute that shows itself, that shines forth in the medium. On the contrary, the image worked by repetition and stoppage is a means, a medium, that does not disappear in what it makes visible. It is what I would call a "pure means," one that shows itself as such. The image gives itself to be seen instead of disappearing in what it makes visible. Historians of the cinema have noted, as a disconcerting novelty, the moment when the main character of Bergman's film *Monika,* Harriet Andersson, suddenly stares directly into the lens of the camera. Bergman himself has written of this sequence: "Here, and for the first time in the history of cinema, a direct, shameless contact is established with the viewer." Since then, pornography and advertising have made this procedure banal. We are accustomed to the gaze of the porno star who stares fixedly into the camera while doing what she has to do, as a way of showing that she is more interested in the viewer than in her partner.

Since his early films and ever more clearly as he went along, Debord has shown us the image as such, that is to say, according to one of his principles from *The Society of the Spectacle,* the image as a zone of undecidability between the true and the false. But there are two ways of showing an image. The image exhibited as such is no longer an image of anything; it is itself imageless. The only thing of which one cannot make an image is, if you will, the being-image of the image. The sign can signify anything, *except the fact that it is in the process of signifying.* What cannot be signified or said in a discourse, what is in a certain way unutterable, can nonetheless be shown in the discourse. There are two ways of showing this "imagelessness," two ways of making visible the fact that there is nothing more to be seen. One is pornography and advertising, which act as though there were always something more to be seen, always more images behind the images; while the other way is to exhibit the image as image and thus to allow the appearance of "imagelessness," which, as Benjamin said, is the refuge of all images. It is here, in this difference, that the ethics and the politics of cinema come into play.

NOTE

This text is the translation of a lecture by Giorgio Agamben, delivered on the occasion of the "Sixth International Video Week" at the Centre Saint-Gervais in Geneva in November 1995.

Dismantling the Spectacle: The Cinema of Guy Debord

THOMAS Y. LEVIN

The only interesting undertaking is the liberation of everyday life,
not only within a historical perspective but for us and right away.
This entails the withering away of alienated forms of communication. *The cinema, too, has to be destroyed.*[1]

It is society and not technology that has made cinema what it is. The
cinema could have been historical examination, theory, essay, memories. It could have been the film which I am making at this moment.[2]

I

Among the various social practices that serve Guy Debord as paradigmatic instances of what he calls the "society of the spectacle," the most often cited are
without doubt television and cinema. Typical in this regard is the American edition of Debord's paratactic theoretical text *Society of the Spectacle* (hereafter referred to as *SoS*), where cinematic iconography not only dominates the front and
back covers—which incorporate a photograph of spectators at a 3-D movie[3]—
but also continues throughout the volume in a series of illustrations located
within the socketed frames of a filmstrip.[4] However, although cinema is certainly

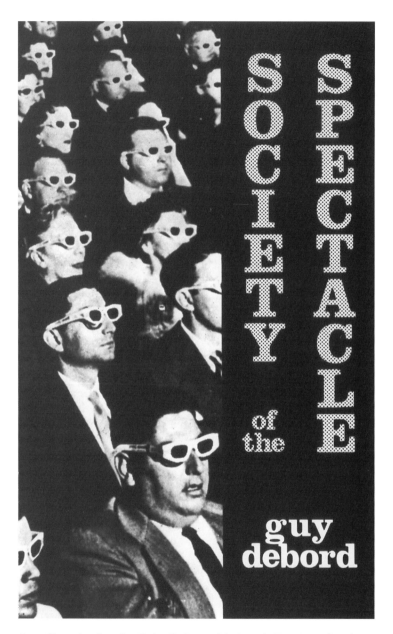

Cover illustration from Guy Debord's *Society of the Spectacle* (American edition).

Filmstrip, illustration in *Society of the Spectacle* (American edition).

a privileged *figure* for the society of the spectacle, it is a mistake to assume that Debord's "spectacle" is synonymous with the "spectacularity" of the filmic medium. On the contrary, as is manifest from the very beginning of Debord's text, the theoretical concept of spectacle is used to designate a historical, socio-economic condition: "The spectacle is not a collection of images, but a social relation among people, mediated by images" (*SoS,* thesis 4).[5] For Debord, the spectacle designates a Weltanschauung (simply put, the alienation of late capitalism) that *manifests* itself in various spectacular phenomena, among them the cinema: "The world at once present and absent which the spectacle *makes visible* is the world of the commodity dominating all that is lived" (*SoS,* thesis 37).

The confusion surrounding the "spectacle" is to some extent produced by a slippage in Debord's employment of the term. Sometimes it does refer to the realm of representation, as is evident in the structural analogy of the opening thesis of *SoS:*

> In societies where modern conditions of production prevail, all of life presents itself as an immense accumulation of *spectacles.* Everything that was directly lived has moved away into a representation.

However, in the next thesis, Debord differentiates between "images of the world" and "the spectacle in general, [which] as the concrete inversion of life, is the autonomous movement of the nonliving." Although this distinction itself merits a close and careful reading, for the present investigation it must suffice to say that the latter use of the expression is *allegorical:* "The spectacle, as the present social organization of the paralysis of history and memory, of the abandonment of history built on the foundation of historical time, is the *false consciousness of time*" (*SoS,* thesis 158). The conflation in turn stems from Debord's rhetorical employment of the notion of spectacles qua images or representation to concretize his reading of "spectacle" as *the* allegory of late capital.

A characteristic instance of this strategy can be found among the illustrations in the journal *Internationale situationniste* (hereafter, *IS*)—a rich collection of montage/collage work on pieces of commodity culture, including such *détourne-*

ments[6] as recaptioned or reworked advertisements, comic strips, newspaper photographs, problematic depictions of scantily clad women, illustrations from industrial manuals, graphs, and so forth.[7] In one of the last issues of the journal, there is a reproduction of a magazine advertisement for German Eumig home movie cameras, whose text reads, "I love my camera because I love to live: I record the best moments of life and revive them at will in all their richness." Underneath the image there is a caption entitled "The Domination of Life by the Spectacle" that reads as follows:

> This advertisement for Eumig cameras (summer 1967) *evokes* very well the petrification of individual life that has reversed itself into a spectacular economy: the present can now be lived immediately *as memory*. Time is submitted to the illusory order of a permanently available present and, through this spatialization of time, both time and life have been lost together.[8]

Here film functions not as the cause but as an illustration, an "evocation" or figure—albeit a privileged one—for a sociopolitical and epistemological shift that has taken place under late capitalism. An attitude toward the production of spectacle (home movies) is taken as a symptom of a "spectacular economy" (the temporality of an alienated social condition). As Debord puts it, years later, in a veiled reference to this advertisement: "When one loves life, one goes to the movies."[9]

The resistance to a facile collapsing of cinema and spectacle is imperative if one is to understand the complex relationship between the Situationist International (SI) and the filmic medium. To the extent that cinema is synonymous with spectacle—a spatialization of time, a staging of separation, a fostering of passivity, alienation, and so on—it is simply unacceptable and must be eliminated. Along with similar forms of spectacle, Debord insists that "the cinema, too, must be destroyed."[10] The question remains, however, to what extent the condemnation of cinema here is a critique of the politics of the "apparatus" analogous to arguments put forth by Martin Heidegger and later by Jean-Louis

"I Love My Camera Because I Love to Live," illustration in *Internationale situationniste* 11 (October 1967), 57.

"London, September 1960: The situationists at the cinema," illustration in *Internationale situationniste* 5 (December 1960), 8.

Baudry and Jean-Louis Comolli regarding the objectification inherent in the very structure of representation.[11] For it might be that what is at issue here is not the cinema as such, but rather a historically specific set of cinematic *practices,* a certain *cinema*—classic, commercial, industrialized, narrativized, and so forth. As Debord notes: "It is society and not technology that has made cinema what it is. The cinema could have been historical examination, theory, essay, memories."[12] This leaves open the possibility of an alternative sort of cinematic activity incompatible with the economy of spectacle, a nonspectacular, antispectacular, or other-than-spectacular cinema. Such a realm of possibility is the precondition of what one might call situationist cinema.

The interest in film on the part of the SI must be understood in light of the significance in its genealogy of the artistic avant-garde: an important dimension of what could be called the "situationist project" involved the production of (art) works. It was essential, however, that such works be critiques of the current historical moment and contain their own negation—that is, they should be in a sense anti-works. As Raoul Vaneigem phrased it in a statement put forth at the fifth SI conference in Göteborg, Sweden (August 1961):

> It is a question not of elaborating the spectacle of refusal, but rather of refusing the spectacle. In order for their elaboration to be *artistic* in the new and authentic sense defined by the SI, the elements of the destruction of the spectacle must precisely cease to be works of art. There is no such thing as *situationism* or a situationist work of art nor for that matter a spectacular situationist.[13]

Indeed, the conference members subsequently approved a suggestion by Attila Kotányi to call the products of such aesthetic activity on the part of the SI "antisituationist," given that truly situationist conditions had yet to be realized. Similarly, Debord insists—in a formulation astonishingly reminiscent of Adorno's *Aesthetic Theory*—that "only the real negation of culture can preserve its meaning. It can no longer be *cultural.* Thus it is what in some way remains at the level of culture, but with a completely different meaning."[14] The contradictions and dangers of a radically negative cultural critique that nevertheless insists on the production of (anti)art objects were a topic of continuing polemical debate within the ranks of the SI. Yet they were very aware of what they themselves described as the

> ambiguous and dangerous policy whose risks the SI had to run by consenting to act *in* culture while being against the entire present organization of this culture and even against all culture as a separate sphere. Nor is this most intransigent oppositional attitude and program any less ambiguous and dangerous because it nevertheless has to coexist with the present order.[15]

This strategic concession is perhaps nowhere more evident than in the SI's relationship to that most compromised medium, the cinema.

The first official articulation of the SI position on cinema occurs in a subsection of one of the first articles in the first issue of *IS* in 1958 entitled, indicatively, "For and against the Cinema."[16] "Cinema is the central art of our society," the editorial begins, and the formal and anecdotal expression in the cinema as well as its material infrastructure are "the best *representation* of an epoch of anarchically juxtaposed inventions (not articulated but simply combined)."[17] But rather than making use of the extraordinary capacities opened up by its technical innovations, so the argument continues, the cinema offers a passive substitute to unitary artistic activity, an exponential increase in the reactionary power of nonparticipatory spectacle. The text makes it clear, however, that this could be otherwise:

> Those that want to construct this [new] world must simultaneously fight the tendency of cinema to constitute the anticonstruction of situations (the construction of a slave atmosphere, the succession of the cathedrals) while recognizing the significance of the new technological developments (stereo sound, odorama) that are valuable in and of themselves.[18]

The opposite of a knee-jerk Luddite rejection of cinematic technology as such, the editorial attributes the reactionary state of the medium (the absence of avant-garde developments manifest in the plastic arts and in literature) to economic and ideological constraints, but also to the *social importance* of the medium. It is this importance, in turn, that makes it necessary that the medium remain in the control of the hegemonic class.

Instead of abandoning film as hopelessly contaminated, the article closes instead with a call for its appropriation. Cinema is likened to architecture (another major SI concern) in terms of its significance within daily life, the difficulties facing any attempt at its renovation, and the imperative for just such a transformation. This leads to the following conclusion:

> One must therefore struggle to appropriate a truly experimental sector within the cinema. We can envisage two distinct ways of using cinema: first, its employment as a form of propaganda in the presituationist transition period; then its direct employment as a constitutive element of an actual situation.[19]

One could read this as the first, rough outline of a manifesto for an (anti)situationist film practice.

To gain a more detailed understanding of the motivations behind the SI espousal of film as a revolutionary weapon, one must examine remarks scattered throughout their publications. In one of the more programmatic of these statements, the concluding section of the article "The Situationists and the New Forms of Action against Politics and Art," René Viénet argues that the SI must make use of the cinema—"the newest and without doubt most useful means of expression of our epoch"—as a didactic, analytic, and critical tool:

> Among other possibilities, the cinema lends itself particularly well to studying the present as a historical problem, to dismantling processes of reification. Historical reality can, of course, be apprehended, known, and filmed only in the course of a complicated process of

mediations. . . . This mediation would be difficult if the empirical existence of facts themselves was not already a mediated existence that only takes on an appearance of immediateness because of and to the extent that, on the one hand, consciousness of the mediation is lacking and, on the other hand, the facts have been uprooted from the network of their determinations, placed in an artificial isolation, and poorly linked together again by the montage of classical cinema. It is precisely this mediation that has been lacking, and inevitably so, in presituationist cinema, which has limited itself to so-called objective forms or re-presentation of politico-moral concepts, whenever it has not been a merely academic type of narrative with all its hypocrisies.[20]

Viénet's conception of an SI film practice enlists the specific capacities of the medium (above all, photographic documentation, voice-over, and analytic montage) to expose the always already mediated status of the seemingly immediate and "natural" world constructed in classical, or presituationist, cinema. The present is studied as a historical problem, history is recast as a problem of representation, and, above all, the practice of representation itself is continuously subjected to critical interrogation. This staging of mediation takes the form of a work on other mediations, primarily by means of cinema's elective affinity to the important strategy of citation and reinscription referred to as *détournement*. Indeed, in a programmatic essay, the editorial collective of *IS* goes so far as to say that "the signature of the movement, the trace of its presence and its contestation in contemporary cultural reality . . . is first and foremost the employment of *détournement*."[21]

It is in this capacity for visual-acoustic *détournement* that cinema finds its single most important justification as an instrument of SI activity. As Debord and Gil J. Wolman confirm in their user's guide to this hallmark SI activity, among the various vehicles for *détournement* such as posters, records, radio broadcasts, and comic strips, none lends itself better than cinema: "It is obviously in the framework of the cinema that *détournement* can attain its greatest efficacity, and undoubtedly, for those concerned with this aspect, its greatest beauty."[22] As will become evident below, such *détournement* can take a number of forms. On the other hand, in the double movement of this "powerful cultural weapon," the context and meaning of both insignificant phenomena (newspaper clippings, advertisements, quotidian phrases) and significant elements (citations from Marx or Saint-Just, a sequence from an Eisenstein film) can be displaced and estranged before being subsequently reinscribed and transformed through radical juxtaposition.

On the other hand, entire films can be "détourned": Debord and Wolman propose *Birth of a Nation,* for example, because of its combination of formal innovations unprecedented in the history of cinema with a racist plot that is utterly intolerable. Rather than censoring it, they suggest, it would be better to détourn it as a whole, without necessarily even altering the montage, by adding a sound track that made a powerful denunciation of the horrors of imperialist war and of the activities of the Ku Klux Klan that, they point out, continue in the United States to this very day.[23] *Détournement* could also be used, they go on to say, for the filmic rewriting of history and in order to illustrate theoretical claims.[24] In an early text, there is also an amusing suggestion as to how one can recuperate hopelessly commercial films through the use of *détournement* as a mode of spectatorship. At one point during the itinerary of a *dérive,* one should stop into a movie theater for slightly less than an hour and interpret the currently playing adventure film as follows:

> Let the heros be some more or less historical people who are close to us, connect the events of the inept scenario to the real reasons which we understand are behind the actions, and connect them also to the events of the current week. Here you have an acceptable collective distraction.[25]

Besides *détournement,* however, there are a number of other arguments for the importance of the cinema within the corpus of SI writings. Viénet insists that the SI must require each of its members to be just as capable of making a film as writing an article because film is just as powerful and accessible a polemical medium as articles, books, leaflets, or posters. Moreover, he argues, such cinematic experience would in turn "intensify" the written articulation of the same problems.[26] In an untranslated text entitled "For the Debate on Orientation, Spring 1970: A Note on the First Series of Texts," Debord makes a similar argument, convinced that the production of films is important not only for rhetorical but also for financial reasons.[27] Under the heading "Le cinéma," the last of a series of "Modest Propositions," he writes:

> Each film could give one or two situationists working as assistants the opportunity to master their own style in this language; and the inevitable success of our works would also provide the economic base for the future production of these comrades. *The expansion of our audience is of decisive importance.*[28]

For these and other reasons, Debord claims that of the many young filmmakers in various countries attempting to use film as instruments of revolutionary critique, at present

> only situationist positions and methods, following the arguments set out by René Viénet in our last issue, have direct access to a revolutionary use of cinema today—while acknowledging that politico-economic conditions are, of course, still able to pose problems.[29]

This claim is fleshed out in a series of LI and SI film reviews of movies by Julien Duvivier, the "cinematographic ruin"[30] (an indignant critique of *Marianne de ma jeunesse*), Federico Fellini (a pan of *La Strada*), Agnès Varda (*La pointe courte* faulted for its vacuous politics), Alain Resnais (praised for *Hiroshima mon amour,* then lambasted for *L'année dernière à Marienbad*), Norman McLaren (*Blinkity Blank* accused of plagiarizing the lettrist cinema), and Jean-Luc Godard, "the dumbest of the pro-Chinese Swiss" (attacked in a number of articles for his cinematic politics, especially in *A bout de souffle* and *Le gai savoir*).[31] The greatest insight into the "contemporary revolutionary usage of the cinema" by the SI, however, is to be had from the films they themselves—that is, first and foremost Guy Debord—made.

II

Je veux un ciné qua non![32]

Yes. Guy Debord, theorist and critic of the spectacle par excellence, was—as he himself often pointed out—a filmmaker.[33] It is a most curious and rather ignored fact that besides writing, organizing, and editing the *IS,* adjudicating schisms, and denouncing traitors and fools, Debord also directed no less than six 35mm black-and-white sound films over a period of twenty-six years from 1952 to 1978 and had plans for numerous others as well.[34] If this seems surprising, it is no accident: these films were attended by only a very few in Paris, have rarely been seen outside France, have never been screened in the U.S., and have provoked almost no critical literature whatsoever beside a number of more or less incidental newspaper reviews.[35]

To some extent this is due to the fact that the films are hard to watch (for reasons that will become clearer below). But until recently, at least, the films *could* be seen. Indeed, Debord's patron and friend Gérard Lebovici—a French film producer whom he had met in 1971—not only supported Debord's work by financing what was effectively a situationist press, Editions Champ Libre, he also bought a cinema—the Studio Cujas in Saint-Germain-des-Prés—that projected Debord's complete cinematographic production on a continuous and exclusive basis. This lasted only through 1984, however, when following the mysterious and still unsolved murder of Lebovici in a parking garage off the Champs Elysées, Debord suddenly withdrew his films in a gesture of protest and mourning classically situationist in its decisiveness. Incensed by the murder of his friend and by the manner in which the press reported it, he then wrote *Considérations sur l'assassinat de Gérard Lebovici* (Reflections on the Assassination of Gérard Lebovici), in which he announced that the outrageous manner in which the newspapers have discussed his assassination has led me to decide that none of my films will ever be shown again in France. This absence will be the most fitting homage.[36]

Today all efforts to view the films in Paris prove futile: the distributor acknowledges that he has the prints but requires Debord's permission to screen them and this permission, for reasons that must be respected, is not to be had.[37]

While Debord's films are thus now, strictly speaking, invisible, they fortunately are not entirely unavailable since Debord published detailed scenarios of his film works in both journals and books on a number of occasions. The first three scenarios appeared in a volume entitled (indicatively) *Contre le cinéma* (Against the Cinema) published by the Scandinavian Institute for Comparative Vandalism in 1964,[38] and in 1978 the scenarios of all six of Debord's films were made available in the collection *Oeuvres cinématographiques complètes, 1952–1978* (Complete Cinematographic Works).[39] With only one exception, which will be articulated below, the study of Debord's antispectacular cinema is forced to take recourse to the only available traces, the appropriately nonspectacular *textual* scenarios.

In the opening moments of Debord's first film, *Hurlements en faveur de Sade* (Howls in Favor of Sade; 1952), Debord himself provides the audience with the cinematic tradition in which to situate his work:

> Memory aid for a history of cinema: 1902—Voyage dans la lune. 1920—The Cabinet of Dr. Caligari. 1924—Entr'acte. 1926—Battleship Potemkin. 1928—Un chien andalou. 1931—City Lights. Birth of Guy-Ernest Debord. 1951—Traité de bave et d'éternité. 1952—L'Anticoncept—Hurlements en faveur de Sade.[40]

This whirlwind tour of landmarks in film history—genre classics of the early cinema (Georges Méliès), expressionist cinema (Robert Wiene), dada cinema (René Clair), Russian revolutionary cinema (Sergei Eisenstein), surrealist cinema (Louis Buñuel and Salvador Dalí), and socially engaged comedy (Charlie Chaplin)—

Cover illustration from Guy Debord, *Contre le cinéma* (1964).

also sketches the contours of a film aesthetic if one considers each entry as short-hand for a catalogue of formal devices and concerns. This is particularly true of the last two works listed prior to Debord's *Hurlements,* the extraordinary and largely unfamiliar films of Isidore Isou and Gil J. Wolman who, along with Maurice Lemaître, are the principal figures of what is known as lettrist cinema, the cinematic avant-garde that was probably the single greatest influence on Debord's cinematic practice.

In the largely neglected history of postwar French experimental cinema, it was the lettrist movement whose remarkable films, or "movie performances," in the 1950s took up a wide range of radical practices (first explored decades earlier by the dadaists) that later became the basic vocabulary of the American and continental "underground" cinema.[41] These practices include, to take just a few examples, the use of flicker, radical sound-image discontinuity, negative sequences, multiple simultaneous acoustic inputs, direct manipulation of the celluloid surface through tearing, writing, and scratching, and an active engagement of the spectator à la "expanded cinema." According to Dominique Noguez, the historian of the French experimental cinema and virtually the only scholar of avant-garde film to recognize the significance of the lettrist cinema,

> it was really the lettrist movement (Isidore Isou, Maurice Lemaître) that laid the foundations in the early fifties for an avant-garde revival. At the same time as, or even before, the American avant-garde, the lettrists invented a great many of the working methods, the forms and the structures widely used today throughout the international experimental cinema.[42]

Indeed, as will become clearer below, the lettrist cinema not only provided a formative context for the films by Debord but also anticipated and to some extent may have provoked aspects of the work of filmmakers such as Peter Kubelka, Tony Conrad, Malcolm LeGrice, and Norman McLaren, to name just a few.

The theoretical basis of lettrist film finds its most eloquent—and extensive—expression in the *Esthétique du cinéma* by Jean-Isidore Isou, a Romanian

Jew who was the founder of the lettrist movement.[43] It is in this impressively elaborated philosophical architectonic that Isou makes a distinction (fundamental to the lettrist aesthetic) between two successive tendencies in the development of any artistic medium: the *phase amplique* (amplic phase) and the *phase ciselante* (chiseling phase). The former refers to the period during which an art form is elaborated, develops its stylistic vocabularies, and employs them to explore and give expression to subjects other than itself. In cinema this would correspond to the development of narrative techniques (flashback, subjective camera), the evolution of various genres, the exploration of the camera's documentary capacities, and so on. The second, "chiseling" phase occurs when the first has run its course and the medium finds itself at a point of exhaustion or of bloated, decadent excess. This leads to a renunciation of subjects external to the medium itself, a reflexive involution during which basic formal and technical presuppositions are subjected to a radical interrogation.[44]

The polemical claim of the lettrist film aesthetic is that the cinematic medium has exhausted its amplic resources and must now move into the subsequent chiseling phase. This is proclaimed in one of the first of numerous manifestos for the new era of "discrepant" cinema, a manifesto that is itself, as it explicitly points out, a film: the first section of Isou's *Traité de bave et d'éternité* (Treatise of Slobber and Eternity; 1951).[45] Here the protagonist Daniel, expounding his new ideas on the "art of film" to the unruly members of a ciné-club audience, declares:

> I think first of all that the cinema is too rich. It is obese. It has reached its limits, its maximum. The moment it attempts to grow any further, cinema will explode. Suffering from a case of congestion, this *pig stuffed with fat* will rip apart into a thousand pieces. I announce the *destruction of cinema,* the first apocalyptic sign of disjunction, of the rupture of this *bloated and pot-bellied* organism called film.[46]

Rather than attempting to create new masterpieces, Daniel insists, the future of the cinema lies in the chewing up, digesting, and regurgitating of the master-

"Photograph—on intentionally damaged footage—published in 1952 in the journal *Ion*," of Guy Debord. (Debord, *Contre le cinéma*, 11.)

pieces of the past. In formal terms, this imperative—which could be read as a call for cinematic *détournement*—manifests itself in two practices that have become the hallmark of lettrist cinema, the radical suspension of sound-image coordination and the intentional mutilation of images:

> The rupture between words and the photograph will constitute what I call THE DISCREPANT CINEMA. *I proclaim the manifesto of discrepant cinema!* I call for filmstrips that have been lacerated or willfully worked over by the filmmaker, *chiseled filmstrips.*[47]

Indeed, referring to what he calls the "sadism of the photo," Daniel explains that the more the filmstrip is decomposed, gangrened, and infected, the more beautiful it will seem to the filmmaker.

Isou's *Esthétique du cinéma* was first published in April 1952 as the lead article in the first (and only) issue of the journal *Ion,* a "special issue on cinema" that also includes virtually all of the major figures and works of lettrist cinema.[48] Besides Isou's text—which is cited in the introductory remarks as the shared basis of the entire issue[49]—the table of contents includes an important piece by Serge Berna entitled "Jusqu'à l'os" (To the Bone), texts by Poucette, Yolande de Luart, and Monique Geoffroy, Marc'O's "Première manifestation d'un cinéma nucléaire," as well as the scenarios of Gil J. Wolman's *L'Anticoncept,* François Dufrêne's *Tambours du jugement premier,* of Gabriel Pomerand's *La légende cruelle,* and of Guy Debord's first film, *Hurlements en faveur de Sade.* It was this very same group that, almost simultaneously with the publication of *Ion,* undertook a "systematic sabotage" of the 1952 Cannes Film Festival that ultimately led to their arrest.[50] As part of their actions, these "men of a new cinema" signed and distributed a polemical tract entitled "Fini le cinéma français" (French Cinema is Over) that condemned current commercial film production and announced the advent of the new "insurrectional" phase of lettrist cinema:

> A number of men [sic], dissatisfied with what they have been given, surpass the world of official expressions and the festival of its poverty.

After **L'ESTHETIQUE DU CINEMA** by Isidore **ISOU**, **TAM-BOURS DU JUGEMENT PREMIER**, the essay in imaginary cinema by François **DUFRENE**, systematizes to the utmost extreme the exhaustion of filmic means, by locating it beyond all of its technology.

Guy-Ernest **DEBORD** with

HURLEMENTS EN FAVEUR DE SADE arrives at the end of cinema in its insurrectional phase.

After these refusals, definitively outside the norms which you like, the

CINEMA NUCLEAIRE by **MARC'O.** integrates the exhibition space and the spectator into the cinematographic representation.

From now on, cinema can no longer be anything but **NUCLEAR**. Thus we want to go beyond these derisory competitions of sub-products between little businessmen who are either already illiterate or destined to soon become so. Our mere presence here makes them die.

And here are the men [sic] of a new cinema: Serge **BERNA**, **G. E. DEBORD**, François **DUFRENE**, Monique **GEOFFROY**, Jean Isidore **ISOU**, Yolande du **LUART**, **MARC'O.**, Gabriel **POME-RAND**, **POUCETTE**, Gil J. **WOLMAN**.[51]

The scenario of *Hurlements* published in *Ion,* a first version later abandoned, is a veritable catalogue of lettrist cinematic strategies and citations. These include acoustic material by (and/or references to) Dufrêne, Marc'O, and Isou, as well as improvisations of lettrist poetry, citations of Apollinaire, shouts, noises, and music by Vivaldi. The image track, which includes newsreel footage (a boxing match, young people killed in the streets of Athens, the Indian army), images of Paris, of Debord, and of Marc'O, also contains much graphical work on language, black frames, and film scratched to the point of total destruction. At times, however, it is, as is spelled out on the screen, "T,e,l,l,e,m,e,n,t, v,i,d,e, à, h,u,r,l,e,r, à, h,u,r,l,e,r" (So empty one could scream, one could scream). The function of these and other devices are elucidated by Debord in an epigrammatic preface to the scenario entitled "Prolegomenes à tout cinéma futur" (Prolegomena to all Future Cinema).[52] In this programmatic one-page text (whose first and last lines reappear in the scenario) Debord guides the reader through the various lettrist techniques that will be employed in his film. These techniques, Debord states in a slightly ironic appropriation of Isouian rhetoric, will assure that his film "will remain among the most important in the history of the reductive hypostasis of cinema by means of a terrorist disorganization of the discrepant."[53] According to Debord's poetics of lettrist cinema, the chiseling or defacement of the image and the lettrist sound performances "are here envisaged as the expression as such of revolt"; censored phrases "denounce repressive forces"; words spelled out "sketch an even more total dislocation," a "destruction" that continues in the aleatory relation of sound and image that reciprocally invade, duplicate, succeed, or ignore each other.

In the second and final version of *Hurlements en faveur de Sade* that premiered barely two months after the publication of *Ion,* there is hardly a trace of the lettrist idiom so manifest in the scenario described above.[54] Stripped of all its "chiseled" aspects in both the visual and acoustic domains, the notorious *Hurlements* is a black-and-white sound film *without images.*[55] Its sound track, devoid of any music or noise, consists of dialogue spoken without expression by Wolman, Isou, Debord, Serge Berna, and Barbara Rosenthal. The image track is literally black and white: when one of the five voices is speaking, the screen is white; during the remainder of the film the sound track is silent, the screen is black, and the entire screening space is dark. The dialogue consists primarily of phrases that have been détourned from journals, works by James Joyce, the French *code civil,* Isou's *Esthétique du cinéma,* and John Ford's *Rio Grande,* supplemented by quotidian banalities.[56] More remarkable still is the fact that the sound track runs only for a total of approximately twenty minutes in a film lasting one hour and twenty minutes. Needless to say, the audience has become bored and nervous, if not violent, long before the twenty-four-minute black silence that makes up the final sequence—a sequence that Debord claims was the inspiration for Yves Klein's monochrome paintings.[57]

The history of the early screenings of *Hurlements* suggests to what extent the film successfully realized the concluding credo of the "Prolegomena" that is also heard on the film's sound track: "The arts of the future will be radical transformations of situations, or nothing at all."[58] At its Paris premier on June 30 at the Ciné-Club d'Avant-Garde in the Musée de l'Homme, *Hurlements* was almost immediately brought to a halt by Armand-Jean Cauliez, director of the film club, and yet still managed to provoke violence in the audience. The film was first screened in its entirety on October 13, 1952, at the Ciné-Club du Quartier Latin in the rooms of the Sociétés Savantes.[59] This time there was no disturbance thanks to the presence of a group of "left lettrists" who enforced the peace.[60] Screenings of *Hurlements* at the ICA (London) in May 1957 and then again in June 1960 also caused amusing scandals, the latter event described as follows by Guy Atkins in his study of Asger Jorn:

> During a final silence of twenty-four minutes, when the only sound in the room was the turning of the reel, a member of the audience got up, thanked Mrs [Dorothy] Morland [Director of the ICA] for an interesting evening and apologized for having to leave early. Everyone else stayed to the end, hoping that a sensational tidbit might still be coming. When the lights went up there was an immediate babble of protest. People stood around and some made angry speeches. One man threatened to resign from the ICA unless the money for his ticket was refunded. Another complained that he and his wife had come all the way from Wimbledon and had paid for a babysitter, because neither of them wanted to miss the film. . . .
>
> The noise from the lecture room was so loud that it reached the next audience, queueing on the stairs for the second house. Those who had just seen the film came out of the auditorium and tried to persuade their friends on the stairs to go home, instead of wasting their time and money. But the atmosphere was so charged with excitement that this well-intentioned advice had the opposite

343

effect. The newcomers became all the more anxious to see the film, since nobody imagined that the show would be a complete blank![61]

Atkins's account demonstrates rather clearly the extent to which Debord's "blank," this "nothing" of a film, was the very means by which the "radical transformation of [a] situation" was realized, the transformation of an event that would otherwise have been a mere iteration of the avant-garde cinematic spectacle-ritual.

Despite its renunciation of an overtly lettrist vocabulary, *Hurlements* remains a decidedly lettrist work. In fact, in abandoning the image track entirely, Debord pushes the gesture of chiseling—the damaging treatment of the film-strip—to the limit: namely, the total destruction of the image. As Debord observes in a passage from an important article in *Potlatch:*

> Last June witnessed a scandal when a film I had made in 1952 was screened in London. It was not a hoax and still less a situationist achievement, but one that depended on complex literary motivations of that time (works on the cinema of Isou, Marc'O, Wolman), and thus fully participated in the phase of decay, precisely in its most extreme form, without even having—except for a few programmatic allusions—the wish for positive developments that characterized the works to which I have just alluded.[62]

Indeed, as Debord acknowledges, the reductive gesture of *Hurlements* is a radicalization of a negative moment that had already been articulated at various points in the pages of *Ion*. In Serge Berna's essay, "Jusqu'à l'os," for example, which calls for a transformation of cinema that goes beyond the mere flesh of the medium and attacks it at the skeletal level, the opening lines read:

> Today, faced with the imperatives imposed upon us by the cinematographic tradition, we must smash the double magic circle that protects this citadel. The first is the sacred barrier within which one guards the credo: "Cinema-is-images."[63]

This is precisely the project, for example, of François Dufrêne's *Tambours du juge-ment premier* (1952), a "film" (consisting of only a sound track) that "puts in doubt the very essence of cinema by means of the IMAGINARY CINEMA."[64]

Berna's imperative also characterizes the films of Wolman and Isou. In Wolman's *L'Anticoncept* (1951),[65] the image track consists of nothing but a white circular field that flashes on and off randomly, sometimes at almost psychedelic speed.[66] The result is a dramatic foregrounding of the sound track, a combination of polemical pronouncement, lettrist sound poetry, and improvised narrative. Following a section toward the end of the hour-long work that plays with the possibilities offered by varying the speeds of the sound recording—an exploration of the creative capacities offered by a manipulation of the apparatus of mechanical reproduction that anticipates by nearly thirty years the "scratch aesthetic" of black street music in the late 1970s—there is a break marked by the line "la vie n'est pas retrospective" (life is not retrospective). Subsequently, the sound track degenerates into a hilarious cacophony of regurgitory and defecatory acoustics.

In Isou's film *Traité,* the assault on the image track takes place not so much on a formal level as in terms of its *"readying of rupture."*[67] While the print of *Traité* shown on April 20, 1951, at a special screening for journalists at Cannes was without images, according to numerous accounts this absence was due to the simple fact that only the sound track had been completed at the time.[68] By the time of its Paris debut, the film included an image track in high lettrist style: chiseled and random images, shots of Indochina, the Seine, skiers, portraits of lettrists, and so on.[69] The issue of the priority of the visual is nevertheless raised in the voice-over. One must, as Daniel puts it,

> destroy the photograph for the sake of speech, do the inverse of what one has done in this domain, the contrary of what one *thought was the cinema.* Who ever said that the cinema, whose meaning is *movement,* must absolutely be *the movement of the photograph* and not the *movement of the word?* . . . The photograph bothers me in the cinema.[70]

It is crucial to note, however, that the devaluation of the image is here motivated by a passion for the sound or, elsewhere, for the letter as such.[71] This classically lettrist concern is, however, at root *aesthetic* and as such far from the imperatives governing the only *apparently* similar gesture by Debord.

The very different impetus behind the elimination of the image track in Debord's film is best understood in light of a hypothetical narrative in Isou's *Esthétique du cinéma* that recounts, curiously enough, what could be considered as the very first conception of *Hurlements:*

> At the Cannes Festival everyone was speaking about *Traité de bave et d'éternité,* which had only been presented at the last moment. The day of the projection it was confirmed that the film did not even exist. A journalist from *Combat* named Arlaud had cried out in the theater: "It would be great if there is no film; we could write our headlines right away." Fortunately (or *unfortunately*), in the end the film did turn up.
>
> Had there been no film, Marc-Gilbert Guillaumin [Marc'O] and Guy-Ernest Debord would have concretely and willingly realized this *lack.* They had planned to speak to a director of a ciné-club that had shown a number of works of our group and to announce an even more sensational creation. The title was already set: *Hurlements en faveur de Sade.* They would have sent out invitations, made posters, and called the journalists. They would have then brought the reels from another film in order to reassure the director, who, by the way, had taken us at our word. [Footnote #1: And our word would have been kept since, in any case, we would have *offered him a spectacle.*] At the point when the projection was to have begun, Debord would have gotten up on stage in order to say a few words of introduction. He would have simply said: "There is no film." I thought I would get involved and link up their destructive scandal with the theory of the constructive *pure debate.* Debord should have said: "The cinema is dead. There can be no more film. [Footnote #2: The scandal would thereby have acquired a new meaning within a holistic conception.] Let us proceed, if you

like, to the debates." [Footnote #3: Since, in any case, the debate would have been presented as an oeuvre, the journalists would have had to chronicle the *premiere* of a new form of work.][72]

The importance of this passage—whose last few lines are cited (albeit in slightly altered form) in the opening moments of *Hurlements*[73]—must be stressed. Unlike both Wolman and Isou, Debord does not critique the image simply in order to invest the spoken or written "letter" with a new poetic vitality. Rather, the absence of the film—and similarly the lack of images in *Hurlements*—is employed as the essential ingredient in a recipe of provocation intended to "radically transform" the cinematic "situation" from a shrine of passive consumption into an arena of active discussion, a shift *away* from the spectacular and *toward* critical engagement. As will become increasingly evident in Debord's later films, already here the focus has begun to shift toward the problem of cinematic *reception,* that is, the issue of spectatorship. In the "Prolegomena," following the enumeration and theoretical articulations of various lettrist tactics, the concluding remarks read: "But all this belongs to an epoch that is ending, and that no longer interests me. Creative values are shifting toward a conditioning of the spectator."[74]

Debord describes *Hurlements* as a "negation and a move beyond the Isouian conception of 'discrepant cinema.'"[75] Despite its indebtedness to the lettrist cinema, the negativity of Debord's film is in fact much closer in its gesture to what one could call "dada cinema."[76] The term is here employed not as a historical designation (according to which a film is "dada" because it was made by a dadaist) but rather as a description of a type of "anti-object" that frustrates contemplative immersion on the part of the spectator and incites public indignation. The distinction is all the more urgent in light of the fact that most historically dada films were not successful as "dada" events. Even *Entr'acte,* that most paradigmatic of historic dada films, was unable to produce the disruptive effects that had been anticipated despite the film's formal radicality.[77] The spectacular structure of the cinematic event itself, so it seems, is at odds with the disconcerting thrust of the dada gesture. Indeed if, as Thomas Elsaesser points out, "film [was] a less than perfect medium at Dada events," this is a function of the very apparatus itself:

For the conditions of a reception in the cinema—the dark room, the stable rectangle of the screen, the fixed voyeuristic position of the spectator—all counteract not only the sense of provocation, but they also compensate for the absence of a coherent diegesis and for the non-narrative organization in the filmed material.[78]

The condition of possibility of "dada" *as* cinema then, requires that the "fundamental degradation of their material," which Walter Benjamin describes as a hallmark dada practice,[79] be carried even further than the suspension of narrative coherence. It is precisely this extreme that is realized in the elimination of the image track in *Hurlements*. Here, Debord suspends even the residual referentiality of the white disc in *L'Anticoncept* (which can still be seen as lens, keyhole, eye) and also attenuates the continuous visual absence of *Tambours* by alternating the black imageless void with a blank white field that, although present, is not readable as anything but the apparatus itself—the screen, the projection, the lamp, and so on. Here that which is always—necessarily—present in the mode of absence, "covered" by the representation that it serves to convey, is staged as such. The spectators, confronted with their *desires and expectations* for a (the) spectacle, are provoked to the point of screams (*hurlements*) when it is revealed to what extent they themselves are an integral part of this spectacular economy.[80] It is in this light that *Hurlements* can be called a—indeed perhaps the first—truly dada film.[81] As Debord states with his own voice at a privileged point in his next film where for the first time the screen becomes entirely white: "One never really contests an organization of existence without contesting all of that organization's forms of language."[82]

III

New forces must be hurled into the battle over leisure, and we will take up our position there.[83]

The year 1952, during which *Hurlements* was completed and premiered, was also the year in which a number of the more radical lettrists split off and formed the

Lettrist International (LI), a scission that could be read as the political analogon to the aesthetic distanciation from certain aspects of the lettrist project manifested in *Hurlements*. Curiously, this key development in the genealogy of the SI—whose initial stages were virtually simultaneous with the first screening of Debord's film—subsequently came to a head in the polemics around another cinematic event: the controversial intervention at Charlie Chaplin's press conference held on October 29, 1952, at the Ritz Hotel in Paris on the occasion of the release of *Limelight*. Here, Debord, Wolman, Serge Berna, and Jean-L. Brau broke through police barriers and bombarded Chaplin with an insulting, denunciatory tract entitled "Finis les pieds plats" (No More Flat Feet)[84] in which they insisted that the very act of holding a press conference indicated Chaplin's sullied commercial values. The tract further lambasted Chaplin's "turn-the-other-cheek" attitude toward oppression, arguing instead that one should respond to suffering with revolution. The attack did not meet with the approval of all the lettrists, however. Despite an initial endorsement of the undertaking, Isou, along with Lemaître and Gabriel Pomerand, expressed reservations in a public disavowal of the gesture published in *Combat* on November 1, 1952.[85] This in turn prompted Debord, Wolman, Brau, and Serge Berna to disassociate themselves from what they perceived as the "reactionary" lettrist faction.[86] Their declaration that "the most compelling exercise of freedom is the destruction of idols, especially when they speak in the name of freedom,"[87] reads both as a justification of their attack on Chaplin and of their break (through the formation of the LI) with Isou, Lemaître, and Pomerand as well.

Just as *Hurlements* was a response to the lettrist movement from a position already beyond it, Debord's next film, which appeared seven years later, *Sur le passage de quelques personnes à travers une assez courte unité de temps* (On the Passage of a Few People through a Rather Brief Moment in Time; 1959), is largely a retrospective account of the activities of the Lettrist International.[88] As the voice-over "announcer" proclaims: "Our camera has captured for you a few aspects of a provisional microsociety,"[89] a group of young people who congregated in Saint-Germain-des-Prés ("the strange setting of our story"), where they "carried out the systematic questioning of all the diversions and labors of a society as well as a global critique of its idea of happiness."[90] While *Sur le passage* is a sometimes slightly nostalgic depiction of the LI, it is at the same time an involuted theoretical meditation. Debord formulates this simultaneity as follows:

> This short film can be taken as a series of notes on the origins of the situationist movement; notes that, as a result, obviously contain a reflection on their own language.[91]

Indeed, the combination of personal reflection and theoretically articulated reflexivity is not only characteristic of *Sur le passage* but, as will become clearer below, is also one of the hallmarks of all of Debord's subsequent films.

Initially, the most striking feature of Debord's second film is the reintroduction of photographic representation. However, following the filmic tabula rasa produced by the elimination of the visual track in *Hurlements,* the images here have a very special status: they are, for the most part, visual citations. Like the sound track in *Hurlements* that, as described above, was composed of "invisible" citations of fragments from various sources, the visual track in *Sur le passage* is a veritable catalogue of *détournement,* employing found footage of policemen in Paris, England, and Japan, colonialists demonstrating in Algiers, parachutists, a speech by de Gaulle, and a solar eruption, to take just a few examples. The film, described in a methodological discussion of *détournement* as a "détourned documentary,"[92] also makes extensive use of a publicity film for Monsavon. In all these cases Debord is doing what Viénet called for years later:

> Let us appropriate the stammerings of this new form of writing; let us, above all, appropriate its most accomplished and modern examples, those that have escaped the ideology of art to an even greater extent than American B-movies: I mean, of course, newsreels, trailers, and most of all filmed advertisements.
>
> Made in the service of the commodity and the spectacle, indeed, but when freed from that support, filmed advertisements can lay the foundations for what Eisenstein foresaw when he spoke of filming *The Critique of Political Economy* or *The German Ideology.*[93]

"Tracking shot of the starlet in her bathtub": Anna Karina in a détourned soap commercial in *Sur le passage de quelques personnes à travers une assez courte unité de temps*. (Debord, *Oeuvres cinématographiques complètes*, 29; image from Debord, *Contre le cinéma*, 55.)

In fact, an initial version of *Sur le passage* included many more *détournements* of scenes from other films, "limit cases of citation"[94] that ultimately had to be removed because—anticipating by almost thirty years the contemporary legal battles over "sampling"—the film companies who owned the reworked scenes refused to sell the rights for reuse. Like *Mémoires* (1959) and its antecedent *Fin de Copenhague* (1957),[95] the collective collage projects by Debord and Asger Jorn that were composed entirely of prefabricated elements subjected to *détournement, Sur le passage* (produced the same year) is also a collage of *détournement.*

The citational quality of the image track in *Sur le passage* is manifest in the sound track as well, beginning with the opening credit sequence during which one hears a recording of the debates—primarily in French and German—of the third SI conference that was held in Munich in April 1959. Throughout the remainder of the film the voice-over consists largely of détourned phrases taken from various classical thinkers, from science fiction novels, or from current pop sociology and read in a generally indifferent manner by either Jean Harnois (using the tone of the radio announcer), Guy Debord (sad and muted in tone), or Claude Brabante (voice of a young girl). In general, the sound track in *Sur le passage*—which also includes music by Handel and Michel-Richard Delalande— has a status equal or superior to the image track, a reversal of the historical and formal priority of the image and a revalorization of the sound track that Debord brought about by suspending the visual dimension in *Hurlements.* This preeminence of the sound track is manifest graphically in the very layout of the scenario in which the film "texts" are presented in their entirety in large type, whereas only a very small selection of the images, described *underneath* in a smaller italic script, are reproduced at the end of the scenario.

In homage to the paradigmatic LI practice of the *dérive, Sur le passage* also includes another class of images: sympathetic depictions of favorite LI haunts such as the cafés in Saint-Germain-des-Prés, Les Halles by night and at dawn, the place Saint-Sulpice, the rue de la Montagne-Sainte-Geneviève, and so forth. As the voice-over accompanying one such image explains, the members of the LI rejected the impoverished and myopic relation to the city manifested by most people:

"In the process of movement and therefore by their ephemeral side" (Karl Marx), *Sur le passage de quelques personnes.* (Debord, *Oeuvres cinématographiques complètes,* 22.)

"In the prestigious décor especially constructed for this purpose," *Sur le passage de quelques personnes.* (Debord, *Oeuvres cinématographiques complètes,* 23.)

"A photograph of two couples drinking wine at a café table is subjected to an examination by the camera in the style of an art film," *Sur le passage de quelques personnes.* Guy Debord, Michèle Bernstein, Asger Jorn, and an unidentified friend. (Debord, *Oeuvres cinématographiques complètes,* 17.)

"Numerous views of dawn at Les Halles," *Sur le passage de quelques personnes.* (Debord, *Oeuvres cinématographiques complètes,* 20.)

We wanted to break out of this conditioning, in search of an alternative use of the urban landscape, in search of new passions. The atmosphere of a few places gave us intimations of the future powers of an architecture that it would be necessary to create as the support and framework for less mediocre games. We could expect nothing of anything we had not altered ourselves.[96]

Debord's description of this quotidian adventure so central to the LI program also reads like a description of the film itself: "It was a trompe-l'oeil reality by means of which one had to discover the potential richness of reality."[97]

Sur le passage is, however, in no sense an unproblematic documentation of LI exploits. This has its material/political reasons. As one hears in the voice-over at a privileged moment in the film where—in a gesture reminiscent of *Hurlements*—the screen is suddenly entirely white:

The ruling class monopoly of the instruments we should have had at our disposal in order to realize the collective art of our time had excluded us even from a cultural production officially dedicated to illustrating and repeating the past. An art film on this generation can only be a film on the absence of its works.[98]

As a result the Parisian scenes, sometimes interrupted by text frames,[99] are also subjected to a number of operations that problematize their documentary character. One of the various strategies employed to refashion traditional scenes is explained as follows:

In order to adopt a position opposed to that of documentary film in terms of the construction of the spectacle, every time there was a danger of encountering a monument we avoided filming it by shooting instead the *point of view of the monument* (just as the young Abel Gance was able to position his camera to shoot from *the snowball's point of view*).[100]

Another important strategy of distanciation involves the depiction of the film crew, images of the clapper, the repeated refilming of a still photograph, and the staging of intentionally inept sequences in which the "apparatus" (camera, projection equipment, off-camera spectators) is visible. During one such sequence, Debord makes the following comment on the sound track:

> Of course, one could make it into a film. But even if such a film were to succeed in being as fundamentally incoherent and unsatisfying as the reality with which it is concerned, it will never be more than a re-creation—impoverished and false like this botched tracking shot.[101]

Here Debord articulates two of the leitmotifs of his cinematic production: the calculated violation and/or analysis of cinematographic convention as a means of exposing the syntax—and in turn the ideological stakes—of the spectacle; and the deliberate staging of confusion as both a refusal of a false and reductive pseudocoherence of (narrative) spectacle and as a reflection of the fundamental *incoherence* of the reality of late capitalism.

In *Sur le passage,* the analysis/exposure of the economy of spectacle includes, beside the examples already cited above, an extensive—and very early— critique of auteurism, dismissed as hopelessly naive in light of the contemporary utter bankruptcy of individual expression.[102] There is also a lengthy dissection of the function and appeal of the "star." Accompanying the last of a number of shots of the "heroine" of a Monsavon soap commercial in a bathtub is the following voice-over text:

> In the final analysis, stars are created by the need we have for them and not by talent or lack of talent or even by the film industry or by advertising. It is the misery of this need, the dismal and anonymous life that would love to swell to the dimensions of the life of the cinema. The imaginary life on the screen is the product of this real need. The star is the projection of this need.[103]

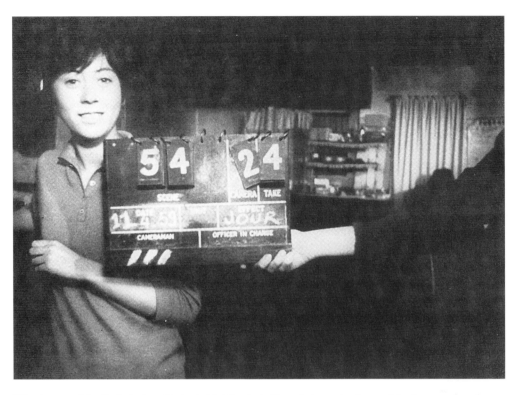

"Two images of the film's clapboard being held at the start of two shots previously seen," *Sur le passage de quelques personnes*. (Debord, *Oeuvres cinématographiques complètes*, 31.)

Like the desire for the star, the appetite for narrative continuity and general intelligibility is fueled by a (repressed) sense of the absence of just such continuity and intelligibility. Debord in turn justifies the refusal of just such transparency (for example, that the sound track be semantically redundant so as not to overwhelm the spectator) by arguing that incomprehensibility is a quotidian experience and its appearance in a film therefore justified. With the screen entirely white, the sound track of *Sur le passage* proclaims:

> Usually what allows one to understand documentaries is the arbitrary limitation of their subject matter. They describe the atomization of social functions and the isolation of their products. One can, in contrast, envisage the entire complexity of a moment that is not resolved into a work, a moment whose movement irreducibly contains facts and values and whose meaning is not yet apparent. The subject matter of the documentary would then be this confused totality.[104]

Throughout Debord's early films, one finds variations of this polemic whose logic one could call the *mimesis of incoherence:* the film is unsatisfying because the world is unsatisfying, the incoherence of the film reflects that of the reality; the poverty of the film's materials serves to emphasize the poverty of its subject, and so on. The task of a radical documentary is thus to refuse the false reduction of a pseudocoherence and to present as such an incoherence that, in its inpenetrable density, holds out the possibility of an alternative, not yet accessible meaning.[105] If one recalls the false coherence of the quotidian that psychogeographical explorations were meant to shatter, one can see how, in short, Debord's films are to the spectacle of traditional documentary or narrative cinema what the *dérive* is to daily life. They thus confirm Ivan Chtcheglov's prediction (under the pseudonym Gilles Ivain) that "later, once the gestures [of the continuous *dérive*] grow stale, this *dérive* will move partially from the realm of lived experience to the realm of representation."[106]

In Debord's next film, *Critique de la séparation* (Critique of Separation; 1961),[107] the only one of the six films that can still be seen today,[108] the nostalgic and retrospective tone of *Sur le passage* has been almost entirely displaced by critique and analysis. This is evident from the film's very first sequence, a series of random images punctuated by text frames that announce: "Coming soon on this screen—one of the greatest anti-films of all time!—Real people! A true story! On a subject that the cinema has never dared to broach." Simultaneously, on the sound track one hears the voice of Caroline Rittener reading the following citation from André Martinet's *Eléments de linguistique générale*:

> When one considers how natural and beneficial it is for man to identify his language with reality, one realizes the level of sophistication he had to reach in order to be able to dissociate them and make each an object of study.[109]

The unbroached subject of the film, it soon becomes clear, is its own operation, the "real people" its audience, and the "true" story that of the alienated relationship produced/staged by the spectacle.

Through a series of remarks spoken by Debord on the voice-over, the film articulates even the considerations that gave rise to the imperative of its own relentlessly involuted focus. It is a striking contradiction, the film insists, that our so-called rational culture develops greater and greater technological powers—among them cinema—whose utopian capacities remain unexplored, however, because those who stand to gain the most from such employment do not have access to them. Even worse, as most people are totally unaware of what is being denied them, they are blind to the need for any transformation. And yet, in a world marked by constant change, where modification is the rule not the exception, most people have been schooled in transformation on a quotidian basis. It would suffice, perhaps, to simply redirect the capacity for technological and other sorts of quotidian revolutions away from the commodity realm. Then, Debord states, "I am sure that those who produce [the world] day after day against their own interests could appropriate it for themselves."[110]

For Debord, contestation of the totality—which is to say, first and foremost, of an entire mode of existence—is without doubt the only worthwhile adventure. However, such an undertaking must confront the fact that in the end, no adventure constitutes itself for us directly. As an adventure, it is linked to the whole range of legends transmitted by the cinema or by other means, which is to say the entire spectacular sham of history.[111]

The always already historically mediated status of all endeavors, no matter how critical their orientation—a crucial point—is simultaneously emphasized on the image track, where a photograph of two situationists is intercut with a shot of King Arthur and his Knights of the Round Table taken from a Hollywood film (a chivalric figure also employed elsewhere as emblematic for aspects of situationist practice).[112] Work on the totality must thus always also be work on mediations and, in a world increasingly dominated by visual spectacle, this in turn means work on the spectacle.

A critique of the spectacle is all the more imperative since, as Debord reminds the viewer in a variation of Benjamin's oft-cited formulation, the spectacle is always the spectacle of the victor. Accompanying images of the UN Security Council, Krushchev, and de Gaulle, as well as Eisenhower receiving de Gaulle, talking with the Pope, and embracing Franco, the sound track provides the following commentary:

> The image that society projects for itself of its own history is limited to the superficial and static history of its rulers, that is, those that incarnate the external fatality of what takes place. The domain of the rulers is the very domain of the spectacle. The cinema suits them well. Moreover, the cinema is constantly presenting exemplary actions and constructing heros based on the same old model as these rulers along with everything that this implies.[113]

This has numerous ramifications: on the one hand, it is important to gain access to the means of spectacle production in order to begin producing "other" types of images that explore the heretofore largely unexamined utopian capacities of this technology; on the other hand, a media literacy must be developed

"In a Hollywood photograph, a knight defies another knight," *Critique de la séparation*. (Debord, *Oeuvres cinématographiques complètes*, 42.)

"Eisenhower in the arms of Franco," *Critique de la séparation*. (Debord, *Oeuvres cinématographiques complètes,* 45.)

that will expose the politics of hegemonic spectacle and thereby also simultaneously prepare a sensibility for an alternative employment of the medium in the future. In almost didactic fashion Debord's voice explains on the sound track:

> The cinematic spectacle has its rules, which enable one to produce satisfactory products. But dissatisfaction is the reality that must be taken as a point of departure. The function of the cinema is to present a false, isolated coherence, either dramatic or documentary, as a substitute for an absent communication and activity. To demystify documentary cinema, it is necessary to dissolve what is called its subject matter.[114]

One of the best vehicles for just such a dismantling of the spectacular structure of documentary cinema, it turns out, is the cinema itself.

Having set itself the task of a polemical interrogation of the politics of cinematic representation, Debord's "antifilm" deploys a full arsenal of *détournement* in its frontal attack on the conflation of the iconico-indexical signifiers of the cinema with reality. Through a relentless superimposition of détourned images (comic strips, press photos, documentary footage, scenes from other films), language (both on the sound track, in text frames, and in subtitles) and music (pieces by François Couperin and Bodin de Boismortier), Debord constructs a work that continuously violates the semiotic redundancy of sound and image characteristic of commercial cinema. Instead of being governed by such reassuring "overcoding," Debord's third film is structured in a radically heterogeneous, contrapuntal manner: written texts interrupt or are superimposed on images, subtitles are often accompanied by other texts read on the voice-over, and so on.[115] According to Debord: "The relation between the images, the commentary and the subtitles is neither complementary nor indifferent. It itself aims to be critical."[116]

The sound-image relations in *Critique de la séparation,* its paratactic formal structure, and its refusal of the economy of "suture" (the catalogue of techniques employed to efface the marks of its own operation and to provide a coherent

"Image from the cover of a book of science fiction," *Critique de la séparation.* (Debord, *Oeuvres cinématographiques complètes,* 41; image from Debord, *Contre le cinéma,* 85.)

"Comic strip image of a blonde with an exhausted expression on her face. The caption reads: 'But she failed. The jeep had sunk too deeply into the mud of the swamp,'" *Critique de la séparation*. (Debord, *Oeuvres cinématographiques complètes*, 39.)

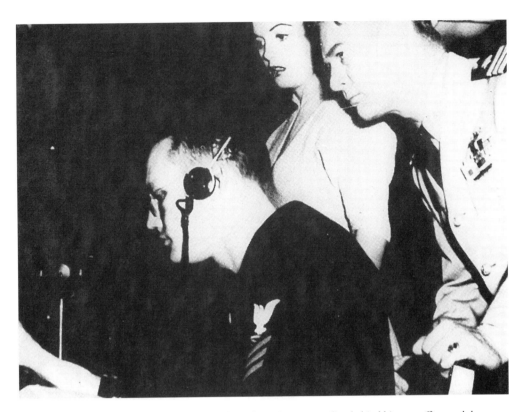

"Photograph taken from a film; a radio operator from the U.S. navy; standing behind him, an officer and the heroine," *Critique de la séparation.* (Debord, *Oeuvres cinématographiques complètes,* 40; image from Debord, *Contre le cinéma,* 40.)

spectatorial position for the viewer to occupy) are justified first of all by the argument for the mimesis of incoherence already manifest in Debord's previous film. Debord's cinema is not a broken mirror fragmenting a homogeneous reality but an unbroken mirror reflecting a fragmented "reality" (only an unsatisfactory film can correspond to an unsatisfactory reality). At one point in the film just before the screen goes black and the sound track becomes silent, we are reminded that it is also "a documentation of the conditions of noncommunication."[117] The formal specificity of *Critique de la séparation* is also justified, however, in terms of the rhetoric of its address. A construction—or rather destruction—that makes no claim to totalization thereby denies the viewer the quietistic, substitute satisfaction offered by the pseudo-intelligibility of most forms of cinema. Because Debord links the very form of narrative and (usually narratively constructed) documentary films with a specific mode of alienated spectatorship, these reigning strategies of cinematic intelligibility must be rejected. Formal coherence, in its own self-sufficiency, maintains the spectator in the comfortable position of consumer: "All coherent artistic expression already expresses the coherence of the past, already expresses passivity."[118] Incoherence, in turn, expresses if not active engagement, then at least a resistance to this passivity.

Critique de la séparation is thus, as its title indicates, a critique of one historically specific relation between viewer and viewed. As is explained in the voice-over accompanying an image of a riot by "natives" in the Belgian Congo (later Zaire), it does not suffice for a film to present an image of some unknown men trying to live differently (politics of the signified). Although such a depiction does have something of a radical, consciousness-raising effect, this is muted and ultimately compromised by its status *as a spectacle,* which is to say, by our nonintervention as spectators (politics of the signifier). As Debord notes in an important essay written at the time this film was being made:

A revolutionary alteration of the present forms of culture can be nothing other than the supersession of all aspects of the aesthetic and technological apparatus, an apparatus that constitutes an aggregation of spectacles separated from life. It is not in its surface meanings that we should look for a spectacle's relation to the problems of the society, but at the deepest level, at the level of *its function as spectacle.*[119]

Debord's recognition that the question of politics in the cinema cannot be limited to a question of "content" but is always already also located in the very structure and operation of the representation leads him to link—in a manner reminiscent of the contemporaneous theoretical work of the *Tel Quel* group—ideological critique with modernist formal radicality.

Not unlike Barthes's distinction between "readerly" and "writerly" texts, Debord distinguishes between a form that fosters facile consumption and one that enlists, provokes, and engages the spectator in an active response. Consider the following remarks that constitute the final sequence of the film's sound track:

> This is a film that interrupts itself and does not come to an end. All conclusions remain to be drawn, everything has to be recalculated. The problem continues to be posed, its expression is becoming more complicated. We have to resort to other measures. Just as there was no profound reason to begin this abstract message, so there is none for concluding it. I have scarcely begun to make you understand that I don't intend to play the game.[120]

The emphasis on the disjunctive, incomplete form that calls upon the reader/spectator to articulate conclusions, the acknowledgment of the need for new means of expression, and the explicit refusal to privilege beginning and end (the distinguishing feature of a paratactic construction) is central to Debord's film practice. However, Debord does not depend upon a political formalism that mistakenly presupposes a necessary relationship between a radical aesthetic form and a nonalienated, nonseparated mode of spectatorship. The film makes no positive claims for any sort of nonspectacular, alternative mode as such. Instead, as summarized by the film's concluding self-description as a refusal to "play the game," Debord's position, while didactic, is rigorously negative.

In its denunciation of the operations of the reigning economy of spectacle, *Critique de la séparation* sketches the contours of an alternative only negatively, by means of its relentless violation, refusal, and critique of the contemporary politics of representation. Indeed, as Debord explains in a rather Brechtian formulation from a very early programmatic essay, such negativity is the condition of possibility of the construction of situations:

> The construction of situations begins on the other side of the modern collapse of the idea of the theater. It is easy to see to what extent the very principle of the theater—nonintervention—is attached to the alienation of the old world. Inversely, we see how the most valid of revolutionary cultural explorations have sought to break the spectator's psychological identification with the hero, so as to incite this spectator into activity by provoking his capacities to revolutionize his own life. The situation is thus made to be lived by its constructors. The role of the "public," if not passive at least a walk-on, must ever diminish, while the share of those who cannot be called actors but, in a new meaning of the term, "livers," will increase.[121]

It is a strategy captured visually in an image of another "game" that occurs on a number of occasions in the film: a sequence, filmed from above, of a pinball session. What is crucial in this representation of a mass cultural practice that in many ways could be read as a figure for late capitalism—for example, the reward of success in both cases is that one is allowed to continue to play—is that the sequence always ends with a "tilt," that is, the moment when the limit of legal "participation" is transgressed and the mechanism punishes the violation by ceasing to function. As a result of this infraction, however, certain aspects of the game—its limits, its principles of operation, the character of tolerated pseudo-engagement, and so forth—are revealed. Thus one can see how the tilt—together with its semantic associations of medieval contestations—captures a number of the essential features of what one might call Debord's aesthetic of countercinema. In *Critique de la séparation* and increasingly in the subsequent films, Debord "tilts" the spectacle and thereby violently brings to a halt a game marked by nonintervention or separation.

In the concluding sequence of *Critique de la séparation,* the new direction charted by the didactic documentation and critique of the spectacle—the itinerary of the tilt—is effectively announced as the program for future cinematographic work. Superimposed onto alternating images of Debord and Asger Jorn one reads the following exchange in the subtitles:

> [Jorn:] One could make a number of documentaries like this, lasting three hours. A sort of "serial."
> [Debord:] The "Mysteries of New York" of alienation.
> [Jorn:] Yes, that would be better; it would be more boring, more meaningful.
> [Debord (as the camera pulls away from him):] More convincing.[122]

However, the next installation of the "Mysteries of Alienation"—which, as the closing subtitle announced, was "to be continued"—did not appear until six years later and then not in the shape of a film. Following an extended period during which, perhaps also as a result of insights developed through his earlier cinematic practice, the question of the spectacle remained one of his primary concerns, Debord presented the continuation of his analysis of the spectacle in the not entirely uncinematic form of a paratactic series of numbered aphorisms published in 1967 under the title *La société du spectacle.*

IV

> The point is not to undertake a critique of revolutionary art, but rather to undertake a revolutionary critique of all art.[123]

Shortly after the publication of Debord's theoretical tour de force, the following announcement appeared in the pages of the September 1969 issue of *IS* as the concluding paragraph of an unsigned article lambasting Godard:

We know that Eisenstein hoped to film *Capital.* We might wonder, however, given that filmmaker's formal ideas and political submissiveness, whether his film would have been faithful to Marx's text. As for us, we have no doubt that we will do better. For example, as soon as it is possible, Guy Debord will himself produce a film adaptation of *The Society of the Spectacle* that will certainly not fall short of his book.[124]

The opportunity to realize this project did not present itself, however, for quite a number of years. In fact, it was not until after May '68 and the final dissolution of the SI in 1972 that Debord could make what would be his first feature-length film, the long-announced cinematic treatment of *La société du spectacle* (1973).[125]

Whatever the multiple motivations behind Debord's interruption in 1973 of what was effectively a twelve-year hiatus from filmmaking, the cinematic translation of *La société du spectacle* underscores the fact that the dissolution of the SI as an organization was not necessarily synonymous with the abandonment of a (postsituationist) revolutionary agenda. Indeed, in the 1972 volume that constitutes the last public expression of the SI, *La véritable scission dans l'Internationale,* Debord and Gianfranco Sanguinetti characterize the post-'68 period in the following, markedly optimistic manner:

> The new epoch is profoundly revolutionary and *it knows that it is.* At every level of the global society *one no longer can, and one no longer wants to* continue to do things as they were done before.[126]

Similar considerations were behind the production of Debord's first post-SI film, as evidenced by the pages of a handsome jet-black glossy brochure that was distributed to the press in 1973. "Coming soon to a cinema near you," the cover reads in large white letters that continue on the following pages, "*La société du spectacle,*" (next page) "and soon thereafter, everywhere else," (next page) "its destruction."[127] Preceding the pages that announce the full credits of the new cinematic

Publicity brochure for Debord's film *La société du spectacle.*

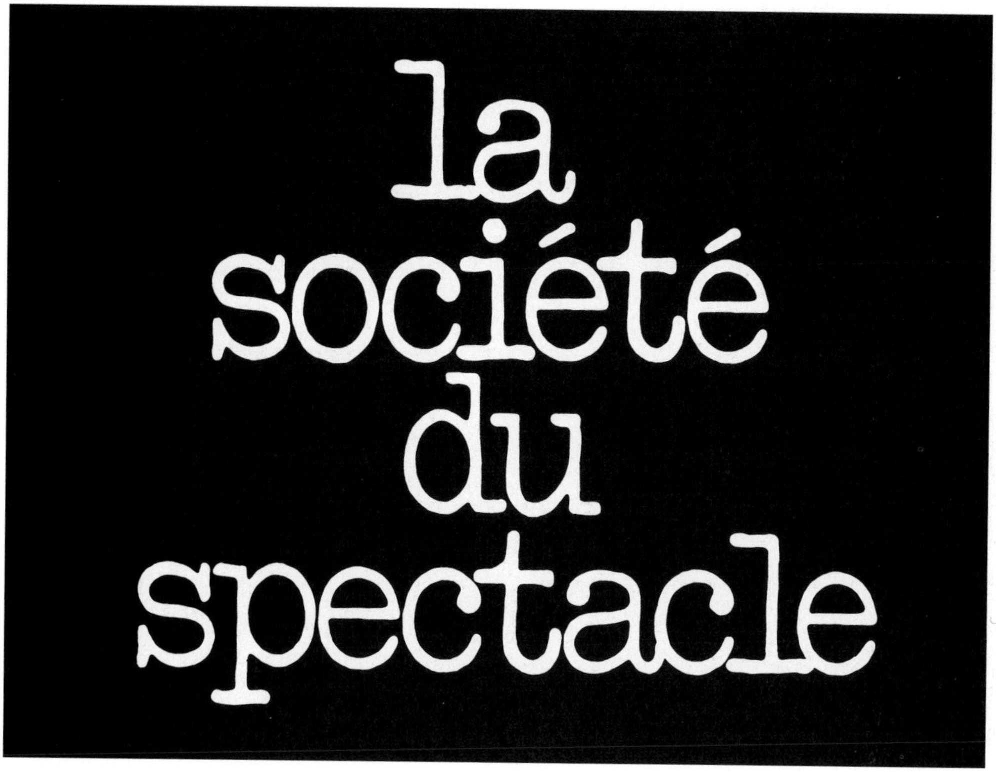
la
société
du
spectacle

et
ultérieurement
partout ailleurs

sa destruction

Que la tentative révolutionnaire de mai 1968 ait marqué le changement d'une époque, voilà ce que démontre le simple fait qu'un livre de théorie subversive comme La Société du Spectacle de Guy Debord puisse être aujourd'hui porté à l'écran par son auteur lui-même, et qu'il existe un producteur pour financer une telle entreprise.

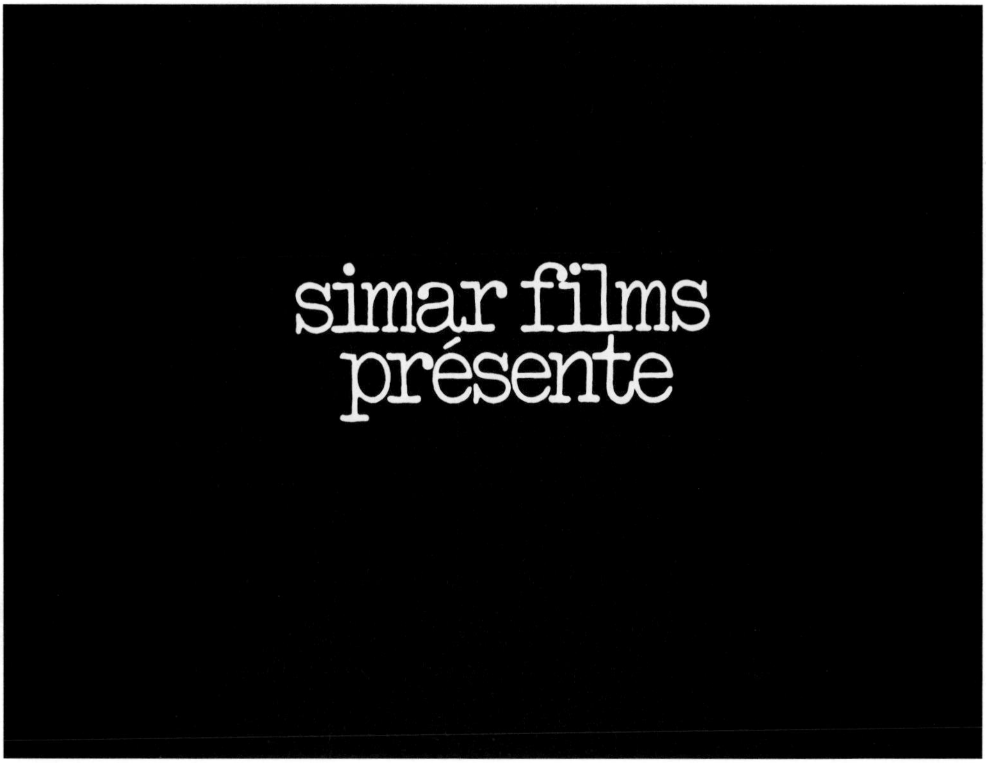
simar films
présente

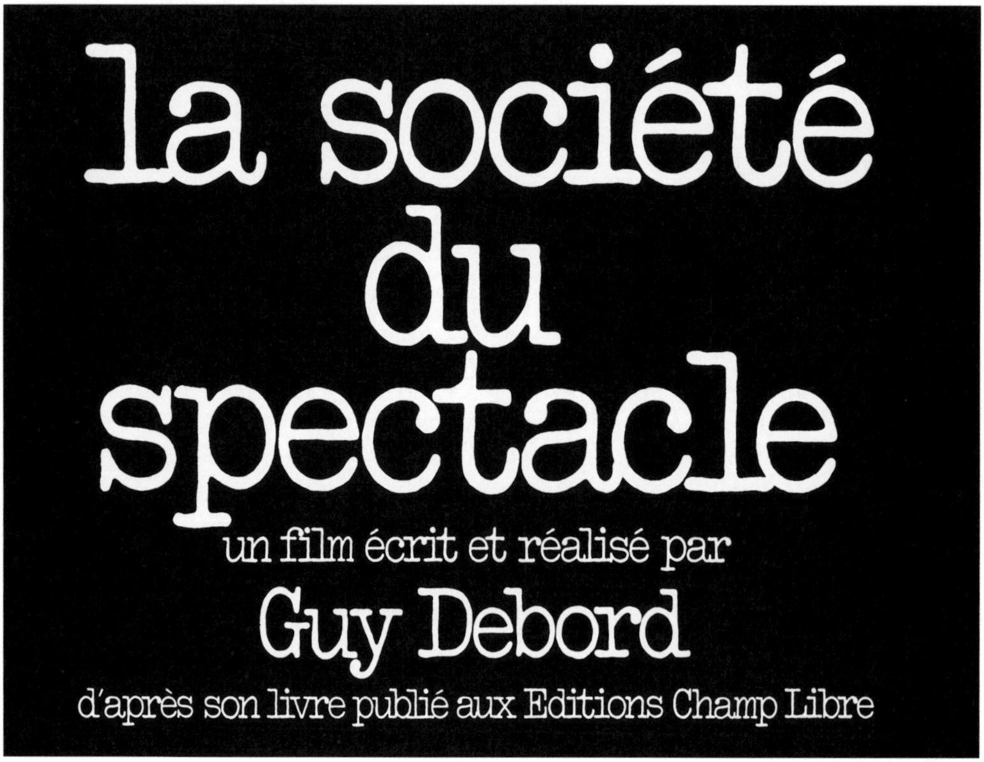

la société
du
spectacle
un film écrit et réalisé par
Guy Debord
d'après son livre publié aux Editions Champ Libre

work—presented by Simar Films and "written and directed by Guy Debord based on his book published by Editions Champ Libre"—one encounters the following statement:

> The extent to which the revolutionary attempt of May 1968 marked the transformation of an epoch is demonstrated precisely by the simple fact that a book of subversive theory like *La société du spectacle* by Guy Debord could be brought to the screen by the author himself, and that there is a producer willing to finance such an undertaking.[128]

The producer in question, the man behind Simar Films, the production company that also went on to produce two more films by Debord, was Gérard Lebovici. Indeed, as Debord explicitly points out in the same brochure, his complete liberty in the working relation with Lebovici/Simar was a very unusual but absolutely essential precondition for his renewed engagement with the cinematic medium.[129]

La société du spectacle is not, however, as it is often described, simply the film version of the book (whatever that might mean, given the work in question). First of all, of the 221 theses in the printed version less than half—Debord insists the best ones[130]—are incorporated into the sound track; second, the order in which they are presented is not identical to the original sequence; and third, various additional texts not contained in the book have been introduced in text frames and subtitles. In short, the film offers, among other things, a rereading (one is tempted to say reediting) by Debord of his own work. This is especially true with regard to the inserted texts by Clausewitz, Emile Pouget, Machiavelli, Marx, Soloviev, Debord, and the Comité d'Occupation de la Sorbonne. These citations—differentiated by their visual presentation in text frames—serve not only as punctuation, marking the points where the original sequence of the theses has been interrupted, but also as elaborations, comments, and critique. One passage in particular, a quotation of August von Cieszkowski, can be read as an elucidation of the impetus behind Debord's cinematic rearticulation of his theoretical study:

Thus, after the immediate production of art had ceased to be the most eminent activity and the predicate of eminence had shifted to theory as such, at present it has detached itself from the latter to the extent that there has developed a posttheoretical, synthetic practice whose primary purpose is to be the foundation and truth of both art and philosophy.[131]

According to the Hegelian logic of this assertion, it is the *theoretical art-work*—which features both the particularity of the object and the generality of the philosophical—that is uniquely capable of fulfilling goals previously assigned to art and/or philosophy. *La société du spectacle* thus represents Debord's attempt to produce just such a "posttheoretical, synthetic" work. As such it could be read as the culmination of the avant-garde artistic project begun in the early 1950s, temporarily suspended in favor of theoretical inquiry and political engagement in the years preceding May 1968, and now reactivated *as* theory. In this light, it is precisely the interrelation of the visual/artistic and the theoretical—an object lesson in spectacle analysis—that is of great significance.

As the theses from Debord's book are impassively read on the sound track, the image track presents an unending stream of détourned visual material. In fact, unlike the previous films that included some original film material shot by De-bord, *La société du spectacle* employs *exclusively* found materials. These include— to cite only a selection from the first section of the film—street scenes, publicity stills (the majority focusing on the objectification of women), scenes from American Westerns and from Soviet and Polish films, fashion commercials, news footage of Nixon meeting Mao, the Sorbonne General Assembly in May '68, the earth filmed from space, astronauts, a police panoptical headquarters with TV monitors showing Métro stations and streets, the footage of the "live" murder of Lee Harvey Oswald, speeches by Giscard d'Estaing, Servan-Schreiber, Séguy, and Castro, bombing runs in Vietnam, and a depiction of a couple watching television. One also encounters sequences appropriated from numerous classics of film history, including *Battleship Potemkin, October, New Babylon, Shanghai Gesture, For Whom the Bell Tolls, Rio Grande, The Charge of the Light Brigade, Johnny Guitar,* and

"A long striptease," *La société du spectacle.* (Debord, *Oeuvres cinématographiques complètes,* 61.)

"A couple, stretched out on a sofa, watches television," *La société du spectacle.* (Debord, *Oeuvres cinématographiques complètes,* 68.)

Sterling Hayden and Joan Crawford in Nicholas Ray's *Johnny Guitar* (1954), *La société du spectacle*. (Debord, *Oeuvres cinématographiques complètes,* 74–75.)

"The Stalinist [Georges] Marché speaks . . . ," *La société du spectacle*. (Debord, *Oeuvres cinématographiques complètes,* 76.)

"The camera pulls back from a photograph of a nude girl, then pans across another," *La société du spectacle.* (Debord, *Oeuvres cinématographiques complètes,* 76.)

"Mao with his closest lieutenant Lin Piao," *La société du spectacle.* (Debord, *Oeuvres cinématographiques complètes,* 93.)

"A few models and a few realizations of recent architecture for vacation spots, so-called 'marinas' at the seashore that can also be found, however, in the mountains," *La société du spectacle*. (Debord, *Oeuvres cinématographiques complètes*, 99.)

"The cruiser *Aurora* sails up the Neva at the end of the night," *La société du spectacle.* (Debord, *Oeuvres cinématographiques complètes,* 9.)

"The Tower of Babel," *La société du spectacle*. (Debord, *Oeuvres cinématographiques complètes*, 101.)

"The forces that maintain order in action . . . in the streets of Nantes [May 1968]," *La société du spectacle*. (Debord, *Oeuvres cinématographiques complètes*, 138.)

"Christian Sebastiani," *La société du spectacle.* (Debord, *Oeuvres cinématographiques complètes,* 135.)

"Guy Debord," *La société du spectacle.* (Debord, *Oeuvres cinématographiques complètes,* 135.)

"Arkadin ends another story: 'Logical?' cries the frog as it drowns with the scorpion, 'Where is the logic in this?' 'I can't help it,' says the scorpion, 'it's my character. . . . Let's drink to character!'" Shot of Orson Welles as Arkadin in *La société du spectacle*. (Debord, *Oeuvres cinématographiques complètes,* 143.)

Confidential Report. As the intricate and multifarious imbrications of the theoretical and the visual cannot be examined in detail here, I will limit myself to a few general observations on Debord's cinematic translation of critical theory, a language of contradiction—dialectical both in content and form—that "is not the negation of style but rather the style of negation."[132]

Like the book *La société du spectacle,* Debord remarks, "its current cinematographic adaptation also does not offer a few partial political critiques but proposes instead a holistic critique of the extant world, which is to say, of all aspects of modern capitalism and its general system of illusions."[133] As the cinema is one of the tools of this "system of illusions," its language must be revolutionized for it to serve other ends. The coherence of the text-image relations is thus neither one of illustration nor of demonstration but rather of *détournement*—"the fluid language of anti-ideology"[134]—here defined as a mode of communication that contains its own critique. Employing a strategy reminiscent of Benjamin's *Passagenwerk* (Arcades Project) in its practice of citation without quotation marks, Debord insolently throws back at spectacular society the images with which it depicts itself.[135] Indeed, one could say that Debord's critique consists in an *incriminating, analytical quotation of the spectacle.* This marks a turning point in the history of cinema that, according to Debord's Hegelian logic, is nothing less than the *Aufhebung* (sublation) of the medium: "In a way, in this film, the cinema, at the end of its pseudo-autonomous history, gathers up its memories."[136] Debord's film is simultaneously a historical film, a Western, a love story, a war film—and none of the above; it is a "critique without concessions," a spectacle of spectacle that as such, like the double negative, reverses the (hegemonic) ideological marking of the medium.

As one might expect, *La société du spectacle* was hardly a box office success. But then, the telos of this cinematic production had never been financial gain: even prior to its release, the hostility toward its violation of the syntax and economy of pleasure characteristic of spectacle was anticipated in the official "preview" for the film at the Studio Gît-le-Coeur. This announcement of what one can only call a "coming un-attraction" consisted of the following message—a *détournement* of an infamous reaction to Schiller's *Die Räuber*—slowly spelled out on a black screen:

> When the idea occurred to me to create the world, I foresaw that there, one day, someone would make a film as revolting as *La Société du Spectacle.* Therefore, I thought it better not to create the world. (signed): God.[137]

Many of the industry critics that reviewed the film seemed to have been of similar opinion: Alain Remond of *Télérama,* for whom the theoretical voice-over was incompatible with the images, concluded that "Debord has almost completely failed"; for S. L. P. of *Téléciné* "the result was far from convincing," and Bernard Pauly of *Cinéma 74* wrote that the film, despite some interesting aspects, was "disappointing and annoying . . . a total failure." Curiously, enthusiastic responses to the film came not only from an informed leftist cinephile camp—*Zoom* critic J. F., for example, places *La société du spectacle* in the avant-garde pantheon of *Un chien andalou* and *Entr'acte*—but also in intelligent reviews in more establishment (conservative) papers. In an extensive article in *Le Monde* entitled "The 'Theoretical' Western by Guy Debord," François Bott describes in careful detail how "the collision of the images against each other and against the text gives rise to the truth of the spectacle," and in *Le nouvel observateur* Claude Roy not only praises Debord as a remarkable writer but raves about a film that is described as "powerfully thought-out . . . a masterpiece of joyous irony and critical humor."[138]

The critical response to *La société du spectacle* is important not only because it was far more extensive than that accorded any of Debord's previous films, but also because of the hostility that Debord insists was much greater and much more univocal in the reaction to his films than it had ever been in response to his writings.[139] Given the radical thrust of *La société du spectacle,* the contempt for the book on the part of the society it criticized at its roots was inevitable and even welcome. Indeed, to a certain extent the resistance confirmed aspects of the book's diagno-

sis, as was pointed out in an often hilarious survey of misreadings of SI works entitled "How Situationist Books Are Not Understood," published in the last issue
of *Internationale situationniste*.[140] Continuing the longstanding SI tradition of targeting and analyzing criticism, Debord also plundered the commentaries on *La
société du spectacle* for symptomatic material. This was then presented in a montage
sampling across the full ideological spectrum under the title "Some Judgments on
the Book" on the last four pages of the publicity brochure for the film.[141]

It is not surprising, then, that the responses to the film *La société du spectacle*
were also, in turn, subjected to a similar ideological dissection. What is remarkable, however, is that this treatment itself *took the form of a film*. Less than two years
after the release of *La société du spectacle,* Debord completed his fifth cinematic
work, a short film adorned with the impudent, polemical title *Réfutation de tous
les jugements, tant élogieux qu'hostiles, qui ont été jusqu'ici portés sur le film "La société
du spectacle"* (Refutation of All the Judgments, Both Complimentary and Hostile, That Have Been Brought to Bear up until Now Concerning the Film "The
Society of the Spectacle"; 1975).[142] A landmark in the history of cinema, this film
is (to my knowledge) the first to take as its explicit and exclusive focus the analysis of the *reception* of a prior film. In its elaboration of an aspect of the *institutional*
critique of spectacle nowhere to be found in the various traditions of avant-garde
film—ontomaterialist, subjectivist, and so on—*Réfutation* performs a sociological analysis reminiscent in many ways of Brecht's symptomatic investigation of
the juridical wrangling in conjunction with his project to film *The Threepenny
Opera*.[143]

Through an examination of the few real arguments to be found in eight
representative reviews of his most recent film, Debord is able to establish a catalogue of the blind spots in their rhetorical strategies and to demonstrate their
integral function in the economy of spectacle. If the focus here seems to have
shifted from the analysis of spectacle proper to an investigation of the economy
of its reception—that is, film criticism or, more generally, art criticism—this is
only because the two are, as Debord demonstrates, effectively synonymous. As
Debord had already noted over ten years earlier in the context of a discussion of
the limits and significance of film criticism within a revolutionary project:

"Pan across a large group of television screens that are broadcasting simultaneously all the sports events that are taking place at any moment at the Olympic games in Munich," *Réfutation de tous les jugements, tant élogieux qu'hostiles, qui ont été jusqu'ici portés sur le film "La société du spectacle."* (Debord, *Oeuvres cinématographiques complètes,* 163.)

"In a newsreel film from July 12, 1936, [Robert] Salengro speaks on stage at a socialist meeting. A ridiculous and odious little man doing everything he can to give his appearance a Mussolini quality," *Réfutation de tous les jugements.* (Debord, *Oeuvres cinématographiques complètes,* 172.)

"A publicity film pushing a brand of pants: on a music hall stage, some men get dressed to the sound of music applauded by a female audience," *Réfutation de tous les jugements.* (Debord, *Oeuvres cinématographiques complètes,* 178.)

Art criticism is second-degree spectacle. The critic is someone who makes a spectacle out of his very condition as spectator—a specialized and therefore ideal spectator, expressing his ideas and feelings *about* a work in which he does not really participate. He re-presents, restages, his own nonintervention in the spectacle. The weakness of random and largely arbitrary fragmentary judgments concerning spectacles that do not really concern us is imposed upon all of us in many banal discussions in private life. But the art critic makes a show of this kind of weakness, presenting it as *exemplary*.[144]

According to this logic, one can read *Réfutation* as a rearticulation at the institutional level of the earlier "critique of separation."

While the polemical thrust of *Réfutation* is directed at the practice of the "exemplary" spectators, they are not the film's intended audience. Those who will be capable of understanding the film, the voice-over explains, are those who understand

that when, according to a very old power strategy, the French people were given a new minister called "The Minister of the Quality of Life," it was quite simply, as Machiavelli put it, "in order to retain at least in name that which they had lost."[145]

The lambasting of the critics, on the other hand, is sustained throughout the film, as indicated by the opening quotation of Chateaubriand: "There are times when one must be economical in one's expenditure of contempt, because of the large number of those in need of it."[146] Despite the variety of critical responses—analogous to the seeming variety of commodities in late capitalism—they all stem from the same culture industry. *Both* of the two general types of critical responses—naive falsification and incompetent approbation—are equally marked, Debord points out, by the position from which they speak. Whatever their position on the film, the critics remain "writing employees of the system of spectacular lying."[147]

The bulk of the comments dissected in *Réfutation* are ones that deal specifically with the cinematic spectacularization of *La société du spectacle*. The most popular objection, for example, is that the film is too difficult: according to one critic the theory on the sound track is too dense to follow, and according to another the images distract one from concentrating on the words. Such arguments not only imply that the critic was able to understand the text in book form (which Debord doubts), but they also disguise as aesthetic objections to a certain conception of cinema what are at root political objections to a certain critique of society. To this Debord responds with a series of variations on the mimesis of incoherence argument discussed earlier: "The stupidity of their reactions goes hand in hand with the decadence of their world"; "The difficulty does not reside in my film; it is in their supine heads"; and "No film is more difficult than its epoch."[148] Dismissing the charge that his work marginalizes itself and thereby becomes a "ghetto cinema," Debord insists that he prefers "to remain in obscurity together with these masses rather than consenting to harangue them in the artificial illumination manipulated by those who hypnotize them."[149] As a final example, one must cite the almost clichéd move that points out the contradiction involved in a public denunciation and examination of the spectacle by means of the spectacle. Such a logically unimpeachable, ultrapurist stance—Debord calls it "Jesuitical"—is of course strategically naive in its insistence that nobody appear within the spectacle as its enemy. It fails to recognize, above all, that the spectacle can be made to serve various ends, including those of a critical theory that "understands, describes and works to overthrow a movement that is effectively taking place under our eyes."[150] Taken together, the films *La société du spectacle* and *Réfutation* are perhaps the most powerful realizations of a critical anticinematic film aesthetic already articulated over a decade before either of them were made. As formulated in the concluding lines of an important and largely ignored essay on the politics of communication, for the situationists,

> every use of the permitted forms of communication has therefore to both be and not be a refusal of this communication: it must, that is, be a communication that contains its refusal and a refusal containing

communication, i.e., the inversion of this refusal into a constructive project. All this must lead somewhere. Communication will now contain *its own critique*.[151]

V

Revolution is not "showing" life to people, rather it is making them live.[152]

In 1978—a decade after May '68—Editions Champ Libre published the collection of Debord's complete cinematographic works, *Oeuvres cinématographiques complètes*. It contained the film scripts, shot descriptions, and illustrations as well as indications regarding text frames and sound material for all five of the films discussed above, as well as for a new, as yet unknown cinematic work by Debord: *In girum imus nocte et consumimur igni* (We Go Around in Circles in the Night and Are Consumed by Fire).[153] Produced the same year that the book was brought out, *In girum,* Debord's second feature-length film, was not actually screened until three years later because no cinema was willing to take it. This created a predicament curiously similar to the current situation: from the outset *In girum* was a film that existed first and, for a number of years, *exclusively* as a text. Furthermore, it was a film that only premiered years after Debord's relation to the cinema was— as indicated by the adjective *complete* in the title of the volume of his cinematographic works—already over. Thus *In girum* was not only Debord's sixth film, it was also his last—a finality that is perceptible in the retrospective, historical, and subjective quality of the film. A coda not only to Debord's relation to the cinematic medium (and, one might argue, to artistic practice as such), *In girum* is, more than any other work since *Mémoires* (with which it shares both structural and thematic features), Debord's commemorative review and homage to the Lettrist and Situationist Internationals.

From the outset, *In girum* raises the question of spectatorship that dominated the previous films. As the voice-over announces that this movie will make no concessions to the viewers, the opening image depicts, in Debord's words, "a contemporary audience in a movie theater, staring straight ahead and looking right at the spectators—in a perfect reverse shot—who thus see nothing but themselves on this screen."[154] In the subsequent remarks on the current state of "separation," the "pseudo-experience" of the film audience is taken to be paradigmatic for the "pseudolife" of quotidian alienation. Parallel with images of daily life in suburban "neohouses," of spectators waiting in line to go to the cinema, of people playing Monopoly as they eat dinner, and so on, the voice-over argues that in fact the situation of employer and employee are quite similar, not least in their shared delusion—described as that of the "unhappy spectator"—that they are truly participating (in government, in success, in happiness, and so on) despite all evidence to the contrary. According to Debord, the mimetic appeal of a cinema based on the principle "when one loves life one goes to the movies" stems not from the supposed "realism" of the depiction but rather from the fact that, since this cinema is *just as impoverished as the real world,* both film and world are similar in that they are contemplated with the same indifference.

Rejecting what he sees as the dominant cinematic practice of simply portraying meaningless events—a cinema "able to deceive boredom for the space of an hour by means of the reflection of that very same boredom"[155]—Debord characterizes his film as part of a project to destabilize the forms of "false consciousness" that have flourished under the current relations of production.[156] Having alerted the viewers that this film will not presuppose the "innocence" of its audience in order to lull them with scenes to be viewed through the "keyhole of a vulgar familiarity," Debord states:

> Since the cinema audience above all must be brought to think about a number of harsh truths that are of direct concern to it, but most of the time kept hidden, one cannot deny that a film which for once renders the difficult service of revealing to that audience that its own affliction is not as mysterious as it thinks, and may even not be incurable if only we could one day go so far as to abolish classes and the State; one cannot deny, I say, that such a film has, at least in this regard, some merit. It will have no others.[157]

"A contemporary audience in a movie theater, staring straight ahead and looking right at the spectators—in a perfect reverse shot—who thus see nothing but themselves on the screen," *In girum imus nocte et consumimur igni.* (Debord, *Oeuvres cinématographiques complètes,* 189.)

This program, which determines the overall structure of *In girum,* has ramifications for both the sound track (which carries the burden of responsibility) and the image track as well.

Responding to the criticism that because he does not "prove" his claims with images, his films are simply dogmatic, Debord lambasts the dominant fetishism of the image. In a move reminiscent of the lettrist disdain for the photographic component of the cinema, Debord contends that, in fact, images as such can prove nothing, save perhaps the reigning deception. By *mis*using images however, by subjecting the cornerstones of the cinematic edifice to *détournement,* something may perhaps be revealed about the medium itself, Debord suggests, even if only negatively. The visual citations in *In girum*—including sequences from *Les visiteurs du soir* (Marcel Carné, 1942), *Les enfants du paradis* (Marcel Carné, 1943–1945), *Orphée* (Jean Cocteau, 1950), *The Charge of the Light Brigade* (Michael Curtiz, 1936), *The Third Man* (Carol Reed, 1939), *They Died with Their Boots On* (Raoul Walsh, 1941), and many others—are thus either inserted into new contexts or provided with new voice-over texts taken, to cite just a few examples, from works by Bossuet, Shakespeare, Villiers de l'Isle-Adam, Pascal, Omar Khàyyàm, Gracian, Sun Tze, and Homer. Debord's position on the status of the image is actually articulated explicitly at an early point in the film. As we watch a scene in which the masked Zorro, leg trapped in the train tracks, frees himself in the last moment before the train passes by, the voice-over states:

> This is a film, for example, in which I only state truths about images that are all either insignificant or false; this is a film that has contempt for the visual dust of which it is composed. I want to conserve nothing of the language of this outdated art, except perhaps the reverse shot of the only world that it has observed and a *tracking shot* along the fleeting ideas of an epoch.[158]

Such disrespect is imperative, we learn, in order to counteract the impression (conveyed by hegemonic cinematic production in order to justify itself) that virtually nothing other than commercial spectacle has ever existed or *was even possible.* On the contrary, Debord asserts it is society and not technology that has made cinema what it is. The cinema could have been historical examination, theory, essay, memories. It could have been the film which I am making at this moment.[159]

The resistance manifested in the refusal on the part of the culture industry to allow *In girum* to be screened is perhaps the best indication of the extent to which such "otherness" (and the unexplored possibilities it reveals) poses a very real threat.

Even more than the previous films, much of *In girum* is about "an important subject": Guy Debord himself. Far from facile autobiography or narcissistic indulgence, however, this focus encompasses—as Debord puts it citing a line borrowed from *Orlando furioso*—"'the ladies, the knights, the weapons, the loves, the conversations and the audacious undertakings' of a unique era."[160] Indeed, the tenor of historical retrospection in *In girum* is best conveyed by the title Debord had initially proposed in 1964 when planning a film on the exploits of the previous years: *Eloge de ce que nous avons aimé* (Homage to the Things We Loved). Foremost among these cherished memories are Debord's world (Paris, the "short-lived capital of perturbation"), his haunts (Saint-Germain-des-Prés), his heroes, his friends, and also his work. Images of a nineteen-year-old Debord, a nineteenth-century Parisian map, and aerial views of Paris are coupled with citations from Dante, Li Po, and Machiavelli to evoke the quality of a bygone urban landscape—at this point there appears a scene from *Les enfants du paradis*—a magical Paris that no longer exists and on whose Left Bank there was "a neighborhood where the negative held court."[161] It was here, Debord notes, among a group of people whose only guiding principle was "Nothing is true, everything is permitted,"[162] that an extremism burst forth independent of any particular cause. At this point, the screen suddenly becomes entirely white as the sound track broadcasts a series of citations of phrases from *Hurlements* (themselves in turn already citations) until an image of an indignant audience at a theater appears, screaming from the balcony for the curtain to be drawn.[163]

What follows is in effect an extended tribute to the members of the Lettrist and Situationist Internationals, to that group of individuals whose

"She who was the most beautiful that year" (photograph by Ed Van der Elsken), *In girum imus nocte et consumimur igni*. (Debord, *Oeuvres cinématographiques complètes*, 237.)

intention was nothing other than to trace, through [their] practice, a line of division between those who want to maintain the existing world and those who want nothing of it.[164]

As we hear accounts of various adventures—the Notre-Dame event, the planned bombing of the Eiffel Tower, and so on—we see images of Gil J. Wolman, Ghislain de Marbaix, Asger Jorn, Giuseppe Gallizio, Attila Kotányi, and Donald Nicholson-Smith interspersed with depictions of favorite SI spots in Paris—Les Halles, cafés in Saint-Germain-des-Prés, the Île de la Cité—as well as photographs of Debord. A short sequence about Ivan Chtcheglov, taken from an earlier unrealized film project entitled *Portrait d'Ivan Chtcheglov*, juxtaposes photographs of Chtcheglov with comic strip representations of Prince Valiant. Debord's voice-over commentary indicates that, despite the history of the SI's exclusions, scissions, and disputes, a profound allegiance toward these figures endured:

> When I speak about these people, I perhaps may seem to be grinning: but one should not take this seriously. I drank their wine. I remain faithful to them. And I do not believe that I have subsequently become, in any way, better than what they themselves were at that time.[165]

Scattered among the above photo portraits are sequences of Venice—the only new footage shot expressly for *In girum*—that are suddenly given new significance by a subsequent shot that pans across the people involved in "mapping out the program best suited to throw the totality of social life into total suspicion"[166]—the participants at the eighth conference of the SI in Venice in 1969.

A tracking shot of the *Kriegspiel* [sic], a board game based on Clausewitz's theory of war developed by Debord in the 1950s as an exercise in strategy and dialectic,[167] sets the tone for the next section of *In girum,* one that is concerned with the problem of strategy. Following a pan across a map of the Old World from the Roman to the Chinese empires, there are shots of West Point cadets about to set out for battle in the U.S. Civil War and then various détourned images of the Light Brigade making its famous charge in the "Valley of Death" at Balaklava. These are accompanied by voice-over observations on the unavoidable

"The 6th Arrondissement seen from above, with the Seine in the foreground," *In girum imus nocte et consumimur igni*. (Debord, *Oeuvres cinématographiques complètes*, 223.)

"The Seine and western tip of the Île de la Cité," *In girum imus nocte et consumimur igni*. (Debord, *Oeuvres cinématographiques complètes,* 239.)

"Establishing shots and close-ups of a *Kriegspiel* [board game] in which two armies are deployed," *In girum imus nocte et consumimur igni*. (Debord, *Oeuvres cinématographiques complètes*, 213.)

"The Light Brigade, in battle formation behind its flag bearers, begins its famous charge through the 'Valley of Death' at Balaklava" (both shots taken by Debord from *The Charge of the Light Brigade*, directed by Michael Curtiz, 1936), *In girum imus nocte et consumimur igni*. (Debord, *Oeuvres cinématographiques complètes*, 257.)

"The Russian chief of staff is astonished at the strange recklessness of this frontal attack. Cannons open fire. The soldiers, advancing directly toward them, fall by the dozens. The Light Brigade begins to gallop and continues its charge in open ranks. It is almost entirely annihilated" (shots taken from *The Charge of the Light Brigade*), *In girum imus nocte et consumimur igni*. (Debord, *Oeuvres cinématographiques complètes*, 258.)

compromises that arise in the course of the reality of actual struggle: politics, Debord reminds the "spectators of history," always takes place in the dirty, risky space of uncertainty. Theoretical work, Debord points out, also has a tactical dimension. It is just one of many weapons in a revolutionary arsenal and, like these, it too must be deployed at the strategic moment. Furthermore, he adds,

> just as theories must be replaced because they become worn out by their decisive victories and even more so by their partial defeats, so too no living epoch has ever arisen from a theory: rather, such an epoch is, above all, a game, a conflict, a voyage.[168]

As an example of tactical practice, Debord unpacks the logic behind his self-imposed "strategy" of obscurity. His resolute refusal of the media stems from the commonplace insight "that this society signs a sort of peace treaty with its most outspoken enemies by giving them a spot in its spectacle."[169] It is precisely this recuperation that Debord prides himself in having resisted. And as if to underscore his tactic of obscurity, the next image is followed by a text frame that announces: "Here the spectators, having been deprived of everything, will even be deprived of images."[170] Then, in a move by now readable as an auto-citation, the screen goes black and remains so for the entire duration of the subsequent monologue. This is finally punctuated by a series of shots of the *Kriegspiel* and the announcement of the "only good news of the current presentation": that the results of Debord's extensive research into strategy will *not* be presented in cinematic form.

What Debord *does* present in the final section of *In girum* is an answer to the nagging question: "What now?" The effect of the SI, Debord had claimed on the sound track, was to destroy once and for all the air of innocence cultivated by the "dominant system of deception."[171] Yet, as he is careful to point out,

> Avant-gardes have only one sole moment; and the best thing that can happen to them is, in the fullest sense of the term, for them to have *made their moment*.[172]

Where does this leave Debord in 1978? In visual terms, the response takes the form of a juxtaposition of a topography of Debord's previous endeavors (as well as a selection of the comrades—intellectual, amorous, revolutionary, and other-wise—that accompanied him at various stages) with the more recent traces of the violence (in urban planning, commodity production, and elsewhere) of advanced capitalism. Images of Florence (where Debord lived during a period of exile), of various houses that Debord lived in at different times, of Alice Becker-Ho, Cardinal de Retz, Clausewitz, of the dadaists and various situationists, as well as a series of photographs taken of Debord from age nineteen to age forty-five, are juxtaposed with shots of "neo-Paris" with its "neohouses," of breweries of "neobeer," of industrial waste sites and "other landscapes ravaged for sake of the surplus of merchandise." On the one hand, the situation is grim. Seen dialecti-cally, however, the victories of the enemy are themselves a negative articulation of everything that still needs to be changed. Such optimism in the face of over-whelming setbacks was even expressed by Marx, as Debord points out in a cita-tion that conveys the concluding tone of film:

> It was already the dawn of that tiresome day that we now see com-ing to an end when the young Marx wrote to Ruge: "You can hardly say that I value the present time too highly; and yet if I nevertheless do not despair, it is only because of the desperate situation of this time, which fills me with hope."[173]

The polyvalence of the present development is also captured by the palin-dromic structure of the Latin title (as emphasized by the opening credit sequence, it can be read in both directions). Within the film, the title is read as a figure for the hopelessness of the current epoch:

> But nothing translated the dead end and the restlessness of the pres-ent time better than the old phrase that circles back around itself completely, given its construction letter by letter as a labyrinth from

"Alice [Becker-Ho] and Celeste," *In girum imus nocte et consumimur igni.* (Debord, *Oeuvres cinématographiques complètes,* 269.)

"Debord: age nineteen," *In girum imus nocte et consumimur igni.* (Debord, *Oeuvres cinématographiques complètes,* 273.)

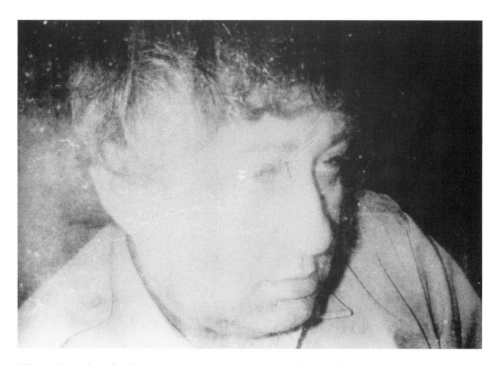

"[Debord:] age forty-five," *In girum imus nocte et consumimur igni*. (Debord, *Oeuvres cinématographiques complètes*, 273.)

which one cannot exit, and thereby conveying perfectly the form and the content of perdition.[174]

However, in the concluding text frame of the film, which reads "To be recommenced from the start," the palindromic structure reappears, now as the more positive appeal to reread (the text of the film), to remake, rewrite, or rethink from the start (the history, the revolutionary ideals, the lives which *In girum* describes).

When it was finally screened in 1981, *In girum* provoked a great variety of critical responses, ranging from the by now standard anti-intellectual accusations of boring obscurantism (*Le Monde*) and intolerable pretentiousness (*Télérama*) to hymns of praise that placed the film in a pantheon alongside Mallarmé and Cocteau (*Les nouvelles littéraires*), compared the film with the modernist subjectivity developed in Marguerite Duras's *Aurelia Steiner* and Straub/Huillet's *Fortini cani* (*Feuille foudre*), and included Debord in the "exclusive club of great filmmakers" (*Quinzaine littéraire*). The focus on the "second-degree spectacle" of the film's journalistic reception that was undertaken cinematographically for *La société du spectacle* then took on yet another form. One year after the screenings (and pirate broadcast)[175] of *In girum,* a modest volume appeared from Champ Libre entitled *Ordures et décombres déballés à la sortie du film "In girum imus nocte et consumimur igni"* (Refuse and Rubble Unpacked upon the Release of "In girum imus nocte et consumimur igni"). This small book contains nothing but the reprints of fourteen reviews of *In girum,* without a single word of commentary![176] Here, at its culmination, Debord's cinematic practice has functioned as a means of provoking a highly indicative reception that is then presented as material to be subjected, in turn, to a political symptomatology.

VI

In "Guy Debord et le problème du maudit" (Guy Debord and the Problem of the Accursed), the opening essay in the first collection of Debord's film scenarios *Contre le cinéma,* Asger Jorn warns against canonizing Debord as a filmmaker. To do so, he argues, would have the anesthetizing effect of inserting him within the very economy of stardom and cinephilic "achievement" that his work attempts to undermine. Furthermore it would fail to recognize that for Debord the cinema *as a medium* was incidental, just one of a number of vehicles—including journals, pamphlets, "metagraphical" collages, board games, translations, and radio programs[177]—employed at various points to explore different questions and make certain points. Despite its focus on Debord's six films, the present essay does not propose to enshrine Debord as an avant-garde cinematic "auteur." Rather, it hopes to direct attention to an important site of creative activity within the SI project whose significance both for the SI and for the history of experimental film and film theory has been heretofore ignored. For Debord's theoretical and artistic production, the films constitute an important and largely unexplored domain by means of which numerous problems can be cast in a new light. Read together with Debord's prolific output as a writer, the films function sometimes as an elaboration, sometimes as an experiment in practice, and sometimes as a translation into another language of central theoretical concerns such as the analysis of spectacle. This is true not only of films such as *La société du spectacle,* where the intimate connection with Debord's theoretical work is manifest, but also of his other films as well. It is in these films—veritable laboratories of *détournement*— that one finds, for example, the most sustained examples of Debord's artistic practice and an important meditation and instantiation of the practice and politics of citation, as well as a critical review of the theory and practice of the SI itself.

The members of both the Lettrist and the Situationist Internationals were very aware of the importance of their films within the development of cinema. Although the lettrist films from the early 1950s are described in an editorial note in a 1954 issue of *Potlatch* as being "of mere historical significance,"[178] it is acknowledged in a later issue of the same journal that the scarcity of these films also permits subsequent filmmakers to claim as theirs innovations introduced by the lettrists many years earlier. Always alert to the plagiarism of their ideas (despite an often proclaimed nonproprietary relation to the products of intellectual labor), the editors regret the current unavailability of their films, thanks to which Norman McLaren's *Blinkity Blank* (1955)—a film that incorporates extended black sequences and various lettrist practices of *cinéma ciselant*—was given honorable mention at the eighth Cannes Film Festival. It is not without some bitterness that McLaren is warmly congratulated for providing hard evidence that, as they put it, "despite various interdictions, the most scandalous innovations can make their way even into the heart of the official propaganda organizations of our enemies."[179] It is thus not entirely surprising that when the plans were drawn up a few years later for a situationist library in Silkeborg (Denmark), the conception of the envisaged archive included a "cinema annex" to house copies of all SI films.[180]

Without any doubt, there is much in the lettrist cinema and the later cinematic works by Debord that has subsequently been taken up and explored—whether consciously or not is unimportant here—in "pioneering" works of the postwar American and European avant-garde, "underground" cinema.[181] As space considerations preclude an exploration here of the full extent of the revisionist ramifications entailed by the rediscovery of the films of the LI and SI, I will limit myself to the following preliminary suggestions. In its radical reduction of expressive means and the slowness of its pace, for example, *Hurlements* antedates both Stan Brakhage's *Reflections on Black* (1955) and Peter Kubelka's *Arnulf Rainer* (1958–1960), as well as certain films made by Warhol or Michael Snow over a decade later. The aesthetic of cinematic *détournement* developed in Debord's subsequent films could be productively compared in turn with the more aestheticized work on found footage undertaken in the late 1950s and early 1960s by Bruce Connor. Debord's films also could be argued to be a crucial moment in the genealogy of the "theory film," a largely ignored genre that one could trace back to Eisenstein's project to film *Kapital* and that, by way of Godard, Marker, and Resnais, would also include works by Laura Mulvey and Peter Wollen (*Penthesilea* [1974] and *Riddles of the Sphinx* [1977]), Yvonne Rainer (*The Man Who Envied Women* [1985]), and Manuel de Landa (*Raw Nerves: A Lacanian Thriller* [1979]).[182]

Godard's indebtedness to Debord, from whom he learned a great deal, itself merits a particularly detailed examination. In what appears to be a rather marked instance of unacknowledged appropriation, an inordinate amount of

Debord's concerns reappear in later works by Godard, both in terms of iconographic or thematic concerns and on a formal level as well. As regards the former, one encounters in Godard's films the sociological interest in Paris (*Two or Three Things I Know about Her*), the *détournement* of advertisements, legal documents, and citations (in *Weekend* there are quotations from Emily Brontë, Balsamo, and Saint-Just!), and of sequences from other films (*Le petit soldat* employs the "Tell me lies" sequence from *Johnny Guitar*). One even encounters the same "stars": years before she became the leading actress in numerous films by Godard as well as his wife, Anna Karina appeared as the actress in the Monsavon commercial détourned by Debord in *Sur le passage.* In formal terms, Godard takes up the philosophical voice-over, the use of black sequences (in *Le gai savoir* and *Vladimir and Rosa*), paratactic, nonnarrative constructions, refusal of sound-image synchrony, extended use of text frames, the exposure of the "means of production," intensive intertextuality, and so on. Indeed, well over a decade before Godard's *Vent d'est,* Debord was producing a revolutionary, materialist "countercinema" that met all criteria established in Peter Wollen's discussion of this alternative cinematographic practice: narrative intransitivity, estrangement, foregrounding, multiple diegesis, aperture, unpleasure, reality.[183]

The comparison with Godard is motivated not only by the fact that for many years Godard was the "good object" of an historically, semiologically, and politically informed film theory. Nor is this simply a question of locating "originality" or of establishing vectors of influence. What is at stake here is the claim that, well before Godard, Debord's "epistemological" cinema had already resolved the dichotomy of the "two avant-gardes," representing a "third avant-garde" that synthesizes a formal modernism (a politics of the signifier) and a semiotic and ideological reflexivity (politics of the signified). Moreover, what one might call the "political modernism" of Debord's cinema avoids, I would argue, the various pitfalls—formalist essentialism, aestheticist myopia, politically naive fetishism of reflexivity, and so on—typical of certain avant-garde cultural practices linked to radical political agendas.[184] Specifically, Debord's films do not manifest the problematic characteristics of the "epistemological modernism"

"Image of the cover of a detective novel entitled *Imposture*. A woman in profile; a bit further stands a man with a glass in his hand," *Critique de la séparation*. (Debord, *Oeuvres cinématographiques complètes,* 51–52; image from Debord, *Contre le cinéma,* 87.)

identified by Sylvia Harvey in her study *May '68 and Film Culture:* they do *not* "replace an interest in the *relationship* between specific means of aesthetic representation and a social reality conceived of as distinct from those means, with an exclusive concern with the means of representation"; they do *not* make any essentialist claims regarding the inherent politics of any specific cinematic form; they do *not* articulate the problem of formal innovation solely in terms of the internal architectonic of the "filmic text" but rather insist on "the insertion of that text within a particular apparatus, within a distribution or exchange specific to a particular society and a particular historical moment"; and finally, in their repeated emphasis on spectatorship and the structure of separation, they do *not* disparage pleasure and "offer a puritanical defense of the 'work' (of reading, of meaning production) that the modernist text invites the reader to perform."[185] Rather, in the sociohistorical analysis of the separation that structures the spectacle, the possibility of an engaged, *enjoyable,* nonseparated experience—such as that of the *dérive*—is always held out as the aim of an alternative model of cinematic practice. In Debord's own words:

> It seems to me that my work [in the cinema], very succinct but extended over a period of twenty-six years, did indeed correspond to the principal criteria of modern art: (1) a very marked originality from the start and the firm decision never to do "the same thing" two times in a row, while still maintaining a personal style and a set of thematic concerns that are always easily recognizable; (2) an understanding of contemporary society, *id est* explaining it by criticizing it, since ours is a time that is distinctly lacking less in apologetics than in criticism; (3) finally, to have been revolutionary *in form as well as in content,* something that always struck me as following the direction of all the "unitary" aspirations of modern art, toward the point where that art attempted to go beyond art.[186]

In its dismantling of the spectacle, the cinema of Guy Debord is thus also the dismantling of the (modernist, avant-garde, political) cinema as well.

NOTES

Originally published in *On the Passage of a Few People through a Rather Brief Moment in Time: The Situationist International, 1957–1972* (Cambridge: MIT Press; Boston: Institute of Contemporary Art, 1989), 72–123. An earlier version of this essay was presented at the Society for Cinema Studies annual conference in Montreal (May 1987) on a panel entitled "Dismantling the Spectacle." I am grateful to the panel chair, Edward Dimendberg (UC Santa Cruz), for provoking that initial engagement with the topic, and to Lindsay Waters (Harvard University Press) and Greil Marcus for the critical mediation that made this further exploration possible.

1. Ken Knabb, ed. and trans., *Situationist International Anthology* (Berkeley: Bureau of Public Secrets, 1981), 33. (Where published translations are employed within the body of the text, the original language citations are provided following the translated reference. Where no English-language source is given, the translation is mine.) Guy Debord, *Sur le passage de quelques personnes à travers une assez courte unité de temps,* in *Oeuvres cinématographiques complètes, 1952–1978* (Paris: Editions Champ Libre, 1978), 31.

2. Debord, *In girum imus nocte et consumimur igni,* in *Oeuvres cinématographiques,* 207–208.

3. This picture, taken by J. R. Eyerman, has since become a veritable cliché not only for the alienation of late consumer culture but also for the ten years following World War II: it appears, for example, on T-shirts, bags, and buttons as well as on the cover of the brochure that accompanied an exhibition of photographs from *Life* magazine held at the International Center of Photography (New York) and entitled: "The Second Decade, 1946–1955." Few realize, however, that this depiction of the latest stage in the drive toward cinematic verisimilitude exists in at least two versions: the one, employed for the cover of the *Society of the Spectacle* (Detroit: Black & Red, 1970, repr. 1977 and 1983), depicts its elegantly attired audience in a virtually trance-like state of absorption, their faces grim, their lips pursed. In the other shot of the same audience, however, the 3-D spectators are laughing, their expressions of hilarity conveying the pleasure of an uproarious, active spectatorship.

4. It is entirely appropriate that these illustrations appear only in the unauthorized translation of *Society of the Spectacle* published in America, the country in many ways paradigmatic for the culture of consumption and alienation that is the focus of the study. In the first edition of *La société du spectacle* (Paris: Buchet-Chastel, 1967), the pirate German edition of *Die Gesellschaft des Spektakels* (Düsseldorf: Projektgruppe Gegengesellschaft, 1971), and the "authorized [German] translation" by Jean-Jacques Raspaud (Hamburg: Edition Nautilus, 1978), there are no illustrations whatsoever. Only one French reprint (Paris: Editions Champ Libre, 1971) has an image

on its cover, a reproduction of a turn-of-the-century world map whose colors indicate the current and projected state of global commercial development. Debord's account of the choice of this map can be found in his small book, *Considérations sur l'assassinat de Gérard Lebovici* (Paris: Editions Gérard Lebovici, 1985), 33–34.

5. The first thirty-four theses of *La société du spectacle* were first published under the title "La séparation achevée" in the SI journal *Internationale situationniste* 11 (October 1967), 43–48 (hereafter *IS*).

6. The translation of *détournement,* one of the key terms of situationist aesthetic practice, poses a number of problems. Its rendition as "diversion" in the American edition of *Society of the Spectacle* (see, for example, thesis 208) is unacceptable because it is burdened with the connotation of "distraction." In French, *détournement*—deflection, turning in a different direction—is also employed to signal detours and to refer to embezzlement, swindle, abduction, and hijacking. The criminal and violent quality of the latter four connotations are closer to the SI practice of illicitly appropriating the products of culture and abducting or hijacking them to other destinations. Nevertheless, these terms are also too marked to be employed. Instead, I have followed the practice adopted by Ken Knabb in his *Anthology* (cf. his footnote on this subject on p. 371) and have simply anglicized the term.

7. This visual material, an important supplement to the articles in the journal, is unfortunately not available to the English reader since, unlike the two-volume German edition of the journal, *Situationistische Internationale* (Hamburg: Edition Nautilus, 1977), which retains the images and even the layout of the original French version, the selections published in translation in the Knabb anthology have no illustrations.

8. *IS* 11 (October 1967), 57; first emphasis in translation is mine.

9. Debord, *In girum,* in *Oeuvres cinématographiques,* 190.

10. Knabb, ed., *Anthology,* 33; cf. the epigraph that opens this essay.

11. Martin Heidegger, "Die Zeit des Weltbildes" in *Holzwege,* ed. Friedrich-Wilhelm von Herrmann (1938; Frankfurt am Main: Klostermann, 1977), 73–110; translated as "The Age of the World Picture," in Heidegger, *The Question Concerning Technology and Other Essays,* trans. William Lovitt (New York: Garland Publishers, 1977), 115–154, esp. 128ff.; Jean-Louis Baudry, *L'effet cinéma* (Paris: Editions Albatros, 1978) and "The Apparatus: Metaphysical Approaches to the Impression of Reality in the Cinema," in Phil Rosen, ed., *Narrative, Apparatus, Ideology: A Film Theory Reader* (New York: Columbia University Press, 1986), 299–318; Jean-Louis Comolli, "Machines of the Visible," in Teresa de Lauretis and Stephen Heath, eds., *The Cinematic Apparatus* (New York: St. Martin's Press, 1980), 121–142.

12. Debord, *In girum,* in *Oeuvres cinématographiques,* 207–208; cf. the second epigraph that opens this essay.

13. Knabb, ed., *Anthology,* 88; "La cinquième conférence de l'I.S. à Göteborg," *IS* 7 (April 1962), 26–27. Compare also "Le sens du déperissement de l'art," *IS* 3 (December 1959), 4 and 7; trans. in this volume, 86–87, 91.

14. Debord, *Society of the Spectacle,* thesis 210.

15. Knabb, ed., *Anthology,* 111, translation modified; "L'opération contre-situationniste dans divers pays," *IS* 8 (January 1963), 24.

16. "Avec et contre le cinéma," *IS* 1 (June 1958), 8–9.

17. Ibid., 8.

18. Ibid., 9.

19. Ibid.

20. René Viénet, "The Situationists and the New Forms of Action against Politics and Art," in this volume, 184–185; "Les situationnistes et les nouvelles formes d'action contre la politique et l'art," *IS* 11 (October 1967), 35.

21. Knabb, ed., *Anthology,* 55–56; "Le détournement comme négation et comme prelude," *IS* 3 (December 1959), 11.

22. Guy Debord and Gil J. Wolman, "Instructions for the Use of Detournement," in Knabb, ed., *Anthology,* 12 (translation of title modified); "Mode d'emploi du détournement," in *Les lèvres nues* 8 (May 1956), 6. For the epistemological genealogy of the SI, it is important to note that the authors of this theoretically central article were listed on the cover of *Les lèvres nues* as "Aragon and André Breton"! Both the text and the cover are reprinted in the very useful collection of reprints of rare original materials edited by Gérard Berreby, *Documents relatifs à la fondation de l'Internationale situationniste* (Paris: Editions Allia, 1985), 301–309. Another important aesthetic affinity is evident from the publication of a German translation of this essay—"Gebrauchs-anweisung für die Entwendung"—in a collection of the poetry of Lautréamont [Isidore Ducasse], *Poésie* (Hamburg: Edition Nautilus, 1979).

23. Knabb, ed., *Anthology,* 12; Berreby, ed., *Documents,* 306.

24. *La dialectique peut-elle casser des briques* is an amusing example of the use of *détournement* to rewrite or refunction—to use a rendition of Brecht's term *Umfunktionierung* that is most appropriate here—an otherwise highly compromised product of the culture industry. This full-length 35mm color film by Doo Kwang Gee is a transformation by Gerard Cohen and René Viénet of a classic Hong Kong kung-fu film (originally titled *The Crush*) into a didactic suspense narrative illustrating the conflict between the proletariat and the bureaucrats! Produced in 1973 by 'L'Oiseau de Minerve,' the movie—which introduces itself as "the first entirely

'détourned' film in the history of cinema"—effects this metamorphosis simply by supplying a new synchronized sound track. As it is (curiously) part of the permanent collection of the ultra-hightech Vidéothèque de Paris, it can be screened upon demand. Another Chinese film détourned by Inez Tan and René Viénet through the use of French subtitles, *Du sang chez les Taoïsts* (1971; color, 80 min.), seems to be currently unavailable. Very little information is available concerning the three further films that Viénet and his collaborators are supposed to have detourned: *Une petite culotte pour l'été, Une soutanne n'a pas de braguette,* and *L'aubergine est farcie.*

25. "Panorama intelligent de l'avant-garde à la fin de 1955," *Potlatch* 24 (November 1955); all issues of the journal have been reprinted in a single volume with an introduction by Guy Debord, *Potlatch, 1954–1957* (Paris: Editions Gérard Lebovici, 1985), above citation, 186; the journal can also be found in Berreby, ed., *Documents,* 161–261, above citation, 231.

26. Viénet, "The Situationists and the New Forms of Action against Politics and Art," in this volume, 185; "Les situationnistes et les nouvelles formes d'action contre la politique et l'art," *IS* 11 (October 1967), 35.

27. Guy Debord, "Pour le debat d'orientation du printemps 1970: Note sur la première série de textes," in his *Textes rares: 1957–1970* (Paris: n.p., 1981), 34–36.

28. "Chaque film pourrait donner à un ou deux situs travaillant comme assistants l'occasion de maîtriser leur propre style dans ce langage; et l'immanquable succès de nos oeuvres apporterait aussi la base économique de la production future de ces camarades. *L'élargissement de notre audience serait décisif*" (ibid., 36).

29. "The Practice of Theory: Cinema and Revolution," in this volume, 188; "Le cinéma et la révolution," *IS* 12 (September 1969), 105.

30. This description as well as the label for Godard further on stem from the "List of Insulted Names" included in the very useful index volume by Jean-Jacques Raspaud and Jean-Pierre Voyer, *L'Internationale situationniste: Chronologie/Bibliographie/Protagonistes* (Paris: Editions Champ Libre, 1972), 25–65.

31. The following chronological list offers a preliminary bibliography of the film reviews and/or texts on film published in the journals of the Lettrist and Situationist Internationals. Where no author is listed, the texts appeared unsigned; lead articles are indicated as such; data regarding reprints and short summaries of content follow the main entry:

> "Le grand âge du cinéma: Le 8ᵉ festival de Cannes sera mauvais," *Potlatch* 19 (lead article; April 1955); *Potlatch, 1954–1957,* 124–125; also in Berreby, ed., *Documents,* 205.

> "Encore la jeunesse pourrie," *Potlatch* 19 (April 1955); *Potlatch, 1954–1957,* 126–127; also in Berreby, *Documents,* 205–206: review of *Marianne de ma jeunesse* (Julien Duvivier, 1955)

"Le grand chemin qui mène a Rome," *Potlatch* 21 (lead article; June 1955); *Potlatch, 1954–1957,* 142–143; also in Berreby, *Documents,* 213: review of *La Strada* (Federico Fellini, 1954)

"La Bible est le seul scénariste qui ne déçoive pas Cecil B. de Mille," *Potlatch* 21 (June 1955); *Potlatch, 1954–1957,* 147; Berreby, *Documents,* 215: review of *Blinkity Black* [sic] (Norman McLaren, 1955) [correct title is *Blinkity Blank*]

"Au vestaire," *Potlatch* 25 (lead article; January 1956); *Potlatch, 1954–1957,* 191–195; also in Berreby, ed., *Documents,* 233–234: review of *La pointe courte* (Agnès Varda, 1956)

"Le cinéma après Alain Resnais," *IS* 3 (December 1959), 8–10: review of *Hiroshima mon amour* (Alain Resnais, 1959)

Michèle Bernstein, "Sunset Boulevard," *IS* 7 (April 1962), 42–46: review of *L'année dernière à Marienbad* (Alain Resnais, 1961)

G.-E. Debord, "Pour un jugement révolutionnaire de l'art," *Notes critiques: Bulletin de recherche et d'orientation révolutionnaire* 3 (Bordeaux) (2 trimestre 1962); reprinted in Debord, *Textes rares,* 13–17; for a translation, see Knabb, ed., *Anthology,* 310–314. Debord's text was a position paper intended as the basis for a discussion between the SI and the group Pouvoir Ouvrier that ultimately did not take place. It was a response to a review of Godard's *A bout de souffle* by S. Chatel published in *Socialisme ou barbarie* 6 (December 1960–February 1961), 104–107.

"L'I.S. vous l'avait bien dit!" *IS* 9 (August 1964), 23: a series of citations about Alain Resnais

"Le rôle de Godard," *IS* 10 (March 1966), 58–59; for a translation, see Knabb, ed., *Anthology,* 175–176: on the films of Jean-Luc Godard

"Le cinéma et la révolution," *IS* 12 (September 1969), 104–105; trans. in this volume, 187–188: review of *Le gai savoir* (Jean-Luc Godard, 1968).

32. François Dufrêne, "Tambours du jugement premier," *Ion* 1 (April 1952), Numéro spécial sur le cinéma, Marc-Gilbert Guillaumin [Marc'O], general editor, 195 (footnote 1).

33. Beneath a full-page photograph of Debord on the second page of the catalogue *Destruktion af RSG-6: En kollektiv manifestation af Situationistisk Internationale* (Odense, Denmark: Galerie EXI, 1963), for example, one reads the following caption: "GUY DEBORD: filminstruktør og redaktør—film director and editor—cinéaste et directeur de revue. c/o 'Internationale Situationiste,' B.P. 75–06 Paris." Similarly, the description of the author of *La société du spectacle*

on the back cover of the Editions Champ Libre reprint (Paris, 1971) begins: "Se disant cinéaste" (Calls himself a filmmaker).

34. Debord at various times announced films that he was planning or hoping to make. These include the following four titles of *films prévus* that are listed on the back cover of *Contre le cinéma* (see note 38 below), framed by the two lines "Prochainement sur les écrans . . . Des films écrits et réalisés par Guy Debord" (Coming soon to the screen . . . Films written and directed by Guy Debord): *Portrait d'Ivan Chtcheglov, Les aspects ludiques manifestes et la tents dans la fronde, Eloge de ce que nous avons aimé dans les images d'une époque,* and *Préface à une nouvelle théorie du mouvement révolutionnaire.* Elsewhere, Debord states that he wanted to make a film of Raoul Vaneigem's *Traité de savoir-vivre à l'usage des jeunes générations* (Paris: Gallimard, 1967, repr. 1981), translated as *The Revolution of Everyday Life* (London: Practical Paradise Publications, 1975); see "Pour le débat d'orientation du printemps 1970: Note sur la première série de textes," in Debord, *Textes rares,* 36.

35. One of the few exceptions is an intelligent article in a rather obscure Austrian art journal by Roberto Ohrt, "Wäre ich nicht Alexander wäre ich gern Diogenes," *Durch* 3/4 (November 1987), 27–48, translated by Ian Brunskill in the same issue as "If I Wasn't Alexander, I Would Like to Be Diogenes," 161–175. Ohrt has also published an interesting piece on the SPUR group and the German side of the SI story: "Die Spur von der Kunst zur Situationistischen Internationale," in Veit Loers, ed., *Gruppe SPUR, 1958–1965* (Regensburg: Städtische Galerie, 1986), 33–44.

36. Debord, *Considérations sur l'assassinat,* 48. Debord's most recent book, *Commentaires sur la société du spectacle* (Paris: Editions Gérard Lebovici, 1988), is also dedicated to Lebovici: "A la mémoire de Gérard Lebovici, assassiné à Paris, le 5 mars 1984, dans un guet-apens resté mystérieux."

37. In response to a query as to whether the films could ever be seen *outside* France, Debord explained to me in a letter of May 29, 1987, that his emphasis on France was in response to the particular injustice perpetrated by the French press. "Naturally I should have said: never again anywhere." In the remainder of the missive Debord goes on to articulate why, in light of the recent restructuration of the film industry, he was concerned about the manner in which his films might be exploited and thus decided to disavow in advance any and all screenings of his work. However, as he notes in conclusion: "It goes without saying that I do not disavow a single word or even a single image of my entire cinematographic work."

38. Guy Debord, *Contre le cinéma* (Aarhus, Denmark: L'Institut scandinave de vandalisme comparé/Bibliothèque d'Alexandrie, 1964). This volume, now out of print, includes the complete scenarios and selected images from Debord's first three films (*Hurlements en faveur de Sade, Sur*

le passage de quelques personnes à travers une assez courte unité de temps, and *Critique de la séparation*) along with a prefatory essay by Asger Jorn entitled "Guy Debord et le problème du maudit" (3–8). The German translation by Pierre Gallissaires and Hanna Mittelstädt entitled *Gegen den Film: Filmskripte* (Hamburg: Edition Nautilus, 1978) drops three of the four explanatory notes that follow the scenario of *Hurlements,* but provides the full text of "Grande fête de nuit" under the title "Eine große Nachtfete."

39. Debord, *Oeuvres cinématographiques.* This hardback volume, which features a map of metropolitan Paris with subway routes on its dust jacket, includes the scenarios from *Contre le cinéma* (minus the introductory essay by Asger Jorn and the technical data supplied for each film). It also contains a selection of stills from each film; the format for these images, however, is slightly smaller than in *Contre le cinéma.* An Italian translation of the collection by Paolo Salvadori was published under the title *Opere cinematografiche complete, 1952–1978* (Rome: Arcana Editrice, 1980).

40. Debord, *Hurlements,* in *Oeuvres cinématographiques,* 7.

41. The standard work on lettrist poetry is Jean-Paul Curtay's *La poésie lettriste* (Paris: Seghers, 1974). For English-language material on lettrism, see *Visible Language* 17 (Summer 1983), a special issue that includes introductory discussions of various aspects of the movement, translations of primary texts by Isou and Lemaître, as well as a chronology and bibliography. For a short illustrated discussion of lettrist work in the plastic arts, see Carol Cutler, "Paris: The Lettrist Movement," *Art in America* 58 (January–February 1970), 117–119. The literature on lettrist cinema is almost as limited as that on the cinema of the SI: see, for example, the short piece by Frédérique Devaux, "Approaching Letterist Cinema," trans. David W. Seaman, in the abovementioned issue of *Visible Language,* 48–56. Devaux has also published a very useful "Petite introduction au cinéma lettriste" in her journal *7ème Art* 12 (Spring–Summer 1988), unpaginated. I am grateful to Ms. Devaux for her generosity in providing me with material that was a valuable source of general orientation for my research on the lettrist genealogy of Debord's early work in film. In Italian, a discussion of "Il cinema lettrista francese," complete with bibliography and short sections on Isou and Lemaître, can be found in the well-documented catalogue *Cine qua non* (Florence: Vallecchi Editore, 1979), 67–76.

42. Dominique Noguez, "The Experimental Cinema in France," trans. Alister Sanderson, *Millennium Film Journal* 1 (Spring–Summer 1978). In light of the fact that none of the studies of avant-garde, underground, or experimental cinema (for example, those by Jean Mitry, Parker Tyler, and David Curtis) as much as mentions lettrist cinema, Noguez must be credited as the first to point out in print both its aesthetic significance and its revisionist ramifications for the

history of postwar avant-garde cinema. In a 1976 essay on the state of experimental cinema in France, Noguez remarks in a footnote that the work of Isou and Lemaître constitutes "an 'underground' French cinema whose historical and aesthetic importance has not yet been grasped. To do so is today one of the most pressing tasks of a criticism worthy of the name" (Dominique Noguez, "Qu'est-ce que le cinéma expérimental? Sa situation en France," in *Une histoire du cinéma* [Paris: Musée national d'art moderne, Centre Georges Pompidou, 1976], 51, note 23). A few years later, in his study *Eloge du cinéma expérimental: Definitions, jalons, perspectives* (Paris: Musée national d'art moderne, Centre Georges Pompidou, 1979), Noguez follows up on his earlier claim and devotes a short section to the lettrist cinema (101–104), which is described as "a movement that has been ignored for much too long and whose innovations are so numerous and go in so many different directions that one should stress their *avant-garde* character (in the strong sense of the term) as well as the fact that these preceded a number of the works produced by the American 'underground' cinema" (101). In the years following this publication, lettrist films began to be "rediscovered" with increasing regularity: in 1980 the Pompidou Center held a retrospective of the films of Lemaître, and in 1982 the show *Thirty Years of Experimental Cinema in France* curated by Noguez (which subsequently travelled to the U.S., Canada, and Japan) included a number of lettrist works.

43. Jean-Isidore Isou, *Esthétique du cinéma* (Paris: Ur, 1953). The following cursory remarks can hardly do justice to a work that deserves a much more detailed treatment than is possible here. A helpful overview can be found in Frédérique Devaux's "Notes sur *Esthétique du cinéma* de Isidore Isou," in *Revue d'histoire du cinéma* 5 (Spring 1981).

44. In a text by Maurice Lemaître "written especially for American readers" the Isouian distinction is explained as follows: "The *Amplic (amplique) phase* is the period in which the art 'swells' and in which public interest is high because it is constructed around *pretexts exterior to the art itself:* anecdotes (battles, epics, divine struggles), sentiments (romantic) or ideas (philosophical, social, etc.). . . . The second phase is called the *Chiseling (ciselante) phase,* and is the period in which the art turns in upon itself" (Maurice Lemaître, "What Is Letterism?" [sic], trans. and adapted by Lowell Blair, in *Ur: La dictature lettriste* 3 (1952), 47–48.

45. "This is the first time that one presents a *manifesto of cinema in the cinema.* It is the first time that one shows a ciné-club in the cinema, which is to say, that one prefers reflection or *debates on cinema in the cinema* to ordinary cinema as such" (Jean-Isidore Isou, *Traité de bave et d'éternité,* 35mm BW, sound, 175 min.). The scenario is contained in Isou, *Oeuvres de spectacle* (Paris: Gallimard, 1964), 7–88; above citation, 27. This volume comes with a red banderole wrapped around it on which the publisher announces: "The transformation of the theater and the cinema." Begun on

August 15, 1950, and completed in May of the following year, the film's original length of four and a half hours was reduced for "practical reasons." At the premiere of the first version of the film (which caused a near riot among the journalist audience) on April 20, 1951, the last day of the Cannes Film Festival, *Traité* was awarded the "Prix des spectateurs d'avant garde" and also the "Prix en marge du Festival de Cannes" by a renegade jury that included Jean Cocteau (some of the press reactions to this screening are reprinted in 7*ème* *Art* 8). It premiered in Paris on May 23, 1951—the very day the final version was completed—at the Cinéma Alexandra and then ran from January 25 to February 7 at the Studio de l'Etoile. The poster for the Paris premiere, designed by Jean Cocteau, is reproduced in small format on the cover of 7*ème* *Art* 12.

46. Isou, *Traité,* in *Oeuvres de spectacle,* 15. Isou's rhetoric is strikingly similar to a proclamation by Dziga Vertov published (admittedly under very different circumstances but with surprisingly analogous imperatives) nearly 30 years earlier:

> WE declare old films, the romantic, the theatricalized etc., to be leprous.
> —Don't come near!
> —Don't look!
> —Mortally dangerous!
> —Contagious.
> WE affirm the future of cinema art by rejecting its present. The death of "cinematography" is necessary so that the art of cinema may live. WE *call for the acceleration of its death.*

Dziga Vertov, "We. A Version of a Manifesto," in Richard Taylor and Ian Christie, eds., *The Film Factory: Russian and Soviet Cinema in Documents,* trans. Richard Taylor (Cambridge: Harvard University Press, 1988), 69.

47. Isou, *Traité,* in *Oeuvres de spectacle,* 24. Further on Isou employs a classically philosophical rhetorical device in order to argue that a destroyed photograph *must* be superior to the ordinary photograph since otherwise the former could not have destroyed the latter (75)!

48. *Ion* 1 (April 1952) (see note 32 above). The table of contents of *Ion* and the Debord scenario are reprinted in Berreby, ed., *Documents,* pp. 111–125. Although Maurice Lemaître's film *Le film est déjà commencé* is missing from this lettrist pantheon, there is a full page advertisement for the published scenario, Maurice Lemaître, *Le film est déjà commencé? Séance de cinéma* (Paris: Editions André Bonne, 1952). This volume also contains a lengthy preface by Isidore Isou.

49. In the notice to the reader that prefaces the volume, one reads: "The only set of values with which the members of this journal are in agreement remains Isou's complete system which has been revealed to us either in written or oral form. It is the point around which our traditional or original opinions are unified for the moment." *Ion* 1 (April 1952), 6.

50. "Doyen des Lettristes: Wolman a 24 ans," in Berreby, ed., *Documents,* 281.

51. "Des hommes insatisfaits de ce qu'on leur a donné dépassent le monde des expressions officielles et le festival de sa pauvreté.

Après **L'ESTHETIQUE DU CINEMA** d'Isidore **ISOU,**

TAMBOURS DU JUGEMENT PREMIER, l'essai de cinéma imaginaire de François **DUFRENE,** systématise à l'extrême l'épuisement des moyens du film, en le situant au delà de toutes ses mécaniques.

Guy-Ernest **DEBORD** avec

HURLEMENTS EN FAVEUR de SADE, arrive au bout du cinéma, dans sa phase insurrectionnelle.

Après ces refus, définitivement en dehors des normes que vous aimez, le **CINEMA NUCLE-AIRE** de **MARC'O.** intègre la salle et le spectateur dans la représentation cinématographique. Désormais, le cinéma ne peut être que **NUCLEAIRE.**

Alors nous voulons dépasser ces dérisoires concours de sous-produits entre petits commerçants analphabètes ou destinés à le devenir. Notre seul présence ici les fait mourir.

Et voici les hommes d'un cinéma neuf: Serge **BERNA, G. E. DEBORD,** François **DUFRENE,** Monique **GEOFFROY,** Jean Isidore **ISOU,** Yolande du **LUART, MARC'O,** Gabriel **POMERAND, POUCETTE,** Gil J. **WOLMAN.**"

(Pamphlet found in the archive of the Silkeborg Kunstmuseum, Silkeborg, Denmark; see also the remark in Berreby, ed., *Documents,* 205. Indicatively, the first statement of this tract reappears in the opening moments of Debord's *Hurlements:* compare *Oeuvres cinématographiques,* 7, and Berreby, ed., *Documents,* 295.)

52. Guy Debord, "Prolégomènes à tout cinéma futur," *Ion* 1 (April 1952), 217; reprinted in Berreby, ed., *Documents,* 109; a German translation by Ursula Panhans Bühler and Roberto Ohrt, "Prolegomena für jedes zukünftige Kino," can be found in *Durch* 3/4 (November 1987), 69.

53. Ibid.

54. Guy Debord, *Hurlements en faveur de Sade* (1952): 16mm BW, sound, 80 min.; production company: Films lettristes. The various scenarios of the film—which was dedicated to Gil J. Wolman—were published in (a) *Ion* 1 (April 1952), 219–230; reprinted in Berreby, ed., *Documents,* 111–123 (this first version, with images, was never made); (b) *Les lèvres nues* 7 (December 1955),

18–23; reprinted in Berreby, ed., *Documents,* pp. 293–298 (a new version without images preceded by a short descriptive text entitled "Grande fête de nuit"; German translation of the latter as "Eine große Nachtfete" in Debord, *Gegen den Film,* 35–36); (c) Debord, *Contre le cinéma,* 13–22 (a final version with sections not included in *Les lèvres nues,* followed by a short prose description [p. 9] and four short statements relating to the film [21–22]; German translation of the scenario in Debord, *Gegen den Film,* 23–34); and (d) Debord, *Oeuvres cinématographiques,* 5–14.

55. Although Isou claims that *Hurlements did* have an image track that was suppressed during the projection upon the suggestion of a sympathetic colleague (Isidore Isou, *Contre le cinéma situationniste, néo-nazi* [Paris: n.p., 1979], 24), in discussion with me Debord insisted that the first scenario was never more than a conceptual experiment and the second version *never* had an image track.

56. On the cowboy motif that reappears with astonishing regularity in situationist and neo-situationist productions well into the 1980s, see Greil Marcus, "The Cowboy Philosopher," *Artforum* 24 (March 1986), 85–91.

57. Although Debord criticizes the notion of originality, he nevertheless resents the failure of film historians and critics to recognize the innovation of his cinema without images. Objecting to a description of himself in *France-Soir* of March 8, 1984, as an "extravagant writer and filmmaker," Debord notes: "Anyone else would have been credited with a bit of originality. Some filmmakers since have taken twenty or thirty years to move towards a cinema without images and one has praised their patience. To give another amusing example, the painter Yves Klein, whom I knew at the time and who was present at the first very tumultuous public projection of this film, was overwhelmed by a convincing black sequence lasting twenty-four minutes. Out of this experience he developed, a few years later, his 'monochrome' painting which, to tell the truth, wrapped in a bit of zen mysticism for his famous 'blue period,' was what provoked many an expert to call him a genius. Some still insist that he is one today. As far as painting is concerned, however, it is not I who could obscure Yves Klein's glory, but rather what Malevich did much earlier and which was momentarily forgotten by these very same experts" (Debord, *Considérations,* 45–46).

58. "Les arts futurs seront des bouleversements de situations, ou rien" (Debord, *Hurlements,* in *Oeuvres cinématographiques,* 8). The phrasing of this line, similar to many formulations in Breton's *L'amour fou,* is also reminiscent of the last line of *Nadja* that reads: "La beauté sera CONVULSIVE ou ne sera pas" (André Breton, *Oeuvres complètes,* I [Paris: Gallimard, 1988], 753). As noted by Marguerite Bonnet, one of the editors of this Pléiade volume, this is a *revolutionary* syntax, as it is the very form employed by Thiers in his famous speech to the National

Assembly on November 13, 1872: "La République sera conservatrice ou ne sera pas" (ibid., 1,564).

59. Cf. *Les lèvres nues* 7 (December 1955), 18, footnote; also in Berreby, ed., *Documents,* 294.

60. A few months later the same group also precluded a *Squelette sadique* in the same ciné-club that had been publicized and attributed to a certain René Guy Babord and that was to consist of turning out the lights in the hall for fifteen minutes (Debord, *Contre le cinéma,* 9).

61. Guy Atkins (with Troels Andersen), *Asger Jorn: The Crucial Years, 1954–1964* (New York: Wittenborn Art Books, 1977), 57–59.

62. G.-E. Debord, "Encore un effort si vous voulez être situationnistes," *Potlatch* 29 (November 1957); *Potlatch, 1954–1957,* 239, also in Berreby, ed., *Documents,* 251; translated in this volume as "One More Try If You Want to Be Situationists (The SI *in* and *against* Decomposition)," 58. This passage is also quoted as the last of the four "explanations" following the scenario of *Hurlements* in Debord, *Contre le cinéma,* 22. In this issue of *Potlatch* it was announced that following the formation of the Situationist International as resolved by the Cosio d'Arroscia conference in July, the journal would heretofore appear under the auspices of the SI: consequently, *Potlatch* 29, the last issue of the journal, carries for the first and last time the subheading "Information Bulletin of the Situationist International."

63. Serge Berna, "Jusqu'à l'os," *Ion* 1 (April 1952), 187. After explaining that the second "chastity belt" is the financial dimension, Berna again calls for a reexamination of "the categorical imperative of cinema . . . which is—the image, the image, the image is what constitutes the cinema" (188).

64. *Ion* 1 (April 1952), 196; the complete scenario of Dufrène's work is contained in this issue, 193–214.

65. Completed on September 25, 1951, it was first screened at the Ciné-Club d'Avant-Garde on February 11, 1952. The projection—onto a large meteorological balloon—caused an uproar and soon thereafter the film was officially censored (cf. *Potlatch* 12 [September 1954]; *Potlatch, 1954–1957,* 69; also in Berreby, ed., *Documents,* 281). For Debord's polemical condemnation of the censorship of a film he praised as "more offensive today than Eisenstein's images which had been so threatening in Europe for such a long time," see "Totem et Tabou," *Internationale lettriste* 3 (August 1953), reprinted in Berreby, ed., *Documents,* 156–157. The scenario of the film, first published in *Ion,* is reprinted in Berreby, ed., *Documents,* 87–107. See also Wolman's "explanatory" text, "Le cinématochrone—nouvelle amplitude," first published in *Ur: La dictature lettriste* 2, no. 10; reprinted in Berreby, ed., *Documents,* 141.

66. Compare the following description of a film attended by the narrator in Robert Desnos's *Nouvelles Hébrides,* written over 30 years earlier: "On the blank screen, a luminous disk was pro-

jected without any images of people or landscapes. The assembly of empty seats attentively followed some magnificent spectacle invisible to me" (Robert Desnos, *Nouvelles Hébrides et autres textes, 1922–1930,* ed. Marie-Claire Dumas [Paris: Gallimard, 1978], 100). The translation cited above is taken from an article by David Wills, "Slit Screen," *Dada/Surrealism* 15 (1986), 88. I am grateful to I. L. Bifidus for pointing out this striking similarity.

67. Isou, *Oeuvres de spectacle,* 87.

68. The generally negative accounts of the debut of the festival's "enfant terrible" in the press make no mention of images: see, for example, R. M. Arlaud's report in *Combat* (April 21–22), 2. Jean Cocteau describes the "Isou affair" on the Rue d'Antibes as follows: "Isidore Isou had invited us to *see* his film—a nine thousand meter spool—in the off-circuit of the festival. However, he had only finished the soundtrack. He considered his ideas sufficient to destroy the unstomachable cinema" (Jean Cocteau, *Entretiens autour du cinématographe* [Paris: Editions André Bonne, 1951], 90; English translation in Jean Cocteau, *Cocteau on the Film,* trans. Vera Traill [London: Dennis Dobson, 1954], 135). Maurice Lemaître recounts more or less the same story: "As Isou and I had not finished the film in time, we projected only the *soundtrack*" (Maurice Lemaître, *Jean Cocteau et le lettrisme* [Paris: Centre de créativité, 1976], 2, note 3). In Isou's own account of the Cannes screening of *Traité,* the first "chapter," entitled "Le principe," *did* have an image track and it was only following this section that the audience was plunged into darkness due to the lack of images, which in turn caused the uproar (Isou, *Contre le cinéma situationniste, néo-nazi,* 24). During the ensuing commotion, Cocteau recounts, Isou had asked him to speak, but he had declined. However, Cocteau appends to the above description the text of the statement that he would have liked to have made on the occasion. Here he discusses the cleansing function of the void in Isou's work, citing as a proleptic comment an episode from the beginning of his own film *Orphée,* in which the journal *Nudisme* contains only blank pages: "'This is ridiculous,' Orpheus says, to which the man from the Café des Poètes responds: 'Less ridiculous than if these pages were filled with ridiculous texts. No excess is ridiculous.' This is why I was content to say to the audience that an insolent attitude is always alive and that they would do well to take Isou's strange screening seriously" (Cocteau, *Entretiens autour du cinématographe,* 90).

69. Frame enlargements from the film depicting Isou and Lemaître can be found in *Une histoire du cinéma,* 144.

70. Isou, *Traité,* in *Oeuvres de spectacle,* 17.

71. As in the following passage from Isou's subsequent film, *Apologie d'un personnage unique* (Apology of a Unique Personality): "One day the cinema will be disgusted by its images, even when they have been *destroyed.* It will not dare present anything but *subtitles.* The film of

tomorrow will be *lettrist* and composed of *subtitles.* If at its inception cinema was by virtue of its images an attack on *reading,* the day will come when the cinema will be a mere *form of reading*" (Isou, *Oeuvres de spectacle,* 269).

72. Isou, *Esthétique du cinéma,* in *Ion* 1 (April 1952), 147–148.

73. Much to Isou's annoyance, years later Debord simply integrates his suggested amplifications, without acknowledging their provenance. Compare Debord, *Hurlements,* in *Oeuvres ciné-matographiques,* 7. For Isou's protest, see his delirious polemic *Contre le cinéma situationniste, néo-nazi,* 25, footnote 1.

74. Debord, "Prolégomènes à tout cinéma futur," in *Ion* 1 (April 1952), 219; reprinted in Berreby, ed., *Documents,* 109.

75. Debord, *Contre le cinéma,* 9.

76. In response to the question "Lettrism: A Neo-Dadaism?" Jean-Paul Curtay writes: "So if lettrism, like Dada, came out of a reaction against a world war, Lettrism did not remain a protest . . . [but became] an exaltation of permanently renewed arts, philosophy, scientific knowledge, technology; a fight for a conversion of destructive powers and trends into constructive powers through original education, planning, administration, and banking systems [!]; a global positive move" (Jean-Paul Curtay, "Lettrism, Abstract Poetry, Mouth Symbols, and More . . ." *Dada/Surrealism* 12 ([1983], 72).

77. Conceived together with Picabia's ballet *Relâche* as an event that would challenge and out-rage the spectators, *Entr'acte* took place in a theater adorned with large signs that read, "If you are not satisfied, go to hell" or "Whistles for sale at the door." The plan was that during the *en-tr'acte* (intermission) the sound track for the film would be provided by the traditional acoustics of intermission: small talk, coughing, drinking, and general murmur. Instead, the audience re-mained obediently seated and watched the film in silence, not even provoked by the film's dra-matic violations of the conventions of cinematic narrative.

78. Thomas Elsaesser, "Dada/Cinema?" *Dada/Surrealism* 15 (1986), 20.

79. In the original, Benjamin's phrase reads "grundsätzliche Entwürdigung ihres Materi-als"; Walter Benjamin, "Das Kunstwerk im Zeitalter seiner technischen Reproduzierbarkeit" (zweite Fassung), *Gesammelte Schriften,* II (Frankfurt am Main: Suhrkamp Verlag, 1980), trans-lated by Harry Zohn as "The Work of Art in the Age of Mechanical Reproduction," in *Illumi-nations* (New York: Schocken, 1969), 237; translation modified.

80. As Raoul Vaneigem puts it in *The Revolution of Everyday Life:* "The more we contemplate, as spectators, the degradation of all values, the less likely we are to get on with a little real de-struction" (173).

81. It is important to distinguish the *cinematic* "dada" dimension of Debord's film from practices employed to similar ends that are in a strict sense *extracinematic*. Typical of the latter is Maurice Lemaître's project to educate film audiences in critical viewing by employing trained spectators to strategically interrupt the screenings of commercial films, a hilarious plan outlined in scrupulous detail in Lemaître's "Base d'une éducation cinématographique du public par la critique permanente," *Ur: La dictature lettriste* 2, 19–20. Similarly one must make a distinction (purely descriptive, not normative) between Debord's reductive strategy and those adopted in Lemaître's film *Le film est déjà commencé* (1951; 35mm, BW, hand-colored, sound, 60 min.; scenario published as *Le film est déjà commencé? Séance de cinéma* [Paris: Editions André Bonne, 1952]). In this work, whose dada gesture is of the "happening" variety, "trained" spectators were to converse with the film, the screen was covered with cloth, the spectators were showered with water, and so on. A filmography of Lemaître's extensive cinematic production can be found in *Une histoire du cinéma,* 87; this volume also reproduces a (incorrectly identified) sequence from the film (143).

82. Knabb, ed., *Anthology,* 30; "On ne conteste jamais réellement une organisation de l'existence sans contester toutes les formes de langage qui appartiennent à cette organisation" (Debord, *Sur le passage,* in *Oeuvres cinématographiques,* 22).

83. Guy Debord, "Report on the Construction of Situations and on the Terms of Organization and Action of the International Situationist Tendency," in this volume, 46; originally published as *Rapport sur la construction des situations et sur les conditions de l'organisation et de l'action de la tendence situationniste internationale* (Paris, n.p., 1957), 16. This seminal text, an internal report published in Paris in June 1957 and presented to the members of the Lettrist International, the International Movement for an Imaginist Bauhaus, and the London Psychogeographical Society, served as the basis of discussion at the Cosio d'Arroscia conference where, on July 27, 1957, the Situationist International was founded. Largely unavailable for many years, the text has been reprinted in Berreby, ed., *Documents,* 607–619, followed by an Italian version, 621–637; it is also reprinted in facsimile in the pamphlet produced by the Centre Georges Pompidou to accompany the exhibit *Sur le passage de quelques personnes à travers une assez courte unité de temps* (Paris, 1989).

84. A facsimile of the tract can be found in Berreby, ed., *Documents,* 262.

85. Following the distribution of "Finis les pieds plats" both the tract and the disavowal were reprinted in the first issue of *Internationale lettriste* under the title: "Mort d'un commis voyageur" together with an introduction by Debord, an open letter by Berna, Brau, Debord, and Wolman to *Combat* (which refused publication) in response to the disavowal, and a letter by Brau

admonishing Isou for his cowardice; this dossier is reprinted in Berreby, ed., *Documents,* 146–151. See also the unsigned "Doyen des lettristes: Wolman a 24 ans," in Berreby, ed., *Documents,* 281. Debord could hardly have been unaware of the overdetermination of attacking Chaplin given that the surrealists had explicitly endorsed Chaplin in their statement "Hands Off Love" signed by Breton, Aragon, Desnos, Leiris, and many others and published in *La révolution sur-réaliste* 9–10 (October 1927), 1–6.

86. In this context the line from Debord's "Prolegomena"—"I made this film before it was too late"—takes on a new significance when it reappears in the sound track of the final version of *Hurlements* followed by the phrase "Jean-Isidore, to get out of that ephemeral crowd." It is tempting to read it along with Debord's renunciation of the explicit lettrist vocabulary as a pro-leptic indication within the realm of the aesthetic of a multiply motivated alienation from the lettrist program that would soon thereafter manifest itself decisively in the scission.

87. *Internationale lettriste* 1; reprinted in Berreby, ed., *Documents,* 151.

88. Guy Debord, *Sur le passage de quelques personnes à travers une assez courte unité de temps:* 35mm BW, sound, 20 min.; produced by Dansk-Fransk Experimentalfilmskompagni; shot in April 1959, cut in September 1959. Scenario in Debord, *Contre le cinéma,* 23–50 (followed by 12 stills); reprinted in *Oeuvres cinématographiques,* 15–35 (followed by six stills). An English transla-tion (without shot descriptions, subtitles, text frame information, or images), "On the Passage of a Few Persons through a Rather Brief Period of Time," can be found in Knabb, ed., *An-thology,* 29–33. Another still image from the film is reproduced in *IS* 11 (October 1967), 36.

89. Knabb, ed., *Anthology,* 29; Debord, *Sur le passage,* in *Oeuvres cinématographiques,* 19.

90. Knabb, ed., *Anthology,* 29 (translation modified); Debord, *Sur le passage,* in *Oeuvres ciné-matographiques,* 17.

91. Technical notes on *Sur le passage* in Debord, *Contre le cinéma,* 3. This technical data is not included in either Debord's *Oeuvres cinématographiques* nor in the translations of the two scenar-ios in the Knabb *Anthology.*

92. "Le détournement comme négation et comme prelude," *IS* 3 (December 1959), 11.

93. Viénet, "The Situationists and the New Forms of Action against Politics and Art" (1967), trans. in this volume, 184; "Les situationnistes et les nouvelles formes d'action," 34. Viénet also calls for increased activity in the domains of (1) experimentation with photo-novels; (2) the pro-motion of guerilla tactics in the mass media; and (3) the perfection of situationist comics. In his reference to the work by Marx that Eisenstein intended to film, Viénet most probably was think-ing of the project to film *Das Kapital* for which there are a series of highly illuminating notes pub-lished in *Iskousstvo Kino* 1 (Moscow 1973). These notes from Eisenstein's work journal are also

available in translation in both English and French: Sergei Eisenstein, "Notes for a Film of *Capital*," trans. Maciej Sliwowski, Jay Leyda, and Annette Michelson, *October* 2 (Summer 1976), 3–26; Sergei Eisenstein, "Filmer le Capital," trans. Jean and Luda Schnitzer, *Ecran 74* 31 (December 1974). For contextualization and analysis, see, above all, Annette Michelson, "Reading Eisenstein Reading *Capital*," *October* 2 (Summer 1976), 27–38, and *October* 3 (Spring 1977), 82–89. Further material can be found in the following two articles: Barthélemy Amengual, "L'aventureux projet d'Eisenstein: Filmer *Le Capital*," *Vertigo* 2 (Paris) (November 1988), 19–20; Raymonde Hébraud-Carasco, "Dialectique Einsenstein [sic]: 'Filmer le Capital,'" *Macula* 1 (1976), 58–76.

94. Technical notes to *Sur le passage*, in Debord, *Contre le cinéma*, 3.

95. Guy-Ernest Debord, *Mémoires* (Paris: L'Internationale situationniste, 1959); Asger Jorn (conseiller technique pour le détournement G. E. Debord), *Fin de Copenhague* (Copenhagen: Permild & Rosengreen, 1957), published under the auspices of the Bauhaus imaginiste in a limited edition of 200 in May. *Fin de Copenhague* is reproduced in facsimile in Berreby, ed., *Documents*, 553–592, and in a separate paperback facsimile edition published in 1985 by Editions Allia in Paris.

96. Knabb, ed., *Anthology*, 31 (translation slightly modified); Debord, *Sur le passage*, in *Oeuvres cinématographiques*, 26.

97. Knabb, ed., *Anthology*, 30 (translation modified); Debord, *Sur le passage*, in *Oeuvres cinématographiques*, 21.

98. Knabb, ed., *Anthology*, 31 (translation slightly modified); Debord, *Sur le passage*, in *Oeuvres cinématographiques*, 25.

99. One such text frame is reproduced as an illustration in Viénet, "Les situationnistes et les nouvelles formes d'action," 36.

100. Technical notes to Debord, *Sur le passage*, in *Contre le cinéma*, 3.

101. Knabb, ed., *Anthology*, 32–33 (translation modified); Debord, *Sur le passage*, in *Oeuvres cinématographiques*, 30.

102. Cf. Knabb, ed., *Anthology*, 33; Debord, *Oeuvres cinématographiques*, 30–31.

103. Knabb, ed., *Anthology*, 33 (translation modified); Debord, *Sur le passage*, in *Oeuvres cinématographiques*, 31–32.

104. Knabb, ed., *Anthology*, 31 (translation modified); Debord, *Sur le passage*, in *Oeuvres cinématographiques*, 23–24.

105. To the extent that Debord's insistence on the documentation of incoherence is motivated by a utopian hope that once the confusion of the world is revealed it will provoke a long-overdue political and social change, it is not unlike the theory of radical distraction articulated

by Siegfried Kracauer in the 1920s. Compare, for example, Kracauer's recognition of the redemptive and mimetic aspects of Weimar mass culture:

> In a profound sense, Berlin audiences act truthfully when increasingly they shun these art events (which, for good reason, remain caught in mere pretension), preferring instead the superficial glamor of the stars, films, revues and production values. Here, in pure externality, the audience encounters itself; its own reality is revealed in the fragmented sequence of splendid sense impressions. Were this reality to remain hidden from the audience, it could neither attack nor change it; its disclosure in the practice of distraction is therefore of *moral* significance.
>
> However, this is the case only if distraction is not an end in itself. Indeed the very fact that the shows which cater to distraction are composed of the same mixture of externalities as the world of the urban masses; the fact that these shows lack any authentic and materially motivated coherence, except possibly the cement [glue?] of sentimentality which covers up this lack but only in order to make it all the more visible; the fact that these shows convey in a precise and undisguised manner to thousands of eyes and ears the *disorder* of society—this is precisely what enables such shows to evoke and maintain that tension which must precede the inevitable radical change.

Siegfried Kracauer, "Cult of Distraction," trans. Thomas Y. Levin, *New German Critique* 40 (Winter 1987), 94–95.

106. Gilles Ivain [Ivan Chtcheglov], "Formula for a New Urbanism," in Knabb, ed., *Anthology,* 4 (translation modified); "Formulaire pour un urbanisme nouveau," *IS* 1 (June 1958), 19.

107. Guy Debord, *Critique de la séparation:* 35mm BW, sound, 20 min.; shot in September–October 1960; cut during January–February 1961; produced by Dansk-Fransk Experimentalfilmskompagni. Scenario in Debord, *Contre le cinéma,* 57–81 (followed by 12 stills); reprinted in *Oeuvres cinématographiques,* 37–58 (followed by six stills). An English translation (without shot descriptions, subtitles, text frame information, or images) can be found under the title "Critique of Separation," in Knabb, ed., *Anthology,* 34–37.

108. This print, part of the collection of the Silkeborg Kunstmuseum (Silkeborg, Denmark), belonged to Asger Jorn (who set up and largely bankrolled the Dansk-Fransk Experimentalfilmskompagni that financed both *Sur le passage* and *Critique de la séparation*). According to Troels Andersen, the curator of the museum, the 35mm print was given to the museum around 1960–

1961 on the condition that it not be shown in public: "The reason for the latter decision was an ideological and artistic quarrel with some of the people involved" (Letter to the author dated October 19, 1987). It can, however, be screened for research purposes upon special request.

109. Not included in either Knabb's *Anthology* nor in Debord's *Oeuvres cinématographiques.* Text frames: "Bientót, sur cet écran—Un des plus grands anti-films de tous les temps!—Des personnages vrais! Une histoire authentique!—Sur un thème comme le cinéma n'a jamais osé en traiter." Citation from André Martinet, *Eléments de linguistique générale* (Paris: Armand Colin, 1970), 2: "Quand on songe combien il est naturel et avantageux pour l'homme d'identifier sa langue et la réalité, on devine quel degré de sophistication il lui a fallu atteindre pour les dissocier et faire de chacune un objet d'études" (technical data on *Critique de la séparation* in Debord, *Contre le cinéma,* 10).

110. Knabb, ed., *Anthology,* 35 (translation modified); Debord, *Critique de la séparation,* in *Oeuvres cinématographiques,* 42.

111. Knabb, ed., *Anthology,* 35 (translation modified); Debord, *Critique de la séparation,* in *Oeuvres cinématographiques,* 42.

112. Compare, for example, the visual references to Robin Hood and Prince Valiant in Debord, *In girum,* in *Oeuvres cinématographiques,* 204 and 245. In the latter case, a comic strip image depicting "Prince Valiant, in search of adventures" alternates with a photograph of Ivan Chtcheglov.

113. Knabb, ed., *Anthology,* 35–36 (translation modified); Debord, *Critique de la séparation,* in *Oeuvres cinématographiques,* 45.

114. Knabb, ed., *Anthology,* 34; Debord, *Critique de la séparation,* in *Oeuvres cinématographiques,* 39–40.

115. In this regard Debord's films are very reminiscent of the montage aesthetic articulated by Theodor W. Adorno and Hanns Eisler in their study of sound-image relations in cinema, *Komposition für den Film* (Munich: Rogner und Bernhard, 1969 and Frankfurt am Main: Suhrkamp Verlag, 1976). For details of the complicated publication history of this seminal study, as well as the status of the English-language edition signed by Hanns Eisler, *Composing for the Films* (New York: Oxford University Press, 1947), cf. the editorial pre- and postfaces in the two German editions cited above.

116. Technical notes to *Critique de la séparation,* in Debord, *Contre le cinéma,* 10.

117. Knabb, ed., *Anthology,* 37 (translation modified); Debord, *Critique de la séparation,* in *Oeuvres cinématographiques,* 50.

118. Knabb, ed., *Anthology,* 37; Debord, *Critique de la séparation,* in *Oeuvres cinématographiques,* 49.

119. Knabb, ed., *Anthology,* 310; "Une modification révolutionnaire des formes présentes de la culture ne peut être rien d'autre que le dépassement de tous les aspects de l'instrumentation esthétique et technique qui constitue un ensemble de spectacles séparés de la vie. Ce n'est pas dans ces significations de surface que l'on doit chercher la relation d'un spectacle avec les problèmes de la société, mais au niveau le plus profond, au niveau de *sa fonction en tant que spectacle*" (Debord, "Pour un jugement révolutionnaire de l'art," 13).

120. Knabb, ed., *Anthology,* 37; Debord, *Critique de la séparation,* in *Oeuvres cinématographiques,* 52–53.

121. Debord, "Report on the Construction of Situations," trans. in this volume, 47; "Rapport sur la construction des situations," 17, reprinted in Berreby, ed., *Documents,* 618. The passage cited above is also employed as an epigraph for one of the first essays in the first issue of *IS* (June 1958), "Problèmes préliminaires à la construction d'une situation," 11, compare Knabb, ed., *Anthology,* 43.

122. Not included in Knabb, ed., *Anthology;* Debord, *Critique de la séparation,* in *Oeuvres cinématographiques,* 52–53. "Les mystères de New York" was a series of 600-meter silent film episodes (twenty-two in all) made by Louis Gasnier in 1915 under the title "The Clutching Hand/Exploits of Elaine" and starring Pearl White. It was based on a serial novel by Pierre Decourcelle that was published in *Le Matin.* Louis Aragon pays an ironic homage to the film in *Anicet ou le panorama* (Paris: NRF, 1921).

123. Knabb, ed., *Anthology,* 310 (translation modified); Debord, "Pour un jugement révolutionnaire de l'art," 141.

124. "The Practice of Theory: Cinema and Revolution," trans. in this volume, 188; "Le cinéma et la révolution," *IS* 12 (September 1969), 105.

125. *La société du spectacle* (1973), 35mm BW, sound, approximately 80 min.; produced by Simar Films (Paris); scenario in Debord, *Oeuvres cinématographiques,* 59–144, followed by twenty stills.

126. *La véritable scission dans l'Internationale* (Paris: Editions Champ Libre, 1972).

127. Publicity brochure for *La société du spectacle* produced by Simar Films (Paris) in 1973.

128. "Que la tentative révolutionnaire de mai 1968 ait marqué le changement d'une époque, voilà ce que démontre le simple fait qu'un livre de théorie subversive comme *La société du spectacle* de Guy Debord puisse être aujourd'hui porté à l'écran par son auteur lui-même, et qu'il existe un producteur pour financer une telle entreprise."

129. As evidenced in the following passage from the contract signed with Simar, Debord's total creative freedom was stipulated in writing: "It is agreed that the author will have complete liberty in the accomplishment of his work, without supervision from anyone, and without even any obligation to take into consideration any comments whatsoever on any aspect of the content or of the cinematic form that he deems appropriate for his film"; "Il est entendu que l'au-

teur accomplira son travail en toute liberté, sans contrôle de qui que ce soit, et sans même tenir compte de quelque observation que ce soit sur aucun aspect du contenu ni de la forme cinématographique qu'il lui paraîtra convenable de donner à son film" (contract between Simar Films and Guy Debord, cited in publicity pamphlet for the film *La société du spectacle* [1973]).

130. In conversation with the author, April 1989 (Paris). The film employs all or part of the following theses in the order listed: 1–4, 6–7, 9–10, 12, 16, 18, 21–24, 29, 31, 33–34; 204–209; 187–188; 195; 35–37, 41, 44, 46, 48, 50, 54–56; 59–60, 63–66, 69–72; 166–169, 171, 173, 178; 147–148, 150, 153, 155–158, 162; 134, 133, 141, 145–146; 75–77, 85–86, 88, 90, 100, 104, 106–107, 114–115, 122–124.

131. August von Cieszkowski, *Prolégomènes à l'historiosophie* (Paris: Editions Champ Libre, 1973), 102; cited in *La société du spectacle,* in Debord, *Oeuvres cinématographiques,* 75.

132. *La société du spectacle* (thesis 204), in Debord, *Oeuvres cinématographiques,* 70.

133. "Sa présente adaptation cinématographique, elle aussi, ne se propose pas quelques critiques politiques partielles, mais une critique totale du monde existant, c'est-à-dire de tous les aspects du capitalisme moderne, et de son système général d'illusions" (publicity brochure for *La société du spectacle*).

134. *La société du spectacle* (thesis 208), in Debord, *Oeuvres cinématographiques,* 72.

135. In the methodological preface to this unfinished project, Benjamin writes that the practice of citation without quotation marks, which he identifies with a strategy of montage, is one of the aims of the work: "Diese Arbeit muß die kunst, ohne Anfuhrungszeichen zu zitieren, zur höchsten Höhe entwickeln. Ihre Theorie hängt aufs engste mit der Montage zusammen" (Walter Benjamin, *Das Passagenwerk,* 1 [Frankfurt am Main: Suhrkamp Verlag, 1985], 572 [thesis N 1, 9]).

136. Ibid.

137. "*Communiqué:* Quand la pensée me vint de créer le monde, je prévis qu'on y tournerait un jour un film aussi révoltant que *La Société du Spectacle.* De sorte que j'ai préféré ne pas créer le monde. (signé): Dieu" (text provided from private archive).

138. Reviews of the film *La société du spectacle: Art Press* 50 (Summer 1981); *Charlie-Hebdo* 181 (May 6, 1974), 15 (D.D.T.) and a reader's letter in *Charlie-Hebdo* 182 (May 13, 1974), 11; *Cinéma 74* 188 (June 1974), 146–147 (Bernard Pauly); *Le Monde* (May 9, 1974), 20 (François Bott); *Le Point* 87 (May 21, 1974), 19; *Nouvel observateur* 494 (April 29, 1974), 62 (Claude Roy); *Nouvel observateur* 496 (May 13, 1974), 28; *Quotidien de Paris* 24 (May 2, 1974), 9; *Téléciné* 189 (June 1974), 24 (S. L. P.); *Télérama* 1,269 (May 11, 1974), 73 (Alain Remond); *Zoom* 22 (January–February 1974), 27 and 29 (J. F.).

139. *In girum,* in Debord, *Oeuvres cinématographiques,* 209.

140. "How Not to Understand Situationist Books," (excerpts) in Knabb, ed., *Anthology,* 265–269 (translation of title modified); "Comment on ne comprend pas des livres situationnistes," *IS* 12 (September 1969), 44–54. It is precisely this practice of symptomatic citation of critical responses that Knabb also employs in an appendix entitled "The Blind Men and the Elephant (Selected Opinions on the Situationists)" (*Anthology,* 381–392).

141. The citations are taken from reviews in *Edmagramme* (December 6, 1967), *Le nouvel observateur* (January 3, 1968; November 8, 1971; May 22, 1972), *La quinzaine littéraire* (February 1, 1968), *La gazette littéraire de Lausanne* (January 13, 1968), *Réforme* (March 9, 1968), *Le Monde* (February 14, 1968), *The Times Literary Supplement* (March 21, 1968), *New York Times* (April 21, 1968), *The Sunday Times* (July 21, 1968), *L'Espresso* (December 15, 1968), *Umanità nuova* (May 15, 1971), *Les temps modernes* 299–300 (June 1971), *Etudes* (June–December 1968).

142. *Réfutation de tous les jugements, tant élogieux qu'hostiles, qui ont été jusqu'ici portés sur le film "La Société du Spectacle"* (1975), 35mm BW, sound, 30 min.; produced by Simar Films (Paris); scenario in Debord, *Oeuvres cinématographiques,* 155–185, followed by six stills.

143. Bertolt Brecht, "Der Dreigroschenprozeß. Ein soziologisches Experiment," in his *Gesammelte Werke* XVIII (Frankfurt am Main: Suhrkamp Verlag, 1967), 139–209. A French translation of this remarkable document can be found in the volume of Brecht's writings entitled *Sur le cinéma* (Paris: L'Arche, 1976).

144. Knabb, ed., *Anthology,* 312; "La critique d'art est un spectacle au deuxième degré. Le critique est celui qui donne en spectacle son état de spectateur même. Spectateur spécialisé, donc spectateur idéal, énonçant ses idées et sentiments *devant* une oeuvre à laquelle il ne participe pas réellement. Il relance, remet en scène, sa propre non-intervention sur le spectacle. La faiblesse des jugements fragmentaires, hasardeux et largement arbitraires, sur des spectacles qui ne nous concernent pas vraiment est notre lot à tous dans beaucoup de discussions banales de la vie privée. Mais le critique d'art fait étalage d'une telle faiblesse, *rendue exemplaire*" (Debord, "Pour un jugement révolutionnaire de l'art," 15).

145. *Réfutation,* in Debord, *Oeuvres cinématographiques,* 166–167.

146. Ibid., 157.

147. Ibid., 162.

148. Ibid., 159 and 166.

149. Ibid., 174.

150. Ibid., 169.

151. "Communication prioritaire," *IS* 7 (April 1962), 24; translated in this volume as "Editorial Notes: Priority Communication," 134.

152. Knabb, ed., *Anthology,* 312; Debord, "Pour un jugement révolutionnaire de l'art," 15.

153. *In girum imus nocte et consumimur igni* (1978); 35mm BW, sound; approximately 80 min.; produced by Simar Films. Scenario in Debord, *Oeuvres cinématographiques,* 187–278, followed by twenty-four black-and-white stills (278ff.). A selection of passages from the film translated into English and introduced by Lucy Forsyth, together with shot illustrations (some cropped, others upside-down) from four of Debord's films, can be found under the title "In girum imus nocte et consumimur igni," in *Block* 14 (Autumn 1988), 27–37; a complete translation has been published by Pelagian Press (London, 1991). A German translation of the scenario is available as *Wir irren des nachts im Kreis umber und werden vom Feuer verzerbt* (Berlin: Edition Tiamat, 1985).

154. *In girum,* in Debord, *Oeuvres cinématographiques,* 189.

155. Ibid., 204.

156. To those who might rightly object to the problematic model of ideology as false consciousness employed here, one should point out that such a critique, while theoretically sound, would do well to attempt to take account of the specificity of the site of the enunciation: the cinema.

157. *In girum,* in Debord, *Oeuvres cinématographiques,* 202.

158. Ibid., 208.

159. Ibid., 207–208.

160. Ibid., 217.

161. Ibid., 223.

162. Ibid., 225.

163. The continued capacity of the absence of any image to dumbfound spectators is confirmed by a critic who describes how, during this sequence, someone in the audience was in the process of going out to complain but then the image reappeared and they returned to their seat (Dominique Païni in *Cinéma 81,* 271–272 [July/August 1981]).

164. *In girum,* in Debord, *Oeuvres cinématographiques,* 256. Elsewhere Debord characterizes the same group as one in which "everybody consumed more glasses of wine daily than the number of lies told by a union leader during the entire duration of a wildcat strike" (232).

165. Ibid., 235.

166. Ibid., 252.

167. For more information on "The Game of War," see the rulebook published by the Société des jeux stratégiques et historiques (Paris, 1977). Together with Alice Becker-Ho, Debord has

published a detailed record of one "game" under the title *Le jeu de la guerre: Relevé des positions successives de toutes les forces au cours d'une partie* (Paris: Editions Gérard Lebovici, 1987).

168. *In girum,* in Debord, *Oeuvres cinématographiques,* 215.

169. Ibid., 265.

170. Ibid., 265.

171. Ibid., 264.

172. Ibid., 262.

173. Ibid., 278.

174. Ibid., 237–238.

175. As announced in an extended article on the film in *Libération* (June 3, 1981), there was a screening of *In girum* at 4 A.M. on the pirate television station "Canal 68" on June 4, 1981.

176. *Ordures et décombres déballés à la sortie du film "In girum imus nocte et consumimur igni"* (Paris: Editions Champ Libre, 1982). There are at least two further reviews of the film not included in this volume: the first, by Régis Jauffret, was published in *Art Press* 50 (Summer 1981), 34; the second, an extended, sympathetic, and quite informed treatment by Lucien Logette, appeared in *Jeune cinéma* 137 (September–October 1981), 23–25.

177. In *Potlatch* 15 (December 1954); *Potlatch, 1954–1957,* 91; also in Berreby, ed., *Documents,* 192, the journal announces the completion of the first LI experiment in radio propaganda, a piece entitled "La valeur éducative" (The educational value). This "unusual" tape, offered to any radio station willing to take the risk of playing it, was composed *entirely* of detourned phrases taken from Bossuet, Demangeon, and Meynier, an article in *France-Soir,* Marx and Engels, Saint-Just, and from the books of Jeremiah, Psalms, and Samuel. The text of the program was then published in its entirety in the subsequent issues of the journal: *Potlatch* 16 (January 1955); *Potlatch, 1954–1957,* 100–102; also in Berreby, ed., *Documents,* 195–196; *Potlatch* 17 (February 1955); *Potlatch, 1954–1957,* 112–113; Berreby, ed., *Documents,* 199–200; *Potlatch* 18 (March 1955); *Potlatch, 1954–1957,* 121–123; also in Berreby, ed., *Documents,* 203–204. It is signed Guy-Ernest Debord.

178. *Potlatch* 15 (December 1954); *Potlatch, 1954–1957,* 91; also in Berreby, ed., *Documents,* 192.

179. *Potlatch* 21 (June 1955); *Potlatch, 1954–1957,* 147; also in Berreby, ed., *Documents,* 215.

180. *IS* 5 (December 1960), 11.

181. This fact, in turn, renders all the more curious (or perhaps symptomatic?) the virtually total lack of any reference to the films by Debord and the lettrists in the secondary literature on the postwar experimental cinema. This striking absence is manifest not only in the already

"classical" English-language accounts of the "international free cinema" by David Curtis, Stephen Dwoskin, P. Adam Sitney, and Parker Tyler, but even in more recent and specialized studies such as Peter Gidal's *Materialist Film* (London: Routledge, 1989).

182. It would be interesting to explore the connections between the "theory film" genre and other cinematic works that explicitly acknowledge their indebtedness to the SI such as Dusan Makavejev's *Sweet Movie* (dedicated to Raoul Vaneigem) and Godfrey Reggio's *La prophétie* (dedicated to Debord).

183. Peter Wollen, "Counter Cinema: *Vent d'est,*" *Afterimage* 4 (Autumn 1972), 6–16.

184. My treatment of the question of "political modernism" has benefited greatly from David Rodowick's impressive discussion of 1970s film theory in his recent study *The Crisis of Political Modernism: Criticism and Ideology in Contemporary Film Theory* (Urbana: University of Illinois Press, 1988), esp. chapter two: "Modernism and Semiology," 42–66.

185. Sylvia Harvey, *May '68 and Film Culture* (London: British Film Institute, 1978), 69–70.

186. "Il me semble qu'ici mon travail, très court mais étendu sur une période de vingt-six ans, a bien correspondu aux principaux critères de l'art moderne: (1) l'originalité fortement marquée au départ et la décision ferme de ne jamais faire 'la même chose' deux fois successivement, tout en ayant un style et une thématique personnelle toujours reconnaissables; (2) comprendre la société de son temps, *id est* l'expliquer en la critiquant, car il s'agissait manifestement d'un temps qui manquait davantage de critique que d'apologétique; (3) enfin, avoir été révolutionnaire *dans la forme et dans le contenu,* ce qui me paraît aller dans le sens de toutes les aspirations 'unitaires' de l'art moderne, vers ce point où il a voulu aller au delà de l'art" (Guy Debord, letter to the author dated April 24, 1989).

Spectacle, Attention, Counter-Memory

Jonathan Crary

Whether or not the term *spectacle* was originally taken from Henri Lefebvre's *Critique de la vie quotidienne,* its currency emerged from the activities in the late 1950s and early 1960s of the various configurations now designated as presituationist or situationist. The product of a radical critique of modernist art practice, a politics of everyday life, and an analysis of contemporary capitalism, its influence was obviously intensified with the publication of Guy Debord's *Society of the Spectacle* in 1967.[1] And years later, the word *spectacle* not only persists but has become a stock phrase in a wide range of critical and not-so-critical discourses. But, assuming it has not become completely devalued or exhausted as an explanation of the contemporary operation of power, does it still mean today what it did in the early '60s? What constellation of forces and institutions does it designate? And if these have mutated, what kind of practices are required now to resist their effects?

One can still well ask if the notion of spectacle is the imposition of an illusory unity onto a more heterogeneous field. Is it a totalizing and monolithic concept that inadequately represents a plurality of incommensurable institutions and events? For some, a troubling aspect of the term *spectacle* is the almost ubiquitous presence of the definite article in front of it, suggesting a single and seamless global system of relations. For others, it is a mystification of the functioning of power, a new opiate-of-the-masses type of explanation, a vague cultural-institutional formation with a suspicious structural autonomy. Or is a concept such as spectacle a necessary tool for the figuration of a radical systemic shift in the way power functions noncoercively within twentieth-century modernity? Is it an indispensable means of revealing as related what would otherwise appear as disparate and unconnected phenomena? Does it not show that a patchwork or mosaic of techniques can still constitute a homogeneous effect of power?

A striking feature of Debord's book was the absence of any kind of historical genealogy of the spectacle, and that absence may have contributed to the sense of the spectacle as having appeared full-blown out of the blue. The question that concerns me is, then: assuming the spectacle does in fact designate a certain set of objective conditions, what are its origins? When might we say it was first effective or operative? And I don't ask this simply as an academic exercise. For the term to have any critical or practical efficacy depends, in part, on how one periodizes it—that is, the spectacle will assume quite different meanings depending on how it is situated historically. Is it more than just a synonym for late capitalism? for the rise of mass media and communication technology? more than an updated account of the culture or consciousness industry and thus chronologically distinct from these?

The "early" work of Jean Baudrillard provides some general parameters for what we might call the prehistory of the spectacle (which Baudrillard sees as having disappeared by the mid-1970s). For Baudrillard, writing in the late '60s, one of the crucial consequences of the bourgeois political revolutions was the ideological force that animated the myths of the Rights of Man: the right to equality and the right to happiness. What he sees happening in the nineteenth century, for the first time, is that observable proof became necessary to demonstrate that happiness had in fact been obtained. Happiness, he says, "had to be *measurable* in terms of signs and objects," signs that would be evident to the eye in terms of "*visible* criteria."[2] Several decades earlier, Walter Benjamin had also written about "the phantasmagoria of equality" in the nineteenth century in terms of the transformation of the citizen into consumer. Baudrillard's account of modernity is one of an increasing destabilization and mobility of signs beginning in the Renaissance, signs that previously had been firmly rooted to relatively secure positions within fixed social hierarchies.[3] Thus, for Baudrillard, modernity is bound up in the struggle of newly empowered classes to overcome this "exclusiveness of signs" and to initiate a "proliferation of signs on demand." Imitations, copies, and counterfeits are all challenges to that exclusivity. The problem of mimesis, then, is not one of aesthetics but one of social power, and the emergence of the Italian theater and perspective painting are at the start of this ever-increasing capacity to produce equivalences. But obviously, for Baudrillard and many others, it is in the nineteenth century, alongside new industrial techniques and forms of circulation, that a new kind of sign emerges: "potentially identical objects produced in indefinite series." For Baudrillard "the relation of objects in such a series is equivalence and indifference . . . and it is on the level of reproduction, of fashion, media, advertising, information and communication (what Marx called the unessential sectors of capitalism) . . . that the global process of capital is held together." The spectacle then would coincide with the moment when sign value takes precedence over use value. But the question of the location of this moment in the history of the commodity remains unanswered.

Guy Debord himself gave a surprisingly precise date for the beginning of the society of the spectacle. In a text published in 1988 he writes that in 1967, the date of his original book, the spectacle was barely forty years old.[4] Not a more approximate kind of number like fifty, but forty. Thus 1927, or roughly the late 1920s. Unfortunately he doesn't provide an indication as to why he singles out this moment. It made me curious about what he might have meant by designating the late '20s as a historical threshold. I offer, then, some fragmentary speculations on some very dissimilar events that might possibly have been implicit in Debord's remark.

1. The first is both symbolic and substantive. The year 1927 saw the technological perfection of television. Vladimir Zworikin, the Russian-born, American-trained engineer and physicist, patented his iconoscope—the first electronic system of a tube containing an electron gun and a screen made out of a mosaic of photoemissive cells, each of which produced a charge proportional to the varying light intensity of the image focused on the screen. Right at the moment when an awareness arose of the age of mechanical reproduction, a new model of circulation and transmission appeared that was to exceed that age, one

that had no need of silver salts or permanent physical support.[5] The spectacle was to become inseparable from this new kind of image and its speed, ubiquity, and simultaneity.

But equally important was that by the late 1920s, when the first experimental broadcasts occurred, the vast interlocking of corporate, military, and state control of television was being settled. Never before had the institutional regulation of a new technique been planned and divided up so far in advance. So, in a sense, much of the territory of spectacle, the intangible domain of the spectrum, had already been diagrammed and standardized before 1930.

2. Perhaps more immediately significant, the movie *The Jazz Singer* premiered in 1927, signaling the arrival of the sound film, and specifically *synchronized* sound. This was not only a transformation in the nature of subjective experience; it was also an event that brought on the complete vertical integration of production, distribution, and exhibition within the film industry and its amalgamation with the corporate conglomerates that owned the sound patents and provided the capital for the costly move to the new technology.[6] Again, as with television, the nascent institutional and economic infrastructure of the spectacle was set in place.

Specifying sound here obviously suggests that spectacular power cannot be reduced to an optical model but is inseparable from a larger organization of perceptual consumption. Sound had of course been part of cinema in various additive forms from the beginning, but the introduction of sync sound transformed the nature of *attention* that was demanded of a viewer. Possibly it is a break that makes previous forms of cinema actually closer to the optical devices of the late nineteenth century. The full coincidence of sound with image, of voice with figure, not only was a crucial new way of organizing space, time, and narrative, but it instituted a more commanding authority over the observer, enforcing a new kind of attention. A vivid sign of this shift can be seen in Fritz Lang's two Mabuse films. In *Dr. Mabuse the Gambler,* a 1922 silent film, the protofascist Mabuse exercises control through his gaze, with a hypnotic optical power; while in *The Testament of Dr. Mabuse* (1932) an incarnation of the same character dominates his underlings only through his voice, emanating from behind a curtain (which, it turns out, conceals not a person but recording technology and a loudspeaker).

And from the 1890s well into the 1930s one of the central problems in mainstream psychology had been the nature of attention: the relation between stimulus and attention, problems of concentration, focalization, and distraction. How many sources of stimulation could one attend to simultaneously? How could novelty, familiarity, and repetition in attention be assessed? It was a problem whose position in the forefront of psychological discourse was directly related to the emergence of a social field increasingly saturated with sensory input. Some of this was the work of James McKeen Cattell, whose experiments on students at Columbia University provided the classical data for the notion of range of attention. Initially much of this research was bound up in the need for information on attention in the context of rationalizing production, but even as early as 1910 hundreds of experimental laboratory studies had been done specifically on the range of attention in advertising (including titles such as "The Attention Value of Periodical Advertisements," "Attention and the Effects of Size in Street Car Advertisements," "Advertising and the Laws of Mental Attention," "Measuring the Attention Value of Color in Advertising," the last a 1913 Columbia dissertation).

The year 1927 was also when Walter Benjamin began his Arcades Project, a work in which he would eventually point to "a crisis in perception itself," a crisis that is the result of a sweeping remaking of the observer by a calculated technology of the individual, derived from new knowledge of the body. In the course of his work on the Arcades Project, Benjamin himself became preoccupied with the question of attention and the related issues of distraction and shock, and he turned to Henri Bergson's *Matter and Memory* for a way out of what he saw as the "standardized and denatured" perception of the masses. Bergson had fought to recover perception from its status as sheer physiological event; for him attention was a question of an engagement of the body, an inhibition of movement, a state of consciousness arrested in the present. But attention could become transformed into something productive only when it was linked to the deeper activity of memory:

Memory thus creates anew present perception . . . strengthening and enriching [it]. . . . If after having gazed on any object, we turn our eyes abruptly away, we obtain an "after-image" [*image consécutive*] of it. It is true we are dealing here with images photographed on the object itself, and with memories following immediately upon the perception of which they are but the echo. But behind these images which are identical with the object, there are others, stored in memory which only resemble it.[7]

What Bergson sought to describe was the vitality of the moment when a conscious rift occurred between memory and perception, a moment in which memory had the capacity to rebuild the object of perception. Deleuze and Guattari have described similar effects of the entry of memory into perception, for example in the perception of a face: one can see a face in terms of a vast set of micromemories and a rich proliferation of semiotic systems, or, what is far more common, in terms of bleak redundancies of representations, which, they say, is where connections can always be effected with the hierarchies of power formations.[8] That kind of redundancy of representation, with its accompanying inhibition and impoverishment of memory, was what Benjamin saw as the standardization of perception, or what we might call an effect of spectacle.

Although Benjamin called *Matter and Memory* a "towering and monumental work," he reproached Bergson for circumscribing memory within the isolated frame of an individual consciousness; the kind of afterimages that interested Benjamin were those of collective historical memory, haunting images of the out-of-date that had the capacity for a social reawakening.[9] And thus Benjamin's apprehension of a present-day crisis in perception is filtered through a richly elaborated afterimage of the mid-nineteenth century.

3. Given the content of Debord's work, we can also assume another crucial development in the late 1920s: the rise of fascism and, soon after, Stalinism, and the way in which they incarnated models of the spectacle. Important, for example, was Goebbels's innovative and synergetic use of every available medium, especially the development of sound/image propaganda, and his devaluation of

the written word, because reading implied time for reflection and thought. In one election campaign in 1930, Goebbels mailed 50,000 phonograph records of one of his own speeches to specially targeted voters. Goebbels also introduced the airplane into politics, making Hitler the first political candidate to fly to several different cities on the same day. Air travel thus functioned as a conveyor of the image of the leader, providing a new sense of ubiquity.

As part of this mixed technology of attention, television was to have played a crucial role. And as recent scholarship has shown, the development of television in Germany was in advance of that of any other country.[10] German TV broadcasting on a regular basis began in 1935, four years ahead of the United States. Clearly, as an instrument of social control, its effectiveness was never realized by the Nazis, but its early history in Germany is instructive for the competing models of spectacular organization that were proposed in the 1930s. A major split emerged early on between the monopolistic corporate forces and the Nazi Party with regard to the development of television in Germany. The Party sought to have television centralized and accessible in public screening halls, unlike the decentralized use of radio in private homes. Goebbels and Hitler had a notion of group reception, believing that this was the most effective form of reception. Public television halls, seating from 40 to 400, were designated, not unlike the subsequent early development of television in the USSR, where a mass viewing environment was also favored. According to the Nazi director of broadcasting, writing in 1935, the "sacred mission" of television was "to plant indelibly the image of the Führer in the hearts of the German people."[11] Corporate power, on the other hand, sought home viewing, for maximization of profit. One model sought to position television as technique within the demands of fascism in general, as a means of mobilizing and inciting the masses, whereas the agents of capitalism sought to privatize, to divide and molecularize, to impose a model of cellularity.

It is easy to forget that in *Society of the Spectacle* Debord outlined two different models of the spectacle; one he called "concentrated" and the other "diffused," preventing the word *spectacle* from simply being synonymous with consumer or late capitalism. Concentrated spectacle was what characterized Nazi

Germany, Stalinist Russia, and Maoist China; the preeminent model of diffused spectacle was the United States: "Wherever the concentrated spectacle rules so does the police . . . it is accompanied by permanent violence. The imposed image of the good envelops in its spectacle the totality of what officially exists and is usually concentrated in one man who is the guarantee of totalitarian cohesion. Everyone must magically identify with this absolute celebrity—or disappear."[12] The diffuse spectacle, on the other hand, accompanies the abundance of commodities. And certainly it is this model to which Debord gives most of his attention in his 1967 book.

I will note in passing Michel Foucault's famous dismissal of the spectacle in *Discipline and Punish:* "Our society is not one of spectacle, but of surveillance; under the surface of images one invests bodies in depth."[13] But the spectacle is also a set of techniques for the management of bodies, the management of attention (I am paraphrasing Foucault) "for assuring the ordering of human multiplicities," "its object is to fix, it is an anti-nomadic technique," "it uses procedures of partitioning and cellularity . . . in which the individual is reduced as a political force."[14] I suspect that Foucault did not spend much time watching television or thinking about it, because it would not be difficult to make a case that television is a further perfecting of panoptic technology. In it *surveillance* and *spectacle* are not opposed terms, as he insists, but collapsed onto one another in a more effective disciplinary apparatus. Recent developments have confirmed literally this overlapping model: television sets that contain advanced image recognition technology in order to monitor and quantify the behavior, attentiveness, and eye movement of a spectator.[15]

But in 1988 Debord sees his two original models of diffused and concentrated spectacle becoming indistinct, converging into what he calls "the integrated society of the spectacle."[16] In this deeply pessimistic book, he describes a more sophisticated deployment of elements from those earlier models, a flexible arrangement of global power adaptable to local needs and circumstances. In 1967 there were still marginalities and peripheries that escaped its reign: in 1988, he insists, the spectacle has irradiated into everything and has absolute control over production, over perception, and especially over the shape of the future and the past.

As much as any single feature, Debord sees the core of the spectacle as the annihilation of historical knowledge—in particular the destruction of the recent past. In its place there is the reign of a perpetual present. History, he writes, had always been the measure by which novelty was assessed, but whoever is in the business of selling novelty has an interest in destroying the means by which it could be judged. Thus there is a ceaseless appearance of the important, and almost immediately its annihilation and replacement: "That which the spectacle ceases to speak of for three days no longer exists."[17]

In conclusion I want to note briefly two different responses to the new texture of modernity taking shape in the 1920s. The painter Fernand Léger writes, in a 1924 essay titled "The Spectacle," published soon after the making of his film *Ballet mécanique,*

> The rhythm of modern life is so dynamic that a slice of life seen from a café terrace is a spectacle. The most diverse elements collide and jostle one another there. The interplay of contrasts is so violent that there is always exaggeration in the effect that one glimpses. On the boulevard two men are carrying some immense gilded letters in a hand cart: the effect is so unexpected that everyone stops and looks. There is the origin of the modern spectacle . . . in the shock of the surprise effect.[18]

But then Léger goes on to detail how advertising and commercial forces have taken the lead in the making of modern spectacle, and he cites the department store, the world of fashion, and the rhythms of industrial production as forms that have conquered the attention of the public. Léger's goal is the same: wanting to win over that public. Of course, he is writing at a point of uncertainty about the direction of his own art, facing the dilemma of what a public art might mean, but the confused program he comes up with in this text is an early instance of the ploys of all those—from Warhol to more recent "appropriationists"—who believe, or at least claim, that they are outwitting the spectacle at its own game. Léger summarizes this kind of ambition: "Let's push the system to the extreme," he states, and offers vague suggestions for polychroming the exterior of factories and apartment buildings, for using new materials and setting them in motion. But this ineffectual inclination to outdo the allure of the spectacle becomes complicit with its annihilation of the past and fetishization of the new.

But the same year, 1924, the first surrealist manifesto suggests a very different aesthetic strategy for confronting the spectacular organization of the modern city. I am referring to what Walter Benjamin called the "anthropological" dimension of surrealism.[19] It was a strategy of turning the spectacle of the city inside out through countermemory and counteritineraries. These would reveal the potency of outmoded objects excluded from its slick surfaces, and of derelict spaces off its main routes of circulation. The strategy incarnated a refusal of the imposed present, and in reclaiming fragments of a demolished past it was implicitly figuring an alternative future. And despite the equivocal nature of many of these surrealist gestures, it is no accident that they were to reappear in new forms in the tactics of situationism in the 1960s, in the notion of the *dérive* or drift, of *détournement,* of psychogeography, the exemplary act, and the constructed situation.[20] Whether these practices have any vitality or even relevance today depends in large measure on what an archaeology of the present tells us. Are we still in the midst of a society that is organized as appearance? Or have we entered a nonspectacular global system arranged primarily around the control and flow of information, a system whose management and regulation of attention would demand wholly new forms of resistance and memory?[21]

Notes

This paper was originally presented at the Sixth International Colloquium on Twentieth Century French Studies, "Revolutions 1889–1989," at Columbia University, March 30–April 1, 1989. Originally published in *October* 50 (Fall 1989), 97–107.

1. Guy Debord, *Society of the Spectacle* (Detroit: Red and Black, 1977).

2. Jean Baudrillard, *La société de consommation: ses mythes, ses structures* (Paris: Gallimard, 1970), 60. Emphasis in original.

3. A well-known passage from the "later" Baudrillard amplifies this: "There is no such thing as fashion in a society of caste and rank since one is assigned a place irrevocably. Thus class-

mobility is non-existent. A prohibition protects the signs and assures them a total clarity; each sign refers unequivocally to a status. . . . In caste societies, feudal or archaic, the signs are limited in number and are not widely diffused. . . . Each is a reciprocal obligation between castes, clans, or persons." Jean Baudrillard, *Simulations,* trans. Paul Foss (New York: Semiotexte, 1983), 84.

4. Guy Debord, *Commentaires sur la société du spectacle* (Paris: Editions Gérard Lebovici, 1988), 13.

5. The historian of science François Dagognet cites the revolutionary nature of this development in his *Philosophie de l'image* (Paris: J. Vrin, 1986), 57–58.

6. See Steven Neale, *Cinema and Technology: Image, Sound, Colour* (Bloomington: Indiana University Press, 1985), 62–102; and Douglas Gomery, "Toward an Economic History of the Cinema: The Coming of Sound to Hollywood," in Teresa de Lauretis and Stephen Heath, eds., *The Cinematic Apparatus* (London: Macmillan, 1980), 38–46.

7. Henri Bergson, *Matter and Memory,* trans. N. M. Paul and W. S. Palmer (New York: Zone Books, 1988), 101–103.

8. See, for example, Félix Guattari, "Les machines concrètes," in his *La révolution moléculaire* (Paris: Encres, 1977), 364–376.

9. "On the contrary he [Bergson] rejects any historical determination of memory. He thus manages above all to stay clear of that experience from which his own philosophy evolved or, rather, in reaction to which it arose. It was the inhospitable, blinding age of big-scale industrialism." Walter Benjamin, *Illuminations,* trans. Harry Zohn (New York: Schocken, 1969), 156–157.

10. I have relied on the valuable research in William Uricchio, "Rituals of Reception, Patterns of Neglect: Nazi Television and Its Postwar Representation," *Wide Angle* 10, no. 4, 48–66. See also Robert Edwin Herzstein, *The War That Hitler Won: Goebbels and the Nazi Media Campaign* (New York: Paragon, 1978).

11. Quoted in Uricchio, "Rituals of Reception," 51.

12. Debord, *Society of the Spectacle,* thesis 64.

13. Michel Foucault, *Discipline and Punish,* trans. Alan Sheridan (New York: Pantheon, 1976), 217.

14. Ibid., 218–219.

15. See, for example, Bill Carter, "TV Viewers, Beware: Nielsen May Be Looking," *New York Times,* June 1, 1989, A1.

16. Debord, *Commentaires,* 17–19.

17. Ibid., 29.

18. Fernand Léger, *Functions of Painting,* trans. Alexandra Anderson (New York: Viking, 1973), 35.

19. Walter Benjamin, *One Way Street,* trans. Edmund Jephcott and Kingsley Shorter (London: New Left Books, 1979), 239. Christopher Phillips suggested to me that the late 1920s would also likely be crucial for Debord as the moment when surrealism became coopted, that is, when its original revolutionary potential was nullified in an early instance of spectacular recuperation and absorption.

20. On these strategies, see the documents in Ken Knabb, ed. and trans., *Situationist International Anthology* (Berkeley: Bureau of Public Secrets, 1981).

21. See my "Eclipse of the Spectacle," in Brian Wallis, ed., *Art after Modernism* (Boston: David Godine, 1984), 283–294.

Why Art Can't Kill the Situationist International

T. J. Clark and Donald Nicholson-Smith

What does it matter to us what judgments may later be passed upon our obscure personalities? If we have seen fit to record the political differences that exist between the majority of the Commune and ourselves, this is not in order to apportion blame to the former and praise to the latter. It is simply to ensure that, should the Commune be defeated, people will know that it was not what it has appeared to be up to now.

Gustave Lefrançais addressing constituents, May 20, 1871[1]

Le passé nous réserve bien des surprises.

No sooner were Guy Debord's ashes safely cast from the Pointe du Vert-Galant into the Seine, no sooner had death quelled his remorseless tendency to respond to everyone who made the least mention of him, than an emboldened pack of commentators bounded from their kennels, all desperately eager to position themselves, pro, con, or otherwise, with respect to Debord's person, writings, and *faits et gestes.*

A case in point is the intrepid dabbler Régis Debray, sometime focal point of Guevarism, sometime advisor to President Mitterrand. Debray, who by his own account had never before engaged with Debord in any way, now felt an urgent need to denounce Debord's ideas, and specifically the concept of the spectacle, for their supposed idealism, for their young-Marxism and young-Hegelianism, for their unreconstructed Feuerbachianism—but most of all for their strict incompatibility with Debray's own positivist sociology of mass communications, which goes by the name of "mediology."[2]

Sometimes modestly described as a small thing (Debray is prone to talking about "notre petite médiologie"), this wannabe discipline has high ambitions. It pretends to the throne of semiology, no less—even though, to use Debray-speak, "'semio' had a good half-decade's start on 'medio.'" But Debray also needs to keep his neoempiricist baby away from the very slightest taint of totalizing or negative thought, and this is where Debord's global condemnation of the spectacle came in handy: "For the situationists . . . mediation is evil. For us, mediation is not only a necessity, it is civilization itself. For us man is man solely by virtue of technological mediation, and he needs the spectacle to gain access to his truth. It is via illusion that man discovers his reality. [etc., etc.]"[3]

We were members of the Situationist International in 1966–1967. This gives us no special vantage point with respect to the really interesting questions about the SI in its final, extraordinary years. In particular the key issue, of how and why the situationists came to have a preponderant role in May 1968—that is, how and why their brand of politics participated in, and to an extent fueled, a crisis of the late-capitalist State—is still wide open to interpretation. (And, for that matter, to simple factual inquiry. The scoffing and evasion and doctoring of the evidence about May 1968 shows no sign of letting up.) We shall get to some of these subjects in a moment. But we make no apology for starting from the bottom. Debray's maunderings are typical. And in a sense necessary. The efforts of organized knowledge to discredit the situationists—to pin on them a final dismissive label and have them be part of "infantile Leftism" or "the 1960s" or some such accredited pseudo-phenomenon—are both entirely sensible (organized knowledge is at least good at identifying its real enemies) and wonderfully self-defeating. For some reason the SI will simply not go away.

All the same, one might well ask why we are responding to *this particular* piece of nonsense. Perhaps the Debray piece was irksome because it really did manage to plumb new depths, even in such a hotly contested field. Certainly we never expect to see it bettered for oily chat show authoritativeness plus bare-faced amnesia—not to mention the more or less lunatic (but, of course, calculated) "esteem" that Debray ends by confessing for Debord "as an individual" and as that rarity, "a professional moralist" who actually had "a personal moral code."

But there was something else, doubtless, that broke the camel's back. It so happened that the British journal *New Left*[4] *Review* chose to publish a (somewhat abbreviated) version of Debray's eulogy in its issue for November-December 1995. This was only the second time in the *Review*'s history that it had addressed—and misrepresented—the question of the situationists (the first, of which more in a moment, came in 1989, after a quarter-century of eloquent silence).[5] But contradictions will out, and as luck (or bad management) would have it, the Debray piece was placed in nice juxtaposition to lengthy and reverential discussions, in the same issue, of Eric Hobsbawm's "history of the short twentieth century"—his "report," as one wag put it, "to a Central Committee that just isn't there any more." The very idea of pressing too hard on Hobsbawm's omissions and excuses as a historian was denounced a priori by *NLR* as "anti-Communist." One law for young-Hegelians, it seems, and another for unrepentant Stalinists. To have been overoptimistic about the revolutionary potential of the Watts proletariat is one thing; to have spent one's life inventing reasons for forced collectivization, show trials, the Great Terror, the suppression of the East German and Hungarian revolutions, and so on ad nauseam, quite another. The former is the ranting of primitive rebels; the latter the hard analytic choices of Marxist history.

Naturally this steered our thoughts back to that earlier effort by *NLR* to invent a history of "situationism" that would somehow avoid dealing with the moment, in the last years of the 1960s, when forms of situationist-influenced politics actually confronted the journal's own so-called mainstream or classical Marxism. Mighty was the labor of *NLR*'s writer on art matters, Peter Wollen,

Moscow, 1917: toppled Alexander III.

when he was finally called in for the issue of March-April 1989; and many were the main currents and imaginative genealogies and thumbnail sketches of this important -ism and that: all in order to buttress the *essential* declaration, on the last page but one of his Shorter and Shorter Twentieth Century, that from 1962 onward in the work of the SI, "the denial by Debord and his supporters of any separation between artistic and political activity . . . led in effect not to a new unity within Situationist practice but to a total elimination of art except in propagandist and agitational forms. . . . Theory displaced art as the vanguard activity, and politics (for those who wished to retain absolutely clean hands) was postponed until the day when it would be placed on the agenda by the spontaneous revolt of those who executed rather than gave orders."[6] Again the Michael Ignatieff authoritativeness is breathtaking. It so happens we remember Wollen in 1968, not yet having transferred his affections from Trotskyite center to avant-garde periphery, making the rounds of the main sites/sights of "student revolution" in Britain as a kind of New Left observer, and recoiling in horror from the ideological impurities he discovered there—of course reserving his full Jonathan Edwards for "those damned situationists, the lowest of the low!" That remark we recall specifically (we wore such verdicts as a badge of honor).

Far be it from us to suggest that this makes Wollen an unreliable guide to the same scene after twenty years' reflection. Age brings wisdom, even repentance. But it means he has—how shall we say?—an interesting perspective on the events he has chosen to narrate.

Enough, enough. In the end the real interest of the Debray/*NLR* proceedings lies in the way they reveal, just a little more flagrantly than usual, the structure (and function) of what now passes for knowledge of the SI from 1960 on. The established wisdom, let us call it. It can be broken down into four essential propositions, though obviously these overlap and repeat themselves.

Proposition 1: The Situationist International was an art organization (a typical late-modernist avant-garde) that strayed belatedly into "art politics." Judged as art, its politics do not amount to much. And surely they are not meant to be judged as politics!

Petrograd, 1918: dedication of a statue of Heinrich Heine (stage center: Lunacharsky).

Proposition 2: The SI in its last ten years was an art-political sect, consumed with the lineaments of its own purity, living on a diet of exclusions and denunciations, and largely ignoring the wider political realm, or the problems of organization and expansion that presented themselves in an apparently prerevolutionary situation. Call this the clean-hands thesis. Or the burning-with-the-pure-flame-of-negativity thesis. (Proposition 2 is subscribed to by many of the SI's admirers.)

Proposition 3: Situationist politics was "subjectivist," post- or hypersurrealist, propelled by a utopian notion of a new "politics of everyday life" that can be reduced to a handful of '68 graffiti: "Take your desires for realities," "Boredom is always counterrevolutionary," etc.

Proposition 4: Situationist theory, especially as represented by Debord's *The Society of the Spectacle,* is hopelessly young-Hegelian—rhetorical, totalizing, resting on a metaphysical hostility to "mere" appearance or representation, and mounting a last-ditch defense of the notion of authenticity, whether of individual or class subject.

Like all good travesties, these four propositions are not simply lies. All of them point to real problems in the work of the situationists after 1960, and the last thing we want to do is suggest those problems did not exist. What we do think, however, is that each of the propositions is a flimsy half-truth, never properly argued by Left opinion-makers, and contradicted by a body of evidence with which these opinion-makers are intimately acquainted but choose not to mention. The reason is not far to seek. Each proposition has a barely hidden corollary, and it is the truth of the corollary that this Left wants (and needs) to affirm.

Corollary 1: Therefore, the bone-hard philistinism of the Left in the 1960s and after—the fact that it called on the likes of Peter Fuller, *Tel Quel,* Roger Garaudy, John Berger, Ernst Fischer, etc.[7] as guides to the new regimes of representation then being ushered in—did not and does not matter.

———

473

Corollary 2: Therefore, the failure of the established Left to pose the problems of revolutionary organization again, and come to terms with the disaster of its Leninist and Trotskyite past, likewise does not matter. Such things are distractions. Dirty hands make light work. And the Left's love affairs with the Great Proletarian Cultural Revolution,[8] or the foci of Che Guevara and the Ecole Normale Supérieure, or the Burmese road to socialism, or the Italian Communist Party, or Tony Benn and Tom Hayden— or a hundred other objects that left the situationists cold for reasons stated by them in detail at the time—are now so much water under the bridge. To each his own elation, apparently. The Left may have prostrated itself in front of Mao's starving and stage-managed utopia. But at least it was not fooled by black uprisings in the United States. So many misled, premature *lumpens,* lacking (the Left's) direction, unaware that the time was not ripe for insurrection (for these guys it never is or will be). "Spontaneity"! The very word brings on a shudder or a giggle.

Corollary 3: Therefore, the grounds of Left theory and practice need not shift. The regime of policy-studies-plus-theory-refereeing needs no renewal to speak of. Raising the problem of the social construction of "subjects" in late capitalism, and possible forms of resistance to such construction, and above all exploring the implications of the invasion and restructuring of whole realms of representation that had once been left largely outside the commodity regime—the set of issues the situationists broached under the rubric "the colonization of everyday life"—all of this leads in the wrong direction. It leads to "identity politics," which every good 1960s survivor is supposed to blame for the demise of the Left.

Corollary 4: Therefore, the Left's infatuation with the wildest and most dubious forms of anti-Hegelianism—semiotic Maoism, PCF paranoid "not-the-subject-but-the-Party-ism," uninhabited universes made up of apparatuses, instances, structures, subcultural tics, and *systèmes de la mode,* weightless skepticisms and eternal battlings with the ghastly specters of "empiricism" and "scientism"—is entirely valid, and has nothing to do

---

with the Left's being listened to these days, on matters of theory, by no one who is not a subscriber to *Representations* and *Diacritics*.

You will notice that the hidden corollaries have a lot more substance than the original arguments about the SI. And that is appropriate. The arguments are ridiculously thin. It is the corollaries that count. It would be tedious, therefore, to go point by point through the cheery misrepresentations and present the evidence for their untruth. Better to take one or two points at random, and convey the general flavor.

Who would ever have thought, for a start, that the SI as pictured by the established wisdom had time, in the intervals between exclusions and anathemata, for analyses of political events in the world outside? For example, the series of interventions in the evolving situation in Algeria, at the time of Ben Bella and Boumedienne, culminating in the long article "Les luttes de classes en Algérie" (published in the situationist journal of March 1966, and then as a wall poster). Or the pamphlet of August 1967 on Mao's Great Proletarian Cultural Revolution, "Le point d'explosion de l'idéologie en Chine" (reprinted in the journal later that year). We are obviously biased judges, but we persist in thinking that these texts are classics of Marxist analysis. (In both cases the SI benefited from having members who possessed real knowledge of the language and history of the countries concerned, as opposed to forming opinions from books by fellow travelers and editorials in *Le Monde*.) But we wonder if those who now dismiss the "political" SI could come up with commentaries on the same or comparable subjects from the same period that strike them, in retrospect, as even roughly as good. "Good" meaning disabused and passionate.

Then there is the question of Debord's *The Society of the Spectacle*. Again, a few points at random. The book was published in November 1967. It was written, that is, at the same time as the political analyses we have just mentioned (along with various others published in the SI journal or as pamphlets: on Watts and the commodity economy, on the Six Day War and the Middle East, on the first peculiar stirrings of "youth revolt," and so on), and it was clearly meant to be

Budapest, October 23, 1956: toppled Stalin.

read alongside those analyses.[9] It is very much more a "political" book than you would ever dream from reading most accounts of it by detractors or enthusiasts. How would anyone suspect, from Debray's account and many others like it, that by far the book's longest chapter is entitled "The Proletariat as Subject and Representation," and that this hinge of the overall argument turns (once again) on the question of Leninism, the Party, and the history of the working-class movement? Of course, our question is *faux naïf.* This aspect of *The Society of the Spectacle* must not be talked about. Either because it would pull commentators back from the dreamworld of simulacra they wish to believe Debord inhabited or predicted, or because arguing with it would involve remembering one's own "positions," then and now.

Let us concede one or two points. Of course *The Society of the Spectacle* was conceived as a work of "high theory," and depends on a dialogue with texts, mostly drawn from the deep past of Marxism, German philosophy, and French classical literature, which it finds a way to ventriloquize and exacerbate. (Debray's suggestion that the book "admits to plagiarism only in extremis"—in a single thesis toward the end—is pure bad faith. Quite apart from the fact that Debray knows perfectly well, as everyone does, that at that moment Debord is quoting Lautréamont on plagiarism, *The Society of the Spectacle* voices its dependence on the past in every paragraph. That dependence is far deeper and weirder than a speed-reader like Debray has time to bother with.) The question to ask is what might have been the strategic point of such a way of writing in 1967. Dates matter. Althusser's *For Marx* and *Reading "Capital"* were two years old, and sweeping the Left in Europe. When Debray says airily that "we were all Feuerbachians in our youth, all great enthusiasts for the young Marx," the little confession conjures away what "we" all became a few years later.[10]

What Debray produced in 1967, the year the Debord book appeared, was *Revolution in the Revolution,* which does for Fidel Castro what Sidney and Beatrice Webb did for Stalin. Fashions in cybernetics and hard-line structuralism had then just promoted (or given new prominence to) the discipline of semiotics. This was the moment, in other words, when the very word *totality,* and the very idea of trying to articulate those forces and relations of production that were

Vilnius, August 30, 1991: toppled Lenin. Courtesy AP/Wide World Photos.

giving capitalism a newly unified and unifying form, were tabooed (as they largely still are) as remnants of a discredited "Hegelian" tradition.[11] These things were on Debord's mind. One of us remembers him at the Collège de France in 1966, sitting in on Hyppolite's course on Hegel's *Logic,* and having to endure a final session at which the master invited two young Turks to give papers. "Trois étapes de la dégénérescence de la culture bourgeoise française," said Debord as the last speaker sat down. "Premièrement, l'érudition classique, quand même basée sur une certaine connaissance générale. Ensuite le petit con stalinien, avec ses mots de passe, 'travail,' 'force' et 'terreur.' Et enfin—dernière bassesse—le sémiologue."[12] In other words, *The Society of the Spectacle* was conceived and written specifically as a book for bad times. It was intended to keep the habit of totalization alive—but of course to express, in every detail of its verbal texture and overall structure, what a labor of rediscovery and revoicing (indeed, of restating the obvious) that project would now involve.

The obvious it has to be, then, once again—since there is such a determination not to face it. For the situationists, the overwhelming reality was Stalinism: the damage and horror it had given rise to, and its capacity to reproduce itself, in ever newer and technically more plausible forms, within a Left that had never faced its own complicity or infection. (We shall never begin to understand Debord's hostility to the concept "representation," for instance, unless we realize that for him the word always carried a Leninist aftertaste. The spectacle is repugnant because it threatens to generalize, as it were, the Party's claim to be the representative of the working class.) *The Society of the Spectacle*'s forced conversation with the early Marx, and with the shades of Feuerbach and Hegel, is an answer to this situation. "Forced" in two senses: it is ostentatious and obviously pushed to excess (so that even Debray cannot miss it); and these qualities are precisely the signs of the tactic being a tactic, forced on the writer by the history—the disaster—he is recounting.

We are not saying that the book does not suffer from the strategy it thinks it has to adopt. Of course it does. But we are saying that the strategy made possible a kind of sanity—inseparable from the book's overweening hubris, its determination to think world-historically in the teeth of specialists from Left and

---

Paris, Place Clichy, March 10, 1969: anarcho-situationist "commandos" installing a replica of Charles Fourier's statue on a plinth left empty since the removal of the original by the Nazis. See *Internationale situationniste* 12 (September 1969), 97–98.

Right—that could be purchased no other way. And we are saying that to choose not to recognize what other modes of Left discourse *The Society of the Spectacle* was launched *against* is to continue the very habits of amnesia and duplicity that the book had full in its sights.

Last, and perhaps centrally, a word on the question of organization. That the SI in the 1960s was a small group is true. That its policy of aiming for constant agreement on key matters, and fighting against the reproduction of hierarchy and ideological freezing within the group, led to repeated splits and exclusions, ditto. We parted company with the situationists in 1968 on just these questions, as applied to the SI's actions in Britain and the U.S. We are not likely, therefore, to think the situationists always got these things right. All the same, what we find nauseating in the received account of them is the implication that concern for problems of internal organization—above all a determination to find a way out of the legacy of "democratic centralism"—is one more token of these art-politicians' lack of seriousness. Anyone who actually reads what the SI wrote in 1966 and 1967 will quickly realize that it could not have issued from a group of people walled into their own factional struggles. There were such struggles. They were thought (sometimes rightly, sometimes wrongly, in our view) to be the necessary condition of the kind of revolutionary clarity that informs the best of situationist writing. But the situationists never got stuck in their own turmoil, and they went on thinking, especially as things heated up in the course of 1967, about how they were to act—to "expand"—if the capitalist State offered them an opportunity. Here, for instance, are extracts from a working document entitled "Réponse aux camarades de Rennes—sur l'organisation et l'autonomie." Signed by Debord, Khayati, and Viénet, and dated July 16, 1967, this text came out of a series of discussions (and joint actions) with other small groups on the Left.

> The discussion begun on July 3 between us and the comrades of two groups affiliated with the Internationale Anarchiste seems to us to have revealed the existence—alongside our agreement on the essential, and indeed as the outcome of that very agreement—of

divergent views on the question of organization. . . . These divergences may be summed up as follows: Whereas we are definitely in favor of *a proliferation of autonomous revolutionary organizations,* Loïc Le Reste [of the Rennes group] thinks far more in terms of a *fusion* of such groups. This is not to say, of course, that Le Reste ultimately favors a single revolutionary organization claiming to "represent" either a class or the revolutionary movement as a whole; nor do we for our part have some kind of formal attachment to artificial distinctions between groups that rightly recognize their own fundamental unity on the main theoretical and practical issues.

The question does not therefore turn on some abstract definition of an absolute organizational model, but rather on a critical examination of present conditions, and on particular choices regarding the prospects for real action.

. . . It is well known that the SI has never "recruited" members, though it is always willing to welcome individuals on an ad hoc basis; and both aspects of this policy have been determined by the concrete conditions which in our view have circumscribed our practical activity—that activity conceived as means and ends, inseparably—and thus the issue does not depend merely on an individual's capacity to understand, or willingness to espouse, particular theoretical positions. (As for those theoretical positions, we naturally hope that all who are able, in the full sense of the term, to *appropriate* them will make free use of what they appropriate.) Very schematically, we may say that the SI considers that what it can do at present is work, on an international level, for the reappearance of certain basic elements of a modern-day revolutionary critique. The activity of the SI is a *moment* that we do not mistake for a *goal:* the workers must organize themselves, they will achieve emancipation through their own efforts, etc. . . . We cannot accept the idea that numerical "reinforcement" is a virtue per se. It can be harmful from an internal point of view, if it produces an imbalance between what we really have to do and a membership that can serve those ends only in an abstract way, and which is thus subordinate, whether for geographical or other reasons. It can be harmful from an external point of view, to the extent that it presents another example of the Will to Pseudo-Power, after the fashion of those many Trotskyite small groups possessed of a "ruling party vocation.". . .

Even more strongly, we disagree with Loïc Le Reste when he argues that the autonomy of different organizations can introduce a *hierarchy* among them. On the contrary, we think that hierarchy threatens to appear within an organization as soon as some of its members can be constrained to approve and execute what the organization decides, while possessing less power than other members to affect the decision. But we do not see how an effectively autonomous organization—and of course one that has rejected any notion of double allegiance—could become subordinate to an outside power. *L'unique et sa propriété*[13] charges that "whenever the SI affects to debate theoretical issues with various other revolutionary organizations . . . things always degenerate into bureaucratic farce, in which judgment is passed on these movements and their programs from the lofty and abstract point of view of a disembodied radicalism." But it is only if the kind of relationship in question was really bureaucratic—that is, aiming at *subordination*—or if our root-and-branch radicalism was indeed abstract and disembodied (which remains to be proven . . .) that one could legitimately talk of the SI seeking a *superior role*—in the first case practically, in the second as empty wish fulfillment. Anyway, what kind of revolutionary organization, composed of what kind of idiots, would actually *let itself* be subordinated in such a way? . . .

As for the possibility of fusions in the future, we believe that they will best take place at revolutionary moments, when the workers' movement is further advanced. . . .

We do not claim to have the secret formula that will solve the organizational problem of the period ahead. In any case, this question can be neither raised nor resolved entirely within the context of today's small radical groups. We (and some others) are sure only of a few basic principles: for instance, the necessity of not following old models, without, however, falling back into the pseudo-innocence of purely informal relationships. These principles are our starting point; and without question one of them is respect for the autonomy of the many groups that are worth talking to, and a determination to go on talking to them in good faith.

This is a working document, as we said, unremarkable in itself, and never published subsequently. To a large extent, its approach to the problems of political organization was overtaken by the events of 1968. (Though of course the text is haunted by a premonition of those events. And to say, as Wollen does, that the May revolution "duly came to the surprise of the Situationists as much as anyone else"[14] is pure face-saving on "anyone else"'s part. Except that the section of the Left Wollen belonged to was not so much surprised as horrified. Events refused to follow the required neo-Gramscian script.)

We cite the "Réponse aux camarades de Rennes" because its contents contradict the current travesty-history of the SI during this period, and not least that travesty-history's favorite *political* claim—that the situationists were simply "council communists," whose only answer to the practical questions of revolutionary politics was to hypostasize past experiments with workers' councils as a way of solving all problems of organization in advance. Again, this charge is not simply empty. The invocation of Kiel and Barcelona could be, at times, a kind of mantra. But in practice the invocation coexisted with a whole range of actions and negotiations that aimed to throw the issue of organization back into the melting pot. And consider the invocation itself! Of course any revolutionary practice has to learn from the past, and no doubt idealize that past in doing so. But better an idealized image of 1918 and 1936 than of the years, and kinds of power, that most of the Left put on a pedestal.

———

We realize that by concentrating on the issues we have selected from the situationists' final years we run the danger of seeming to fall in with the established notion of some form of epistemological (and practical) break in the SI's history, taking place in the early 1960s, by which "art" gave way to "politics." It is a crude model, shedding about as much useful light on the difference between "early" and "late" situationists as Althusser's does on "early" and "late" Marx. All of the activity we have mentioned was conceived as an aspect of a practice in which "art"—meaning those possibilities of representational and antirepresentational action thrown up by fifty years of modernist experiment on the borders of the category—might now be realized. This was the truly utopian dimension of SI activity. And it could and did become a horizon of possibility that meant too little in practice. But only at moments. Surely the remarkable thing, which it now takes a massive effort of historical imagination to recapture, is how active—how instrumental—this utopian dimension was in what the situationists actually did. It was the "art" dimension, to put it crudely—the continual pressure put on the question of representational forms in politics and everyday life, and the refusal to foreclose on the issue of representation versus agency—that made their politics the deadly weapon it was for a while. And gave them the role they had in May 1968. This is the aspect of the 1960s that the official Left wants most of all to forget.

Inevitably we have focused here on the SI and the Left. It was the Left (as opposed to, say, the art world) that the situationists most hated in the 1960s and thought worth targeting. Whether the Left is still worth targeting, we are not sure. We have tried several times to write a conclusion to this article that did so, and come up hard against the emptiness of the present. As usual, Debord is the best guide to this state of affairs. "Long ago," he says in his 1992 preface to *The Society of the Spectacle,*

> Thesis 58 had established as axiomatic that "The spectacle has its roots in the fertile field of the economy, and it is the produce of this field which must in the end come to dominate the spectacular market."
>
> This striving of the spectacle toward modernization and unification, together with all the other tendencies toward the simplification

of society, was what in 1989 led the Russian bureaucracy suddenly, and as one man, to convert to the current *ideology* of democracy—in other words, to the dictatorial freedom of the Market, as tempered by the recognition of the rights of Homo Spectator. No one in the West felt the need to spend more than a single day considering the import and impact of this extraordinary media event—proof enough, were proof called for, of the progress made by the techniques of the spectacle. All that needed recording was the fact that a sort of geological tremor had apparently taken place. The phenomenon was duly noted, dated, and deemed sufficiently well understood; a very simple sign, "the fall of the Berlin Wall," repeated over and over again, immediately attained the incontestability of all the other *signs of democracy*.[15]

The "very simple sign" still rules. It does so for all kinds of reasons, including the utter failure of the Left to face what the sign might mean for *it*—what it might say about its fifty-year collaboration with Stalinist counterrevolution, and the kinds of theoretical and practical monsters that collaboration bred. The sign still rules. Therefore no move to the apodictic or universal rings true, and yet we gag at the current rhetoric of detotalization: "We move from place to place and from time to time,"[16] etc. The history of the SI will someday be of use in a new project of resistance. What that project will be like is guesswork. It will certainly have to struggle to reconceive the tentacular unity of its enemy, and hence will need to articulate the grounds of a unity capable of contesting it. The word *totality* will not put it at panic stations. And it will want to know the past. Maybe it will find itself retelling the stories of moments of refusal and reorganization—the SI being only one of them—that the dreamwork of the Left goes on excluding from consciousness.

NOTES

Originally published in *October* 79 (Winter 1997), 15–31.

1. Cited in *Internationale situationniste* 12 (September 1969), 23.

2. Régis Debray, "A propos du spectacle: Réponse à un jeune chercheur," *Le Débat* 85 (May-August 1995).

———

3. Régis Debray, interview with Nicolas Weill, *Le Monde,* July 19, 1996.

4. The word "Left" recurs in what follows, and inevitably its meaning shifts. Much of the time it is used descriptively, and therefore pessimistically, to indicate a set of interlocking ideological directorships stretching roughly from the statist and workerist fringes of social democracy and laborism to the para-academic journals and think tanks of latter-day Trotskyism, taking in the Stalinist and lightly post-Stalinist center along the way. But of course there would be no point in using this description if we did not think it still worth doing so in the name of, and hopefully for the benefit of, another Left altogether (we ask the indulgence of those, and they are many, who reject the term "Left" as irrevocably compromised). This is a Left whose struggles with the late-capitalist state are at present local and multiform ("identity" and "ecological" politics being merely those forms that the spectacle chooses for now to (mis)represent—and many others will surely be given the same cynical treatment in years to come); a Left, however, that increasingly senses the enormity of its enemy and begins to think the problem of contesting that enemy in terms not borrowed from Marxist-Leninism or its official opposition; a Left whose insubordination is the theme of endless jeremiads from the "actually existing" Left, whose dismal instruction—to unite and fight under the same old phony-communitarian banners—it persists in ignoring.

5. Peter Wollen, "The Situationist International," *New Left Review* 174 (March-April 1989). Versions of the article then appeared in Iwona Blaswick, ed., *An Endless Adventure . . . an Endless Passion . . . an Endless Banquet: A Situationist Scrapbook* (London: ICA/Verso, 1989), and Elisabeth Sussman, ed., *On the Passage of a Few People through a Rather Brief Moment in Time: The Situationist International, 1957–1972* (Cambridge: MIT Press, 1989). The publications accompanied a traveling exhibition designed to illustrate Wollen's thesis.

6. Wollen, "Situationist International," 94.

7. The reader is invited to supply other names. We had a hard job thinking of any.

8. On May 17, 1968, the Sorbonne Occupation Committee, in which the situationists were then still the majority, cabled the Chinese Communist Party as follows: "TREMBLE BUREAUCRATS STOP [etc.] LONG LIVE THE GREAT CHINESE PROLETARIAN REVOLUTION OF 1927 BETRAYED BY THE STALINIST BUREAUCRATS STOP LONG LIVE THE PROLETARIANS OF CANTON AND ELSEWHERE WHO HAVE TAKEN UP ARMS AGAINST THE SO-CALLED PEOPLE'S ARMY STOP LONG LIVE THOSE CHINESE WORKERS AND STUDENTS WHO HAVE ATTACKED THE SO-CALLED CULTURAL REVOLUTION AND THE BUREAUCRATIC MAOIST REGIME STOP LONG LIVE REVOLUTIONARY MARXISM STOP DOWN WITH THE STATE STOP COMITÉ D'OCCUPATION DE LA SORBONNE AUTONOME ET POPULAIRE." Contrast this communication with the fact that for a full decade after 1968,

a large portion of the Left continued to flounder about in myriad versions of Maoism. The consensus of the French Left intelligentsia and its *vedettariat* (naming names would, we assume, be superfluous for readers of *October*) was almost ironclad in this regard—a state of affairs it is now strictly forbidden to recall. At the time, incidentally, one of the few opposing voices raised against the Parisian Mao cult was that of the former situationist René Viénet.

9. Most of these texts can be found in English translation in Ken Knabb's *Situationist International Anthology* (Berkeley: Bureau of Public Secrets, 1981).

10. Not that the "we" became just one thing. Debray's own sinuous trajectory is not our concern here: the curious (if they exist) may trace it through his voluminous autobiographical writings, or take a look at his *Media Manifestoes,* recently published in English translation (London: Verso, 1996). But a shared need to avoid the hard core of Debord makes strange bedfellows. Thus Philippe Sollers's recent discovery that Debord's work is "one of the greatest of the century," that Debord is "un classique parmi les classiques," etc. (see, for example, *Libération,* December 6, 1994, 34), is ridiculed by Debray as so much "brandishing of the mystical corpse" and "psalmodizing of pale *détournements* into dazzling inventions" (Debray, "A propos du spectacle," 6). What all this dueling hyperbole papers over is that both Debray and Sollers, the one disparagingly, the other admiringly, want above all to imprison Debord's negativity in an ivory tower.

11. No one is claiming that the effort at totalization in Debord is risk-free; still less that his example should point us back to some ludicrous Hegel revival. But it is time to retire the claim that "the pursuit of totality" necessarily equals "undifferentiation," "organic unity," "refusal of specificity and autonomy," etc. A rereading of the analytic sections of *The Philosophy of Right* would be a good first step; and a comparison between these sections' accounts of the constitution (and contradictions) of social identities, and, say, the little myths of absence and difference, generalized from a pseudo-psychology to any and every scale and social circumstance, which are all the Left at present has to offer to an "identity politics" in search of a theory and practice.

12. "Three stages in French middle-class culture's degeneration: first, standard scholarship, even if based on a certain general knowledge; next the Stalinist idiot with his passwords, 'labor,' 'force,' and 'terror'; and finally—the lowest of the low—the semiotician."

13. A pamphlet published in 1967 by a group of recent SI excludees known as the "Garnautins."

14. Wollen, "Situationist International," 94.

15. Guy Debord, "Preface to the Third French Edition," *The Society of the Spectacle* (New York: Zone Books, 1994), 9–10.

16. Wollen, "Situationist International," 95.

Letter and Response

To the Editors:

    To begin with, I would like to congratulate you on your special issue on Guy Debord and the Situationist International, which adds considerably to our understanding of the SI and its significance. Next, sadly, I would like to set the record straight on what I myself did, said, and thought nearly thirty years ago, back in 1968. This may seem utterly trivial to others, but a small section of the essay by T. J. Clark and Donald Nicholson-Smith was very hurtful to me personally—designedly so.

    First, I was never ever a "Trotskyite" although, like Clark and Nicholson-Smith, I was certainly on "the Left." Second, I never "[made] the rounds of the main sites/sights of 'student revolution' in Britain" as they assert, thrilling though the missed prospect sounds. I did visit the student occupation at Hornsey College of Art, mainly, as I recall, because my friend Tom Nairn worked there and was involved in the occupation. I don't see how they can remember me being there—I never met T. J. Clark until later, although I may have met Donald Nicholson-Smith in other circumstances, perhaps through mutual friends or acquaintances such as Chris Gray and Bob Mules.

    If they did encounter me at Hornsey, or muddled me up with someone else, I suppose they must have been "revolutionary tourists" too! I certainly never said the words they quote me as saying, which are completely out of character both in style and content. I'm not sure how to envisage "recoiling in horror"— perhaps it's a rhetorical exercise. In fact, I sympathized with the Situationist International at the time, as others can attest. I am not claiming that I was an SI member, like Clark and Nicholson-Smith, but I wasn't some kind of anti-SI New Left agent either. And, despite all, I still think Nicholson-Smith genuinely deserves a badge of honor for his fine new translation of *The Society of the Spectacle*.

On a further point, I was not "called in" or commissioned to write the essay which was published in *New Left Review*. (Nor, in fact, had I ever written for *NLR* on art.) It was written to make sense of all I had learned researching the exhibition at the Beaubourg. I offered it to *NLR* out of the blue and they simply made the decision to publish it, for whatever sinister motives of their own. I did not initiate the 1989 exhibition in order "to illustrate [my own] thesis." It was the other way around. I wanted to show the full extent of the art produced under the aegis of the SI, both before and after 1962, and, more generally, to revive interest in a group of artists, thinkers, and agitators whose important contribution had been overlooked and neglected by far too many and for far too long.

I believe the show was helpful in creating the changed climate in which the *October* special issue became a possibility. My own work was meant to lay a preliminary foundation for future research, which I am glad to see is now beginning to emerge. Naturally, given the controversial and often paradoxical trajectory of the SI, there will be plenty of room for argument and reasoned debate.

As for the substance of Clark and Nicholson-Smith's polemic, there is much I agree with in their essay, despite its bile and flashes of sectarianism. I share their belief in the power of creativity from below, their anti-Stalinism, their reservations about Gramsci, although you wouldn't think so from their incessant jabs and slurs. We do differ radically, it seems clear, in our estimation of Hegel and the need for a certain concept of "totality." Finally, I can see no place for the old SI habit of ad hominem personal invective, which T. J. Clark and Donald Nicholson-Smith still seem to value. I cannot believe it encourages better understanding of anything. In truth, I am really surprised they wish to keep it alive.

Enough. Now, as Arkadin and Debord exhorted us, "Let's drink to friendship!"
—Peter Wollen

T. J. Clark and Donald Nicholson-Smith respond:

They say of the sixties that if you remember them you weren't really there. Selective memory is something else again, and Peter Wollen seems to be suffering from a bad case of it.

Obviously "Why Art Can't Kill the Situationist International" was written in anger, and we make no apology for that. So far as Wollen is concerned, the anger was provoked by his essay on the history of the SI, and specifically his three-sentence treatment of the organization in its last decade. We think he should look again at these sentences (which conclude some thirty pages of discussion of the SI's place in modern art), and ask himself whether they are not lofty, contemptuous, and dismissive. That's how they read to us. They seem to epitomize—and, in view of their publication history, to enshrine—a certain effort to turn the SI safely into an art movement, and thereby to minimize its role in the political and social movements of the sixties. Like Wollen, presumably, we think that those upheavals are of much more than historical interest, and every day they are traduced and trivialized by the culture industry. Much is at stake, therefore. We wanted to denounce a loose conspiracy of silence and misrepresentation which has been the response of a portion of the Left to the challenge the SI poses to their model of political action. If such counterattacks are ad hominem, that is because it is people who misrepresent and keep silent—not just "signs and meanings."

For these very reasons, we do not want to tell lies about Peter Wollen. We gladly accept that he was never a Trotskyite—that was how we understood his politics way back then, but of course the label is vague. And if he prefers not to have his regular articles in *New Left Review* on film and popular music (which were one of the reasons we bought the magazine) count as writings on "art," then so be it. As for Wollen's disclaimers on his later relations with *NLR,* we never really imagined Robin Blackburn or some other editor of the review rapping out specific instructions: "Job for you here, Comrade Wollen!" The fact is that Wollen's piece chimed in perfectly with the *NLR*'s needs. So, more recently, did the repellent Debray offering—about which, incidentally, Wollen says nothing. You can be an active agent or a passive conduit of a political agenda. We do not much mind which of the two Wollen chooses to have been. Much the same sort of thing may be said of the nature of his connection to the fatuous traveling exhibition on the SI.

As for "those damn Situationists," etc., and "setting the record straight," here goes. We are at the University of Essex, not Hornsey College of Art (as if it mattered). It is the spring of 1968, and the place is having its own micro-May, complete with "Marxist" organizers and "Situationist" graffiti-daubers. Peter Wollen is down on a short visit, being shown around by Herbie Butterfield (who will jog his memory if need be). No prizes for guessing which side Wollen is on.

Hey, times are bad. Arkadin's toast is fine by us. We propose a follow-up: "To the Decline and Fall of the Spectacular Commodity Economy! And here's to the next uprising in South Central!"

NOTE

Originally published in *October* 80 (Spring 1997), 149–151.